EVERYMAN, I will go with thee,

and be thy guide,

In thy most need to go by thy side

ROBERT BROWNING

Born in Camberwell in 1812. First visited
Italy in 1834; married Elizabeth Barrett,
1846; lived in Italy, except for brief intervals,
from 1846 to 1861, when he settled in
London. Died at Venice on 16th
December 1889.

Robert Browning's Works in Everyman's
Library:

Vol.   I. *Poems and Plays*, 1833–44. Introduction by John Bryson, M.A.
No. 41.

"   II. *Poems and Plays*, 1844–64. No. 42.

" III. *The Ring and the Book*, 1868–9.
Introduction by John Bryson,
M.A. No. 502.

Vols. IV, V. *Poems and Plays*, 1871–90.
Selected, with an Introduction
by Mildred M. Bozman. Nos. 964,
966.

Robert Browning
Poems and Plays

Introduction by
JOHN BRYSON, M.A.

IN FIVE VOLUMES
VOLUME TWO: 1844–1864

DENT: LONDON
EVERYMAN'S LIBRARY
DUTTON: NEW YORK

NO. 42

SBN: 460 00042 x

CONTENTS

Contents

DRAMATIC ROMANCES AND LYRICS

INSCRIBED

TO

JOHN KENYON, ESQ.,

IN THE HOPE THAT A RECOLLECTION OF HIS OWN

SUCCESSFUL

" RHYMED PLEA FOR TOLERANCE "

MAY INDUCE HIM TO ADMIT GOOD-NATUREDLY THIS

HUMBLER PROSE ONE OF

HIS VERY GRATEFUL AND AFFECTIONATE FRIEND.

R. B.

DRAMATIC ROMANCES AND LYRICS

CAVALIER TUNES.[1]

I.—MARCHING ALONG.

I. KENTISH Sir Byng stood for his King,
   Bidding the crop-headed Parliament swing:
   And, pressing a troop unable to stoop
   And see the rogues flourish and honest folk droop,
   Marched them along, fifty-score strong,
   Great-hearted gentlemen, singing this song.

II. God for King Charles! Pym and such carles
    To the Devil that prompts 'em their treasonous parles!
    Cavaliers, up! Lips from the cup,
    Hands from the pasty, nor bite take nor sup
    Till you're (*Chorus*) *marching along, fifty-score strong,*
    Great-hearted gentlemen, singing this song.

III. Hampden to Hell, and his obsequies' knell
     Serve Hazelrig, Fiennes, and young Harry as well!
     England, good cheer! Rupert is near!
     Kentish and loyalists, keep we not here

   (*Cho.*) *Marching along, fifty-score strong,*
         Great-hearted gentlemen, singing this song!

IV. Then, God for King Charles! Pym and his snarls
    To the Devil that pricks on such pestilent carles!
    Hold by the right, you double your might;
    So, onward to Nottingham, fresh for the fight,

   (*Cho.*) *March we along, fifty-score strong,*
         Great-hearted gentlemen, singing this song!

[1] Such Poems as the following come properly enough, I suppose, under the head of "Dramatic Pieces"; being, though for the most part Lyric in expression, always Dramatic in principle, and so many utterances of so many imaginary persons, not mine.

3

II.—GIVE A ROUSE.

I. King Charles, and who'll do him right now?
King Charles, and who's ripe for fight now?
Give a rouse: here's, in Hell's despite now,
King Charles!

II. Who gave me the goods that went since?
Who raised me the house that sank once?
Who helped me to gold I spent since?
Who found me in wine you drank once?

> (*Cho.*) *King Charles, and who'll do him right now?*
> *King Charles, and who's ripe for fight now?*
> *Give a rouse: here's, in Hell's despite now,*
> *King Charles!*

III. To whom used my boy George quaff else,
By the old fool's side that begot him?
For whom did he cheer and laugh else,
While Noll's damned troopers shot him?

> (*Cho.*) *King Charles, and who'll do him right now?*
> *King Charles, and who's ripe for fight now?*
> *Give a rouse: here's, in Hell's despite now,*
> *King Charles!*

III.—BOOT AND SADDLE.

I. BOOT, saddle, to horse, and away!
Rescue my Castle, before the hot day
Brightens to blue from its silvery gray,

> (*Cho.*) *Boot, saddle, to horse, and away!*

II. Ride past the suburbs, asleep as you'd say;
Many's the friend there, will listen and pray
" God's luck to gallants that strike up the lay,

> (*Cho.*) " *Boot, saddle, to horse, and away!* "

III. Forty miles off, like a roebuck at bay,
Flouts Castle Brancepeth the Roundheads' array:
Who laughs, " Good fellows ere this, by my fay,

> (*Cho.*) " *Boot, saddle, to horse, and away?* "

IV. Who? My wife Gertrude; that, honest and gay,
    Laughs when you talk of surrendering, " Nay!
    " I've better counsellors; what counsel they?

        (*Cho.*) " *Boot, saddle, to horse, and away !* "

MY LAST DUCHESS.

FERRARA.

THAT's my last Duchess painted on the wall,
Looking as if she were alive; I call
That piece a wonder, now: Frà Pandolf's hands
Worked busily a day, and there she stands.
Will't please you sit and look at her? I said
" Frà Pandolf " by design, for never read
Strangers like you that pictured countenance,
The depth and passion of its earnest glance,
But to myself they turned (since none puts by
The curtain I have drawn for you, but I)
And seemed as they would ask me, if they durst,
How such a glance came there; so, not the first
Are you to turn and ask thus. Sir, 'twas not
Her husband's presence only, called that spot
Of joy into the Duchess' cheek: perhaps
Frà Pandolf chanced to say " Her mantle laps
" Over my Lady's wrist too much," or " Paint
" Must never hope to reproduce the faint
" Half-flush that dies along her throat; " such stuff
Was courtesy, she thought, and cause enough
For calling up that spot of joy. She had
A heart . . . how shall I say? . . . too soon made glad,
Too easily impressed; she liked whate'er
She looked on, and her looks went everywhere.
Sir, 'twas all one! My favour at her breast,
The drooping of the daylight in the West,
The bough of cherries some officious fool
Broke in the orchard for her, the white mule
She rode with round the terrace—all and each
Would draw from her alike the approving speech,
Or blush, at least. She thanked men,—good; but thanked
Somehow . . . I know not how . . . as if she ranked

My gift of a nine hundred years old name
With anybody's gift.   Who'd stoop to blame
This sort of trifling?   Even had you skill
In speech—(which I have not)—to make your will
Quite clear to such an one, and say " Just this
" Or that in you disgusts me; here you miss,
" Or there exceed the mark "—and if she let
Herself be lessoned so, nor plainly set
Her wits to yours, forsooth, and made excuse,
—E'en then would be some stooping, and I chuse
Never to stoop.   Oh, Sir, she smiled, no doubt,
Whene'er I passed her; but who passed without
Much the same smile?   This grew; I gave commands;
    Then all smiles stopped together.   There she stands
As if alive.   Will't please you rise?   We'll meet
The company below, then.   I repeat,
The Count your Master's known munificence
Is ample warrant that no just pretence
Of mine for dowry will be disallowed;
Though his fair daughter's self, as I avowed
At starting, is my object.   Nay, we'll go
Together down, Sir!   Notice Neptune, tho',
Taming a sea-horse, thought a rarity,
Which Claus of Innsbruck cast in bronze for me.

COUNT GISMOND.

AIX IN PROVENCE.

I. CHRIST God, who savest men, save most
        Of men Count Gismond who saved me!
    Count Gauthier, when he chose his post,
        Chose time and place and company
    To suit it; when he struck at length
    My honour 'twas with all his strength.

II. And doubtlessly ere he could draw
        All points to one, he must have schemed!
    That miserable morning saw
        Few half so happy as I seemed,
    While being dressed in Queen's array
    To give our Tourney prize away.

III. I thought they loved me, did me grace
        To please themselves; 'twas all their deed;
    God makes, or fair or foul, our face;
        If showing mine so caused to bleed
    My cousins' hearts, they should have dropped
    A word, and straight the play had stopped.

IV. They, too, so beauteous! Each a queen
        By virtue of her brow and breast;
    Not needing to be crowned, I mean,
        As I do. E'en when I was dressed,
    Had either of them spoke, instead
    Of glancing sideways with still head!

V. But no: they let me laugh, and sing
        My birthday song quite through, adjust
    The last rose in my garland, fling
        A last look on the mirror, trust
    My arms to each an arm of theirs,
    And so descend the castle-stairs—

VI. And come out on the morning troop
        Of merry friends who kissed my cheek,
    And called me Queen, and made me stoop
        Under the canopy—(a streak
    That pierced it, of the outside sun,
    Powdered with gold its gloom's soft dun)—

VII. And they could let me take my state
        And foolish throne amid applause
    Of all come there to celebrate
        My Queen's day—Oh, I think the cause
    Of much was, they forgot no crowd
    Makes up for parents in their shroud!

VIII. Howe'er that be, all eyes were bent
        Upon me, when my cousins cast
    Theirs down; 'twas time I should present
        The victor's crown, but . . . there, 'twill last
    No long time . . . the old mist again
    Blinds me as then it did. How vain!

IX. See! Gismond's at the gate, in talk
        With his two boys: I can proceed.

Well, at that moment, who should stalk
  Forth boldly (to my face, indeed)
But Gauthier, and he thundered " Stay! "
And all stayed.   " Bring no crowns, I say! "

x. " Bring torches!   Wind the penance-sheet
    " About her!   Let her shun the chaste,
  " Or lay herself before their feet!
    " Shall she, whose body I embraced
  " A night long, queen it in the day?
  " For Honour's sake no crowns, I say! "

xi. I?   What I answered?   As I live,
    I never fancied such a thing
  As answer possible to give.
    What says the body when they spring
  Some monstrous torture-engine's whole
  Strength on it?   No more says the soul.

xii. Till out strode Gismond; then I knew
    That I was saved.   I never met
  His face before, but, at first view,
    I felt quite sure that God had set
  Himself to Satan; who would spend
  A minute's mistrust on the end?

xiii. He strode to Gauthier, in his throat
    Gave him the lie, then struck his mouth
  With one back-handed blow that wrote
    In blood men's verdict there.   North, South,
  East, West, I looked.   The lie was dead,
  And damned, and truth stood up instead.

xiv. This glads me most, that I enjoyed
    The heart of the joy, with my content
  In watching Gismond unalloyed
    By any doubt of the event:
  God took that on him—I was bid
  Watch Gismond for my part: I did.

xv. Did I not watch him while he let
    His armourer just brace his greaves,
  Rivet his hauberk, on the fret
    The while!   His foot . . . my memory leaves
  No least stamp out, nor how anon
  He pulled his ringing gauntlets on.

XVI. And e'en before the trumpet's sound
    Was finished, prone lay the false Knight,
Prone as his lie, upon the ground:
    Gismond flew at him, used no sleight
Of the sword, but open-breasted drove,
Cleaving till out the truth he clove.

XVII. Which done, he dragged him to my feet
    And said " Here die, but end thy breath
" In full confession, lest thou fleet
    " From my first, to God's second death!
" Say, hast thou lied? " And, " I have lied
" To God and her," he said, and died.

XVIII. Then Gismond, kneeling to me, asked
    —What safe my heart holds, tho' no word
Could I repeat now, if I tasked
    My powers for ever, to a third
Dear even as you are. Pass the rest
Until I sank upon his breast.

XIX. Over my head his arm he flung
    Against the world; and scarce I felt
His sword, that dripped by me and swung,
    A little shifted in its belt,—
For he began to say the while
How South our home lay many a mile.

XX. So 'mid the shouting multitude
    We two walked forth to never more
Return. My cousins have pursued
    Their life, untroubled as before
I vexed them. Gauthier's dwelling-place
God lighten! May his soul find grace!

XXI. Our elder boy has got the clear
    Great brow; tho' when his brother's black
Full eye shows scorn, it . . . Gismond here?
    And have you brought my tercel back?
I just was telling Adela
How many birds it struck since May.

INCIDENT OF THE FRENCH CAMP.

I. You know, we French stormed Ratisbon:
        A mile or so away
    On a little mound, Napoléon
        Stood on our storming-day;
    With neck out-thrust, you fancy how,
        Legs wide, arms locked behind,
    As if to balance the prone brow
        Oppressive with its mind.

II. Just as perhaps he mused " My plans
        " That soar, to earth may fall,
    " Let once my army-leader Lannes
        " Waver at yonder wall,"—
    Out 'twixt the battery-smokes there flew
        A rider, bound on bound
    Full-galloping; nor bridle drew
        Until he reached the mound.

III. Then off there flung in smiling joy,
        And held himself erect
    By just his horse's mane, a boy:
        You hardly could suspect—
    (So tight he kept his lips compressed,
        Scarce any blood came thro')
    You looked twice ere you saw his breast
        Was all but shot in two.

IV. " Well," cried he, " Emperor, by God's grace
        " We've got you Ratisbon!
    " The Marshal's in the market-place,
        " And you'll be there anon
    " To see your flag-bird flap his vans
        " Where I, to heart's desire,
    " Perched him! " The Chief's eye flashed; his plans
        Soared up again like fire.

V. The Chief's eye flashed; but presently
        Softened itself, as sheathes
    A film the mother eagle's eye
        When her bruised eaglet breathes:

" You're wounded! "   " Nay," his soldier's pride
   Touched to the quick, he said:
" I'm killed, Sire! "   And, his Chief beside,
   Smiling the boy fell dead.

SOLILOQUY OF THE SPANISH CLOISTER.

I. GR-R-R—there go, my heart's abhorrence!
   Water your damned flower-pots, do!
If hate killed men, Brother Lawrence,
   God's blood, would not mine kill you!
What? your myrtle-bush wants trimming?
   Oh, that rose has prior claims—
Needs its leaden vase filled brimming?
   Hell dry you up with its flames!

II. At the meal we sit together:
   Salve tibi! I must hear
Wise talk of the kind of weather,
   Sort of season, time of year:
Not a plenteous cork-crop: scarcely
   Dare we hope oak-galls, I doubt:
What's the Latin name for " *parsley* " *?*
   What's the Greek name for Swine's Snout?

III. Whew! We'll have our platter burnished,
   Laid with care on our own shelf!
With a fire-new spoon we're furnished,
   And a goblet for ourself,
Rinsed like something sacrificial
   Ere 'tis fit to touch our chaps—
Marked with L. for our initial!
   (He, he! There his lily snaps!)

IV. *Saint*, forsooth! While brown Dolores
   Squats outside the Convent bank,
With Sanchicha, telling stories,
   Steeping tresses in the tank,
Blue-black, lustrous, thick like horsehairs,
   —Can't I see his dead eye glow
Bright, as 'twere a Barbary corsair's?
   (That is, if he'd let it show!)

v. When he finishes refection,
       Knife and fork he never lays
   Cross-wise, to my recollection,
       As do I, in Jesu's praise.
   I, the Trinity illustrate,
       Drinking watered orange-pulp—
   In three sips the Arian frustrate;
       While he drains his at one gulp!

vi. Oh, those melons! If he's able
       We're to have a feast; so nice!
   One goes to the Abbot's table,
       All of us get each a slice.
   How go on your flowers? None double?
       Not one fruit-sort can you spy?
   Strange!—And I, too, at such trouble,
       Keep 'em close-nipped on the sly!

vii. There's a great text in Galatians,
       Once you trip on it, entails
   Twenty-nine distinct damnations,
       One sure, if another fails.
   If I trip him just a-dying,
       Sure of Heaven as sure can be,
   Spin him round and send him flying
       Off to Hell, a Manichee?

viii. Or, my scrofulous French novel,
       On grey paper with blunt type!
   Simply glance at it, you grovel
       Hand and foot in Belial's gripe:
   If I double down its pages
       At the woeful sixteenth print,
   When he gathers his greengages,
       Ope a sieve and slip it in't?

ix. Or, there's Satan!—one might venture
       Pledge one's soul to him, yet leave
   Such a flaw in the indenture
       As he'd miss till, past retrieve,
   Blasted lay that rose-acacia
       We're so proud of! *Hy, Zy, Hine* . . .
   'St, there's Vespers! *Plena gratiâ*
       Ave, Virgo ! Gr-r-r—you swine!

IN A GONDOLA.

He sings.

I SEND my heart up to thee, all my heart
 In this my singing!
For the stars help me, and the sea bears part:
 The very night is clinging
Closer to Venice' streets to leave one space
 Above me, whence thy face
May light my joyous heart to thee its dwelling-place.

She speaks.

Say after me, and try to say
My very words, as if each word
Came from you of your own accord,
In your own voice, in your own way:
" This woman's heart, and soul, and brain
" Are mine as much as this gold chain
" She bids me wear; which " (say again)
" I choose to make by cherishing
" A precious thing, or choose to fling
" Over the boat-side, ring by ring."
And yet once more say . . . no word more!
Since words are only words. Give o'er!
Unless you call me, all the same,
Familiarly by my pet-name
Which, if the Three should hear you call,
And me reply to, would proclaim
At once our secret to them all:
Ask of me, too, command me, blame—
Do break down the partition-wall
'Twixt us, the daylight world beholds
Curtained in dusk and splendid folds.
What's left but—all of me to take?
I am the Three's; prevent them, slake
Your thirst! 'Tis said, the Arab sage
In practising with gems can loose
Their subtle spirit in his cruce
And leave but ashes: so, sweet mage,
Leave them my ashes when thy use
Sucks out my soul, thy heritage!

He sings.

I. Past we glide, and past, and past!
   What's that poor Agnese doing
Where they make the shutters fast?
   Grey Zanobi's just a-wooing
To his couch the purchased bride:
   Past we glide!

II. Past we glide, and past, and past!
   Why's the Pucci Palace flaring
Like a beacon to the blast?
   Guests by hundreds—not one caring
If the dear host's neck were wried:
   Past we glide!

She sings.

I. The Moth's kiss, first!
   Kiss me as if you made believe
You were not sure, this eve,
How my face, your flower, had pursed
Its petals up; so, here and there
You brush it, till I grow aware
Who wants me, and wide open burst.

II. The Bee's kiss, now!
   Kiss me as if you entered gay
My heart at some noonday,
A bud that dares not disallow
The claim, so all is rendered up,
And passively its shattered cup
Over your head to sleep I bow.

He sings.

I. What are we two?
   I am a Jew,
And carry thee, farther than friends can pursue,
To a feast of our tribe,
Where they need thee to bribe
The devil that blasts them unless he imbibe
Thy . . . Shatter the vision for ever! And now,
As of old, I am I, Thou art Thou!

II. Say again, what we are?
      The sprite of a star,
      I lure thee above where the Destinies bar
      My plumes their full play
      Till a ruddier ray
      Than my pale one announce there is withering away
      Some . . . Shatter the vision for ever!   And now,
      As of old, I am I, Thou art Thou!

He muses.

Oh, which were best, to roam or rest?
The land's lap or the water's breast?
To sleep on yellow millet-sheaves,
Or swim in lucid shallows, just
Eluding water-lily leaves,
An inch from Death's black fingers, thrust
To lock you, whom release he must;
Which life were best on Summer eves?

He speaks, musing.

Lie back; could thought of mine improve you?
From this shoulder let there spring
A wing; from this, another wing;
Wings, not legs and feet, shall move you!
Snow-white must they spring, to blend
With your flesh, but I intend
They shall deepen to the end,
Broader, into burning gold,
Till both wings crescent-wise enfold
Your perfect self, from 'neath your feet
To o'er your head, where, lo, they meet
As if a million sword-blades hurled
Defiance from you to the world!
Rescue me thou, the only real!
And scare away this mad Ideal
That came, nor motions to depart!
Thanks!   Now, stay ever as thou art!

Still he muses.

I. What if the Three should catch at last
     Thy serenader?   While there's cast

Paul's cloak about my head, and fast
Gian pinions me, Himself has past
His stylet thro' my back; I reel;
And . . . is it Thou I feel?

They trail me, these three godless knaves,
Past every church that sains and saves,
Nor stop till, where the cold sea raves
By Lido's wet accursed graves,
They scoop mine, roll me to its brink,
And . . . on Thy breast I sink!

She replies, musing.

Dip your arm o'er the boat-side, elbow-deep,
As I do: thus: were Death so unlike Sleep,
Caught this way? Death's to fear from flame, or steel,
Or poison doubtless; but from water—feel!

Go find the bottom! Would you stay me? There!
Now pluck a great blade of that ribbon-grass
To plait in where the foolish jewel was,
I flung away: since you have praised my hair,
'Tis proper to be choice in what I wear.

He speaks.

Row home? must we row home? Too surely
Know I where its front's demurely
Over the Giudecca piled;
Window just with window mating,
Door on door exactly waiting,
All's the set face of a child:
But behind it, where's a trace
Of the staidness and reserve,
And formal lines without a curve,
In the same child's playing-face?
No two windows look one way
O'er the small sea-water thread
Below them. Ah, the autumn day
I, passing, saw you overhead!
First, out a cloud of curtain blew,
Then, a sweet cry, and last, came you—
To catch your loory that must needs

Escape just then, of all times then,
To peck a tall plant's fleecy seeds,
And make me happiest of men.
I scarce could breathe to see you reach
So far back o'er the balcony,
(To catch him ere he climbed too high
Above you in the Smyrna peach)
That quick the round smooth cord of gold,
This coiled hair on your head, unrolled,
Fell down you like a gorgeous snake
The Roman girls were wont, of old,
When Rome there was, for coolness' sake
To let lie curling o'er their bosoms.
Dear loory, may his beak retain
Ever its delicate rose stain
As if the wounded lotus-blossoms
Had marked their thief to know again!
Stay longer yet, for others' sake
Than mine! what should your chamber do?
—With all its rarities that ache
In silence while day lasts, but wake
At night-time and their life renew,
Suspended just to pleasure you
—That brought against their will together
These objects, and, while day lasts, weave
Around them such a magic tether
That they look dumb: your harp, believe,
With all the sensitive tight strings
That dare not speak, now to itself
Breathes slumbrously as if some elf
Went in and out the chords, his wings
Make murmur wheresoe'er they graze,
As an angel may, between the maze
Of midnight palace-pillars, on
And on, to sow God's plagues have gone
Through guilty glorious Babylon.
And while such murmurs flow, the nymph
Bends o'er the harp-top from her shell,
As the dry limpet for the lymph
Come with a tune he knows so well.
And how your statues' hearts must swell
And how your pictures must descend
To see each other, friend with friend!

Oh, could you take them by surprise,
You'd find Schidone's eager Duke
Doing the quaintest courtesies
To that prim Saint by Haste-thee-Luke:
And, deeper into her rock den,
Bold Castelfranco's Magdalen
You'd find retreated from the ken
Of that robed counsel-keeping Ser—
As if the Tizian thinks of her,
And is not, rather, gravely bent
On seeing for himself what toys
Are these, his progeny invent,
What litter now the board employs
Whereon he signed a document
That got him murdered! Each enjoys
Its night so well, you cannot break
The sport up, so, indeed must make
More stay with me, for other's sake.

She speaks.

ı. To-morrow, if a harp-string, say,
Is used to tie the jasmine back
That overfloods my room with sweets,
Contrive your Zorzi somehow meets
My Zanze: if the ribbon's black,
The Three are watching; keep away.

ıı. Your gondola—let Zorzi wreathe
A mesh of water-weeds about
Its prow, as if he unaware
Had struck some quay or bridge-foot stair;
That I may throw a paper out
As you and he go underneath.

There's Zanze's vigilant taper; safe are we!
Only one minute more to-night with me?
Resume your past self of a month ago!
Be you the bashful gallant, I will be
The lady with the colder breast than snow:
Now bow you, as becomes, nor touch my hand
More than I touch yours when I step to land,
And say, All thanks, Siora!—

                    Heart to heart,

And lips to lips!   Yet once more, ere we part,
Clasp me, and make me thine, as mine thou art!

He is surprised and stabbed.

It was ordained to be so, Sweet,—and best
Comes now, beneath thine eyes, and on Thy breast.
Still kiss me!   Care not for the cowards!   Care
Only to put aside thy beauteous hair
My blood will hurt!   The Three, I do not scorn
To death, because they never lived: but I
Have lived indeed, and so—(yet one more kiss)—can die!

ARTEMIS PROLOGUIZES.

I AM a Goddess of the ambrosial courts,
And save by Here, Queen of Pride, surpassed
By none whose temples whiten this the world.
Thro' Heaven I roll my lucid moon along;
I shed in Hell o'er my pale people peace;
On earth, I, caring for the creatures, guard
Each pregnant yellow wolf and fox-bitch sleek,
And every feathered mother's callow brood,
And all that love green haunts and loneliness.
Of men, the chaste adore me, hanging crowns
Of poppies red to blackness, bell and stem,
Upon my image at Athenai here;
And this dead Youth, Asclepios bends above,
Was dearest to me.   He my buskined step
To follow thro' the wild-wood leafy ways,
And chase the panting stag, or swift with darts
Stop the swift ounce, or lay the leopard low,
Neglected homage to another God:
Whence Aphrodite, by no midnight smoke
Of tapers lulled, in jealousy dispatched
A noisome lust that, as the gadbee stings,
Possessed his stepdame Phaidra for himself
The son of Theseus her great absent spouse.
Hippolutos exclaiming in his rage
Against the miserable Queen, she judged
Life insupportable, and, pricked at heart

An Amazonian stranger's race should dare
To scorn her, perished by the murderous cord:
Yet, ere she perished, blasted in a scroll
The fame of him her swerving made not swerve,
Which Theseus read, returning, and believed,
So, exiled in the blindness of his wrath,
The man without a crime, who, last as first,
Loyal, divulged not to his sire the truth.
Now Theseus from Poseidon had obtained
That of his wishes should be granted Three,
And this he imprecated straight—alive
May ne'er Hippolutos reach other lands!
Poseidon heard, ai, ai! And scarce the prince
Had stepped into the fixed boots of the car,
That gave the feet a stay against the strength
Of the Henetian horses, and around
His body flung the reins, and urged their speed
Along the rocks and shingles of the shore,
When from the gaping wave a monster flung
His obscene body in the coursers' path!
These, mad with terror as the sea-bull sprawled
Wallowing about their feet, lost care of him
That reared them; and the master-chariot-pole
Snapping beneath their plunges like a reed,
Hippolutos, whose feet were trammeled fast,
Was yet dragged forward by the circling rein
Which either hand directed; nor was quenched
The frenzy of that flight before each trace,
Wheel-spoke and splinter of the woeful car,
Each boulder-stone, sharp stub, and spiny shell,
Huge fish-bone wrecked and wreathed amid the sands
On that detested beach, was bright with blood
And morsels of his flesh: then fell the steeds
Head-foremost, crashing in their mooned fronts,
Shivering with sweat, each white eye horror-fixed.
His people, who had witnessed all afar,
Bore back the ruins of Hippolutos.
But when his sire, too swoln with pride, rejoiced,
(Indomitable as a man foredoomed)
That vast Poseidon had fulfilled his prayer,
I, in a flood of glory visible,
Stood o'er my dying votary, and deed
By deed revealed, as all took place, the truth.

Then Theseus lay the woefullest of men,
And worthily; but ere the death-veils hid
His face, the murdered prince full pardon breathed
To his rash sire.   Whereat Athenai wails.
So, I who ne'er forsake my votaries,
Lest in the cross-way none the honey-cake
Should tender, nor pour out the dog's hot life;
Lest at my fain the priests disconsolate
Should dress my image with some faded poor
Few crowns, made favours of, nor dare object
Such slackness to my worshippers who turn
The trusting heart and loaded hand elsewhere
As they had climbed Oulumpos to report
Of Artemis and nowhere found her throne—
I interposed: and, this evenful night,
While round the funeral pyre the populace
Stood with fierce light on their black robes that blind
Each sobbing head, while yet their hair they clipped
O'er the dead body of their withered prince,
And, in his palace, Theseus prostrated
On the cold hearth, his brow cold as the slab
'Twas bruised on, groaned away the heavy grief—
As the pyre fell, and down the cross logs crashed,
Sending a crowd of sparkles thro' the night,
And the gay fire, elate with mastery,
Towered like a serpent o'er the clotted jars
Of wine, dissolving oils and frankincense,
And splendid gums, like gold,—my potency
Conveyed the perished man to my retreat
In the thrice venerable forest here.
And this white-bearded Sage who squeezes now
The berried plant, is Phoibos' son of fame,
Asclepios, whom my radiant brother taught
The doctrine of each herb and flower and root,
To know their secret'st virtue and express
The saving soul of all—who so has soothed
With lavers the torn brow and murdered cheeks,
Composed the hair and brought its gloss again,
And called the red bloom to the pale skin back
And laid the strips and jagged ends of flesh
Even once more, and slacked the sinew's knot
Of every tortured limb—that now he lies
As if mere sleep possessed him underneath

II—B 42

These interwoven oaks and pines.   Oh, cheer,
Divine presenter of the healing rod
Thy snake, with ardent throat and lulling eye,
Twines his lithe spires around!   I say, much cheer!
Proceed thou with thy wisest pharmacies!
And ye, white crowd of woodland sister-nymphs,
Ply, as the Sage directs, these buds and leaves
That strew the turf around the Twain! While I
Await, in fitting silence, the event.

WARING.

I.

1. WHAT'S become of Waring
    Since he gave us all the slip,
    Chose land-travel or seafaring,
    Boots and chest, or staff and scrip,
    Rather than pace up and down
    Any longer London-town?

II. Who'd have guessed it from his lip,
    Or his brow's accustomed bearing,
    On the night he thus took ship,
    Or started landward?—little caring
    For us, it seems, who supped together,
    (Friends of his too, I remember)
    And walked home thro' the merry weather,
    The snowiest in all December;
    I left his arm that night myself
    For what's-his-name's, the new prose-poet,
    That wrote the book there, on the shelf—
    How, forsooth, was I to know it
    If Waring meant to glide away
    Like a ghost at break of day?
    Never looked he half so gay!

III. He was prouder than the Devil:
    How he must have cursed our revel!
    Ay, and many other meetings,
    Indoor visits, outdoor greetings,

As up and down he paced this London,
With no work done, but great works undone,
Where scarce twenty knew his name.
Why not, then, have earlier spoken,
Written, bustled? Who's to blame
If your silence kept unbroken?
" True, but there were sundry jottings,
" Stray-leaves, fragments, blurrs and blottings,
" Certain first steps were achieved
" Already which "—(is that your meaning?)
" Had well borne out whoe'er believed
" In more to come! " But who goes gleaning
Hedge-side chance-blades, while full-sheaved
Stand cornfields by him? Pride, o'erweening
Pride alone, puts forth such claims
O'er the day's distinguished names.

IV. Meantime, how much I loved him,
I find out now I've lost him:
I, who cared not if I moved him,
Who could so carelessly accost him,
Henceforth never shall get free
Of his ghostly company,
His eyes that just a little wink
As deep I go into the merit
Of this and that distinguished spirit—
His cheeks' raised colour, soon to sink,
As long I dwell on some stupendous
And tremendous (Heaven defend us!)
Monstr'-inform'-ingens-horrend-ous
Demoniaco-seraphic
Penman's latest piece of graphic.
Nay, my very wrist grows warm
With his dragging weight of arm!
E'en so, swimmingly appears,
Thro' one's after-supper musings,
Some lost Lady of old years,
With her beauteous vain endeavour,
And goodness unrepaid as ever;
The face, accustomed to refusings,
We, puppies that we were . . . Oh never
Surely, nice of conscience, scrupled
Being aught like false, forsooth, to?

Telling aught but honest truth to?
What a sin, had we centupled
Its possessor's grace and sweetness!
No! she heard in its completeness
Truth, for truth's a weighty matter,
And, truth at issue, we can't flatter!
Well, 'tis done with: she's exempt
From damning us thro' such a sally;
And so she glides, as down a valley,
Taking up with her contempt,
Past our reach; and in, the flowers
Shut her unregarded hours.

v. Oh, could I have him back once more.
This Waring, but one half-day more!
Back, with the quiet face of yore,
So hungry for acknowledgment
Like mine! I'd fool him to his bent!
Feed, should not he, to heart's content?
I'd say, " to only have conceived
" Your great works, tho' they ne'er make progress,
" Surpasses all we've yet achieved! "
I'd lie so, I should be believed.
I'd make such havoc of the claims
Of the day's distinguished names
To feast him with, as feasts an ogress
Her sharp-toothed golden-crowned child!
Or, as one feasts a creature rarely
Captured here, unreconciled
To capture; and completely gives
Its pettish humours licence, barely
Requiring that it lives.

vi. Ichabod, Ichabod,
The glory is departed!
Travels Waring East away?
Who, of knowledge, by hearsay,
Reports a man upstarted
Somewhere as a God,
Hordes grown European-hearted,
Millions of the wild made tame
On a sudden at his fame?
In Vishnu-land what Avatar?

Or who, in Moscow, toward the Czar,
With the demurest of footfalls
Over the Kremlin's pavement, bright
With serpentine and syenite,
Steps, with five other Generals,
That simultaneously take snuff,
For each to have pretext enough
To kerchiefwise unfurl his sash
Which, softness' self, is yet the stuff
To hold fast where a steel chain snaps,
And leave the grand white neck no gash?
Waring, in Moscow, to those rough
Cold northern natures borne, perhaps,
Like the lambwhite maiden dear
From the circle of mute kings,
Unable to repress the tear,
Each as his sceptre down he flings,
To Dian's fame at Taurica,
Where now a captive priestess, she alway
Mingles her tender grave Hellenic speech
With theirs, tuned to the hailstone-beaten beach,
As pours some pigeon, from the myrrhy lands
Rapt by the whirlblast to fierce Scythian strands
Where breed the swallows, her melodious cry
Amid their barbarous twitter!
In Russia?   Never!   Spain were fitter!
Ay, most likely 'tis in Spain
That we and Waring meet again—
Now, while he turns down that cool narrow lane
Into the blackness, out of grave Madrid
All fire and shine—abrupt as when there's slid
Its stiff gold blazing pall
From some black coffin-lid.
Or, best of all,
I love to think
The leaving us was just a feint;
Back here to London did he slink;
And now works on without a wink
Of sleep, and we are on the brink
Of something great in fresco-paint:
Some garret's ceiling, walls and floor,
Up and down and o'er and o'er
He splashes, as none splashed before

Since great Caldara Polidore:
Or music means this land of ours
Some favour yet, to pity won
By Purcell from his Rosy Bowers,—
" Give me my so long promised son,
" Let Waring end what I begun! "
Then down he creeps and out he steals
Only when the night conceals
His face—in Kent 'tis cherry-time,
Or, hops are picking; or, at prime
Of March, he wanders as, too happy,
Years ago when he was young,
Some mild eve when woods grew sappy,
And the early moths had sprung
To life from many a trembling sheath
Woven the warm boughs beneath;
While small birds said to themselves
What should soon be actual song,
And young gnats, by tens and twelves,
Made as if they were the throng
That crowd around and carry aloft
The sound they have nursed, so sweet and pure,
Out of a myriad noises soft,
Into a tone that can endure
Amid the noise of a July noon,
When all God's creatures crave their boon,
All at once, and all in tune,
And get it, happy as Waring then,
Having first within his ken
What a man might do with men,
And far too glad, in the even-glow,
To mix with your world he meant to take
Into his hand, he told you, so—
And out of it his world to make,
To contract and to expand
As he shut or oped his hand.
Oh, Waring, what's to really be?
A clear stage and a crowd to see!
Some Garrick—say—out shall not he
The heart of Hamlet's mystery pluck?
Or, where most unclean beasts are rife,
Some Junius—am I right?—shall tuck
His sleeve, and out with flaying-knife!

Some Chatterton shall have the luck
Of calling Rowley into life!
Some one shall somehow run amuck
With this old world, for want of strife
Sound asleep: contrive, contrive
To rouse us, Waring! Who's alive?
Our men scarce seem in earnest now:
Distinguished names!—but 'tis, somehow,
As if they played at being names
Still more distinguished, like the games
Of children. Turn our sport to earnest
With a visage of the sternest!
Bring the real times back, confessed
Still better than our very best!

II.

1. " WHEN I last saw Waring . . ."
   (How all turned to him who spoke—
   You saw Waring? Truth or joke?
   In land-travel, or sea-faring?)

II. " We were sailing by Triest,
   " Where a day or two we harboured:
   " A sunset was in the West,
   " When, looking over the vessel's side,
   " One of our company espied
   " A sudden speck to larboard.
   " And, as a sea-duck flies and swims
   " At once, so came the light craft up,
   " With its sole lateen sail that trims
   " And turns (the water round its rims
   " Dancing, as round a sinking cup)
   " And by us like a fish it curled,
   " And drew itself up close beside,
   " Its great sail on the instant furled,
   " And o'er its planks, a shrill voice cried,
   " (A neck as bronzed as a Lascar's)
   " ' Buy wine of us, you English Brig?
   " ' Or fruit, tobacco and cigars?
   " ' A Pilot for you to Triest?
   " ' Without one, look you ne'er so big,
   " ' They'll never let you up the bay!

      " ' We natives should know best.'
      " I turned, and ' just those fellows' way,'
      " Our captain said, ' The 'long-shore thieves
      " ' Are laughing at us in their sleeves.'

III. " In truth, the boy leaned laughing back;
      " And one, half-hidden by his side
      " Under the furled sail, soon I spied,
      " With great grass hat, and kerchief black,
      " Who looked up, with his kingly throat,
      " Said somewhat, while the other shook
      " His hair back from his eyes to look
      " Their longest at us; then the boat,
      " I know not how, turned sharply round,
      " Laying her whole side on the sea
      " As a leaping fish does; from the lee
      " Into the weather, cut somehow
      " Her sparkling path beneath our bow;
      " And so went off, as with a bound,
      " Into the rose and golden half
      " Of the sky, to overtake the sun,
      " And reach the shore, like the sea-calf
      " Its singing cave; yet I caught one
      " Glance ere away the boat quite passed,
      " And neither time nor toil could mar
      " Those features: so I saw the last
      " Of Waring! "—You?   Oh, never star
Was lost here, but it rose afar!
Look East, where whole new thousands are!
In Vishnu-land what Avatar?

RUDEL TO THE LADY OF TRIPOLI.

I. I know a Mount, the gracious Sun perceives
First when he visits, last, too, when he leaves
The world; and, vainly favoured, it repays
The day-long glory of his steadfast gaze
By no change of its large calm front of snow.
And underneath the Mount, a Flower I know,
He cannot have perceived, that changes ever
At his approach; and, in the lost endeavour

To live his life, has parted, one by one,
With all a flower's true graces, for the grace
Of being but a foolish mimic sun;
With ray-like florets round a disk-like face.
Men nobly call by many a name the Mount,
As over many a land of theirs its large
Calm front of snow like a triumphal targe
Is reared, and still with old names, fresh ones vie,
Each to its proper praise and own account:
Men call the Flower, the Sunflower, sportively.

II. Oh, Angel of the East, one, one gold look
   Across the waters to this twilight nook,
   —The far sad waters, Angel, to this nook!

III. Dear Pilgrim, art thou for the East indeed?
    Go! Saying ever as thou dost proceed,
    That I, French Rudel, choose for my device
    A sunflower outspread like a sacrifice
    Before its idol. See! These inexpert
    And hurried fingers could not fail to hurt
    The woven picture; 'tis a women's skill
    Indeed; but nothing baffled me, so, ill
    Or well, the work is finished. Say, men feed
    On songs I sing, and therefore bask the bees
    On my flower's breast as on a platform broad:
    But, as the flower's concern is not for these
    But solely for the sun, so men applaud
    In vain this Rudel, he not looking here
    But to the East—the East! Go, say this, Pilgrim
        dear!

CRISTINA.

I. She should never have looked at me,
   If she meant I should not love her!
   There are plenty . . . men, you call such,
   I suppose . . . she may discover
   All her soul to, if she pleases,
   And yet leave much as she found them:
   But I'm not so, and she knew it
   When she fixed me, glancing round them.

II. What? To fix me thus meant nothing?
  But I can't tell . . . there's my weakness . . .
What her look said!—no vile cant, sure,
  About " need to strew the bleakness
" Of some lone shore with its pearl-seed,
  " That the Sea feels "—no " strange yearning
" That such souls have, most to lavish
  " Where there's chance of least returning."

III. Oh, we're sunk enough here, God knows!
  But not quite so sunk that moments,
Sure tho' seldom, are denied us,
  When the spirit's true endowments
Stand out plainly from its false ones,
  And apprise it if pursuing
Or the right way or the wrong way,
  To its triumph or undoing.

IV. There are flashes struck from midnights,
  There are fire-flames noondays kindle,
Whereby piled-up honours perish,
  Whereby swoln ambitions dwindle,
While just this or that poor impulse,
  Which for once had play unstifled,
Seems the sole work of a life-time
  That away the rest have trifled.

V. Doubt you if, in some such moment,
  As she fixed me, she felt clearly,
Ages past the soul existed,
  Here an age 'tis resting merely,
And hence, fleets again for ages:
  While the true end, sole and single,
It stops here for is, this love-way,
  With some other soul to mingle?

VI. Else it loses what it lived for,
  And eternally must lose it;
Better ends may be in prospect,
  Deeper blisses, if you choose it,
But this life's end and this love-bliss
  Have been lost here. Doubt you whether
This she felt, as, looking at me,
  Mine and her souls rushed together?

VII. Oh, observe! Of course, next moment,
　　The world's honours, in derision,
　Trampled out the light for ever:
　　Never fear but there's provision
　Of the Devil's to quench knowledge
　　Lest we walk the earth in rapture!
　—Making those who catch God's secret
　　Just so much more prize their capture.

VIII. Such am I: the secret's mine now!
　　She has lost me—I have gained her!
　Her soul's mine: and, thus, grown perfect,
　　I shall pass my life's remainder,
　Life will just hold out the proving
　　Both our powers, alone and blended—
　And then, come the next life quickly!
　　This world's use will have been ended.

I.—MADHOUSE CELL.

JOHANNES AGRICOLA IN MEDITATION.

THERE's Heaven above, and night by night,
　I look right through its gorgeous roof:
No sun and moons though e'er so bright
　Avail to stop me; splendour-proof
I keep the broods of stars aloof:
For I intend to get to God,
　For 'tis to God I speed so fast,
For in God's breast, my own abode,
　Those shoals of dazzling glory past,
I lay my spirit down at last.
I lie where I have always lain,
　God smiles as he has always smiled;
Ere suns and moons could wax and wane,
　Ere stars were thundergirt, or piled
The Heavens, God thought on me his child;
Ordained a life for me, arrayed
　Its circumstances, every one
To the minutest; ay, God said
　This head this hand should rest upon

Thus, ere he fashioned star or sun.
And having thus created me,
   Thus rooted me, he bade me grow,
Guiltless for ever, like a tree
   That buds and blooms, nor seeks to know
   The law by which it prospers so:
But sure that thought and word and deed
   All go to swell his love for me,
Me, made because that love had need
   Of something irrevocably
Pledged solely its content to be.
Yes, yes, a tree which must ascend,—
   No poison-gourd foredoomed to stoop!
I have God's warrant, could I blend
   All hideous sins, as in a cup,
To drink the mingled venoms up,
Secure my nature will convert
   The draught to blossoming gladness fast,
While sweet dews turn to the gourd's hurt,
   And bloat, and while they bloat it, blast,
As from the first its lot was cast.
For as I lie, smiled on, full fed
   By unexhausted power to bless,
I gaze below on Hell's fierce bed,
   And those its waves of flame oppress,
Swarming in ghastly wretchedness;
Whose life on earth aspired to be
   One altar-smoke, so pure!—to win
If not love like God's love to me,
   At least to keep his anger in,
And all their striving turned to sin!
   Priest, doctor, hermit, monk grown white
With prayer, the broken-hearted nun,
   The martyr, the wan acolyte,
The incense-swinging child,—undone
Before God fashioned star or sun!
God, whom I praise; how could I praise,
   If such as I might understand,
Make out, and reckon on, his ways,
   And bargain for his love, and stand,
Paying a price, at his right hand?

II.—MADHOUSE CELL.

PORPHYRIA'S LOVER.

THE rain set early in to-night
  The sullen wind was soon awake,
It tore the elm-tops down for spite,
  And did its worst to vex the lake,
I listened with heart fit to break;
When glided in Porphyria: straight
  She shut the cold out and the storm,
And kneeled and made the cheerless grate
  Blaze up, and all the cottage warm;
Which done, she rose, and from her form
Withdrew the dripping cloak and shawl,
  And laid her soiled gloves by, untied
Her hat and let the damp hair fall,
  And last, she sate down by my side
And called me.   When no voice replied,
She put my arm about her waist,
  And made her smooth white shoulder bare,
And all her yellow hair displaced,
  And, stooping, made my cheek lie there,
And spread o'er all her yellow hair,
Murmuring how she loved me; she
  Too weak, for all her heart's endeavour,
To set its struggling passion free
  From pride, and vainer ties dissever,
And give herself to me for ever:
But passion sometimes would prevail,
  Nor could to-night's gay feast restrain
A sudden thought of one so pale
  For love of her, and all in vain;
So, she was come through wind and rain.
Be sure I looked up at her eyes
  Proud, very proud; at last I knew
Porphyria worshipped me; surprise
  Made my heart swell, and still it grew
While I debated what to do.
That moment she was mine, mine, fair,
  Perfectly pure and good: I found
A thing to do, and all her hair
  In one long yellow string I wound

Three times her little throat around,
And strangled her.   No pain felt she;
    I am quite sure she felt no pain.
As a shut bud that holds a bee
    I warily oped her lids; again
Laughed the blue eyes without a stain.
And I untightened next the tress
    About her neck; her cheek once more
Blushed bright beneath my burning kiss:
    I propped her head up as before,
Only, this time *my* shoulder bore
Her head, which droops upon it still:
    The smiling rosy little head,
So glad it has its utmost will,
    That all it scorned at once is fled,
And I, its love, am gained instead!
Porphyria's love: she guessed not how
    Her darling one wish would be heard.
And thus we sit together now,
    And all night long we have not stirred,
And yet God has not said a word!

THROUGH THE METIDJA TO ABD-EL-KADR.
1842.

I. As I ride, as I ride,
   With a full heart for my guide,
   So its tide rocks my side,
   As I ride, as I ride,
   That, as I were double-eyed,
   He, in whom our Tribes confide,
   Is described, ways untried
   As I ride, as I ride.

II. As I ride, as I ride
   To our Chief and his Allied,
   Who dares chide my heart's pride
   As I ride, as I ride?
   Or are witnesses denied—
   Through the desert waste and wide
   Do I glide unespied
   As I ride, as I ride?

III. As I ride, as I ride,
    When an inner voice has cried,
    The sands slide, nor abide
    (As I ride, as I ride)
    O'er each visioned Homicide
    That came vaunting (has he lied?)
    To reside—where he died,
    As I ride, as I ride.

IV. As I ride, as I ride,
    Ne'er has spur my swift horse plied,
    Yet his hide, streaked and pied,
    As I ride, as I ride,
    Shows where sweat has sprung and dried,
    —Zebra-footed, ostrich-thighed—
    How has vied stride with stride
    As I ride, as I ride!

V. As I ride, as I ride,
    Could I loose what Fate has tied,
    Ere I pried, she should hide
    As I ride, as I ride,
    All that's meant me: satisfied
    When the Prophet and the Bride
    Stop veins I'd have subside
    As I ride, as I ride!

THE PIED PIPER OF HAMELIN;

A CHILD'S STORY.

(WRITTEN FOR, AND INSCRIBED TO, W. M. THE YOUNGER.)

I.   HAMELIN Town's in Brunswick,
    By famous Hanover city;
        The River Weser, deep and wide,
        Washes its wall on the southern side;
        A pleasanter spot you never spied;
    But, when begins my ditty,
        Almost five hundred years ago,
        To see townsfolk suffer so
            From vermin, was a pity.

II.   Rats!
They fought the dogs, and killed the cats,
    And bit the babies in the cradles,
    And ate the cheeses out of the vats,
        And licked the soup from the cook's own ladles,
Split open the kegs of salted sprats,
Made nests inside men's Sunday hats,
And even spoiled the women's chats,
      By drowning their speaking
      With shrieking and squeaking
In fifty different sharps and flats.

III. At last the people in a body
    To the Town Hall came flocking:
    " 'Tis clear," cried they, " our Mayor's a noddy;
      " And as for our Corporation—shocking
    " To think we buy gowns lined with ermine
    " For dolts that can't or won't determine
    " What's best to rid us of our vermin!
    " You hope, because you're old and obese,
    " To find in the furry civic robe ease?
    " Rouse up, Sirs!   Give your brains a racking
    " To find the remedy we're lacking,
    " Or, sure as fate, we'll send you packing!"
At this the Mayor and Corporation
Quaked with a mighty consternation.

IV. An hour they sate in council,
    At length the Mayor broke silence:
    " For a guilder I'd my ermine gown sell;
    " I wish I were a mile hence!
    " It's easy to bid one rack one's brain—
    " I'm sure my poor head aches again
    " I've scratched it so, and all in vain.
    " Oh for a trap, a trap, a trap!"
Just as he said this, what should hap
At the chamber door but a gentle tap?
    " Bless us," cried the Mayor, " what's that?"
(With the Corporation as he sat,
Looking little though wondrous fat;
Nor brighter was his eye, nor moister
Than a too-long-opened oyster,
Save when at noon his paunch grew mutinous
For a plate of turtle green and glutinous)

The Pied Piper of Hamelin

" Only a scraping of shoes on the mat?
" Anything like the sound of a rat
" Makes my heart go pit-a-pat!

v. " Come in! "—the Mayor cried, looking bigger:
And in did come the strangest figure!
His queer long coat from heel to head
Was half of yellow and half of red;
And he himself was tall and thin,
With sharp blue eyes, each like a pin,
And light loose hair, yet swarthy skin,
No tuft on cheek nor beard on chin,
But lips where smiles went out and in—
There was no guessing his kith and kin!
And nobody could enough admire
The tall man and his quaint attire:
Quoth one: " It's as my great-grandsire,
" Starting up at the Trump of Doom's tone,
" Had walked this way from his painted tombstone! "

vi. He advanced to the council-table:
And, " Please your honours," said he, " I'm able,
" By means of a secret charm, to draw
" All creatures living beneath the sun,
" That creep, or swim, or fly, or run,
" After me so as you never saw!
" And I chiefly use my charm
" On creatures that do people harm,
" The mole, and toad, and newt, and viper;
" And people call me the Pied Piper."
(And here they noticed round his neck
A scarf of red and yellow stripe,
To match with his coat of the self same cheque;
And at the scarf's end hung a pipe;
And his fingers, they noticed, were ever straying
As if impatient to be playing
Upon this pipe, as low it dangled
Over his vesture so old-fangled.)
" Yet," said he, " poor piper as I am.
" In Tartary I freed the Cham,
" Last June, from his huge swarms of gnats;
" I eased in Asia the Nizam
" Of a monstrous brood of vampire-bats:
" And, as for what your brain bewilders,

" If I can rid your town of rats
" Will you give me a thousand guilders? "
" One? fifty thousand! "—was the exclamation
Of the astonished Mayor and Corporation.

VII. Into the street the Piper stept,
    Smiling first a little smile,
As if he knew what magic slept
    In his quiet pipe the while;
Then, like a musical adept,
To blow the pipe his lips he wrinkled,
And green and blue his sharp eyes twinkled
Like a candle flame where salt is sprinkled;
And ere three shrill notes the pipe uttered,
You heard as if an army muttered;
And the muttering grew to a grumbling;
And the grumbling grew to a mighty rumbling;
And out of the houses the rats came tumbling:
Great rats, small rats, lean rats, brawny rats,
Brown rats, black rats, grey rats, tawny rats,
Grave old plodders, gay young friskers,
    Fathers, mothers, uncles, cousins,
Cocking tails and pricking whiskers,
    Families by tens and dozens,
Brothers, sisters, husbands, wives—
Followed the Piper for their lives.
From street to street he piped advancing,
And step for step they followed dancing,
Until they came to the river Weser
Wherein all plunged and perished
—Save one who, stout as Julius Cæsar,
Swam across and lived to carry
(As he the manuscript he cherished)
To Rat-land home his commentary,
Which was, " At the first shrill notes of the pipe,
" I heard a sound as of scraping tripe,
" And putting apples, wondrous ripe,
" Into a cider-press's gripe:
" And a moving away of pickle-tub boards,
" And a leaving ajar of conserve-cupboards,
" And the drawing the corks of train-oil-flasks,
" And a breaking the hoops of butter-casks;
" And it seemed as if a voice

" (Sweeter far than by harp or by psaltery
" Is breathed) called out, Oh rats, rejoice!
" The world is grown to one vast drysaltery!
" So munch on, crunch on, take your nuncheon,
" Breakfast, supper, dinner, luncheon!
" And just as a bulky sugar-puncheon,
" All ready staved, like a great sun shone
" Glorious scarce an inch before me,
" Just as methought it said, Come, bore me!
" —I found the Weser rolling o'er me."

VIII. You should have heard the Hamelin people
    Ringing the bells till they rocked the steeple;
    " Go," cried the Mayor, " and get long poles!
    " Pike out the nests and block up the holes!
    " Consult with carpenters and builders,
    " And leave in our town not even a trace
    " Of the rats! "—when suddenly up the face
    Of the Piper perked in the market-place,
    With a, " First, if you please, my thousand guilders!"

IX. A thousand guilders! The Mayor looked blue;
    So did the Corporation too.
    For council dinners made rare havock
    With Claret, Moselle, Vin-de-Grave, Hock;
    And half the money would replenish
    Their cellar's biggest butt with Rhenish.
    To pay this sum to a wandering fellow
    With a gipsy coat of red and yellow!
    " Beside," quoth the Mayor with a knowing wink,
    " Our business was done at the river's brink;
    " We saw with our eyes the vermin sink,
    " And what's dead can't come to life, I think.
    " So, friend, we're not the folks to shrink
    " From the duty of giving you something for drink,
    " And a matter of money to put in your poke;
    " But, as for the guilders, what we spoke
    " Of them, as you very well know, was in joke.
    " Beside, our losses have made us thrifty;
    " A thousand guilders! Come, take fifty!"

X. The Piper's face fell, and he cried,
    " No trifling! I can't wait, beside!
    " I've promised to visit by dinner time
    " Bagdat, and accept the prime

" Of the Head Cook's pottage, all he's rich in,
" For having left, in the Caliph's kitchen,
" Of a nest of scorpions no survivor—
" With him I proved no bargain-driver,
" With you, don't think I'll bate a stiver!
" And folks who put me in a passion
" May find me pipe to another fashion."

XI. " How? " cried the Mayor, " d'ye think I'll brook
" Being worse treated than a Cook?
" Insulted by a lazy ribald
" With idle pipe and vesture piebald?
" You threaten us, fellow?   Do your worst,
" Blow your pipe there till you burst! "

XII. Once more he stept into the street;
        And to his lips again
    Laid his long pipe of smooth straight cane;
        And ere he blew three notes (such sweet
    Soft notes as yet musician's cunning
        Never gave the enraptured air)
    There was a rustling, that seemed like a bustling
    Of merry crowds justling at pitching and hustling.
    Small feet were pattering, wooden shoes clattering,
    Little hands clapping, and little tongues chattering,
    And, like fowls in a farm-yard when barley is scattering,
    Out came the children running.
    All the little boys and girls,
    With rosy cheeks and flaxen curls,
    And sparkling eyes and teeth like pearls,
    Tripping and skipping, ran merrily after
    The wonderful music with shouting and laughter.

XIII. The Mayor was dumb, and the Council stood
    As if they were changed into blocks of wood,
    Unable to move a step, or cry
    To the children merrily skipping by—
    And could only follow with the eye
    That joyous crowd at the Piper's back.
    But how the Mayor was on the rack,
    And the wretched Council's bosoms beat,
    As the Piper turned from the High Street
    To where the Weser rolled its waters
    Right in the way of their sons and daughters!
    However he turned from South to West,

And to Koppelberg Hill his steps addressed,
And after him the children pressed;
Great was the joy in every breast.
" He never can cross that mighty top!
" He's forced to let the piping drop,
" And we shall see our children stop!"
When, lo, as they reached the mountain's side,
A wondrous portal opened wide,
As if a cavern was suddenly hollowed;
And the Piper advanced and the children followed,
And when all were in to the very last,
The door in the mountain side shut fast.
Did I say, all? No! One was lame,
And could not dance the whole of the way;
And in after years, if you would blame
His sadness, he was used to say,—
" It's dull in our town since my playmates left!
" I can't forget that I'm bereft
" Of all the pleasant sights they see,
" Which the Piper also promised me;
" For he led us, he said, to a joyous land,
" Joining the town and just at hand,
" Where waters gushed and fruit-trees grew,
" And flowers put forth a fairer hue,
" And everything was strange and new;
" The sparrows were brighter than peacocks here,
" And their dogs outran our fallow deer,
" And honey-bees had lost their stings,
" And horses were born with eagles' wings;
" And just as I became assured
" My lame foot would be speedily cured,
" The music stopped and I stood still,
" And found myself outside the Hill,
" Left alone against my will,
" To go now limping as before,
" And never hear of that country more!"

XIV. Alas, alas for Hamelin!
     There came into many a burgher's pate
     A text which says, that Heaven's Gate
     Opes to the Rich at as easy rate
As the needle's eye takes a camel in!
The Mayor sent East, West, North, and South

To offer the Piper by word of mouth,
  Wherever it was men's lot to find him,
Silver and gold to his heart's content,
If he'd only return the way he went,
  And bring the children behind him.
But when they saw 'twas a lost endeavour,
And Piper and dancers were gone for ever,
They made a decree that lawyers never
  Should think their records dated duly
If, after the day of the month and year,
These words did not as well appear,
" And so long after what happened here
  " On the Twenty-second of Júly,
" Thirteen hundred and Seventy-six: "
And the better in memory to fix
The place of the Children's last retreat,
They called it, the Pied Piper's Street—
Where any one playing on pipe or tabor
Was sure for the future to lose his labour.
Nor suffered they Hostelry or Tavern
  To shock with mirth a street so solemn;
But opposite the place of the cavern
  They wrote the story on a column,
And on the Great Church Window painted
The same, to make the world acquainted
How their children were stolen away;
And there it stands to this very day.
And I must not omit to say
That in Transylvania there's a tribe
Of alien people that ascribe
The outlandish ways and dress
On which their neighbours lay such stress,
To their fathers and mothers having risen
Out of some subterraneous prison
Into which they were trepanned
Long time ago in a mighty band
Out of Hamelin town in Brunswick land,
But how or why, they don't understand.

xv. So, Willy, let you and me be wipers
  Of scores out with all men—especially pipers:
  And, whether they pipe us free, from rats or from mice,
  If we've promised them aught, let us keep our promise.

"HOW THEY BROUGHT THE GOOD NEWS FROM GHENT TO AIX."

[16—.]

I.

I SPRANG to the stirrup, and Joris, and he;
I galloped, Dirck galloped, we galloped all three;
" Good speed! " cried the watch, as the gate-bolts undrew;
" Speed! " echoed the wall to us galloping through;
Behind shut the postern, the lights sank to rest,
And into the midnight we galloped abreast.

II.

Not a word to each other; we kept the great pace
Neck by neck, stride by stride, never changing our place;
I turned in my saddle and made its girths tight,
Then shortened each stirrup, and set the pique right,
Rebuckled the cheek-strap, chained slacker the bit,
Nor galloped less steadily Roland a whit.

III.

'Twas moonset at starting; but while we drew near
Lokern, the cocks crew and twilight dawned clear;
At Boom, a great yellow star came out to see;
At Düffield, 'twas morning as plain as could be;
And from Mecheln church-steeple we heard the half-chime,
So Joris broke silence with, " Yet there is time! "

IV.

At Aerschot, up leaped of a sudden the sun,
And against him the cattle stood black every one,
To stare thro' the mist at us galloping past,
And I saw my stout galloper Roland at last,
With resolute shoulders, each butting away
The haze, as some bluff river headland its spray.

V.

And his low head and crest, just one sharp ear bent back
For my voice, and the other pricked out on his track;
And one eye's black intelligence,—ever that glance
O'er its white edge at me, his own master, askance!

And the thick heavy spume-flakes which aye and anon
His fierce lips shook upwards in galloping on.

VI.

By Hasselt, Dirck groaned; and cried Joris, " Stay spur!
" Your Roos galloped bravely, the fault's not in her,
" We'll remember at Aix "—for one heard the quick wheeze
Of her chest, saw the stretched neck and staggering knees,
And sunk tail, and horrible heave of the flank,
As down on her haunches she shuddered and sank.

VII.

So we were left galloping, Joris and I,
Past Looz and past Tongres, no cloud in the sky;
The broad sun above laughed a pitiless laugh,
'Neath our feet broke the brittle bright stubble like chaff;
Till over by Dalhem a dome-spire sprang white,
And " Gallop," gasped Joris, " for Aix is in sight! "

VIII.

" How they'll greet us! "—and all in a moment his roan
Rolled neck and croup over, lay dead as a stone;
And there was my Roland to bear the whole weight
Of the news which alone could save Aix from her fate,
With his nostrils like pits full of blood to the brim,
And with circles of red for his eye-sockets' rim.

IX.

Then I cast loose my buffcoat, each holster let fall,
Shook off both my jack-boots, let go belt and all,
Stood up in the stirrup, leaned, patted his ear,
Called my Roland his pet-name, my horse without peer;
Clapped my hands, laughed and sang, any noise, bad or good,
Till at length into Aix Roland galloped and stood.

X.

And all I remember is, friends flocking round
As I sate with his head 'twixt my knees on the ground,
And no voice but was praising this Roland of mine,
As I poured down his throat our last measure of wine,
Which (the burgesses voted by common consent)
Was no more than his due who brought good news from Ghent.

PICTOR IGNOTUS.

[FLORENCE, 15—.]

I COULD have painted pictures like that youth's
   Ye praise so.   How my soul springs up!   No bar
Stayed me—ah, thought which saddens while it soothes!—
   Never did fate forbid me, star by star,
To outburst on your night with all my gift
   Of fires from God: nor would my flesh have shrunk
From seconding my soul, with eyes uplift
   And wide to Heaven, or, straight like thunder, sunk
To the centre, of an instant; or around
   Turned calmly and inquisitive, to scan
The licence and the limit, space and bound,
   Allowed to Truth made visible in Man.
And, like that youth ye praise so, all I saw,
   Over the canvas could my hand have flung,
Each face obedient to its passion's law,
   Each passion clear proclaimed without a tongue;
Whether Hope rose at once in all the blood,
   A tip-toe for the blessing of embrace,
Or Rapture drooped the eyes, as when her brood
   Pull down the nesting dove's heart to its place,
Or Confidence lit swift the forehead up,
   And locked the mouth fast, like a castle braved,—
O Human faces, hath it spilt, my cup?
   What did ye give me that I have not saved?
Nor will I say I have not dreamed (how well!)
   Of going—I, in each new picture,—forth,
As, making new hearts beat and bosoms swell,
   To Pope or Kaiser, East, West, South or North,
Bound for the calmly satisfied great State,
   Or glad aspiring little burgh, it went,
Flowers cast upon the car which bore the freight,
   Through old streets named afresh from its event,
Till it reached home, where learned Age should greet
   My face, and Youth, the star not yet distinct
Above his hair, lie learning at my feet!—
   Oh, thus to live, I and my picture, linked
With love about, and praise, till life should end,
   And then not go to Heaven, but linger here,

Here on my earth, earth's every man my friend,—
   The thought grew frightful, 'twas so wildly dear!
But a voice changed it! Glimpses of such sights
   Have scared me, like the revels thro' a door
Of some strange House of Idols at its rites;
   This world seemed not the world it was before!
Mixed with my loving trusting ones there trooped
   . . . Who summoned those cold faces that begun
To press on me and judge me? Tho' I stooped
   Shrinking, as from the soldiery a nun,
They drew me forth, and spite of me . . . enough!
   These buy and sell our pictures, take and give,
Count them for garniture and household-stuff,
   And where they live our pictures needs must live,
And see their faces, listen to their prate,
   Partakers of their daily pettiness,
Discussed of,—" This I love, or this I hate,
   " This likes me more, and this affects me less!"
Wherefore I chose my portion. If at whiles
   My heart sinks, as monotonous I paint
These endless cloisters and eternal aisles
   With the same series, Virgin, Babe, and Saint,
With the same cold, calm, beautiful regard,
   At least no merchant traffics in my heart;
The sanctuary's gloom at least shall ward
   Vain tongues from where my pictures stand apart,
Only prayer breaks the silence of the shrine
   While, blackening in the daily candle-smoke,
They moulder on the damp wall's travertine,
   'Mid echoes the light footstep never woke.
So die, my pictures; surely, gently die!
   Oh, youth, men praise so,—holds their praise its worth?
Blown harshly, keeps the trump its golden cry?
   Tastes sweet the water with such specks of earth?

THE ITALIAN IN ENGLAND.

THAT second time they hunted me
From hill to plain, from shore to sea,
And Austria, hounding far and wide
Her blood-hounds thro' the country-side,
Breathed hot and instant on my trace,—
I made six days a hiding-place
Of that dry green old aqueduct
Where I and Charles, when boys, have plucked
The fire-flies from the roof above,
Bright creeping thro' the moss they love.
—How long it seems since Charles was lost!
Six days the soldiers crossed and crossed
The country in my very sight;
And when that peril ceased at night,
The sky broke out in red dismay
With signal-fires; well, there I lay
Close covered o'er in my recess,
Up to the neck in ferns and cress,
Thinking on Metternich our friend,
And Charles's miserable end,
And much beside, two days; the third,
Hunger o'ercame me when I heard
The peasants from the village go
To work among the maize; you know,
With us, in Lombardy, they bring
Provisions packed on mules, a string
With little bells that cheer their task,
And casks, and boughs on every cask
To keep the sun's heat from the wine;
These I let pass in jingling line,
And, close on them, dear noisy crew,
The peasants from the village, too;
For at the very rear would troop
Their wives and sisters in a group
To help, I knew; when these had passed,
I threw my glove to strike the last,
Taking the chance: she did not start,
Much less cry out, but stooped apart
One instant, rapidly glanced round,

And saw me beckon from the ground:
A wild bush grows and hides my crypt;
She picked my glove up while she stripped
A branch off, then rejoined the rest
With that; my glove lay in her breast:
Then I drew breath: they disappeared:
It was for Italy I feared.

An hour, and she returned alone
Exactly where my glove was thrown.
Meanwhile came many thoughts; on me
Rested the hopes of Italy;
I had devised a certain tale
Which, when 'twas told her, could not fail
Persuade a peasant of its truth;
I meant to call a freak of youth
This hiding, and give hopes of pay,
And no temptation to betray.
But when I saw that woman's face,
Its calm simplicity of grace,
Our Italy's own attitude
In which she walked thus far, and stood,
Planting each naked foot so firm,
To crush the snake and spare the worm—
At first sight of her eyes, I said,
" I am that man upon whose head
" They fix the price, because I hate
" The Austrians over us: the State
" Will give you gold—oh, gold so much,
" If you betray me to their clutch!
" And be your death, for aught I know,
" If once they find you saved their foe.
" Now, you must bring me food and drink,
" And also paper, pen, and ink,
" And carry safe what I shall write
" To Padua, which you'll reach at night
" Before the Duomo shuts; go in,
" And wait till Tenebræ begin;
" Walk to the third Confessional,
" Between the pillar and the wall,
" And kneeling whisper *whence comes peace?*
" Say it a second time; then cease;
" And if the voice inside returns,

" *From Christ and Freedom ; what concerns*
" *The cause of Peace ?*—for answer, slip
" My letter where you placed your lip;
" Then come back happy we have done
" Our mother service—I, the son,
" As you the daughter of our land!"

   Three mornings more, she took her stand
In the same place, with the same eyes:
I was no surer of sun-rise
Than of her coming: we conferred
Of her own prospects, and I heard
She had a lover—stout and tall,
She said—then let her eyelids fall,
" He could do much "—as if some doubt
Entered her heart,—then, passing out,
" She could not speak for others—who
" Had other thoughts; herself she knew: "
And so she brought me drink and food.
After four days, the scouts pursued
Another path: at last arrived
The help my Paduan friends contrived
To furnish me: she brought the news:
For the first time I could not choose
But kiss her hand and lay my own
Upon her head—" This faith was shown
" To Italy, our mother;—she
" Uses my hand and blesses thee!"
She followed down to the sea-shore;
I left and never saw her more.

   How very long since I have thought
Concerning—much less wished for—aught
Beside the good of Italy
For which I live and mean to die!
I never was in love; and since
Charles proved false, nothing could convince
My inmost heart I had a friend;
However, if I pleased to spend
Real wishes on myself—say, Three—
I know at least what one should be;
I would grasp Metternich until
I felt his red wet throat distil

In blood thro' these two hands: and next,
—Nor much for that am I perplexed—
Charles, perjured traitor, for his part,
Should die slow of a broken heart
Under his new employers: last
—Ah, there, what should I wish? For fast
Do I grow old and out of strength.—
If I resolved to seek at length
My father's house again, how scared
They all would look, and unprepared!
My brothers live in Austria's pay
—Disowned me long ago, men say;
And all my early mates who used
To praise me so—perhaps induced
More than one early step of mine—
Are turning wise; while some opine
" Freedom grows Licence," some suspect
" Haste breeds Delay," and recollect
They always said, such premature
Beginnings never could endure!
So, with a sullen " All's for best,"
The land seems settling to its rest.
I think, then, I should wish to stand
This evening in that dear, lost land,
Over the sea the thousand miles,
And know if yet that woman smiles
With the calm smile; some little farm
She lives in there, no doubt; what harm
If I sate on the door-side bench,
And, while her spindle made a trench
Fantastically in the dust,
Inquired of all her fortunes—just
Her children's ages and their names,
And what may be the husband's aims
For each of them—I'd talk this out,
And sit there, for an hour about,
Then kiss her hand once more, and lay
Mine on her head, and go my way.

So much for idle wishing—how
It steals the time! To business now!

THE ENGLISHMAN IN ITALY.

[PIANO DI SORRENTO.]

FORTÙ, Fortù, my beloved one,
  Sit here by my side,
On my knees put up both little feet!
  I was sure, if I tried,
I could make you laugh spite of Scirocco:
  Now, open your eyes—
Let me keep you amused till he vanish
  In black from the skies,
With telling my memories over
  As you tell your beads;
All the memories plucked at Sorrento
  —The flowers, or the weeds.

Time for rain! for your long hot dry Autumn
  Had net-worked with brown
The white skin of each grape on the bunches,
  Marked like a quail's crown,
Those creatures you make such account of,
  Whose heads,—specked with white
Over brown like a great spider's back,
  As I told you last night,—
Your mother bites off for her supper;
  Red-ripe as could be.
Pomegranates were chapping and splitting
  In halves on the tree:
And betwixt the loose walls of great flintstone,
  Or in the thick dust
On the path, or straight out of the rock side,
  Wherever could thrust
Some burnt sprig of bold hardy rock-flower
  Its yellow face up,
For the prize were great butterflies fighting,
  Some five for one cup.
So I guessed, ere I got up this morning,
  What change was in store,
By the quick rustle-down of the quail-nets
  Which woke me before

I could open my shutter, made fast
    With a bough and a stone,
And look thro' the twisted dead vine-twigs,
    Sole lattice that's known!
Quick and sharp rang the rings down the net-poles,
    While, busy beneath,
Your priest and his brother tugged at them,
    The rain in their teeth:
And out upon all the flat house-roofs
    Where split figs lay drying,
The girls took the frails under cover:
    Nor use seemed in trying
To get out the boats and go fishing,
    For, under the cliff,
Fierce the black water frothed o'er the blind-rock.
    No seeing our skiff
Arrive about noon from Amalfi,
    —Our fisher arrive,
And pitch down his basket before us,
    All trembling alive
With pink and grey jellies, your sea-fruit,
    —You touch the strange lumps,
And mouths gape there, eyes open, all manner
    Of horns and of humps,
Which only the fisher looks grave at,
    While round him like imps
Cling screaming the children as naked
    And brown as his shrimps;
Himself too as bare to the middle—
    —You see round his neck
The string and its brass coin suspended,
    That saves him from wreck.
But to-day not a boat reached Salerno,
    So back to a man
Came our friends, with whose help in the vineyards
    Grape-harvest began:
In the vat, half-way up in our house-side,
    Like blood the juice spins,
While your brother all bare-legged is dancing
    Till breathless he grins
Dead-beaten, in effort on effort
    To keep the grapes under,
Since still when he seems all but master,

In pours the fresh plunder
From girls who keep coming and going
    With basket on shoulder,
And eyes shut against the rain's driving,
    Your girls that are older,—
For under the hedges of aloe,
    And where, on its bed
Of the orchard's black mould, the love-apple
    Lies pulpy and red,
All the young ones are kneeling and filling
    Their laps with the snails
Tempted out by this first rainy weather,—
    Your best of regales,
As to-night will be proved to my sorrow,
    When, supping in state,
We shall feast our grape-gleaners (two dozen,
    Three over one plate)
With lasagne so tempting to swallow
    In slippery ropes,
And gourds fried in great purple slices,
    That colour of popes.
Meantime, see the grape-bunch they've brought you,—
    The rain-water slips
O'er the heavy blue bloom on each globe
    Which the wasp to your lips
Still follows with fretful persistence—
    Nay, taste, while awake,
This half of a curd-white smooth cheese-ball,
    That peels, flake by flake,
Like an onion's, each smoother and whiter;
    Next, sip this weak wine
From the thin green glass flask, with its stopper,
    A leaf of the vine,—
And end with the prickly-pear's red flesh
    That leaves thro' its juice
The stony black seeds on your pearl-teeth
    . . . Scirocco is loose!
Hark! the quick, whistling pelt of the olives
    Which, thick in one's track,
Tempt the stranger to pick up and bite them,
    Tho' not yet half black!
How the old twisted olive trunks shudder!
    The medlars let fall

Their hard fruit, and the brittle great fig-trees
  Snap off, figs and all,—
For here comes the whole of the tempest!
  No refuge, but creep
Back again to my side and my shoulder,
  And listen or sleep.

O how will your country show next week,
  When all the vine-boughs
Have been stripped of their foliage to pasture
  The mules and the cows?
Last eve, I rode over the mountains;
  Your brother, my guide,
Soon left me, to feast on the myrtles
  That offered, each side,
Their fruit-balls, black, glossy, and luscious,—
  Or strip from the sorbs
A treasure, so rosy and wondrous,
  Of hairy gold orbs!
But my mule picked his sure, sober path out,
  Just stopping to neigh
When he recognised down in the valley
  His mates on their way
With the faggots, and barrels of water;
  And soon we emerged
From the plain, where the woods could scarce follow;
  And still as we urged
Our way, the woods wondered, and left us,
  As up still we trudged
Though the wild path grew wilder each instant,
  And place was e'en grudged
'Mid the rock-chasms, and piles of loose stones
  (Like the loose broken teeth
Of some monster, which climbed there to die
  From the ocean beneath)
Place was grudged to the silver-grey fume-weed
  That clung to the path,
And dark rosemary, ever a-dying,
  That, 'spite the wind's wrath,
So loves the salt rock's face to seaward,—
  And lentisks as staunch
To the stone where they root and bear berries,—
  And . . . what shows a branch

Coral-coloured, transparent, with circlets
   Of pale seagreen leaves—
Over all trod my mule with the caution
   Of gleaners o'er sheaves,
Still, foot after foot like a lady—
   So, round after round,
He climbed to the top of Calvano,
   And God's own profound
Was above me, and round me the mountains,
   And under, the sea,
And within me, my heart to bear witness
   What was and shall be!
Oh heaven, and the terrible crystal!
   No rampart excludes
Your eye from the life to be lived
   In the blue solitudes!
Oh, those mountains, their infinite movement!
   Still moving with you—
For, ever some new head and breast of them
   Thrusts into view
To observe the intruder—you see it
   If quickly you turn
And, before they escape you, surprise them—
   They grudge you should learn
How the soft plains they look on, lean over,
   And love (they pretend)
—Cower beneath them; the flat sea-pine crouches,
   The wild fruit-trees bend,
E'en the myrtle-leaves curl, shrink and shut—
   All is silent and grave:
'Tis a sensual and timorous beauty—
   How fair, but a slave!
So, I turned to the sea,—and there slumbered
   As greenly as ever
Those isles of the siren, your Galli;
   No ages can sever
The Three, nor enable their sister
   To join them,—half way
On the voyage, she looked at Ulysses—
   No farther to-day;
Tho' the small one, just launched in the wave,
   Watches breast-high and steady
From under the rock, her bold sister

Swum half-way already.
Fortù, shall we sail there together
    And see from the sides
Quite new rocks show their faces—new haunts
    Where the siren abides?
Shall we sail round and round them, close over
    The rocks, tho' unseen,
That ruffle the gray glassy water
    To glorious green?
Then scramble from splinter to splinter,
    Reach land and explore,
On the largest, the strange square black turret
    With never a door,
Just a loop to admit the quick lizards;
    Then, stand there and hear
The birds' quiet singing, that tells us
    What life is, so clear!
The secret they sang to Ulysses,
    When, ages ago,
He heard and he knew this life's secret,
    I hear and I know!

Ah, see! The sun breaks o'er Calvano—
    He strikes the great gloom
And flutters it o'er the mount's summit
    In airy gold fume!
All is over! Look out, see the gypsy,
    Our tinker and smith,
Has arrived, set up bellows and forge,
    And down-squatted forthwith
To his hammering, under the wall there;
    One eye keeps aloof
The urchins that itch to be putting
    His jews'-harps to proof,
While the other, thro' locks of curled wire,
    Is watching how sleek
Shines the hog, come to share in the windfalls
    —An abbot's own cheek!
All is over! Wake up and come out now,
    And down let us go,
And see the fine things got in order
    At Church for the show
Of the Sacrament, set forth this evening;

To-morrow's the Feast
Of the Rosary's Virgin, by no means
   Of Virgins the least—
As you'll hear in the off-hand discourse
   Which (all nature, no art)
The Dominican brother, these three weeks,
   Was getting by heart.
Not a post nor a pillar but's dizened
   With red and blue papers;
All the roof waves with ribbons, each altar
   A-blaze with long tapers;
But the great masterpiece is the scaffold
   Rigged glorious to hold
All the fiddlers and fifers and drummers,
   And trumpeters bold,
Not afraid of Bellini nor Auber,
   Who, when the priest's hoarse,
Will strike us up something that's brisk
   For the feast's second course.
And then will the flaxen-winged Image
   Be carried in pomp
Thro' the plain, while in gallant procession
   The priests mean to stomp.
And all round the glad church lie old bottles
   With gunpowder stopped,
Which will be, when the Image re-enters,
   Religiously popped.
And at night from the crest of Calvano
   Great bonfires will hang,
On the plain will the trumpets join chorus,
   And more poppers bang!
At all events, come—to the garden,
   As far as the wall,
See me tap with a hoe on the plaster
   Till out there shall fall
A scorpion with wide angry nippers!
   . . . "Such trifles "—you say?
Fortù, in my England at home,
   Men meet gravely to-day
And debate, if abolishing Corn-laws
   Is righteous and wise
—If 'tis proper, Scirocco should vanish
   In black from the skies!

THE LOST LEADER.

I.

JUST for a handful of silver he left us,
    Just for a riband to stick in his coat—
Found the one gift of which fortune bereft us,
    Lost all the others she lets us devote;
They, with the gold to give, doled him out silver,
    So much was their's who so little allowed:
How all our copper had gone for his service!
    Rags—were they purple, his heart had been proud!
We that had loved him so, followed him, honoured him,
    Lived in his mild and magnificent eye,
Learned his great language, caught his clear accents,
    Made him our pattern to live and to die!
Shakespeare was of us, Milton was for us,
    Burns, Shelley, were with us,—they watch from their
        graves!
He alone breaks from the van and the freemen,
    He alone sinks to the rear and the slaves!

II.

We shall march prospering,—not thro' his presence;
    Songs may inspirit us,—not from his lyre;
Deeds will be done,—while he boasts his quiescence,
    Still bidding crouch whom the rest bade aspire:
Blot out his name, then,—record one lost soul more,
    One task more declined, one more footpath untrod,
One more triumph for devils, and sorrow for angels,
    One wrong more to man, one more insult to God!
Life's night begins: let him never come back to us!
    There would be doubt, hesitation and pain,
Forced praise on our part—the glimmer of twilight,
    Never glad confident morning again!
Best fight on well, for we taught him,—strike gallantly,
    Aim at our heart ere we pierce through his own;
Then let him receive the new knowledge and wait us,
    Pardoned in Heaven, the first by the throne!

THE LOST MISTRESS.

I. ALL's over, then—does truth sound bitter
    As one at first believes?
Hark, 'tis the sparrows' good-night twitter
    About your cottage eaves!

II. And the leaf-buds on the vine are woolly,
    I noticed that, to-day;
One day more bursts them open fully
    —You know the red turns gray.

III. To-morrow we meet the same then, dearest?
    May I take your hand in mine?
Mere friends are we,—well, friends the merest
    Keep much that I'll resign:

IV. For each glance of that eye so bright and black,
    Though I keep with heart's endeavour,—
Your voice, when you wish the snowdrops back,
    Though it stays in my soul for ever!—

V. —Yet I will but say what mere friends say,
    Or only a thought stronger;
I will hold your hand but as long as all may,
    Or so very little longer!

HOME-THOUGHTS, FROM ABROAD.

I. OH, to be in England
Now that April's there,
And whoever wakes in England
Sees, some morning, unaware,
That the lowest boughs and the brush-wood sheaf
Round the elm-tree bole are in tiny leaf,
While the chaffinch sings on the orchard bough
In England—now!

II. And after April, when May follows,
    And the whitethroat builds, and all the swallows—
    Hark! where my blossomed pear-tree in the hedge
    Leans to the field and scatters on the clover
    Blossoms and dewdrops—at the bent-spray's edge—
    That's the wise thrush; he sings each song twice over,
    Lest you should think he never could recapture
    The first fine careless rapture!
    And though the fields look rough with hoary dew,
    All will be gay when noontide wakes anew
    The buttercups, the little children's dower
    —Far brighter than this gaudy melon-flower!

HOME-THOUGHTS, FROM THE SEA.

NOBLY, nobly Cape Saint Vincent to the north-west died away;
Sunset ran, one glorious blood-red, reeking into Cadiz Bay;
Bluish mid the burning water, full in face Trafalgar lay;
In the dimmest north-east distance, dawned Gibraltar grand
    and gray;
"Here and here did England help me,—how can I help
    England?"—say,
Whoso turns as I, this evening, turn to God to praise and pray,
While Jove's planet rises yonder, silent over Africa.

NATIONALITY IN DRINKS.

I. My heart sunk with our Claret-flask,
        Just now, beneath the heavy sedges
    That serve this pond's black face for mask;
        And still at yonder broken edges
    Of the hole, where up the bubbles glisten,
    After my heart I look and listen.

II. Our laughing little flask, compell'd
        Thro' depth to depth more bleak and shady;
    As when, both arms beside her held,
        Feet straightened out, some gay French lady
    Is caught up from Life's light and motion,
        And dropped into Death's silent ocean!

Up jumped Tokay on our table,
Like a pygmy castle-warder,
Dwarfish to see, but stout and able,
Arms and accoutrements all in order;
And fierce he looked north, then, wheeling south
Blew with his bugle a challenge to Drouth,
Cocked his flap-hat with the tosspot-feather,
Twisted his thumb in his red moustache,
Jungled his huge brass spurs together,
Tightened his waist with its Buda sash,
And then with an impudence nought could abash,
Shrugged his hump-shoulder,
To tell the beholder,
For twenty such knaves he should laugh but the bolder,
And so with his sword-hilt gallantly jutting,
And dexter-hand on his haunch abutting,
Went the little man, Sir Ausbruch, strutting!

Here's to Nelson's memory!
'Tis the second time that I, at sea,
Right off Cape Trafalgar here,
Have drunk it deep in British beer:
Nelson for ever—any time
Am I his to command in prose or rhyme!
Give me of Nelson only a touch,
And I guard it, be it little or much;
Here's one the Captain gives, and so
Down at the word, by George, shall it go!
He says that at Greenwich they show the beholder
Nelson's coat, "still with tar on the shoulder,
" For he used to lean with one shoulder digging,
" Jigging, as it were, and zig-zag-zigging,
" Up against the mizen rigging!"

THE BISHOP ORDERS HIS TOMB AT ST.
PRAXED'S CHURCH.

[ROME, 15—.]

VANITY, saith the preacher, vanity!
Draw round my bed: is Anselm keeping back?
Nephews—sons mine . . . ah God, I know not! Well—
She, men would have to be your mother once,
Old Gandolf envied me, so fair she was!
What's done is done, and she is dead beside,
Dead long ago, and I am bishop since,
And as she died so must we die ourselves,
And thence ye may perceive the world's a dream.
Life, how and what is it? As here I lie
In this state-chamber, dying by degrees,
Hours and long hours in the dead night, I ask
" Do I live, am I dead?" Peace, peace seems all.
St. Praxed's ever was the church for peace;
And so, about this tomb of mine. I fought
With tooth and nail to save my niche, ye know:
—Old Gandolf cozened me, despite my care;
Shrewd was that snatch from out the corner South
He graced his carrion with, God curse the same!
Yet still my niche is not so cramped but thence
One sees the pulpit o' the epistle-side,
And somewhat of the choir, those silent seats,
And up into the aery dome where live
The angels, and a sunbeam's sure to lurk:
And I shall fill my slab of basalt there,
And 'neath my tabernacle take my rest,
With those nine columns round me, two and two,
The odd one at my feet where Anselm stands:
Peach-blossom marble all, the rare, the ripe
As fresh-poured red wine of a mighty pulse
—Old Gandolf with his paltry onion-stone,
Put me where I may look at him! True peach,
Rosy and flawless: how I earned the prize!
Draw close: that conflagration of my church
—What then? So much was saved if aught were missed!
My sons, ye would not be my death? Go dig
The white-grape vineyard where the oil-press stood,
Drop water gently till the surface sinks,

And if ye find . . . Ah, God I know not, I! . . .
Bedded in store of rotton figleaves soft,
And corded up in a tight olive-frail,
Some lump, ah God, of *lapis lazuli,*
Big as a Jew's head cut off at the nape,
Blue as a vein o'er the Madonna's breast . . .
Sons, all have I bequeathed you, villas, all,
That brave Frascati villa with its bath,
So, let the blue lump poise between my knees,
Like God the Father's globe on both his hands
Ye worship in the Jesu Church so gay,
For Gandolf shall not choose but see and burst!
Swift as a weaver's shuttle fleet our years:
Man goeth to the grave, and where is he?
Did I say basalt for my slab, sons? Black—
'Twas ever antique-black I meant! How else
Shall ye contrast my frieze to come beneath?
The bas-relief in bronze ye promised me,
Those Pans and Nymphs ye wot of, and perchance
Some tripod, thyrsus, with a vase or so,
The Saviour at his sermon on the mount,
St. Praxed in a glory, and one Pan
Ready to twitch the Nymph's last garment off,
And Moses with the tables . . . but I know
Ye mark me not! What do they whisper thee,
Child of my bowels, Anselm? Ah, ye hope
To revel down my villas while I gasp
Bricked o'er with beggar's mouldy travertine
Which Gandolf from his tomb-top chuckles at!
Nay, boys, ye love me—all of jasper, then!
'Tis jasper ye stand pledged to, lest I grieve
My bath must needs be left behind, alas!
One block, pure green as a pistachio-nut,
There's plenty jasper somewhere in the world—
And have I not St. Praxed's ear to pray
Horses for ye, and brown Greek manuscripts,
And mistresses with great smooth marbly limbs?
—That's if ye carve my epitaph aright,
Choice Latin, picked phrase, Tully's every word,
No gaudy ware like Gandolf's second line—
Tully, my masters? Ulpian serves his need!
And then how I shall lie through centuries,
And hear the blessed mutter of the mass,

And see God made and eaten all day long,
And feel the steady candle-flame, and taste
Good strong thick stupifying incense-smoke!
For as I lie here, hours of the dead night,
Dying in state and by such slow degrees,
I fold my arms as if they clasped a crook,
And stretch my feet forth straight as stone can point,
And let the bedclothes for a mortcloth drop
Into great laps and folds of sculptor's-work:
And as yon tapers dwindle, and strange thoughts
Grow, with a certain humming in my ears,
About the life before I lived this life,
And this life too, Popes, Cardinals and Priests,
St. Praxed at his sermon on the mount,
Your tall pale mother with her talking eyes,
And new-found agate urns as fresh as day,
And marble's language, Latin pure, discreet,
—Aha, ELUCESCEBAT quoth our friend?
No Tully, said I, Ulpian at the best!
Evil and brief hath been my pilgrimage.
All *lapis*, all, sons! Else I give the Pope
My villas: will ye ever eat my heart?
Ever your eyes were as a lizard's quick,
They glitter like your mother's for my soul,
Or ye would heighten my impoverished frieze,
Piece out its starved design, and fill my vase
With grapes, and add a vizor and a Term,
And to the tripod ye would tie a lynx
That in his struggle throws the thyrsus down,
To comfort me on my entablature
Whereon I am to lie till I must ask
" Do I live, am I dead? "   There, leave me, there!
For ye have stabbed me with ingratitude
To death—ye wish it—God, ye wish it! Stone—
Gritstone, a-crumble! Clammy squares which sweat
As if the corpse they keep were oozing through—
And no more *lapis* to delight the world!
Well, go! I bless ye. Fewer tapers there,
But in a row: and, going, turn your backs
—Ay, like departing altar-ministrants,
And leave me in my church, the church for peace,
That I may watch at leisure if he leers—
Old Gandolf, at me, from his onion-stone,
As still he envied me, so fair she was!

GARDEN-FANCIES.

I.—THE FLOWER'S NAME.

I. HERE's the garden she walked across,
    Arm in my arm, such a short while since:
Hark, now I push its wicket, the moss
    Hinders the hinges and makes them wince!
She must have reached this shrub ere she turned,
    As back with that murmur the wicket swung;
For she laid the poor snail, my chance foot spurned,
    To feed and forget it the leaves among.

II. Down this side of the gravel-walk
    She went while her robe's edge brushed the box:
And here she paused in her gracious talk
    To point me a moth on the milk-white flox.
Roses, ranged in valiant row,
    I will never think that she passed you by!
She loves you noble roses, I know;
    But yonder, see, where the rock-plants lie!

III. This flower she stopped at, finger on lip,
    Stooped over, in doubt, as settling its claim;
Till she gave me, with pride to make no slip,
    Its soft meandering Spanish name.
What a name! was it love, or praise?
    Speech half-asleep, or song half-awake?
I must learn Spanish, one of these days,
    Only for that slow sweet name's sake.

IV. Roses, if I live and do well,
    I may bring her, one of these days,
To fix you fast with as fine a spell,
    Fit you each with his Spanish phrase!
But do not detain me now; for she lingers
    There, like sunshine over the ground,
And ever I see her soft white fingers
    Searching after the bud she found.

V. Flower, you Spaniard, look that you grow not,
    Stay as you are and be loved for ever!

Bud, if I kiss you 'tis that you blow not,
   Mind, the shut pink mouth opens never!
For while thus it pouts, her fingers wrestle,
   Twinkling the audacious leaves between,
Till round they turn and down they nestle—
   Is not the dear mark still to be seen?

VI. Where I find her not, beauties vanish;
   Whither I follow her, beauties flee;
Is there no method to tell her in Spanish
   June's twice June since she breathed it with me?
Come, bud, show me the least of her traces,
   Treasure my lady's lightest foot-fall
—Ah, you may flout and turn up your faces—
   Roses, you are not so fair after all!

II.—SIBRANDUS SCHAFNABURGENSIS

I. Plague take all your pedants, say I!
   He who wrote what I hold in my hand,
Centuries back was so good as to die,
   Leaving this rubbish to cumber the land;
This, that was a book in its time,
   Printed on paper and bound in leather,
Last month in the white of a matin-prime
   Just when the birds sang all together.

II. Into the garden I brought it to read,
   And under the arbute and laurustine
Read it, so help me grace in my need,
   From title-page to closing line.
Chapter on chapter did I count,
   As a curious traveller counts Stonehenge;
Added up the mortal amount;
   And then proceeded to my revenge.

III. Yonder's a plum-tree, with a crevice
   An owl would build in, were he but sage;
For a lap of moss, like a fine pont-levis
   In a castle of the middle age,
Joins to a lip of gum, pure amber;
   When he'd be private, there might he spend
Hours alone in his lady's chamber:
   Into this crevice I dropped our friend.

IV. Splash, went he, as under he ducked,
    —I knew at the bottom rain drippings stagnate;
Next a handful of blossoms I plucked
    To bury him with, my bookshelf's magnate;
Then I went in-doors, brought out a loaf,
    Half a cheese, and a bottle of Chablis;
Lay on the grass and forgot the oaf
    Over a jolly chapter of Rabelais.

V. Now, this morning, betwixt the moss
    And gum that locked our friend in limbo,
A spider had spun his web across,
    And sate in the midst with arms a-kimbo:
So I took pity, for learning's sake,
    And, *de profundis, accentibus lætis,*
Cantate ! quoth I, as I got a rake,
    And up I fished his delectable treatise.

VI. Here you have it, dry in the sun,
    With all the binding all of a blister,
And great blue spots where the ink has run,
    And reddish streaks that wink and glister
O'er the page so beautifully yellow—
    Oh, well have the droppings played their tricks !
Did he guess how toadstools grow, this fellow?
    Here's one stuck in his chapter six !

VII. How did he like it when the live creatures
    Tickled and toused and browsed him all over,
And worm, slug, eft, with serious features,
    Came in, each one, for his right of trover;
When the water-beetle with great blind deaf face
    Made of her eggs the stately deposit,
And the newt borrowed just so much of the preface
    As tiled in the top of his black wife's closet.

VIII. All that life, and fun, and romping,
    All that frisking, and twisting, and coupling,
While slowly our poor friend's leaves were swamping,
    And clasps were cracking, and covers suppling !
As if you had carried sour John Knox
    To the play-house at Paris, Vienna, or Munich,
Fastened him into a front-row box,
    And danced off the Ballet with trousers and tunic.

IX. Come, old Martyr! What, torment enough is it?
    Back to my room shall you take your sweet self!
Good-bye, mother-beetle; husband-eft, *sufficit !*
    See the snug niche I have made on my shelf:
A.'s book shall prop you up, B.'s shall cover you,
    Here's C. to be grave with, or D. to be gay,
And with E. on each side, and F. right over you,
    Dry-rot at ease till the Judgment-day!

THE LABORATORY.

[ANCIEN RÉGIME.]

I. Now that I, tying thy glass mask tightly,
May gaze thro' these faint smokes curling whitely,
As thou pliest thy trade in this devil's-smithy—
Which is the poison to poison her, prithee?

II. He is with her; and they know that I know
Where they are, what they do: they believe my tears
    flow
While they laugh, laugh at me, at me fled to the drear
Empty church, to pray God in, for them!—I am here.

III. Grind away, moisten and mash up thy paste,
Pound at thy powder,—I am not in haste!
Better sit thus, and observe thy strange things,
Than go where men wait me and dance at the King's.

IV. That in the mortar—you call it a gum?
Ah, the brave tree whence such gold oozings come!
And yonder soft phial, the exquisite blue,
Sure to taste sweetly,—is that poison too?

V. Had I but all of them, thee and thy treasures,
What a wild crowd of invisible pleasures!
To carry pure death in an earring, a casket,
A signet, a fan-mount, a fillagree-basket!

VI. Soon, at the King's, a mere lozenge to give
And Pauline should have just thirty minutes to live!
But to light a pastile, and Elise, with her head,
And her breast, and her arms, and her hands, should
    drop dead!

VII. Quick—is it finished? The colour's too grim!
    Why not soft like the phial's, enticing and dim?
    Let it brighten her drink, let her turn it and stir,
    And try it and taste, ere she fix and prefer!

VIII. What a drop! She's not little, no minion like me—
    That's why she ensnared him: this never will free
    The soul from those strong, great eyes,—say, " no! "
    To that pulse's magnificent come-and-go.

IX. For only last night, as they whispered, I brought
    My own eyes to bear on her so, that I thought
    Could I keep them one half minute fixed, she would fall,
    Shrivelled; she fell not; yet this does it all!

X. Not that I bid you spare her the pain!
    Let death be felt and the proof remain;
    Brand, burn up, bite into its grace—
    He is sure to remember her dying face!

XI. Is it done? Take my mask off! Nay, be not morose,
    It kills her, and this prevents seeing it close:
    The delicate droplet, my whole fortune's fee—
    If it hurts her, beside, can it ever hurt me?

XII. Now, take all my jewels, gorge gold to your fill,
    You may kiss me, old man, on my mouth if you will!
    But brush this dust off me, lest horror it brings
    Ere I know it—next moment I dance at the King's!

THE CONFESSIONAL.

[SPAIN.]

I. IT is a lie—their Priests, their Pope,
    Their Saints, their . . . all they fear or hope
    Are lies, and lies—there! thro' my door
    And ceiling, there! and walls and floor,
    There, lies, they lie, shall still be hurled,
    Till spite of them I reach the world!

II. You think Priests just and holy men!
Before they put me in this den,
I was a human creature too,
With flesh and blood like one of you,
A girl that laughed in beauty's pride
Like lilies in your world outside.

III. I had a lover—shame avaunt!
This poor wrenched body, grim and gaunt,
Was kissed all over till it burned,
By lips the truest, love e'er turned
His heart's own tint: one night they kissed
My soul out in a burning mist.

IV. So, next day when the accustomed train
Of things grew round my sense again,
"That is a sin," I said—and slow
With downcast eyes to church I go,
And pass to the confession-chair,
And tell the old mild father there.

V. But when I faulter Beltran's name,
"Ha?" quoth the father; "much I blame
"The sin; yet wherefore idly grieve?
"Despair not,—strenuously retrieve!
"Nay, I will turn this love of thine
"To lawful love, almost divine.

VI. "For he is young, and led astray,
"This Beltran, and he schemes, men say,
"To change the laws of church and state;
"So, thine shall be an angel's fate,
"Who, ere the thunder breaks, should roll
"Its cloud away and save his soul.

VII. "For, when he lies upon thy breast,
"Thou mayst demand and be possessed
"Of all his plans, and next day steal
"To me, and all those plans reveal,
"That I and every priest, to purge
"His soul, may fast and use the scourge."

VIII. That father's beard was long and white,
With love and truth his brow seemed bright,

I went back, all on fire with joy,
And, that same evening, bade the boy,
Tell me, as lovers should, heart-free,
Something to prove his love of me.

IX. He told me what he would not tell
For hope of heaven or fear of Hell;
And I lay listening in such pride,
And, soon as he had left my side,
Tripped to the church by morning-light
To save his soul in his despite.

X. I told the father all his schemes,
Who were his comrades, what their dreams;
" And now make haste," I said, " to pray
" The one spot from his soul away;
" To-night he comes, but not the same
" Will look ! " At night he never came.

XI. Nor next night: on the after-morn,
I went forth with a strength new-born:
The church was empty; something drew
My steps into the street; I knew
It led me to the market-place—
Where, lo,—on high—the father's face !

XII. That horrible black scaffold drest—
The stapled block . . . God sink the rest !
That head strapped back, that blinding vest,
Those knotted hands and naked breast—
Till near one busy hangman pressed—
And—on the neck these arms caressed. . . .

XIII. No part in aught they hope or fear !
No Heaven with them, no Hell,—and here,
No Earth, not so much space as pens
My body in their worst of dens
But shall bear God and Man my cry—
Lies—lies, again—and still, they lie !

THE FLIGHT OF THE DUCHESS.

I. YOU'RE my friend:
  I was the man the Duke spoke to;
  I helped the Duchess to cast off his yoke, too;
  So, here's the tale from beginning to end,
  My friend!

II. Ours is a great wild country:
  If you climb to our castle's top,
  I don't see where your eye can stop;
  For when you've passed the corn-field country,
  Where vineyards leave off, flocks are packed,
  And sheep-range leads to cattle-tract,
  And cattle-tract to open-chase,
  And open-chase to the very base
  Of the mountain, where, at a funeral pace,
  Round about, solemn and slow,
  One by one, row after row,
  Up and up the pine-trees go,
  So, like black priests up, and so
  Down the other side again
  To another greater, wilder country,
  That's one vast red drear burnt-up plain,
  Branched thro' and thro' with many a vein
  Whence iron's dug, and copper's dealt;
  Look right, look left, look straight before,—
  Beneath they mine, above they smelt,
  Copper-ore and iron-ore,
  And forge and furnace mould and melt,
  And so on, more and ever more,
  Till, at the last, for a bounding belt,
  Comes the salt sand hoar of the great sea shore,
  —And the whole is our Duke's country!

III. I was born the day this present Duke was—
  (And O, says the song, ere I was old!)
  In the castle where the other Duke was—
  (When I was hopeful and young, not old!)
  I in the Kennel, he in the Bower:
  We are of like age to an hour.

My father was Huntsman in that day;
Who has not heard my father say
That, when a boar was brought to bay,
Three times, four times out of five,
With his huntspear he'd contrive
To get the killing-place transfixed,
And pin him true, both eyes betwixt?
And that's why the old Duke had rather
Have lost a salt-pit than my father,
And loved to have him ever in call;
That's why my father stood in the hall
When the old Duke brought his infant out
To show the people, and while they passed
The wondrous bantling round about,
Was first to start at the outside blast
As the Kaiser's courier blew his horn,
Just a month after the babe was born.
" And," quoth the Kaiser's courier, " since
" The Duke has got an Heir, our Prince
" Needs the Duke's self at his side: "
The Duke looked down and seemed to wince,
But he thought of wars o'er the world wide,
Castles a-fire, men on their march,
The toppling tower, the crashing arch;
And up he looked, and awhile he eyed
The row of crests and shields and banners,
Of all achievements after all manners,
And " ay," said the Duke with a surly pride.
The more was his comfort when he died
At next year's end, in a velvet suit,
With a gilt glove on his hand, and his foot
In a silken shoe for a leather boot,
Petticoated like a herald,
In a chamber next to an ante-room,
Where he breathed the breath of page and groom,
What he called stink, and they, perfume:
—They should have set him on red Berold,
Mad with pride, like fire to manage!
They should have got his cheek fresh tannage
Such a day as to-day in the merry sunshine!
Had they stuck on his fist a rough-foot merlin!
—Hark, the wind's on the heath at its game!
Oh for a noble falcon-lanner

To flap each broad wing like a banner,
And turn in the wind, and dance like flame!)
Had they broached a cask of white beer from Berlin!
—Or if you incline to prescribe mere wine—
Put to his lips when they saw him pine,
A cup of our own Moldavia fine,
Cotnar, for instance, green as May sorrel,
And ropy with sweet,—we shall not quarrel.

iv. So, at home, the sick tall yellow Duchess
Was left with the infant in her clutches,
She being the daughter of God knows who:
And now was the time to revisit her tribe,
So, abroad and afar they went, the two,
And let our people rail and gibe
At the empty Hall and extinguished fire,
As loud as we liked, but ever in vain,
Till after long years we had our desire,
And back came the Duke and his mother again.

v. And he came back the pertest little ape
That ever affronted human shape;
Full of his travel, struck at himself—
You'd say, he despised our bluff old ways
—Not he! For in Paris they told the elf
That our rough North land was the Land of Lays,
The one good thing left in evil days;
Since the Mid-Age was the Heroic Time,
And only in wild nooks like ours
Could you taste of it yet as in its prime,
And see true castles, with proper towers,
Young-hearted women, old-minded men,
And manners now as manners were then.
So, all that the old Dukes had been, without knowing it,
This Duke would fain know he was, without being it;
'Twas not for the joy's self, but the joy of his show-
          ing it,
Nor for the pride's self, but the pride of our seeing it,
He revived all usages thoroughly worn-out,
The souls of them fumed-forth, the hearts of them
          torn-out:
And chief in the chase his neck he perilled,
On a lathy horse, all legs and length,

With blood for bone, all speed, no strength!
—They should have set him on red Berold,
With the red eye slow consuming in fire,
And the thin stiff ear like an abbey spire!

VI. Well, such as he was, he must marry, we heard:
And out of a convent, at the word,
Came the Lady, in time of spring.
—Oh, old thoughts they cling, they cling!
That day, I know, with a dozen oaths
I clad myself in thick hunting-clothes
Fit for the chase of urox or buffle
In winter-time when you need to muffle;
But the Duke had a mind we should cut a figure,
And so we saw the Lady arrive:
My friend, I have seen a white crane bigger!
She was the smallest lady alive,
Made, in a piece of Nature's madness,
Too small, almost, for the life and gladness
That over-filled her, as some hive
Out of the bears' reach on the high trees
Is crowded with its safe merry bees:
In truth, she was not hard to please!
Up she looked, down she looked, round at the mead,
Straight at the castle, that's best indeed
To look at from outside the walls:
As for us, styled the " serfs and thralls,"
She as much thanked me as if she had said it,
(With her eyes, do you understand?)
Because I patted her horse while I led it;
And Max, who rode on her other hand,
Said, no bird flew past but she enquired
What its true name was, nor ever seemed tired—
If that was an eagle she saw hover,—
If the green and grey bird on the field was the plover.
When suddenly appeared the Duke,
And as down she sprung, the small foot pointed
On to my hand,—as with a rebuke,
And as if his backbone were not jointed,
The Duke stepped rather aside than forward,
And welcomed her with his grandest smile;
And, mind you, his mother all the while
Chilled in the rear, like a wind to Nor'ward;

And up, like a weary yawn, with its pullies
Went, in a shriek, the rusty portcullis;
And, like a glad sky the north-wind sullies,
The Lady's face stopped its play,
As if her first hair had grown grey—
For such things must begin some one day!

VII. In a day or two she was well again;
As who should say, " You labour in vain!
" This is all a jest against God, who meant
" I should ever be, as I am, content
" And glad in his sight; therefore, glad I will be! "
So, smiling as at first went she.

VIII. She was active, stirring, all fire—
Could not rest, could not tire—
To a stone she had given life!
(I myself loved once, in my day,)
—For a Shepherd's, Miner's, Huntsman's wife,
(I had a wife, I know what I say,)
Never in all the world such an one!
And here was plenty to be done,
And she that could do it, great or small,
She was to do nothing at all.
There was already this man in his post,
This in his station, and that in his office,
And the Duke's plan admitted a wife, at most,
To meet his eye, with the other trophies,
Now outside the Hall, now in it,
To sit thus. stand thus, see and be seen,
At the proper place in the proper minute,
And die away the life between.
And it was amusing enough, each infraction
Of rule (but for after-sadness that came)
To hear the consummate self-satisfaction
With which the young Duke and the old Dame
Would let her advise, and criticise,
And, being a fool, instruct the wise,
And, child-like, parcel out praise or blame:
They bore it all in complacent guise,
As tho' an artificer, after contriving
A wheel-work image as if it were living,
Should find with delight it could motion to strike him!

So found the Duke, and his mother like him,—
The Lady hardly got a rebuff—
That had not been contemptuous enough,
With his cursed smirk, as he nodded applause,
And kept off the old mother-cat's claws.

IX. So, the little Lady grew silent and thin,
    Paling and ever paling,
As the way is with a hid chagrin;
    And the Duke perceived that she was ailing,
And said in his heart, " 'Tis done to spite me,
" But I shall find in my power to right me!"
Don't swear, friend—the Old One, many a year,
Is in Hell, and the Duke's self . . . you shall hear.

X. Well, early in autumn, at first winter-warning,
When the stag had to break with his foot, of a morning,
A drinking-hole out of the fresh tender ice
That covered the pond till the sun, in a trice,
Loosening it, let out a ripple of gold,
And another and another, and faster and faster,
Till, dimpling to blindness, the wide water rolled:
Then it so chanced that the Duke our master
Asked himself what were the pleasures in season,
And found, since the calendar bade him be hearty,
He should do the Middle Age no treason
In resolving on a hunting-party.
Always provided, old books showed the way of it!
What meant old poets by their strictures?
And when old poets had said their say of it,
How taught old painters in their pictures?
We must revert to the proper channels,
Workings in tapestry, paintings on pannels,
And gather up Woodcraft's authentic traditions:
Here was food for our various ambitions,
As on each case, exactly stated,
—To encourage your dog, now, the properest chirrup,
Or best prayer to St. Hubert on mounting your stirrup—
We of the household took thought and debated.
Blessed was he whose back ached with the jerkin
His sire was wont to do forest-work in;
Blesseder he who nobly sunk " ohs "
And " ahs " while he tugged on his grandsire's trunk-
    hose;

What signified hats if they had no rims on,
Each slouching before and behind like the scallop,
And able to serve at sea for a shallop,
Loaded with lacquer and looped with crimson?
So that the deer now, to make a short rhyme on't,
What with our Venerers, Prickers, and Verderers,
Might hope for real hunters at length, and not murderers,
And oh, the Duke's tailor—he had a hot time on't!

XI. Now you must know, that when the first dizziness
Of flap-hats and buff-coats and jackboots subsided,
The Duke put this question, "The Duke's part provided,
" Had not the Duchess some share in the business?"
For out of the mouth of two or three witnesses,
Did he establish all fit-or-unfitnesses:
And, after much laying of heads together,
Somebody's cap got a notable feather
By the announcement with proper unction
That he had discovered the lady's function;
Since ancient authors held this tenet,
" When horns wind a mort and the deer is at siege,
" Let the dame of the Castle prick forth on her jennet,
" And with water to wash the hands of her liege
" In a clean ewer with a fair toweling,
" Let her preside at the disemboweling."
Now, my friend, if you had so little religion
As to catch a hawk, some falcon-lanner,
And thrust her broad wings like a banner
Into a coop for a vulgar pigeon;
And if day by day, and week by week,
You cut her claws, and sealed her eyes,
And clipped her wings, and tied her beak,
Would it cause you any great surprise
If when you decided to give her an airing
You found she needed a little preparing?
—I say, should you be such a curmudgeon,
If she clung to the perch, as to take it in dudgeon?
Yet when the Duke to his lady signified,
Just a day before, as he judged most dignified,
In what a pleasure she was to participate,—
And, instead of leaping wide in flashes,
Her eyes just lifted their long lashes,
As if pressed by fatigue even he could not dissipate,

And duly acknowledged the Duke's forethought,
But spoke of her health, if her health were worth aught,
Of the weight by day and the watch by night,
And much wrong now that used to be right,
So, thanking him, declined the hunting,—
Was conduct ever more affronting?
With all the ceremony settled—
With the towel ready, and the sewer
Polishing up his oldest ewer,
And the jennet pitched upon, a piebald,
Black-barred, cream-coated and pink eye-ball'd,—
No wonder if the Duke was nettled!
And when she persisted nevertheless,—
Well, I suppose here's the time to confess
That there ran half round our Lady's chamber
A balcony none of the hardest to clamber;
And that Jacynth the tire-woman, ready in waiting,
Stayed in call outside, what need of relating?
And since Jacynth was like a June rose, why, a fervent
Adorer of Jacynth, of course, was your servant;
And if she had the habit to peep through the casement,
How could I keep at any vast distance?
And so, as I say, on the Lady's persistence,
The Duke, dumb stricken with amazement,
Stood for awhile in a sultry smother,
And then, with a smile that partook of the awful,
Turned her over to his yellow mother
To learn what was decorous and lawful;
And the mother smelt blood with a cat-like instinct,
As her cheek quick whitened thro' all its quince-tinct—
Oh, but the Lady heard the whole truth at once!
What meant she?—Who was she?—Her duty and
    station,
The wisdom of age and the folly of youth, at once,
Its decent regard and its fitting relation—
In brief, my friend, set all the devils in hell free
And turn them out to carouse in a belfry,
And treat the priests to a fifty-part canon,
And then you may guess how that tongue of hers
    ran on!
Well, somehow or other it ended at last
And, licking her whiskers, out she passed;
And after her,—making (he hoped) a face

Like Emperor Nero or Sultan Saladin,
Stalked the Duke's self with the austere grace
Of ancient hero or modern paladin,—
From door to staircase—oh, such a solemn
Unbending of the vertebral column!

xii. However, at sunrise our company mustered,
And here was the huntsman bidding unkennel,
And there 'neath his bonnet the pricker blustered,
With feather dank as a bough of wet fennel;
For the court-yard's four walls were filled with fog
You might cut as an axe chops a log.
Like so much wool for colour and bulkiness;
And out rode the Duke in a perfect sulkiness,
Since before breakfast, a man feels but queasily,
And a sinking at the lower abdomen
Begins the day with indifferent omen:
And lo, as he looked around uneasily,
The sun ploughed the fog up and drove it asunder
This way and that from the valley under;
And, looking thro' the court-yard arch,
Down in the valley, what should meet him
But a troop of Gypsies on their march,
No doubt with the annual gifts to greet him.

xiii. Now, in your land, Gypsies reach you, only
After reaching all lands beside;
North they go, south they go, trooping or lonely,
And still, as they travel far and wide,
Catch they and keep now a trace here, a trace there.
That puts you in mind of a place here, a place there:
But with us, I believe they rise out of the ground,
And nowhere else, I take it, are found
With the earth-tint yet so freshly embrowned;
Born, no doubt, like insects which breed on
The very fruit they are meant to feed on:
For the earth—not a use to which they don't turn it,
The ore that grows in the mountain's womb,
Or the sand in the pits like a honeycomb,
They sift and soften it, bake it and burn it—
Whether they weld you, for instance, a snaffle
With side-bars never a brute can baffle;
Or a lock that's a puzzle of wards within wards;

Or, if your colt's fore-foot inclines to curve inwards,
Horseshoes they'll hammer which turn on a swivel
And won't allow the hoof to shrivel;
Then they cast bells like the shell of the winkle,
That keep a stout heart in the ram with their tinkle:
But the sand—they pinch and pound it like otters;
Commend me to Gypsy glass-makers and potters!
Glasses they'll blow you, crystal-clear,
Where just a faint cloud of rose shall appear,
As if in pure water you dropped and let die
A bruised black-blooded mulberry;
And that other sort, their crowning pride,
With long white threads distinct inside,
Like the lake-flower's fibrous roots which dangle
Loose such a length and never tangle,
Where the bold sword-lily cuts the clear waters,
And the cup-lily couches with all the white daughters:
Such are the works they put their hand to,
And the uses they turn and twist iron and sand to.
And these made the troop which our Duke saw sally
Towards his castle from out of the valley,
Men and women, like new-hatched spiders,
Come out with the morning to greet our riders!
And up they wound till they reached the ditch,
Whereat all stopped save one, a witch,
That I knew, as she hobbled from the group,
By her gait, directly, and her stoop,
I, whom Jacynth was used to importune
To let that same witch tell us our fortune.
The oldest Gypsy then above ground;
And, so sure as the autumn season came round,
She paid us a visit for profit or pastime,
And every time, as she swore, for the last time.
And presently she was seen to sidle
Up to the Duke till she touched his bridle,
So that the horse of a sudden reared up
As under its nose the old witch peered up
With her worn-out eyes, or rather eye-holes
Of no use now but to gather brine,
And began a kind of level whine
Such as they used to sing to their viols
When their ditties they go grinding
Up and down with nobody minding:

And, then as of old, at the end of the humming
Her usual presents were forthcoming
—A dog-whistle blowing the fiercest of trebles,
(Just as a sea-shore stone holding a dozen fine pebbles,)
Or a porcelain mouth-piece to screw on a pipe-end,—
And so she awaited her annual stipend.
But this time, the Duke would scarcely vouchsafe
A word in reply; and in vain she felt
With twitching fingers at her belt
For the purse of sleekpine-martin pelt,
Ready to put what he gave in her pouch safe,—
Till, either to quicken his apprehension,
Or possibly with an after-intention,
She was come, she said, to pay her duty
To the new Duchess, the youthful beauty.
No sooner had she named his Lady,
Than a shine lit up the face so shady,
And its smirk returned with a novel meaning—
For it struck him, the babe just wanted weaning;
If one gave her a taste of what life was and sorrow,
She, foolish to-day, would be wiser to-morrow;
And who so fit a teacher of trouble
As this sordid crone bent well nigh double?
So, glancing at her wolf-skin vesture,
(If such it was, for they grow so hirsute
That their own fleece serves for natural fur suit)
He was contrasting, 'twas plain from his gesture,
The life of the lady so flower-like and delicate
With the loathsome squalor of this helicat.
I, in brief, was the man the Duke beckoned
From out of the throng, and while I drew near
He told the crone, as I since have reckoned
By the way he bent and spoke into her ear
With circumspection and mystery,
The main of the Lady's history,
Her frowardness and ingratitude;
And for all the crone's submissive attitude
I could see round her mouth the loose plaits tightening,
And her brow with assenting intelligence brightening,
As tho' she engaged with hearty good will
Whatever he now might enjoin to fulfil,
And promised the lady a thorough frightening.
And so, just giving her a glimpse

Of a purse, with the air of a man who imps
The wing of the hawk that shall fetch the hernshaw.
He bade me take the gypsy mother
And set her telling some story or other
Of hill or dale, oak-wood or fernshaw,
To while away a weary hour
For the Lady left alone in her bower,
Whose mind and body craved exertion
And yet shrank from all better diversion.

XIV. Then clapping heel to his horse, the mere curvetter,
Out rode the Duke, and after his hollo
Horses and hounds swept, huntsman and servitor,
And back I turned and bade the crone follow.
And what makes me confident what's to be told you
Had all along been of this crone's devising,
Is, that, on looking round sharply, behold you,
There was a novelty quick as surprising:
For first, she had shot up a full head in stature,
And her step kept pace with mine nor faultered,
As if age had foregone its usurpature,
And the ignoble mien was wholly altered,
And the face looked quite of another nature,
And the change reached too, whatever the change
    meant,
Her shaggy wolf-skin cloak's arrangement,
For where its tatters hung loose like sedges,
Gold coins were glittering on the edges,
Like the band-roll strung with tomans
Which proves the veil a Persian woman's:
And under her brow, like a snail's horns newly
Come out as after the rain he paces,
Two unmistakeable eye-points duly
Lived and aware looked out of their places.
So we went and found Jacynth at the entry
Of the Lady's chamber standing sentry;
I told the command and produced my companion,
And Jacynth rejoiced to admit any one,
For since last night, by the same token,
Not a single word had the Lady spoken:
So they went in both to the presence together,
While I in the balcony watched the weather.

xv. And now, what took place at the very first of all,
     I cannot tell, as I never could learn it:
     Jacynth constantly wished a curse to fall
     On that little head of hers and burn it,
     If she knew how she came to drop so soundly
     Asleep of a sudden and there continue
     The whole time sleeping as profoundly
     As one of the boars my father would pin you
     'Twixt the eyes where the life holds garrison,
     —Jacynth forgive me the comparison!
     But where I begin my own narration
     Is a little after I took my station
     To breathe the fresh air from the balcony,
     And, having in those days a falcon eye,
     To follow the hunt thro' the open country,
     From where the bushes thinlier crested
     The hillocks, to a plain where's not one tree:—
     When, in a moment, my ear was arrested
     By—was it singing, or was it saying,
     Or a strange musical instrument playing
     In the chamber?—and to be certain
     I pushed the lattice, pulled the curtain,
     And there lay Jacynth asleep,
     Yet as if a watch she tried to keep,
     In a rosy sleep along the floor
     With her head against the door;
     While in the midst, on the seat of state,
     Like a queen the Gypsy woman sate,
     With head and face downbent
     On the Lady's head and face intent,
     For, coiled at her feet like a child at ease,
     The lady sate between her knees
     And o'er them the Lady's clasped hands met,
     And on those hands her chin was set,
     And her upturned face met the face of the crone
     Wherein the eyes had grown and grown
     As if she could double and quadruple
     At pleasure the play of either pupil
     —Very like by her hands slow fanning,
     As up and down like a gor-crow's flappers
     They moved to measure like bell clappers
     —I said, is it blessing, is it banning,
     Do they applaud you or burlesque you?

Those hands and fingers with no flesh on?
When, just as I thought to spring in to the rescue,
At once I was stopped by the Lady's expression:
For it was life her eyes were drinking
From the crone's wide pair above unwinking,
Life's pure fire received without shrinking,
Into the heart and breast whose heaving
Told you no single drop they were leaving—
Life, that filling her, past redundant
Into her very hair, back swerving
Over each shoulder, loose and abundant,
As her head thrown back showed the white throat
    curving,
And the very tresses shared in the pleasure,
Moving to the mystic measure,
Bounding as the bosom bounded.
I stopped short, more and more confounded,
As still her cheeks burned and eyes glistened,
As she listened and she listened,—
When all at once a hand detained me,
And the selfsame contagion gained me,
And I kept time to the wondrous chime,
Making out words and prose and rhyme,
Till it seemed that the music furled
Its wings like a task fulfilled, and dropped
From under the words it first had propped,
And left them midway in the world,
And word took word as hand takes hand,
I could hear at last, and understand,
And when I held the unbroken thread,
The Gypsy said:—

" And so at last we find my tribe,
And so I set thee in the midst,
And to one and all of them describe
What thou saidst and what thou didst,
Our long and terrible journey thro',
And all thou art ready to say and do
In the trials that remain:
I trace them the vein and the other vein
That meet on thy brow and part again,
Making our rapid mystic mark;
And I bid my people prove and probe

Each eye's profound and glorious globe
Till they detect the kindred spark
In those depths so dear and dark,
Like the spots that snap, and burst, and flee,
Circling over the midnight sea.
And on that young round cheek of thine
I make them recognise the tinge,
As when of the costly scarlet wine
They drip so much as will impinge
And spread in a thinnest scale afloat
One thick gold drop from the olive's coat
Over a silver plate whose sheen
Still thro' the mixture shall be seen.
For, so I prove thee, to one and all,
Fit, when my people ope their breast,
To see the sign, and hear the call,
And take the vow, and stand the test
Which adds one more child to the rest—
When the breast is bare and the arms are wide,
And the world is left outside.
For there is probation to decree,
And many and long must the trials be
Thou shalt victoriously endure,
If that brow is true and those eyes are sure:
Like a jewel-finder's fierce assay
Of the prize he dug from its mountain tomb,—
Let once the vindicating ray
Leap out amid the anxious gloom,
And steel and fire have done their part
And the prize falls on its finder's heart;
So, trial after trial past,
Wilt thou fall at the very last
Breathless, half in trance
With the thrill of the great deliverance,
Into our arms for evermore;
And thou shalt know, those arms once curled
About thee, what we knew before,
How love is the only good in the world.
Henceforth be loved as heart can love,
Or brain devise, or hand approve!
Stand up, look below,
It is our life at thy feet we throw
To step with into light and joy;

Not a power of life but we'll employ
To satisfy thy nature's want;
Art thou the tree that props the plant,
Or the climbing plant that seeks the tree—
Canst thou help us, must we help thee?
If any two creatures grew into one,
They would do more than the world has done;
Tho' each apart were never so weak,
Yet vainly thro' the world should ye seek
For the knowledge and the might
Which in such union grew their right:
So, to approach, at least, that end,
And blend,—as much as may be, blend
Thee with us or us with thee,
As climbing-plant or propping-tree,
Shall some one deck thee, over and down,
Up and about, with blossoms and leaves?
Fix his heart's fruit for thy garland crown,
Cling with his soul as the gourd-vine cleaves,
Die on thy boughs and disappear
While not a leaf of thine is sere?
Or is the other fate in store,
And art thou fitted to adore,
To give thy wondrous self away,
And take a stronger nature's sway?
I foresee and I could foretell
Thy future portion, sure and well—
But those passionate eyes speak true, speak true,
And let them say what thou shalt do!
Only, be sure thy daily life,
In its peace, or in its strife,
Never shall be unobserved;
We pursue thy whole career,
And hope for it, or doubt, or fear,—
Lo, hast thou kept thy path or swerved,
We are beside thee, in all thy ways,
With our blame, with our praise,
Our shame to feel, our pride to show,
Glad, sorry—but indifferent, no!
Whether it is thy lot to go,
For the good of us all, where the haters meet
In the crowded city's horrible street;
Or thou step alone thro' the morass

Where never sound yet was
Save the dry quick clap of the stork's bill,
For the air is still, and the water still,
When the blue breast of the dipping coot
Dives under, and all again is mute.
So at the last shall come old age,
Decrepit as befits that stage;
How else wouldst thou retire apart
With the hoarded memories of thy heart
And gather all to the very least
Of the fragments of life's earlier feast,
Let fall through eagerness to find
The crowning dainties yet behind?
Ponder on the entire past
Laid together thus at last,
When the twilight helps to fuse
The first fresh, with the faded hues,
And the outline of the whole,
As round eve's shades their framework roll,
Grandly fronts for once thy soul:
And then as, 'mid the dark, a gleam
Of yet another morning breaks,
And like the hand which ends a dream,
Death, with the might of his sunbeam
Touches the flesh and the soul awakes,
Then—"
　　　　　　Ay, then, indeed, something would happen!
But what?　For here her voice changed like a bird's;
There grew more of the music and less of the words;
Had Jacynth only been by me to clap pen
To paper and put you down every syllable,
With those clever clerkly fingers,
All that I've forgotten as well as what lingers
In this old brain of mine that's but ill able
To give you even this poor version
Of the speech I spoil, as it were, with stammering
—More fault of those who had the hammering
Of prosody into me and syntax,
And did it, not with hobnails but tintacks!
But to return from this excursion,—
Just, do you mark, when the song was sweetest,
The peace most deep and the charm completest,
There came, shall I say, a snap—

And the charm vanished!
And my sense returned, so strangely banished,
And, starting as from a nap,
I knew the crone was bewitching my lady,
With Jacynth asleep; and but one spring made I,
Down from the casement, round to the portal,
Another minute and I had entered,
When the door opened, and more than mortal
Stood, with a face where to my mind centred
All beauties I ever saw or shall see,
The Duchess—I stopped as if struck by palsy.
She was so different, happy and beautiful,
I felt at once that all was best,
And that I had nothing to do, for the rest,
But wait her commands, obey and be dutiful.
Not that, in fact, there was any commanding,
—I saw the glory of her eye,
And the brow's height and the breast's expanding,
And I was hers to live or to die.
As for finding what she wanted,
You know God Almighty granted
Such little signs should serve his wild creatures
To tell one another all their desires,
So that each knows what its friend requires,
And does its bidding without teachers.
I preceded her; the crone
Followed silent and alone;
I spoke to her, but she merely jabbered
In the old style; both her eyes had slunk
Back to their pits; her stature shrunk;
In short, the soul in its body sunk
Like a blade sent home to its scabbard.
We descended, I preceding;
Crossed the court with nobody heeding;
All the world was at the chase,
The court-yard like a desert-place,
The stable emptied of its small fry;
I saddled myself the very palfrey
I remember patting while it carried her,
The day she arrived, and the Duke married her.
And, do you know, though its easy deceiving
Oneself in such matters, I can't help believing
The lady had not forgotten it either,

And knew the poor Devil so much beneath her
Would have been only too glad for her service
To dance on hot ploughshares like a Turk dervise,
But unable to pay proper duty where owing it
Was reduced to that pitiful method of showing it:
For though the moment I began setting
His saddle on my own nag of Berold's begetting,
(Not that I meant to be obtrusive)
She stopped me, while his rug was shifting,
By a single rapid finger's lifting,
And, with a gesture kind but conclusive,
And a little shake of the head, refused me,—
I say, although she never used me,
Yet when she was mounted, the gypsy behind her,
And I ventured to remind her,
I suppose with a voice of less steadiness
Than usual, for my feelings exceeded me,
—Something to the effect that I was in readiness
Whenever God should please she needed me,—
Then, do you know, her face looked down on me
With a look that placed a crown on me,
And she felt in her bosom,—mark, her bosom—
And, as a flower-tree drops its blossom,
Dropped me—ah, had it been a purse
Of silver, my friend, or gold that's worse,
Why, you see, as soon as I found myself
So understood,—that a true heart so may gain
Such a reward,—I should have gone home again,
Kissed Jacynth, and soberly drowned myself!
It was a little plait of hair
Such as friends in a convent make
To wear, each for the other's sake,—
This, see, which at my breast I wear,
Ever did (rather to Jacynth's grudgment),
And ever shall, till the Day of Judgment.
And then,—and then,—to cut short,—this is idle,
These are feelings it is not good to foster,—
I pushed the gate wide, she shook the bridle,
And the palfrey bounded,—and so we lost her!

XVI. When the liquor's out, why clink the cannakin?
I did think to describe you the panic in
The redoubtable breast of our master the mannikin,

And what was the pitch of his mother's yellowness,
How she turned as a shark to snap the spare-rib
Clean off, sailors say, from a pearl-driving Carib,
When she heard, what she called, the fight of the
    feloness—
But it seems such child's play
What they said and did with the lady away!
And to dance on, when we've lost the music,
Always made me—and no doubt makes you—sick.
Nay, to my mind, the world's face looked so stern
As that sweet form disappeared thro' the postern,
She that kept it in constant good humour,
It ought to have stopped; there seemed nothing to do more.
But the world thought otherwise and went on,
And my head's one that its spite was spent on:
Thirty years are fled since that morning,
And with them all my head's adorning.
Nor did the old Duchess die outright,
As you expect, of suppressed spite,
The natural end of every adder
Not suffered to empty its poison-bladder:
But she and her son agreed, I take it,
That no one should touch on the story to wake it,
For the wound in the Duke's pride rankled fiery,
So they made no search and small inquiry—
And when fresh gypsies have paid us a visit, I've
Noticed the couple were never inquisitive,
But told them they're folks the Duke don't want here,
And bade them make haste and cross the frontier.
Brief, the Duchess was gone and the Duke was glad of it
And the old one was in the young one's stead,
And took, in her place, the household's head,
And a blessed time the household had of it!
And were I not, as a man may say, cautious
How I trench, more than needs, on the nauseous,
I could favour you with sundry touches
Of the paint-smutches with which the Duchess
Heightened the mellowness of her cheek's yellowness
(To get on faster) until at last her
Cheek grew to be one master-plaster
Of mucus and fucus from mere use of ceruse
Till in short she grew from scalp to udder
Just the object to make you shudder!

xvii. You're my friend—
    What a thing friendship is, world without end!
    How it gives the heart and soul a stir-up,
    As if somebody broached you a glorious runlet,
    And poured out all lovelily, sparkling, and sunlit,
    Our green Moldavia, the streaky syrup,
    Cotnar as old as the time of the Druids—
    Friendship's as good as that monarch of fluids
    To supple a dry brain, fill you its ins-and-outs,—
    Gives your Life's hour-glass a shake when the thin sand
        doubts
    Whether to run on or stop short, and guarantees
    Age is not all made of stark sloth and arrant ease!
    I have seen my little Lady once more,
    Jacynth, the Gypsy, Berold, and the rest of it,
    For to me spoke the Duke, as I told you before;
    I always wanted to make a clean breast of it,
    And now it is made—why, my heart's-blood, that went
        trickle,
    Trickle, but anon, in such muddy dribblets,
    Is pumped up brisk now, thro' the main ventricle,
    And genially floats me about the giblets!
    I'll tell you what I intend to do:
    I must see this fellow his sad life thro'
    —He is our Duke after all,
    And I, as he says, but a serf and thrall;
    My father was born here and I inherit
    His fame, a chain he bound his son with,—
    Could I pay in a lump I should prefer it,
    But there's no mine to blow up and get done with,
    So I must stay till the end of the chapter:
    For, as to our middle-age-manners-adapter,
    Be it a thing to be glad on or sorry on,
    One day or other, his head in a morion,
    And breast in a hauberk, his heels he'll kick up
    Slain by some onslaught fierce of hiccup.
    And then, when red doth the sword of our Duke rust,
    And its leathern sheath lies o'ergrown with a blue crust,
    Then, I shall scrape together my earnings;
    For, you see, in the Churchyard Jacynth reposes,
    And our children all went the way of the roses—
    It's a long lane that knows no turnings—
    One needs but little tackle to travel in,

So, just one stout cloak shall I indue,
And for a staff, what beats the javelin
With which his boars my father pinned you?
And then, for a purpose you shall hear presently,
Taking some Cotnar, a tight plump skinfull,
I shall go journeying, who but I, pleasantly?
Sorrow is vain and despondency sinful.
What's a man's age? He must hurry more, that's all;
Cram in a day, what his youth took a year to hold;
When we mind labour, then only, we're too old—
What age had Methusalem when he begat Saul?
And at last, as its haven some buffeted ship sees,
(Come all the way from the north-parts with sperm
    oil)
I shall get safely out of the turmoil
And arrive one day at the land of the gypsies
And find my lady, or hear the last news of her
From some old thief and son of Lucifer,
His forehead chapletted green with wreathy hop,
Sunburned all over like an Æthiop:
And when my Cotnar begins to operate
And the tongue of the rogue to run at a proper rate,
And our wine-skin, tight once, shows each flaccid dent,
I shall drop in with—as if by accident—
" You never knew then, how it all ended,
" What fortunes good or bad attended
" The little lady your Queen befriended? "
—And when that's told me, what's remaining?
This world's too hard for my explaining—
The same wise judge of matters equine
Who still preferred some slim four-year-old
To the big-boned stock of mighty Berold,
And for strong Cotnar drank French weak wine,
He also must be such a lady's scorner!
Smooth Jacob still robs homely Esau,
Now up, now down, the world's one see-saw!
So, I shall find out some snug corner
Under a hedge, like Orson the wood-knight,
Turn myself round and bid the world good night;
And sleep a sound sleep till the trumpet's blowing
Wakes me (unless priests cheat us laymen)
To a world where's to be no further throwing
Pearls before swine that can't value them. Amen!

EARTH'S IMMORTALITIES.

FAME.

See, as the prettiest graves will do in time,
Our poet's wants the freshness of its prime;
Spite of the sexton's browsing horse, the sods
Have struggled thro' its binding osier-rods;
Headstone and half-sunk footstone lean awry,
Wanting the brick-work promised by and by;
How the minute grey lichens, plate o'er plate,
Have softened down the crisp-cut name and date!

LOVE.

So, the year's done with!
  (*Love me for ever!*)
All March begun with,
  April's endeavour;
May-wreaths that bound me
  June needs must sever!
Now snows fall round me,
  Quenching June's fever—
  (*Love me for ever!*)

SONG.

I. Nay but you, who do not love her,
    Is she not pure gold, my mistress?
  Holds earth aught—speak truth—above her?
    Aught like this tress, see, and this tress,
  And this last fairest tress of all,
  So fair, see, ere I let it fall!

II. Because, you spend your lives in praising;
    To praise, you search the wide world over;
  So, why not witness, calmly gazing,
    If earth holds aught—speak truth—above her?
  Above this tress, and this I touch
  But cannot praise, I love so much!

THE BOY AND THE ANGEL.

MORNING, evening, noon, and night,
" Praise God," sang Theocrite.

Then to his poor trade he turned,
By which the daily meal was earned.

Hard he laboured, long and well;
O'er his work the boy's curls fell:

But ever, at each period,
He stopped and sang, " Praise God."

Then back again his curls he threw,
And cheerful turned to work anew.

Said Blaise, the listening monk, " Well done;
" I doubt not thou art heard, my son:

" As well as if thy voice to-day
" Were praising God, the Pope's great way.

" This Easter Day, the Pope at Rome
" Praises God from Peter's dome."

Said Theocrite, " Would God that I
" Might praise Him, that great way, and die!"

Night passed, day shone,
And Theocrite was gone.

With God a day endures alway,
A thousand years are but a day.

God said in Heaven, " Nor day nor night
" Now brings the voice of my delight."

Then Gabriel, like a rainbow's birth,
Spread his wings and sank to earth;

Entered in flesh, the empty cell,
Lived there, and played the craftsman well:

And morning, evening, noon, and night,
Praised God in place of Theocrite.

And from a boy, to youth he grew;
The man put off the stripling's hue:

The man matured and fell away
Into the season of decay:

And ever o'er the trade he bent,
And ever lived on earth content.

(He did God's will; to him, all one
If on the earth or in the sun.)

God said, " A praise is in mine ear;
" There is no doubt in it, no fear:

" So sing old worlds, and so
" New worlds that from my footstool go.

" Clearer loves sound other ways:
" I miss my little human praise."

Then forth sprang Gabriel's wings, off fell
The flesh disguise, remained the cell.

'Twas Easter Day: he flew to Rome,
And paused above Saint Peter's dome.

In the tiring-room close by
The great outer gallery,

With his holy vestments dight,
Stood the new Pope, Theocrite:

And all his past career
Came back upon him clear,

Since when, a boy, he plied his trade,
Till on his life the sickness weighed:

And in his cell, when death drew near,
An angel in a dream brought cheer:

And rising from the sickness drear
He grew a priest, and now stood here.

To the East with praise he turned,
And on his sight the angel burned.

" I bore thee from thy craftsman's cell,
" And set thee here; I did not well.

" Vainly I left my angel's-sphere,
" Vain was thy dream of many a year.

" Thy voice's praise seemed weak; it dropped—
" Creation's chorus stopped!

" Go back and praise again
" The early way—while I remain.

" With that weak voice of our disdain,
" Take up Creation's pausing strain.

" Back to the cell and poor employ:
" Become the craftsman and the boy! "

Theocrite grew old at home;
A new Pope dwelt in Peter's Dome.

One vanished as the other died:
They sought God side by side.

MEETING AT NIGHT.

1. THE grey sea and the long black land;
And the yellow half-moon large and low;
And the startled little waves that leap
In fiery ringlets from their sleep,
As I gain the cove with pushing prow,
And quench its speed in the slushy sand.

II. Then a mile of warm sea-scented beach;
    Three fields to cross till a farm appears;
    A tap at the pane, the quick sharp scratch
    And blue spurt of a lighted match,
    And a voice less loud, thro' its joys and fears,
    Than the two hearts beating each to each!

PARTING AT MORNING.

ROUND the cape of a sudden came the sea,
And the sun looked over the mountain's rim—
And straight was a path of gold for him,
And the need of a world of men for me.

SAUL.

SAID Abner, " At last thou art come!
  " Ere I tell, ere thou speak,—
" Kiss my cheek, wish me well!" Then I wished it,
  And did kiss his cheek:
And he, " Since the King, oh my friend,
  " For thy countenance sent,
Nor drunken nor eaten have we;
  Nor, until from his tent
Thou return with the joyful assurance
  The king liveth yet,
Shall our lip with the honey be brightened,
  —The water, be wet.

" For out of the black mid-tent's silence,
  A space of three days,
No sound hath escaped to thy servants,
  Of prayer nor of praise,
To betoken that Saul and the Spirit
  Have ended their strife,
And that faint in his triumph the monarch
  Sinks back upon life.

" Yet now my heart leaps, O beloved!
  God's child, with his dew
On thy gracious gold hair, and those lilies
  Still living and blue

As thou brak'st them to twine round thy harp-strings,
  As if no wild heat
Were raging to torture the desert!"
  Then I, as was meet,
Knelt down to the God of my fathers,
  And rose on my feet,
And ran o'er the sand burnt to powder.
  The tent was unlooped;
I pulled up the spear that obstructed,
  And under I stooped;
Hands and knees o'er the slippery grass-patch—
  All withered and gone—
That leads to the second enclosure,
  I groped my way on,
Till I felt where the foldskirts fly open;
  Then once more I prayed,
And opened the foldskirts and entered,
  And was not afraid;
And spoke, " Here is David, thy servant!"
  And no voice replied;
And first I saw naught but the blackness;
  But soon I descried
A something more black than the blackness
  —The vast, the upright
Main-prop which sustains the pavilion,—
  And slow into sight
Grew a figure, gigantic, against it,
  And blackest of all;—
Then a sunbeam, that burst thro' the tent-roof,
  Showed Saul.
He stood as erect as that tent-prop;
  Both arms stretched out wide
On the great cross-support in the centre
  That goes to each side:
So he bent not a muscle, but hung there
  As, caught in his pangs
And waiting his change, the king-serpent
  All heavily hangs,
Far away from his kind, in the pine,
  Till deliverance come
With the Spring-time,—so agonised Saul,
  Drear and stark, blind and dumb.

Then I tuned my harp,—took off the lilies
   We twine round its chords
Lest they snap 'neath the stress of the noontide
   —Those sunbeams like swords!
And I first played the tune all our sheep know,
   As, one after one,
So docile they come to the pen-door
   Till folding be done;
—They are white and untorn by the bushes,
   For lo, they have fed
Where the long grasses stifle the water
   Within the stream's bed:
How one after one seeks its lodging,
   As star follows star
Into eve and the blue far above us,
   —So blue and so far!
Then the tune for which quails on the cornland
   Will leave each his mate
To follow the player; then, what makes
   The crickets elate
Till for boldness they fight one another:
   And then, what has weight
To set the quick jerboa a-musing
   Outside his sand house
—There are none such as he for a wonder—
   Half bird and half mouse!
—God made all the creatures and gave them
   Our love and our fear,
To show, we and they are his children,
   One family here.

Then I played the help-tune of our reapers,
   Their wine-song, when hand
Grasps hand, eye lights eye in good friendship,
   And great hearts expand,
And grow one in the sense of this world's life;
   And then, the low song
When the dead man is praised on his journey—
   " Bear, bear him along
" With his few faults shut up like dead flowrets;
   " Are balm-seeds not here
" To console us? The land is left none such
   " As he on the bier—

"Oh, would we might keep thee, my brother!"
  And then, the glad chaunt
Of the marriage,—first go the young maidens,
  Next, she whom we vaunt
As the beauty, the pride of our dwelling:
  And then, the great march
When man runs to man to assist him,
  And buttress an arch
Nought can break . . . who shall harm them, our friends?
  Then, the chorus intoned
As the Levites go up to the altar
  In glory enthroned—
But I stopped here—for here, in the darkness,
  Saul groaned.

And I paused, held my breath in such silence!
  And listened apart;
And the tent shook, for mighty Saul shuddered,—
  And sparkles gan dart
From the jewels that woke in his turban
  —At once with a start
All its lordly male-sapphires, and rubies
  Courageous at heart;
So the head—but the body still moved not,
  Still hung there erect.
And I bent once again to my playing,
  Pursued it unchecked,
As I sang, "Oh, our manhood's prime vigour!
  —No spirit feels waste,
No muscle is stopped in its playing,
  No sinew unbraced;—
And the wild joys of living! The leaping
  From rock up to rock—
The rending their boughs from the palm-trees,—
  The cool silver shock
Of a plunge in the pool's living water—
  The haunt of the bear,
And the sultriness showing the lion
  Is couched in his lair:
And the meal—the rich dates—yellowed over
  With gold dust divine,
And the locust's-flesh steeped in the pitcher,
  The full draught of wine,

And the sleep in the dried river channel
　　Where tall rushes tell
The water was wont to go warbling
　　So softly and well,—
How good is man's life here, mere living!
　　How fit to employ
The heart and the soul and the senses
　　For ever in joy!
Hast thou loved the white locks of thy father
　　Whose sword thou didst guard
When he trusted thee forth to the wolf hunt
　　For glorious reward?
Didst thou see the thin hands of thy mother
　　Held up, as men sung
The song of the nearly-departed,
　　And heard her faint tongue
Joining in while it could to the witness
　　' Let one more attest,
' I have lived, seen God's hand thro' that life-time,
　　' And all was for best . . .'
Then they sung thro' their tears, in strong triumph,
　　Not much,—but the rest!
And thy brothers—the help and the contest,
　　The working whence grew
Such result, as from seething grape-bundles
　　The spirit so true:
And the friends of thy boyhood—that boyhood
　　With wonder and hope,
Present promise, and wealth in the future,—
　　The eye's eagle scope,—
Till lo, thou art grown to a monarch,
　　A people is thine!
Oh all gifts the world offers singly,
　　On one head combine,
On one head the joy and the pride,
　　Even rage like the throe
That opes the rock, helps its glad labour,
　　And let's the gold go—
And ambition that sees a sun lead it—
　　Oh, all of these—all
Combine to unite in one creature
　　—Saul!"
　　　　　　END OF PART THE FIRST.

TIME'S REVENGES.

I'VE a Friend, over the sea;
I like him, but he loves me;
It all grew out of the books I write;
They find such favour in his sight
That he slaughters you with savage looks
Because you don't admire my books:
He does himself though,—and if some vein
Were to snap to-night in this heavy brain,
To-morrow month, if I lived to try,
Round should I just turn quietly,
Or out of the bedclothes stretch my hand
Till I found him, come from his foreign land
To be my nurse in this poor place,
And make me broth, and wash my face,
And light my fire, and, all the while,
Bear with his old good-humoured smile
That I told him " Better have kept away
" Than come and kill me, night and day,
" With worse than fever's throbs and shoots,
" At the creaking of his clumsy boots."
I am as sure that this he would do,
As that Saint Paul's is striking Two:
And I think I had rather . . . woe is me!
—Yes, rather see him than not see,
If lifting a hand would seat him there
Before me in the empty chair
To-night, when my head aches indeed,
And I can neither think, nor read,
And these blue fingers will not hold
The pen; this garret's freezing cold!

And I've a Lady—There he wakes,
The laughing fiend and prince of snakes
Within me, at her name, to pray
Fate send some creature in the way
Of my love for her, to be down-torn
Upthrust and onward borne
So I might prove myself that sea
Of passion which I needs must be!

Call my thoughts false and my fancies quaint,
And my style infirm, and its figures faint,
All the critics say, and more blame yet,
And not one angry word you get!
But, please you, wonder I would put
My cheek beneath that Lady's foot
Rather than trample under mine
The laurels of the Florentine,
And you shall see how the Devil spends
A fire God gave for other ends!
I tell you, I stride up and down
This garret, crowned with love's best crown,
And feasted with love's perfect feast,
To think I kill for her, at least,
Body and soul and peace and fame,
Alike youth's end and manhood's aim,
—So is my spirit, as flesh with sin,
Filled full, eaten out and in
With the face of her, the eyes of her,
The lips and little chin, the stir
Of shadow round her mouth; and she
—I'll tell you,—calmly would decree
That I should roast at a slow fire,
If that would compass her desire
And make her one whom they invite
To the famous ball to-morrow night.

There may be Heaven; there must be Hell;
Meantime, there is our Earth here—well!

THE GLOVE.

(PETER RONSARD *loquitur.*)

" HEIGHO," yawned one day King Francis,
" Distance all value enhances!
" When a man's busy, why, leisure
" Strikes him as wonderful pleasure,—
" 'Faith, and at leisure once is he?
" Straightway he wants to be busy.
" Here we've got peace; and aghast I'm
" Caught thinking war the true pastime!

" Is there a reason in metre?
" Give us your speech, master Peter! "
I who, if mortal dare say so,
Ne'er am at loss with my Naso,
" Sire," I replied, " joys prove cloudlets:
" Men are the merest Ixions "—
Here the King whistled aloud, " Let's
" . . . Heigho . . . go look at our lions! "
Such are the sorrowful chances
If you talk fine to King Francis.

And so, to the courtyard proceeding,
Our company, Francis was leading,
Increased by new followers tenfold
Before he arrived at the penfold;
Lords, ladies, like clouds which bedizen
At sunset the western horizon.
And Sir De Lorge pressed 'mid the foremost
With the dame he professed to adore most—
Oh, what a face! One by fits eyed
Her, and the horrible pitside;
For the penfold surrounded a hollow
Which led where the eye scarce dared follow,
And shelved to the chamber secluded
Where Bluebeard, the great lion, brooded.
The king hailed his keeper, an Arab
As glossy and black as a scarab.
And bade him make sport and at once stir
Up and out of his den the old monster.
They opened a hole in the wirework
Across it, and dropped there a firework,
And fled; one's heart's beating redoubled;
A pause, while the pit's mouth was troubled,
The blackness and silence so utter,
By the firework's slow sparkling and sputter;
Then earth in a sudden contortion
Gave out to our gaze her abortion!
Such a brute! Were I friend Clement Marot
(Who's experience of nature's but narrow,
And whose faculties move in no small mist
When he versifies David the Psalmist)
I should study that brute to describe you
Illum Juda Leonem de Tribu!

One's whole blood grew curdling and creepy
To see the black mane, vast and heapy,
The tail in the air stiff and straining,
The wide eyes, nor waxing nor waning,
As over the barrier which bounded
His platform, and us who surrounded
The barrier, they reached and they rested
On the space that might stand him in best stead:
For who knew, he thought, what the amazement,
The eruption of clatter and blaze meant,
And if, in this minute of wonder,
No outlet, 'mid lightning and thunder,
Lay broad, and, his shackles all shivered.
The lion at last was delivered?
Ay, that was the open sky o'erhead!
And you saw by the flash on his forehead,
By the hope in those eyes wide and steady,
He was leagues in the desert already,
Driving the flocks up the mountain,
Or catlike couched hard by the fountain
To waylay the date-gathering negress:
So guarded be entrance or egress.
" How he stands!" quoth the King: " we may well swear,
" No novice, we've won our spurs elsewhere,
" And so can afford the confession,
" We exercise wholesome discretion
" In keeping aloof from his threshold;
" Once hold you, those jaws want no fresh hold,
" Their first would too pleasantly purloin
" The visitor's brisket or sirloin;
" But who's he would prove so fool-hardy?
" Not the best man of Marignan, pardie?"

The sentence no sooner was uttered,
Than over the rails a glove fluttered,
Fell close to the lion, and rested:
The dame 'twas, who flung it and jested
With life so, De Lorge had been wooing
For months past; he sate there pursuing
His suit, weighing out with nonchalance
Fine speeches like gold from a balance.

Sound the trumpet, no true knight's a tarrier!
De Lorge made one leap at the barrier,

Walked straight to the glove,—while the lion
Ne'er moved, kept his far-reaching eye on
The palm-tree-edged desert-spring's sapphire,
And the musky oiled skin of the Kaffir,—
Picked it up, and as calmly retreated,
Leaped back where the lady was seated,
And full in the face of its owner
Flung the glove—

    " Your heart's queen, you dethrone her?
" So should I "—cried the King—" 'twas mere vanity,
" Not love, set that task to humanity! "
Lords and ladies alike turned with loathing
From such a proved wolf in sheep's clothing.

Not so, I; for I caught an expression
In her brow's undisturbed self-possession
Amid the Court's scoffing and merriment,—
As if from no pleasing experiment
She rose, yet of pain not much heedful
So long as the process was needful—
As if she had tried in a crucible,
To what " speeches like gold " were reducible,
And, finding the finest prove copper,
Felt the smoke in her face was but proper;
To know what she had *not* to trust to,
Was worth all the ashes, and dust too.
She went out 'mid hooting and laughter;
Clement Marot stayed; I followed after,
And asked, as a grace, what it all meant—
If she wished not the rash deed's recalment?
" For I "—so I spoke—" am a Poet:
" Human nature,—behoves that I know it! "

She told me, " Too long had I heard
" Of the deed proved alone by the word:
" For my love,—what De Lorge would not dare!
" With my scorn—what De Lorge could compare!
" And the endless descriptions of death
" He would brave when my lip formed a breath,
" I must reckon as braved, or, of course,
" Doubt his word—and moreover, perforce,
" For such gifts as no lady could spurn,

" Must offer my love in return.
" When I looked on your lion, it brought
" All the dangers at once to my thought,
" Encountered by all sorts of men,
" Before he was lodged in his den,—
" From the poor slave whose club or bare hands
" Dug the trap, set the snare on the sands,
" With no King and no Court to applaud,
" By no shame, should he shrink, overawed,
" Yet to capture the creature made shift,
" That his rude boys might laugh at the gift,
" To the page who last leaped o'er the fence
" Of the pit, on no greater pretence
" Than to get back the bonnet he dropped,
" Lest his pay for a week should be stopped—
" So, wiser I judged it to make
" One trial what ' death for my sake '
" Really meant, while the power was yet mine,
" Than to wait until time should define
" Such a phase not so simply as I,
" Who took it to mean just ' to die.'
" The blow a glove gives is but weak—
" Does the mark yet discolour my cheek?
" But when the heart suffers a blow,
" Will the pain pass so soon, do you know? "

I looked, as away she was sweeping,
And saw a youth eagerly keeping
As close as he dared to the doorway:
No doubt that a noble should more weigh
His life than befits a plebeian;
And yet, had our brute been Nemean—
(I judge by a certain calm fervor
The youth stepped with, forward to serve her)
—He'd have scarce thought you did him the worst turn
If you whispered " Friend, what you'd get, first earn! "
And when, shortly after, she carried
Her shame from the Court, and they married,
To that marriage some happiness, maugre
The voice of the Court, I dared augur.

For De Lorge, he made women with men vie,
Those in wonder and praise, these in envy;

And in short stood so plain a head taller
That he wooed and won . . . How do you call her?
The beauty, that rose in the sequel
To the King's love, who loved her a week well;
And 'twas noticed he never would honour
De Lorge (who looked daggers upon her)
With the easy commission of stretching
His legs in the service, and fetching
His wife, from her chamber, those straying
Sad gloves she was always mislaying,
While the King took the closet to chat in,—
But of course this adventure came pat in;
And never the King told the story,
How bringing a glove brought such glory,
But the wife smiled—" His nerves are grown firmer—
" Mine he brings now and utters no murmur!"

Venienti occurrite morbo !
With which moral I drop my theorbo.

LURIA

A TRAGEDY

LURIA

PERSONS.

Luria, a Moor, Commander of the Florentine Forces.
Husain, a Moor, his friend.
Puccio, the old Florentine Commander, now Luria's Chief
    Officer.
Braccio, Commissary of the Republic of Florence.
Jacopo (Lapo), his Secretary.
Tiburzio, Commander of the Pisans.
Domizia, a noble Florentine Lady.

TIME, 14—.

SCENE.—Luria's *Camp between Florence and Pisa.*

ACT I.

MORNING.

Braccio, *as dictating to his* Secretary; Puccio *standing by.*

  Brac. [*to* Puc.] Then, you join battle in an hour?
  Puc.   Not I;
Luria, the Captain.
  Brac. [*to the* Sec.] " In an hour, the battle."
[*To* Puc.] Sir, let your eye run o'er this loose digest
And see if very much of your report
Have slipped away through my civilian phrase.
Does this instruct the Signory aright
How army stands with army?
  Puc. [*taking the paper.*]   All seems here:
—That Luria, seizing with our City's force
The several points of vantage, hill and plain,
Shuts Pisa safe from help on every side,
And baffling the Lucchese arrived too late,
Must, in the battle he delivers now,
Beat her best troops and first of chiefs.
  Brac.   So sure?
Tiburzio's a consummate captain too!

Puc. Luria holds Pisa's fortune in his hand.

Brac. [*to the* Sec.] " The Signory hold Pisa in their hand;
Your own proved soldiership's our warrant, sir:
So, while my secretary ends his task,
Have out two horsemen, by the open roads,
To post with it to Florence!

Puc. [*returning the paper.*]   All seems here;
Unless . . . Ser Braccio, 'tis my last report!
Since Pisa's outbreak, and my overthrow,
And Luria's hastening at the city's call
To save her, as he only could, no doubt;
Till now that she is saved or sure to be,—
Whatever you tell Florence, I tell you:
Each day's note you, her Commissary, make
Of Luria's movements, I myself supply.
No youngster am I longer, to my cost;
Therefore while Florence gloried in her choice
And vaunted Luria, whom but Luria, still,
As if zeal, courage, prudence, conduct, faith,
Had never met in any man before,
I saw no pressing need to swell the cry.
But now, this last report and I have done—
So, ere to-night comes with its roar of praise,
'Twere not amiss if some one old i' the trade
Subscribed with, " True, for once rash counsel's best;
" This Moor of the bad faith and doubtful race,
" This boy to whose untried sagacity,
" Raw valour, Florence trusts without reserve
" The charge to save her, justifies her choice;
" In no point has this stranger failed his friends;
" Now praise; " I say this, and it is not here.

Brac. [*to the* Sec.] Write, " Puccio, superseded in the
                charge
" By Luria, bears full witness to his worth,
" And no reward our Signory can give
" Their champion but he'll back it cheerfully."
Aught more? Five minutes hence, both messengers!

[PUCCIO *goes.*

Brac. [*after a pause, and while he slowly tears the paper into
                shreds.*]

I think . . . pray God, I hold in fit contempt
This warfare's noble art and ordering,
And,—once the brace of prizers fairly matched,

Poleaze with poleaxe, knife with knife as good,—
Spit properly at what men term their skill . . .
Yet here I think our fighter has the odds;
With Pisa's strength diminished thus and thus,
Such points of vantage in our hands and such,
With Lucca off the stage, too,—all's assured:
Luria must win this battle.   Write the Court,
That Luria's trial end and sentence pass!

   Sec.   Patron,—
   Brac.   Aye, Lapo?
   Sec.   If you trip, I fall;
'Tis in self-interest I speak—
   Brac.   Nay, nay,
You overshoot the mark, my Lapo!   Nay!
When did I say pure love's impossible?
I make you daily write those red cheeks thin,
Load your young brow with what concerns it least,
And, when we visit Florence, let you pace
The Piazza by my side as if we talked,
Where all your old acquaintances may see:
You'd die for me, I should not be surprised!
Now then!
   Sec.   Sir, look about and love yourself!
Step after step the Signory and you
Tread gay till this tremendous point's to pass;
Which, pass not, pass not, ere you ask yourself,
Bears the brain steadily such draughts of fire,
Or too delicious may not prove the pride
Of this long secret Trial you dared plan,
Dare execute, you solitary here,
With the grey-headed toothless fools at home,
Who think themselves your lords, they are such slaves?
If they pronounce this sentence as you bid,
Declare the treason, claim its penalty,—
And sudden out of all the blaze of life,
On the best minute of his brightest day,
From that adoring army at his back,
Thro' Florence' joyous crowds before his face,
Into the dark you beckon Luria . . .
   Brac.   Then—
Why, Lapo, when the fighting-people vaunt,
We of the other craft and mystery,
May we not smile demure, the danger past?

   Sec.   Sir, no, no, no,—the danger, and your spirit
At watch and ward?   Where's danger on your part,
With that thin flitting instantaneous steel,
'Gainst the blind bull-front of a brute-force world?
If Luria, that's to perish sure as fate,
Should have been really guiltless after all?
   Brac.   Ah, you have thought that;
   Sec.   Here I sit, your scribe,
And in and out goes Luria, days and nights;
This Puccio comes; the Moor his other friend,
Husain; they talk—all that's feigned easily;
He speaks (I would not listen if I could),
Reads, orders, counsels;—but he rests sometimes,—
I see him stand and eat, sleep stretched an hour
On the lynx-skins, yonder; hold his bared black arms
Into the sun from the tent-opening; laugh
When his horse drops the forage from his teeth
And neighs to hear him hum his Moorish songs,
That man believes in Florence, as the Saint
Tied to the wheel believes in God!
   Brac.   How strange—
You too have thought that!
   Sec.   Do but you think too,
And all is saved! I only have to write,
The man seemed false awhile, proves true at last;
Bury it . . . so I write to the Signory . . .
Bury this Trial in your breasts for ever,
Blot it from things or done or dreamed about,
So Luria shall receive his meed to-day
With no suspicion what reverse was near,—
As if no meteoric finger hushed
The doom-word just on the destroyer's lip.
Motioned him off, and let life's sun fall straight.
   Brac. [*looks to the wall of the tent.*]   Did he draw that?
   Sec.   With charcoal, when the watch
Made the report at midnight; Lady Domizia
Spoke of the unfinished Duomo, you remember;
That is his fancy how a Moorish front
Might join to, and complete, the body,—a sketch,—
And again where the cloak hangs, yonder in the shadow.
   Brac.   He loves that woman.
   Sec.   She is sent the spy
Of Florence,—spies on you as you on him:

Florence, if only for Domizia's sake,
Is surely safe.   What shall I write?
  Brac.   I see—
A Moorish front, nor of such ill design!
Lapo, there's one thing plain and positive;
Man seeks his own good at the whole world's cost.
What?   If to lead our troops, stand forth our chiefs,
And hold our fate, and see us at their beck,
Yet render up the charge when peace returned,
Have ever proved too much for Florentines,
Even for the best and bravest of ourselves—
If in the struggle when the soldier's sword
Should sink its point before the statist's pen,
And the calm head replace the violent hand,
Virtue on virtue still have fallen away
Before ambition with unvarying fate,
Till Florence' self at last in bitterness
Be forced to own such falls the natural end,
And, sparing further to expose her sons
To a vain strife and profitless disgrace,
Declare " The Foreigner, one not my child,
" Shall henceforth lead my troops, reach height by height
" The glory, then descend into the shame;
" So shall rebellion be less guilt in him,
" And punishment the easier task for me."
—If on the best of us this brand she set,
Can I suppose an utter alien here,
This Luria, our inevitable foe,
Confessed a mercenary and a Moor,
Born free from any ties that bind the rest
Of common faith in Heaven or hope on Earth,
No Past with us, no Future,—such a Spirit
Shall hold the path from which our staunchest broke,
Stand firm where every famed precursor fell?
My Lapo, I will frankly say, these proofs
So duly noted of the man's intent,
Are for the doting fools at home, not me;
The charges here, they may be true or false,
—What is set down?   Errors and oversights,
This dallying interchange of courtesies
With Pisa's General,—all that, hour by hour,
Puccio's pale discontent has furnished us,
Of petulant speeches, inconsiderate acts,

Now overhazard, overcaution now;
Even that he loves this Lady who believes
She outwits Florence, and whom Florence posted
By my procurement here, to spy on me,
Lest I one minute lose her from my sight—
She who remembering her whole House's fall,
That nest of traitors strangled in the birth,
Now labours to make Luria . . . poor device
As plain . . . the instrument of her revenge!
—That she is ever at his ear to prompt
Inordinate conceptions of his worth,
Exorbitant belief in its reward,
And after, when sure disappointment follows,
Proportionable rage at such a wrong—
Why, all these reasons, while I urge them most,
Weigh with me less than least; as nothing weigh!
Upon that broad Man's heart of his, I go!
On what I know must be, yet while I live
Will never be, because I live and know!
Brute-force shall not rule Florence!   Intellect
May rule her, bad or good as chance supplies,—
But Intellect it shall be, pure if bad,
And Intellect's tradition so kept up
Till the good comes—'twas Intellect that ruled,
Not Brute-force bringing from the battle-field
The attributes of wisdom, foresight's graces
We lent it there to lure its grossness on;
All which it took for earnest and kept safe
To show against us in our market-place,
Just as the plumes and tags and swordsman's gear
(Fetched from the camp where at their foolish best
When all was done they frightened nobody)
Perk in our faces in the street, forsooth,
With our own warrant and allowance.   No!
The whole procedure's overcharged,—its end
In too strict keeping with the bad first step.
To conquer Pisa was sheer inspiration?
Well then, to perish for a single fault,
Let that be simple justice!—There, my Lapo!
A Moorish front ill suits our Duomo's body—
Blot it out—and bid Luria's sentence come!

[LURIA *who, with* DOMIZIA, *has entered unobserved at the
    close of the last phrase, now advancing.*

And Luria, Luria, what of Luria now?

Brac. Ah, you so close, Sir? Lady Domizia too?
I said it needs must be a busy moment
For one like you—that you were now i' the thick
Of your duties, doubtless, while we idlers sate . . .

Lur. No—in that paper,—it was in that paper
What you were saying!

Brac. Oh—my day's dispatch!
I censure you to Florence: will you see?

Lur. See your dispatch, your last, for the first time?
Well, if I should, now? For in truth, Domizia,
He would be forced to set about another,
In his sly cool way, the true Florentine,
To mention that important circumstance;
So while he wrote I should gain time, such time!
Do not send this!

Brac. And wherefore?

Lur. These Lucchese
Are not arrived—they never will arrive!
And I must fight to-day, arrived or not;
And I shall beat Tiburzio, that is sure:
And then will be arriving my Lucchese,
But slowly, oh so slowly, just in time
To look upon my battle from the hills,
Like a late moon, of use to nobody!
And I must break my battle up, send forth,
Surround on this side, hold in check on that—
Then comes to-morrow, we negotiate,
You make me send for fresh instructions home,
—Incompleteness, incompleteness!

Brac. Ah, we scribes!
Why, I had registered that very point,
The non-appearance of our foes' ally,
As a most happy fortune; both at once
Were formidable—singly faced, each falls.

Lur. So no great battle for my Florentines!
No crowning deed, decisive and complete,
For all of them, the simple as the wise,
Old, young, alike, that do not understand
Our wearisome pedantic art of war,
By which we prove retreat may be success,
Delay—best speed,—half loss, at times,—whole gain:
They want results—as if it were their fault!

And you, with warmest wish to be my friend,
Will not be able now to simply say
" Your servant has performed his task—enough!
" You ordered, he has executed: good!
" Now walk the streets in holiday attire,
" Congratulate your friends, till noon strikes fierce,
" Then form bright groups beneath the Duomo's shade!"
No! you will have to argue and explain,
Persuade them all is not so ill in the end,
Tease, tire them out!   Arrive, arrive, Lucchese!
   Dom.   Well, you will triumph for the Past enough,
Whatever be the Present's chance—no service
Falls to the ground with Florence; she awaits
Her saviour, will receive him fittingly.
   Lur.   Ah, Braccio, you know Florence . . . will she,
                 think you,
Receive one . . . what means " fittingly receive? "
—Receive compatriots, doubtless—I am none:
And yet Domizia promises so much!
   Brac.   Kind women still give men a woman's prize.
I know not o'er which gate most boughs will arch,
Nor if the Square will wave red flags or blue—
I should have judged, the fullest of rewards
Our State gave Luria, when she made him chief
Of her whole force, in her best Captain's place.
   Lur.   That my reward?   Florence on my account
Relieved Ser Puccio?—mark you, my reward!
And Puccio's having all the fight's true joy—
Goes here and there, directs, may fight himself,
While I must order, stand aloof, o'ersee!
That was my calling—there was my true place!
I should have felt, in some one over me,
Florence impersonate, my visible Head,
As I am over Puccio,—taking life
Directly from her eye!—They give me you!
But do you cross me, set me half to work?
I enjoy nothing—but I will, for once!
Decide, shall we join battle? may I wait?
   Brac.   Let us compound the matter; wait till noon;
Then, no arrival,—
   Lur.   Ah, noon comes too fast!
I wonder, do you guess why I delay
Involuntarily the final blow

As long as possible? Peace follows it!
Florence at peace, and the calm studious heads
Come out again, the penetrating eyes;
As if a spell broke, all's resumed, each art
You boast, more vivid that it slept awhile!
'Gainst the glad heaven, o'er the white palace-front
The interrupted scaffold climbs anew;
The walls are peopled by the Painter's brush;
The Statue to its niche ascends to dwell;
The Present's noise and trouble have retired
And left the eternal Past to rule once more.—
You speak its speech and read its records plain,
Greece lives with you, each Roman breathes your friend,
—But Luria—where will then be Luria's place?
   Dom.   Highest in honour, for that Past's own sake,
Of which his actions, sealing up the sum
By saving all that went before from wreck,
Will range as part, with which he worshipped too.
   Lur.   Then I may walk and watch you in your streets
Leading the life my rough life helps no more,
So different, so new, so beautiful—
Nor fear that you will tire to see parade
The club that slew the lion, now that crooks
And shepherd-pipes come into use again?
For very lone and silent seems my East
In its drear vastness—still it spreads, and still
No Braccios, no Domizias anywhere—
Not ever more!—Well, well, to-day is ours!
   Dom. [*to* Brac.]   Should he not have been one of us?
   Lur.   Oh, no!
Not one of you, and so escape the thrill
Of coming into you, and changing thus,—
Feeling a soul grow on me that restricts
The boundless unrest of the savage heart!
The sea heaves up, hangs loaded o'er the land,
Breaks there and buries its tumultuous strength;
Horror, and silence, and a pause awhile;
Lo, inland glides the gulf-stream, miles away,
In rapture of assent, subdued and still,
'Neath those strange banks, those unimagined skies!
Well, 'tis not sure the quiet lasts for ever!
Your placid heads still find our hands new work;
Some minutes' chance—there comes the need of mine—

And, all resolved on, I too hear at last.
Oh, you must find some use for me, Ser Braccio!
You hold my strength; 'twere best dispose of it!
What you created, see that you find food for—
I shall be dangerous else!
    Brac.   How dangerous, Sir?
    Lur.   Oh, there are many ways, Domizia warns me,
And one with half the power that I possess,
Grows very formidable! Do you doubt?
Why, first, who holds the army . . .
    Dom.   While we talk
Morn wears, we keep you from your proper place
In the field!—
    Lur.   Nay, to the field I move no more!
My part is done, and Puccio's may begin!
I cannot trench upon his province longer
With any face.—You think yourselves so safe?
Why see—in concert with Tiburzio, now—
One could . . .
    Dom.   A trumpet!
    Lur.   My Lucchese at last!
Arrived, as sure as Florence stands! your leave!
                                 [*Springs out.*
    Dom. How plainly is true greatness charactered
By such unconsciousness as Luria's here,
And sharing least the secret of itself!
Be it with head that schemes or hand that acts,
Such save the world which none but they could save,
Yet think whate'er they did, that world could do.
    Brac. Yes: and how worthy note, that those same
              great ones
In hand or head, with such unconsciousness
And all its due entailed humility,
Should never shrink, so far as I perceive,
From taking up whatever offices
Involve the whole world's safety or mishap,
Into their mild hands as a thing of course!
The Statist finds it natural to lead
The mob who might as easily lead him—
The Soldier marshals men who know as much—
Statist and Soldier verily believe!
While we poor scribes . . . you catch me thinking, now,
That I shall in this very letter write

What none of you are able! To it, Lapo!

[DOMIZIA *goes*.

This last, worst, all affected childish fit
Of Luria's, this be-praised unconsciousness,
Convinces me: the Past was no child's play;
It was a man beat Pisa,—not a child.
All's mere dissimulation—to remove
The fear, he best knows we should entertain.
The utmost danger was at hand. Is't written?
Now make a duplicate, lest this should fail,
And speak your fullest on the other side.

   Sec. I noticed he was busily repairing
My half-effacement of his Duomo sketch,
And, while he spoke of Florence, turned to it,
As the Mage Negro King to Christ the Babe.—
I judge his childishness the true relapse
To boyhood of a man who has worked lately,
And presently will work, so, meantime plays:
Whence more than ever I believe in him.

   Brac. [*after a pause.*] The sword! At best, the soldier,
         as he says,
In Florence—the black face, the barbarous name,
For Italy to boast her show of the age,
Her man of men!—To Florence with each letter!

ACT II.

NOON.

   Dom. Well, Florence, shall I reach thee, pierce thy heart
Thro' all its safeguards? Hate is said to help—
Quicken the eye, invigorate the arm,
And this my hate, made up of many hates,
Might stand in scorn of visible instrument,
And will thee dead:—yet do I trust it not.
Nor Man's devices, nor Heaven's memory
Of wickedness forgot on Earth so soon,
But thy own nature,—Hell and thee I trust,
To keep thee constant in that wickedness,
Where my revenge may meet thee: turn aside
A single step, for gratitude, or shame,—
Grace but this Luria, this wild mass of rage
That I prepare to launch against thee now,

With other payment than thy noblest found,—
Give his desert for once its due reward,—
And past thee would my sure destruction roll.
But thou, who mad'st our House thy sacrifice,
It cannot be thou wilt except this Moor
From the accustomed fate of zeal and truth;
Thou wilt deny his looked-for recompense,
And then—I reach thee! Old and trained, my sire
Could bow down on his quiet broken heart,
Die awe-struck and submissive, when at last
The strange blow came for the expected wreath;
And Porzio passed in blind bewilderment
To exile, never to return,—they say,
Perplexed in his frank simple honest soul,
As if some natural law had changed,—how else
Could Florence, on plain fact pronouncing thus,
Judge Porzio's actions worthy such an end?
But Berto, with the ever-passionate pulse,
—Oh that long night, its dreadful hour on hour,
In which no way of getting his fair fame
From their inexplicable charges free,
Was found, save pouring forth the impatient blood
To show its colour whether false or no!
My brothers never had a friend like me
Close in their need to watch the time, then speak,
—Burst with a wakening laughter on their dream,
Say, Florence was all falseness, so false here,—
And show them what a simple task remained—
To leave dreams, rise, and punish in God's name
The City wedded to its wickedness—
None stood by them as I by Luria stand!
So, when the stranger cheated of his due
Turns on thee as his rapid nature bids,
Then, Florence, think, a hireling at thy throat
For the first outrage, think who bore thy last,
Yet mutely in forlorn obedience died!
He comes . . . his friend . . . black faces in the camp
Where moved those peerless brows and eyes of old!

Enter LURIA *and* HUSAIN.

   Dom. Well, and the movement—is it as you hope?
'Tis Lucca?
   Lur.   Ah, the Pisan trumpet merely!

Tiburzio's envoy, I must needs receive—

Dom. Whom I withdraw before; yet if I lingered
You could not wonder, for my time fleets fast;
The overtaking night brings such reward!—
And where will then be room for me? Yet still
Remember who was first to promise it,
And envies those who also can perform!　　　　　*[Goes.*

　　Lur. This trumpet from the Pisans?—

　　Hus.　　　　　　　　　In the camp;
A very noble presence—Braccio's visage
On Puccio's body—calm and fixed and good;
A man I seem as I had seen before—
Most like, it was some statue had the face.

　　Lur. Admit him! This will prove the last delay!

　　Hus. Ay, friend, go on, and die thou going on!
Thou heard'st what the grave woman said but now:
To-night rewards thee! That is well to hear!
But stop not therefore; hear it, and go on!

　　Lur. Oh, their reward and triumph and the rest
They round me in the ears with, all day long?
All that, I never take for earnest, friend!
Well would it suit us,—their triumphal arch
Or storied pillar,—thee and me, the Moors!
But gratitude in those Italian eyes—
That, we shall get?

　　Hus.　　　　It is too cold an air—
Our sun rose out of yonder mound of mist—
Where is he now? So I trust none of them!

　　Lur. Truly?

　　Hus.　　　　I doubt and fear. There stands a wall
'Twixt our expansive and explosive race
And those absorbing, concentrating men!
They use thee!

　　Lur.　　　And I feel it, Husain; yes,
And care not—yes, an alien force like mine
Is only called to play its part outside
Their different nature; where its sole use seems
To fight with and keep off an adverse force
As alien,—which repelled, mine too withdraws;
Inside, they know not what to do with me;
So I have told them laughingly and oft,
But long since I prepared to learn the worst.

　　Hus. What is the worst?

II—*E 42

Lur.   I will forestall them, Husain,
And speak my destiny, they dare not speak—
Banish myself before they find the heart!
I will be first to say, " the work rewards!
" I know, for all your praise, my use is over,
" So may it be!—meanwhile 'tis best I go,
" And carry safe my memories of you all
" To other scenes of action, newer lands,"—
Thus leaving them confirmed in their belief
They would not easily have tired of me!
You think this hard to say?
Hus.   Say it or not,
So thou but go, so they but let thee go!
This hating people, that hate each the other,
And in one blandness to us Moors unite—
Locked each to each like slippery snakes, I say,
Which still in all their tangles, hissing tongue
And threatening tail, ne'er do each other harm;
While any creature of a better blood,
They seem to fight for, while they circle safe
And never touch it,—pines without a wound,
Withers away before their eyes and breath.
See thou, if Puccio come not safely out
Of Braccio's grasp, this Braccio sworn his foe,
As Braccio safely from Domizia's toils
Who hates him most!—But thou, the friend of all,
. . . Come out of them!
Lur.   The Pisan trumpet now!
Hus.   Breathe free—it is an enemy, no friend!   [*Goes.*
Lur.   He keeps his instincts, no new culture mars
Their perfect use in him; just so the brutes
Rest not, are anxious without visible cause,
When change is in the elements at work,
Which man's trained senses fail to apprehend.
But here,—he takes the distant chariot-wheels
For thunder, festal fire for lightning's flash,
The finer traits of cultivated life
For treachery and malevolence: I see!

Enter TIBURZIO.

Lur.   Quick, sir, your message. I but wait your message
To sound the charge. You bring not overtures
For truce?—I would not, for your General's sake,

You spoke of truce—a time to fight is come,
And whatsoe'er the fight's event, he keeps
His honest soldier's name to beat me with,
Or leaves me all himself to beat, I trust!

Tib. I am Tiburzio.

Lur.   You? 'Tis—yes . . . Tiburzio!
You were the last to keep the ford i' the valley
From Puccio, when I threw in succours there!
Why, I was on the heights—thro' the defile
Ten minutes after, when the prey was lost;
You wore an open scull-cap with a twist
Of water-reeds—the plume being hewn away;
While I drove down my battle from the heights,
—I saw with my own eyes!

Tib.   And you are Luria
Who sent my cohort, that laid down its arms
In error of the battle-signal's sense,
Back safely to me at the critical time—
One of a hundred deeds—I know you! Therefore
To none but you could I . . .

Lur.   No truce, Tiburzio!

Tib. Luria, you know the peril's imminent
On Pisa,—that you have us in the toils,
Us her last safeguard, all that intercepts
The rage of her implacablest of foes
From Pisa,—if we fall to-day, she falls.
Tho' Lucca will arive, yet, 'tis too late.
You have so plainly here the best of it,
That you must feel, brave soldier as you are,
How dangerous we grow in this extreme,
How truly formidable by despair.
Still, probabilities should have their weight—
The extremest chance is ours, but, that chance failing,
You win this battle. Wherefore say I this?
To be well apprehended when I add,
This danger absolutely comes from you.
Were you, who threaten thus, a Florentine . . .

Lur. Sir, I am nearer Florence than her sons.
I can, and have perhaps obliged the State,
Nor paid a mere son's duty.

Tib.   Even so!
Were you the son of Florence, yet endued
With all your present nobleness of soul,

No question, what I must communicate
Would not detach you from her.
    Lur.   Me, detach?
    Tib. Time urges: you will ruin presently
Pisa, you never knew, for Florence' sake
You think you know. I have from time to time
Made prize of certain secret missives sent
From Braccio here, the Commissary, home—
And knowing Florence otherwise, I piece
The entire chain out, from these its scattered links.
Your trial occupies the Signory:
They sit in judgment on your conduct now!
When men at home enquire into the acts
Which in the field e'en foes appreciate . . .
Brief, they are Florentines! You, saving them,
Will seek the sure destruction saviours find.
    Lur. Tiburzio—
    Tib.   All the wonder is of course!
I am not here to teach you, nor direct,
Only to loyally apprise—scarce that.
This is the latest letter, sealed and safe,
As it left here an hour ago. One way
Of two thought free to Florence, I command.
The duplicate is on its road: but this,—
Read it, and then I shall have more to say.
    Lur. Florence!
    Tib.   Now, were yourself a Florentine,
This letter, let it hold the worst it can,
Would be no reason you should fall away—
The Mother city is the mother still,
And recognition of the children's service
Her own affair; reward—there's no reward!
But you are bound by quite another tie;
Nor Nature shows, nor Reason, why at first
A foreigner, born friend to all alike,
Should give himself to any special State
More than another, stand by Florence' side
Rather than Pisa's—'tis as fair a city
You war against as that you fight for—famed
As well as she in story, graced no less
With noble heads, and patriotic hearts,—
Nor to a stranger's eye would either cause,
Stripped of the cumulative loves and hates

Which take importance from familiar view,
Stand as the Right, and Sole to be upheld.
Therefore, should the preponderating gift
Of love and trust, Florence was first to throw,
Which made you hers not Pisa's, void the scale,—
Old ties dissolving, things resume their place
And all begins again. Break seal and read!
At least let Pisa offer for you now!
And I, as a good Pisan, shall rejoice—
Tho' for myself I lose, in gaining you,
This last fight and its opportunity;
The chance it brings of saving Pisa yet,
Or in the turn of battle dying so
That shame should want its extreme bitterness.

    Lur. Tiburzio, you that fight for Pisa now
As I for Florence . . . say my chance were yours!
You read this letter, and you find . . . no, no!
Too mad!

    Tib.   I read the letter, find they purpose
When I have crushed their foe, to crush me: well?

    Lur. You being their captain, what is it you do?

    Tib. Why as it is, all cities are alike—
Pisa will pay me much as Florence you;
I shall be as belied, whate'er the event,
As you, or more: my weak head, they will say,
Prompted this last expedient, my faint heart
Entailed on them indelible disgrace,
Both which defects ask proper punishment.
Another tenure of obedience, mine!
You are no son of Pisa's: break and read!

    Lur. And act on what I read? What act were fit?
If the firm-fixed foundation of my faith
In Florence, which to me stands for Mankind,
—If that breaks up and, disemprisoning
From the abyss . . . Ah friend, it cannot be!
You may be very sage, yet . . . all the world
Having to fail, or your sagacity,
You do not wish to find yourself alone!
What would the world be worth? Whose love be sure?
The world remains—you are deceived!

    Tib.   Your hand!
I lead the vanguard.—If you fall, beside,
The better—I am left to speak! For me,

This was my duty, nor would I rejoice
If I could help, it misses its effect:
And after all you will look gallantly
Found dead here with that letter in your breast!
   Lur. Tiburzio—I would see these people once
And test them ere I answer finally!
At your arrival let the trumpet sound:
If mine returns not then the wonted cry
It means that I believe—am Pisa's!
    Tib.   Well.   [*Goes.*
   Lur. My heart will have it he speaks true! My blood
Beats close to this Tiburzio as a friend.
If he had stept into my watch-tent, night
And the wild desert full of foes around,
I should have broke the bread and given the salt
Secure, and, when my hour of watch was done,
Taken my turn to sleep between his knees,
Safe in the untroubled brow and honest cheek.
Oh, world, where all things pass and nought abides,
Oh, life the long mutation—is it so?
Is it with life as with the body's change?
—Where, e'en tho' better follow, good must pass,
Nor manhood's strength can mate with boyhood's grace,
Nor age's wisdom, in its turn, find strength,
But silently the first gift dies away,
And tho' the new stays, never both at once!
Life's time of savage instinct's o'er with me,
It fades and dies away, past trusting more,
As if to punish the ingratitude
With which I turned to grow in these new lights,
And learned to look with European eyes.
Yet it is better, this cold certain way,
Where Braccio's brow tells nothing,—Puccio's mouth,
Domizia's eyes reject the searcher—yes—
For on their calm sagacity I lean,
Their sense of right, deliberate choice of good,
Sure, as they know my deeds, they deal with me.
Yes, that is better—that is best of all!
Such faith stays when mere wild belief would go!
Yes—when the desert creature's heart, at fault
Amid the scattering tempest's pillared sands,
Betrays its steps into the pathless drift—
The calm instructed eye of man holds fast

By the sole bearing of the visible star,
Sure that when slow the whirling wreck subsides,
The boundaries, lost now, shall be found again,—
The palm-trees and the pyramid over all.
Yes: I trust Florence—Pisa is deceived!

Enter BRACCIO, PUCCIO, *and* DOMIZIA.

Brac. Noon's at an end: no Lucca? You must fight.
Lur. Do you remember, ever, gentle friends,
I am no Florentine?
Dom.　　　　　　It is yourself
Who still are forcing us importunately,
To bear in mind what else we should forget.
Lur. For loss!—For what I lose in being none!
No shrewd man, such as you yourselves respect,
But would remind you of the stranger's loss
In natural friends and advocates at home,
Hereditary loves, even rivalships,
With precedents for honour and reward.
Still, there's a gain, too! If you take it so,
The stranger's lot has special gain as well!
Do you forget there was my own far East
I might have given away myself to, once,
As now to Florence, and for such a gift,
Stood there like a descended Deity?
There, worship greets us! what do I get here?
　　　　　　　　　　　　　[*Shows the letter.*
See! Chance has put into my hand the means
Of knowing what I earn, before I work!
Should I fight better, should I fight the worse,
With your crown palpably before me? see!
Here lies my whole reward! Best know it now,
Or keep it for the end's entire delight?
Brac. If you serve Florence as the vulgar serve,
For swordsman's pay alone,—break seal and read!
In that case, you will find your full desert!
Lur. Give me my one last happy moment, friends!
You need me now, and all the gratitude
This letter can contain will never balance
The after-feeling that your need's at end!
This moment . . . Oh, the East has use with you!
Its sword still flashes—is not flung aside
With the past praise, in a dark corner yet!

How say you? 'Tis not so with Florentines—
Captains of yours—for them, the ended war
Is but a first step to the peace begun
—He who did well in war, just earns the right
To begin doing well in peace, you know!
And certain my precursors,—would not such
Look to themselves in such a chance as this,
Secure the ground they trod upon, perhaps?
For I have heard, by fits, or seemed to hear,
Of strange occurrences, ingratitude,
Treachery even,—say that one of you
Surmised this letter carried what might turn
To harm hereafter, cause him prejudice—
What would he do?

    Dom. [*hastily.*] Thank God and take revenge!
Turn her own force against the city straight,
And even at the moment when the foe
Sounded defiance . . .

               [TIBURZIO'S *trumpet sounds in the distance.*
    Lur.   Ah, you Florentines!
So would you do? Wisely for you, no doubt!
My simple Moorish instinct bids me sink
The obligation you relieve me from,
Still deeper! [*to* PUC.] Sound our answer, I should say!
And thus:—[*tearing the paper*]—The battle! That solves
    every doubt!

ACT III.

AFTERNOON.

PUCCIO, *as making a report to* JACOPO.

    Puc. And here, your Captain must report the rest;
For, as I say, the main engagement over,
And Luria's special part in it performed,
How could subalterns like myself expect
Leisure or leave to occupy the field
And glean what dropped from his wide harvesting?
I thought, when Lucca at the battle's end
Came up, just as the Pisan centre broke,
That Luria would detach me and prevent
The flying Pisans seeking what they found,
Friends in the rear, a point to rally by:
But no—more honourable proved my post!

I had the august captive to escort
Safe to our camp—some other could pursue,
Fight, and be famous; gentler chance was mine—
Tiburzio's wounded spirit must be soothed!
He's in the tent there.

    Jac.   Is the substance down?
I write—" The vanguard beaten, and both wings
In full retreat—Tiburzio prisoner "—
And now,—" That they fell back and formed again
On Lucca's coming."—Why then, after all,
'Tis half a victory, no conclusive one?

    Puc. Two operations where a sole had served.

    Jac. And Luria's fault was—?

    Puc.   Oh, for fault . . . not much!
He led the attack, a thought impetuously,
—There's commonly more prudence; now, he seemed
To hurry measures, otherwise well-judged;
By over concentrating strength, at first,
Against the enemy's van, both sides escaped:
That's reparable—yet it is a fault.

Enter BRACCIO.

    Jac. As good as a full victory to Florence,
With the advantage of a fault beside—
What is it, Puccio?—that by pressing forward
With too impetuous . . .

    Brac.   The report anon!
Thanks, Sir—you have elsewhere a charge, I know.

                        [PUCCIO *goes.*

There's nothing done but I would do again;
Yet, Lapo, it may be the Past proves nothing,
And Luria has kept faithful to the end!

    Jac. I was for waiting.

    Brac.   Yes: so was not I!
He could not choose but tear that letter—true!
Still, certain of his tones, I mind, and looks—
You saw, too, with a fresher soul than I.
So, Porzio seemed an injured man, they say!
Well, I have gone upon the broad, sure ground.

Enter LURIA, PUCCIO, *and* DOMIZIA.

    Lur. [*to* PUC.] Say, at his pleasure I will see Tiburzio:
All's at his pleasure.

Dom. [*to* LUR.]   Were I not so sure
You would reject, as you do constantly,
Praise,—I might tell you what you have deserved
Of Florence by this last and crowning feat:
But words are vain!
Lur.   Nay, you may praise me now!
I want instruction every hour, I find,
On points where once I saw least need of it;
And praise, I have been used to do without,
Seems not so easy to dispense with now,
After a battle half one's strength is gone—
And glorious passion in us once appeased,
Our reason's calm cold dreadful voice begins.
All justice, power and beauty scarce appear
Monopolized by Florence, as of late,
To me, the stranger; you, no doubt, may know
Why Pisa needs must give her rival place;
And I am growing nearer you, perhaps,
For I, too, want to know and be assured,
When a cause ceases to reward itself,
Its friend needs fresh sustainments; praise is one,
And here stand you—you, Lady, praise me well!
But yours—(your pardon)—is unlearned praise:
To the motive, the endeavour, the heart's self,
Your quick sense looks; you crown and call aright
The soul of the purpose, ere 'tis shaped as act,
Takes flesh i' the world, and clothes itself a king;
But when the act comes, stands for what 'tis worth,
—Here's Puccio, the skilled soldier; he's my judge!
Was all well, Puccio?
Puc.   All was . . . must be well:
If we beat Lucca presently, as doubtless . . .
—No, there's no doubt, we must—All was well done.
Lur. In truth? But you are of the trade, my Puccio!
You have the fellow-craftsman's sympathy!
There's none knows like a fellow of the craft,
The all unestimated sum of pains
That go to a success the world can see;
They praise then, but the best they never know:
—But you know!—Oh, if envy mix with it,
Hate even, still the bottom praise of all,
Whatever be the dregs, that drop's pure gold!
—For nothing's like it; nothing else records

Those daily, nightly drippings in the dark
Of the heart's blood, the world lets drop away
For ever . . . So, pure gold that praise must be!
And I have yours, my soldier: yet the best
Is still to come—there's one looks on apart
Whom all refers to, failure or success;
What's done might be our best, our utmost work,
And yet inadequate to serve his need:
Here's Braccio now, for Florence—here's our service—
Well done for us, is it well done for him?
His chosen engine, tasked to its full strength
Answers his end?—Should he have chosen higher?
Do we help Florence, now our best is done?

   Brac. This battle with the foregone services,
Saves Florence.

   Lur.   Why then, all is very well!
Here am I in the middle of my friends,
Who know me and who love me, one and all!
And yet . . . 'tis like . . . this instant while I speak
Is like the turning moment of a dream
When . . . Ah, you are not foreigners like me!
Well then, one always dreams of friends at home,
And always comes, I say, the turning point
When something changes in the friendly eyes
That love and look on you . . . so slight, so slight . . .
And yet it tells you they are dead and gone,
Or changed and enemies, for all their words,
And all is mockery, and a maddening show!
You, now, so kind here, all you Florentines,
What is it in your eyes . . . those lips, those brows . . .
Nobody spoke it . . . yet I know it well!—
Come now—this battle saves you, all's at end,
Your use of me is o'er, for good, for evil,—
Come now, what's done against me, while I speak,
In Florence? Come! I feel it in my blood,
My eyes, my hair, a voice is in my ear
That spite of all this smiling and kind speech
You are betraying me! What is it you do?
Have it your way, and think my use is over;
That you are saved and may throw off the mask—
Have it my way, and think more work remains
Which I could do,—so show you fear me not!
Or prudent be, or generous, as you choose,

But tell me—tell what I refused to know
At noon, lest heart should fail me! Well? That letter?
My fate is known at Florence! What is it?

   Brac. Sir, I shall not conceal what you divine:
It is no novelty for innocence
To be suspected, but a privilege:
The after certain compensation comes.
Charges, I say not whether false or true,
Have been preferred against you some time since,
Which Florence was bound, plainly, to receive,
And which are therefore undergoing now
The due investigation. That is all.
I doubt not but your innocence will shine
Apparent and illustrious, as to me,
To them this evening, when the trial ends.

   Lur. My trial?

   Dom.   Florence, Florence to the end,
My whole heart thanks thee!

   Puc. [*to* Brac.]   What is " Trial," Sir?
It was not for a trial—surely, no—
I furnished you those notes from time to time?
I hold myself aggrieved—I am a man—
And I might speak,—ay, and speak mere truth, too,
And yet not mean at bottom of my heart
What should assist a—Trial, do you say?
You should have told me!

   Dom.   Nay, go on, go on!
His sentence! Do they sentence him? What is it?
The block? Wheel?

   Brac.   Sentence there is none as yet,
Nor shall I give my own opinion here
Of what it should be, or is like to be,
When it is passed, applaud or disapprove!
Up to that point, what is there to impugn?

   Lur. They are right, then, to try me?

   Brac.   I assert,
Maintain, and justify the absolute right
Of Florence to do all she can have done
In this procedure,—standing on her guard,
Receiving even services like yours
With utmost fit suspicious wariness.
In other matters—keep the mummery up!
Take all the experiences of the whole world,

Each knowledge that broke thro' a heart to life,
Each reasoning which, to work out, cost a brain.
—In other cases, know these, warrant these,
And then dispense with them—'tis very well!
Let friend trust friend, and love demand its like,
And gratitude be claimed for benefits,—
There's grace in that—and when the fresh heart breaks,
The new brain proves a martyr, what of it?
Where is the matter of one moth the more
Singed in the candle, at a summer's end?
But Florence is no simple John or James
To have his toy, his fancy, his conceit,
That he's the one excepted man by fate,
And, when fate shows him he's mistaken there,
Die with all good men's praise, and yield his place
To Paul and George intent to try their chance:
Florence exists because these pass away;
She's a contrivance to supply a type
Of Man, which men's deficiencies refuse;
She binds so many, that she grows out of them—
Stands steady o'er their numbers, tho' they change
And pass away—there's always what upholds,
Always enough to fashion the great show!
As, see, yon hanging city, in the sun,
Of shapely cloud substantially the same!
A thousand vapours rise and sink again,
Are interfused, and live their life and die,—
Yet ever hangs the steady show i' the air
Under the sun's straight influence: that is well!
That is worth Heaven to hold, and God to bless!
And so is Florence,—the unseen sun above,
Which draws and holds suspended all of us—
Binds transient mists and vapours into one,
Differing from each and better than they all.
And shall she dare to stake this permanence
On any one man's faith?   Man's heart is weak,
And its temptations many: let her prove
Each servant to the very uttermost
Before she grant him her reward, I say!
   Dom.   And as for hearts she chances to mistake,
That are not destined to receive reward,
Tho' they deserve it, did she only know!
—What should she do for these?

Brac.   What does she not?
Say, that she gives them but herself to serve!
Here's Luria—what had profited his strength,
When half an hour of sober fancying
Had shown him step by step the uselessness
Of strength exerted for its proper sake?
But the truth is, she did create that strength,
Drew to the end the corresponding means.
The world is wide—are we the only men?
Oh, for the time, the social purpose' sake,
Use words agreed on, bandy epithets,
Call any man, sole Great and Wise and Good!
But shall we, therefore, standing by ourselves,
Insult our souls and God with the same speech?
There, swarm the ignoble thousands under Him—
What marks us from the hundreds and the tens?
Florence took up, turned all one way the soul
Of Luria with its fires, and here he stands!
She takes me out of all the world as him,
Fixing my coldness till like ice it stays
The fire! So, Braccio, Luria, which is best?
    Lur. Ah, brave me? And is this indeed the way
To gain your good word and sincere esteem?
Am I the baited tiger that must turn
And fight his baiters to deserve their praise?
Obedience has no fruit then?—Be it so!
Do you indeed remember I stand here
The Captain of the conquering army,—mine—
With all your tokens, praise and promise, ready
To show for what their names were when you gave,
Not what you style them now you take away?
If I call in my troops to arbitrate,
And in their first enthusiastic thrill
Of victory, tell them how you menace me—
Commending to their plain instinctive sense,
My story first, your comment afterward,—
Will they take, think you, part with you or me?
When I say simply, I, the man they know,
Ending my work, ask payment, and find Florence
Has all this while provided silently
Against the day of pay and proving words,
By what you call my sentence that's to come—
Will they sit waiting it complacently?

When I resist that sentence at their head
What will you do, my mild antagonist?

Brac. I will rise up like fire, proud and triumphant
That Florence knew you thoroughly and by me,
And so was saved: " See, Italy," I'll say,
" The need of our precautions—here's a man
" Was far advanced, just touched on the reward
" Less subtle cities had accorded him—
" But we were wiser; at the end comes this! "
And from that minute all your strength will go—
The very stones of Florence cry against
The all-exacting, unenduring Luria,
Resenting her first slight probation thus,
As if he, only, shone and cast no shade,
He, only, walked the earth with privilege
Against suspicion, free from causing fear—
So, for the first inquisitive mother's-word,
He turned, and stood on his defence, forsooth!
Reward? You will not be worth punishment!

Lur. And Florence knew me thus! Thus I have lived,—
And thus you, with the clear fine intellect,
Braccio, the cold acute instructed mind,
Out of the stir, so calm and unconfused,
Reported me—how could you otherwise!
Ay?—and what dropped from *you*, just now, more over?
Your information, Puccio?—Did your skill
And understanding sympathy approve
Such a report of me? Was this the end?
Or is even this the end? Can I stop here—
You, Lady, with the woman's stand apart,
The heart to see with, not those learned eyes,
. . . I cannot fathom why you should destroy
The unoffending man, you call your friend—
So, looking at the good examples here
Of friendship, 'tis but natural I ask
Had you a further end, in all you spoke,
Than profit to me, in those instances
Of perfidy from Florence to her chiefs—
All I remember now for the first time?

Dom. I am a daughter of the Traversari,
Sister of Porzio and of Berto both.
I have foreseen all that has come to pass.
I knew the Florence that could doubt their faith,

Must needs mistrust a stranger's—holding back
Reward from them, must hold back his reward.
And I believed, the shame they bore and died,
He would not bear, but live and fight against—
Seeing he was of other stuff than they.

   Lur. Hear them! All these against one Foreigner!
And all this while, where is in the whole world
To his good faith a single witness?

   Tiburzio [*who has entered during the preceding dialogue.*]
                                Here!

Thus I bear witness to it, not in word
But deed. I live for Pisa; she's not lost
By many chances—much prevents from that!
Her army has been beaten, I am here,
But Lucca comes at last, one chance exists.
I rather had see Pisa three times lost
Than saved by any traitor, even by you.
The example of a traitor's happy fortune
Would bring more evil in the end than good.
Pisa rejects such: save yourself and her!
I, in her name, resign forthwith to you
My charge,—the highest of her offices.
You shall not, by my counsel, turn on Florence
Her army, give her calumny that ground—
Nor bring it with you: be you all we gain,
And all she'll lose, a head to deck some bridge,
And save the crown's cost that should deck the head.
Leave her to perish in her perfidy,
Plague-stricken and stripped naked to all eyes,
A proverb and a by-word in all mouths!
Go you to Pisa—Florence is my place—
Leave me to tell her of the rectitude,
I, from the first, told Pisa, knowing it.
To Pisa!

   Dom. Ah, my Braccio, are you caught?

   Brac. Puccio, good soldier and selected man,
Whom I have ever kept beneath my eye,
Ready, as fit, to serve in this event
Florence, who clear foretold it from the first—
Thro' me, she gives you the command and charge
She takes, thro' me, from him who held it late!
A painful trial, very sore, was yours:
All that could draw out, marshal in array

The selfish passions 'gainst the public good—
Slights, scorns, neglects, were heaped on you to bear:
And ever you did bear and bow the head!
It had been sorry trial, to precede
Your feet, hold up the promise of reward
For luring gleam; your footsteps kept the track
Thro' dark and doubt: take all the light at once!
Trial is over, consummation shines;
Well have you served, as well henceforth command!

   Puc. No, no . . . I dare not . . . I am grateful, glad;
But Luria—you shall understand he's wronged—
And he's my Captain—this is not the way
We soldiers climb to fortune: think again!
The sentence is not even passed, beside!
I dare not . . . where's the soldier could?

   Lur.   Now, Florence—
Is it to be?—You will know all the strength
Of the savage—to your neck the proof must go?
You will prove the brute nature? Ah, I see!
The savage plainly is impassible—
He keeps his calm way thro' insulting words,
Sarcastic looks, sharp gestures—one of which
Would stop you, fatal to your finer sense:
But if he steadily advances, still
Without a mark upon his callous hide,
Thro' the mere brushwood you grow angry with,
And leave the tatters of your flesh upon,
—You have to learn that when the true bar comes,
The thick mid forest, the real obstacle,
Which when you reach, you give the labour up,
Nor dash on, but lie down composed before,
—He goes against it, like the brute he is!
It falls before him, or he dies in his course!
I kept my course thro' past ingratitude—
I saw—it does seem, now, as if I saw,
Could not but see, those insults as they fell,
—Ay, let them glance from off me, very like,
Laughing, perhaps, to think the quality
You grew so bold on, while you so despised
The Moor's dull mute inapprehensive mood,
Was saving you; I bore and kept my course:
Now real wrong fronts me—see if I succumb!
Florence withstands me?—I will punish her!

At night my sentence will arrive, you say!
Till then I cannot, if I would, rebel—
—Unauthorised to lay my office down,
Retaining my full power to will and do:
After—it is to see.   Tiburzio, thanks!
Go—you are free—join Lucca.   I suspend
All further operations till to-night.
Thank you, and for the silence most of all!
[*To Brac.*] Let my complacent bland accuser go,
And carry his self-approving head and heart
Safe thro' the army which would trample him
Dead in a moment at my word or sign!
Go, Sir, to Florence; tell friends what I say—
That while I wait their sentence, theirs waits them!
[*To Dom.*] You, Lady,—you have black Italian eyes!
I would be generous if I might. . . . Oh, yes—
For I remember how so oft you seemed
Inclined at heart to break the barrier down
Which Florence makes God build between us both.
Alas, for generosity! this hour
Demands strict justice—bear it as you may!
I must—the Moor,—the Savage,—pardon you!
[*To Puc.*] Puccio, my trusty soldier, see them forth!—

ACT IV.

EVENING.

Enter PUCCIO *and* JACOPO.

Puc.   What Luria *will* do?   Ah, 'tis yours, fair Sir,
Your and your subtle-witted master's part,
To tell me that; I tell you what he can.
     Jac.   Friend, you mistake my station! I observe
The game, watch how my betters play, no more.
     Puc.   But mankind are not pieces—there's your fault!
You cannot push them, and, the first move made,
Lean back to study what the next should be,
In confidence that when 'tis fixed upon,
You'll find just where you left them, blacks and whites:
Men go on moving when your hand's away.
You build, I notice, firm on Luria's faith
This whole time,—firmlier than I choose to build,

Who never doubted it—of old, that is—
With Luria in his ordinary mind:
But now, oppression makes the wise man mad—
How do I know he will not turn and stand
And hold his own against you, as he may?
Suppose that he withdraws to Pisa—well,—
Then, even if all happens to your wish,
Which is a chance . . .

   Jac.   Nay—'twas an oversight,
Not waiting till the proper warrant came:
You could not take what was not ours to give.
But when at night the sentence really comes,
And Florence authorizes past dispute
Luria's removal and your own advance,
You will perceive your duty and accept?

   Puc.   Accept what? muster-rolls of soldiers' names?
An army upon paper?—I want men,
Their hearts as well as hands—and where's a heart
That's not with Luria, in the multitude
I come from walking thro' by Luria's side?
You gave him to them, set him on to grow,
Head-like, upon their trunk, one blood feeds both,
They feel him there, and live, and well know why!
—For they do know, if you are ignorant,
Who kept his own place and respected theirs,
Managed their ease, yet never spared his own.
All was your deed: another might have served—
There's peradventure no such dearth of men—
But you chose Luria—so they grew to him:
And now, for nothing they can understand,
Luria's removed, off is to roll the head—
The body's mine—much I shall do with it!

   Jac.   That's at the worst!

   Puc.   No—at the best, it is!
Best, do you hear? I saw them by his side;
Only we two with Luria in the camp
Are left that know the secret? You think that?
Hear what I saw: from rear to van, no heart
But felt the quiet patient hero there
Was wronged, nor in the moveless ranks an eye
But glancing told its fellow the whole story
Of that convicted silent knot of spies
Who passed thro' them to Florence; they might pass—

No breast but gladlier beat when free of them!
Our troops will catch up Luria, close him round,
Lead him to Florence as their natural lord,
Partake his fortunes, live or die with him!

Jac. And by mistake catch up along with him
Puccio, no doubt, compelled in self-despite
To still continue Second in Command!

Puc. No, Sir, no second nor so fortunate!
Your tricks succeed with me too well for that!
I am as you have made me, and shall die
A mere trained fighting hack to serve your end;
With words, you laugh at while they leave your mouth,
For my life's rules and ordinance of God!
I have to do my duty, keep my faith,
And earn my praise, and guard against my blame,
As I was trained. I shall accept your charge,
And fight against one better than myself,
And my own heart's conviction of his worth—
That, you may count on!—just as hitherto
I have gone on, persuaded I was wronged,
Slighted, and all the terms we learn by rote,—
All because Luria superseded me—
Because the better nature, fresh-inspired,
Mounted above me to its proper place!
What mattered all the kindly graciousness,
And cordial brother's bearing? This was clear—
I, once the captain, was subaltern now,
And so must keep complaining like a fool!
Go, take the curse of a lost man, I say!
You neither play your puppets to the end,
Nor treat the real man,—for his realness' sake
Thrust rudely in their place,—with such regard
As might console them for their altered rank.
Me, the mere steady soldier, you depose
For Luria, and here's all that he deserves!
Of what account, then, are my services?
One word for all: whatever Luria does,
—If backed by his indignant troops he turns
In self-defence and Florence goes to ground,—
Or for a signal, everlasting shame,
He pardons you, and simply seeks his friends
And heads the Pisan and the Lucchese troops
—And if I, for you ingrates past belief,

Resolve to fight against a man called false,
Who, inasmuch as he is true, fights there—
Whichever way he wins, he wins for me,
For every soldier, for the common good!
Sir, chronicling the rest, omit not this!

As they go, enter LURIA *and* HUSAIN.

   Hus. Saw'st thou?—For they are gone! The world lies bare
Before thee, to be tasted, felt and seen
Like what it is, now Florence goes away!
Thou livest now, with men art man again!
Those Florentines were eyes to thee of old;
But Braccio, but Domizia, gone is each—
There lie beneath thee thine own multitudes—
Sawest thou?
   Lur.   I saw.
   Hus.   Then, hold thy course, my King!
The years return. Let thy heart have its way!
Ah, they would play with thee as with all else?
Turn thee to use, and fashion thee anew,
Find out God's fault in thee as in the rest?
Oh, watch, but listen only to these men
Once at their occupation! Ere ye know,
The free great heaven is shut, their stifling pall
Drops till it frets the very tingling hair—
So weighs it on our head,—and, for the earth,
Our common earth is tethered up and down,
Over and across—here shalt thou move, they say!
   Lur. Ah, Husain?
   Hus.   So have they spoiled all beside!
So stands a man girt round with Florentines,
Priests, greybeards, Braccios, women, boys and spies,
All in one tale, each singing the same song,
How thou must house, and live at bed and board,
Take pledge and give it, go their every way,
Breathe to their measure, make thy blood beat time
With theirs—or—all is nothing—thou art lost—
A savage . . . how shouldst thou perceive as they?
Feel glad to stand 'neath God's close naked hand!
Look up to it! Why, down they pull thy neck,
Lest it crush thee, who feel'st it and wouldst kiss,
Without their priests that needs must glove it first,
Lest peradventure, it should wound thy lip!

Love Woman!   Why, a very beast thou art!
Thou must . . .
 Lur.   Peace, Husain!
 Hus.   Ay, but, spoiling all,
For all, else true, things substituting false,
That they should dare spoil, of all instincts, thine!
Should dare to take thee with thine instincts up,
Thy battle-ardours, like a ball of fire,
And class them and allow them place and play
So far, no farther—unabashed the while!
Thou with the soul that never can take rest—
Thou born to do, undo, and do again,
But never to be still,—wouldst thou make war?
Oh, that is commendable, just and right!
Come over, say they, have the honour due
In living out thy nature!   Fight thy best—
It is to be for Florence not thyself!
For thee, it were a horror and a plague—
For us, when war is made for Florence, see,
How all is changed—the fire that fed on earth
Now towers to heaven!—
 Lur.   And what sealed up so long
My Husain's mouth?
 Hus.   Oh, friend, oh, lord—for me,
What am I?—I was silent at thy side,
That am a part of thee—It is thy hand,
Thy foot that glows when in the heart fresh blood
Boils up, thou heart of me!   Now live again!
Again love as thou likest, hate as free!
Turn to no Braccios nor Domizias now,
To ask, before thy very limbs dare move,
If Florence' welfare be concerned thereby!
 Lur. So clear what Florence must expect of me?
 Hus. Both armies against Florence!   Take revenge!
Wide, deep—to live upon, in feeling now,—
And after, in remembrance, year by year—
And, with the dear conviction, die at last!
She lies now at thy pleasure—pleasure have!
Their vaunted intellect that gilds our sense,
And blends with life, to show it better by,
—How think'st thou?—I have turned that light on them!
They called our thirst of war a transient thing;
The battle-element must pass away

From life, they said, and leave a tranquil world:
—Master, I took their light and turned it full
On that dull turgid vein they said would burst
And pass away; and as I looked on Life,
Still everywhere I tracked this, though it hid
And shifted, lay so silent as it thought,
Changed oft the hue yet ever was the same:
Why, 'twas all fighting, all their nobler life!
All work was fighting, every harm—defeat,
And every joy obtained—a victory!
Be not their dupe!
                —Their dupe? That hour is past!
Here stand'st thou in the glory and the calm!
All is determined! Silence for me now!   [HUSAIN *goes*.
    Lur. Have I heard all?
    Dom. [*advancing from the background*.] No, Luria, I am
        here!
Not from the motives these have urged on thee,
Ignoble, insufficient, incomplete,
And pregnant each with sure seeds of decay,
As failing of sustainment from thyself,
—Neither from low revenge, nor selfishness,
Nor savage lust of power, nor one, nor all,
Shalt thou abolish Florence! I proclaim
The angel in thee, and reject the spirits
Which ineffectual crowd about his strength,
And mingle with his work and claim a share!
—Inconsciously to the augustest end
Thou hast arisen: second not in rank
So much as time, to him who first ordained
That Florence, thou art to destroy, should be—
Yet him a star, too, guided, who broke first
The pride of lonely power, the life apart,
And made the eminences, each to each,
Lean o'er the level world and let it lie
Safe from the thunder henceforth 'neath their arms—
So the few famous men of old combined,
And let the multitude rise underneath,
And reach them, and unite—so Florence grew!
Braccio speaks well, it was well worth the price.
But when the sheltered Many grew in pride
And grudged the station of the glorious ones,
Who, greater than their kind, are truly great

Only in voluntary servitude—
Time was for thee to rise, and thou art here.
Such plague possessed this Florence—who can tell
The mighty girth and greatness at the heart
Of those so noble pillars of the grove
She pulled down in her envy? Who as I,
The light weak parasite born but to twine
Round each of them and, measuring them, so live?
My light love keeps the matchless circle safe,
My slender life proves what has past away!
I lived when they departed; lived to cling
To thee, the mighty stranger; thou would'st rise
And burst the thraldom, and avenge, I knew.
I have done nothing; all was thy strong heart:
But a bird's weight can break the infant tree
Which after holds an aery in its arms,
And 'twas my care that nought should warp thy spire
From rising to the height; the roof is reached—
Break through and there is all the sky above!
Go on to Florence, Luria! 'Tis man's cause!
Fail thou, and thine own fall is least to dread!
Thou keepest Florence in her evil way,
Encouragest her sin so much the more—
And while the bloody past is justified,
Thou all the surelier dost work against
The men to come, the Lurias yet unborn,
Who, greater than thyself, are reached o'er thee
That giv'st the vantage-ground their foes require,
As o'er my prostrate House thyself was't reached!
Man calls thee—God shall judge thee: all is said,
The mission of my House fulfilled at last!
And the mere woman, speaking for herself,
Reserves speech; it is now no woman's time.

                                        [Domizia goes,

   Lur.   So at the last must figure Luria, then!
Doing the various work of all his friends,
And answering every purpose save his own.
No doubt, 'tis well for them to wish; for him—
After the exploit what is left?   Perchance
A little pride upon the swarthy brow,
At having brought successfully to bear
'Gainst Florence' self her own especial arms,—
Her craftiness, impelled by fiercer strength

From Moorish blood than feeds the northern wit—
But after!—once the easy vengeance willed,
Beautiful Florence at a word laid low
—(Not in her Domes and Towers and Palaces,
Not even in a dream, that outrage!)—low,
As shamed in her own eyes henceforth for ever,
Low, for the rival cities round to see
Conquered and pardoned by a hireling Moor!
—For him, who did the irreparable wrong,
What would be left, his life's illusion fled,—
What hope or trust in the forlorn wide world?
How strange that Florence should mistake me so!
How grew this? What withdrew her faith from me?
Some cause! These fretful-blooded children talk
Against their mother,—they are wronged, they say—
Notable wrongs a smile makes up again!
So, taking fire at each supposed offence,
They may speak rashly, suffer for rash speech—
But what could it have been in word or deed
That injured me? Some one word spoken more
Out of my heart, and all had changed perhaps!
My fault, it must have been,—for what gain they?
Why risk the danger? See, what I could do!
And my fault, wherefore visit upon them,
My Florentines? The generous revenge,
I meditate! To stay here passively,
Go at their summons, be as they dispose—
Why, if my very soldiers keep their ranks,
And if I pacify my chiefs, what then?
I ruin Florence—teach her friends mistrust—
Confirm her enemies in harsh belief—
And when she finds one day, as she must find,
The strange mistake, and how my heart was hers,
Shall it console me, that my Florentines
Walk with a sadder step, a graver face,
Who took me with such frankness, praised me so,
At the glad outset! Had they loved me less,
They had less feared what seemed a change in me.
And after all, who did the harm? Not they!
How could they interpose with those old fools
In the council? Suffer for those old fools' sakes—
They, who made pictures of me, sang the songs
About my battles? Ah, we Moors get blind

Out of our proper world where we can see!
The sun that guides is closer to us! There—
There, my own orb! He sinks from out the sky!
Why, there! a whole day has he blessed the land,
My land, our Florence all about the hills,
The fields and gardens, vineyards, olive-grounds
All have been blest—and yet we Florentines
With minds intent upon our battle here,
Found that he rose too soon, or else too late,
Gave us no vantage, or gave Pisa more—
And so we wronged him! Does he turn in ire
To burn the earth, that cannot understand?
Or drop out quietly, and leave the sky,
His task once ended? Night wipes blame away:
Another morning from my East shall rise
And find all eyes at leisure, more disposed
To watch it and approve its work, no doubt.
So, praise the new sun, the successor praise!
Praise the new Luria, and forget the old!
                             [Taking a phial from his breast.
—Strange! This is all I brought from my own Land
To help me—Europe would supply the rest,
All needs beside, all other helps save this!
I thought of adverse fortune, battles lost,
The natural upbraidings of the loser,
And then this quiet remedy to seek
At end of the disastrous day—   *[He drinks.*
                    'Tis sought!
This was my happy triumph-morning: Florence
Is saved: I drink this, and ere night,—die!—Strange!

ACT V.

NIGHT.

LURIA. PUCCIO.

Lur. I thought to do this, not to talk this: well!
Such were my projects for the City's good,
To save her from attack or by defence.
Time, here as elsewhere, soon or late may take
Our foresight by surprise with chance and change:
But not a little we provide against

Luria

—If you see clear on every point.
   Puc.   Most clear.
   Lur. Then all is said—not much, if you count words,
Yet for an understanding ear enough,
And all that my brief stay permits, beside.
Nor must you blame me, as I sought to teach
My elder in command, or threw a doubt
Upon the very skill, it comforts me
To know I leave,—your steady soldiership
That never failed me: yet, because it seemed
A stranger's eye might haply note defect,
Which skill, thro' use and custom, overlooks,
I have gone into the old cares once more,
As if I had to come and save again
Florence—that May—that morning! 'Tis night now—
Well—I broke off with? . . .
   Puc.   Of the past campaign
You spoke—of measures to be kept in mind
For future use.
   Lur.   True, so . . . but, time—no time!
As well end here: remember this, and me!
Farewell now!
   Puc.   Dare I speak?
   Lur.   —The south o' the river—
How is the second stream called . . . no,—the third?
   Puc. Pesa.
   Lur.   And a stone's cast from the fording-place,
To the East,—the little mount's name?
   Puc.   Lupo.
   Lur.   Ay
Ay—there the tower, and all that side is safe!
With San Romano, west of Evola,
San Miniato, Scala, Empoli,
Five towers in all,—forget not!
   Puc.   Fear not me!
   Lur.—Nor to memorialize the Council now,
I' the easy hour, on those battalions' claim
On the other side, by Staggia on the hills,
That kept the Siennese at check!
   Puc.   One word—
Sir, I must speak! That you submit yourself
To Florence' bidding, howsoe'er it prove,
And give up the command to me—is much,

Too much, perhaps: but what you tell me now,
Even will affect the other course you choose—
Poor as it may be, peril even that!
Refuge you seek at Pisa—yet these plans
All militate for Florence, all conclude
Your formidable work to make her queen
Of the country,—which her rivals rose against
When you began it,—which to interrupt,
Pisa would buy you off at any price!
You cannot mean to sue for Pisa's help,
With this made perfect and on record?

   Lur.   I—
At Pisa, and for refuge, do you say?

   Puc. Where are you going, then? You must decide
On leaving us, a silent fugitive,
Alone, at night—you, stealing thro' our lines,
Who were this morning's Luria,—you escape
To painfully begin the world once more,
With such a Past, as it had never been!
Where are you going?

   Lur.   Not so far, my Puccio,
But that I hope to hear, and know, and praise
(If you mind praise from your old captain yet)
Each happy blow you strike for Florence!

   Puc.   —Ay,
But ere you gain your shelter, what may come?
For see—tho' nothing's surely known as yet,
Still . . . truth must out . . . I apprehend the worst,
If mere suspicion stood for certainty
Before, there's nothing can arrest the steps
Of Florence toward your ruin, once on foot.
Forgive her fifty times, it matters not!
And having disbelieved your innocence,
How can she trust your magnanimity?
You may do harm to her—why then, you will!
And Florence is sagacious in pursuit.
Have you a friend to count on?

   Lur.   One sure friend.

   Puc. Potent?

   Lur.   All potent.

   Puc.   And he is apprised?

   Lur. He waits me.

   Puc.   So!—Then I, put in your place,

Making my profit of all done by you,
Calling your labours mine, reaping their fruit,
To these, the State's gift, now add this of yours—
That I may take to my peculiar store
All your instructions to do Florence good;
And if, by putting some few happily
In practice, I should both advantage her
And draw down honour on myself,—what then?

   Lur. Do it, my Puccio! I shall know and praise!

   Puc. Though, so, men say, " mark what we gain by change
"—A Puccio for a Luria! "

   Lur.   Even so!

   Puc. Then, not for fifty hundred Florences,
Would I accept one office save my own,
Fill any other than my rightful post
Here at your feet, my Captain and my Lord,
That such a cloud should break, such trouble be,
Ere a man settle soul and body down
Into his true place and take rest for ever!
Here were my wise eyes fixed on your right hand,
And so the bad thoughts came and the worse words,
And all went wrong and painfully enough,—
No wonder,—till, the right spot stumbled on,
All the jar stops, and there is peace at once!
I am yours now,—a tool your right hand wields!
God's love, that I should live, the man I am,
On orders, warrants, patents and the like,
As if there were no glowing eye i' the world,
To glance straight inspiration to my brain,
No glorious heart to give mine twice the beats!
For, see—my doubt, where is it?—Fear? 'tis flown!
And Florence and her anger are a tale
To scare a child! Why, half a dozen words
Will tell her, spoken as I now can speak,
Her error, my past folly—and all's right,
And you are Luria, our great chief again!
Or at the worst—which worst were best of all—
To exile or to death I follow you!

   Lur. Thanks, Puccio! Let me use the privilege
You grant me: if I still command you,—stay!
Remain here—my vicegerent, it shall be,
And not successor: let me, as of old,

Still serve the State, my spirit prompting yours;
Still triumph, one for both—There! Leave me now!
You cannot disobey my first command?
Remember what I spoke of Jacopo,
And what you promised to observe with him!
Send him to speak with me—nay, no farewell—
You shall be by me when the sentence comes.

[PUCCIO *goes.*

So, there's one Florentine returns again!
Out of the genial morning company,
One face is left to take into the night.

Enter JACOPO.

Jac.   I wait for your commands, Sir.
Lur.   What, so soon?
I thank your ready presence and fair word.
I used to notice you in early days
As of the other species, so to speak,
Those watchers of the lives of us who act—
That weigh our motives, scrutinize our thoughts;
So, I propound this to your faculty
As you would tell me, were a town to take
. . . That is, of old.   I am departing hence
Under these imputations: that is nought—
I leave no friend on whom they may rebound,
Hardly a name behind me in the land,
Being a stranger; all the more behoves
That I regard how altered were the case
With natives of the country, Florentines,
On whom the like mischance should fall; the roots
O' the tree survive the ruin of the trunk—
No root of mine will throb—you understand.
But I had predecessors, Florentines,
Accused as I am now, and punished so—
The Traversari—you know more than I
How stigmatized they are, and lost in shame.
Now, Puccio, who succeeds me in command,
Both served them and succeeded, in due time;
He knows the way, holds proper documents,
And has the power to lay the simple truth
Before an active spirit, as I know yours:
And also there's Tiburzio, my new friend,
Will, at a word, confirm such evidence,

He being the chivalric soul we know.
I put it to your instinct—were't not well,
—A grace, though but for contrast's sake, no more,—
If you who witness, and have borne a share
Involuntarily, in my mischance,
Should, of your proper motion, set your skill
To indicate . . . that is, investigate
The reason or the wrong of what befel
Those famous citizens, your countrymen?
Nay—you shall promise nothing—but reflect,
And if your sense of justice prompt you—good!

   Jac. And if, the trial past, their fame stand clear
To all men's eyes, as yours, my lord, to mine—
Their ghosts may sleep in quiet satisfied!
For me, a straw thrown up into the air,
My testimony goes for a straw's worth.
I used to hold by the instructed brain,
And move with Braccio as the master-wind;
The heart leads surelier: I must move with you—
As greatest now, who ever were the best.
So, let the last and humblest of your servants
Accept your charge, as Braccio's heretofore,
And offer homage, by obeying you!   [JACOPO *goes.*

   Lur. Another!—Luria goes not poorly forth!
If we could wait! The only fault's with Time:
All men become good creatures—but so slow!

Enter DOMIZIA.

   Lur. Ah, you once more?
   Dom.   Domizia, that you knew,
Performed her task, and died with it—'Tis I!
Another woman, you have never known.
Let the Past sleep now.
   Lur.   I have done with it.
   Dom. How inexhaustibly the spirit grows!
One object, she seemed erewhile born to reach
With her whole energies and die content,
So like a wall at the world's end it stood,
With nought beyond to live for,—is it reached?
Already are new undreamed energies
Outgrowing under, and extending further
To a new object;—there's another world!
See! I have told the purpose of my life,—

'Tis gained—you are decided, well or ill—
You march on Florence, or submit to her—
My work is done with you, your brow declares:
But—leave you?   More of you seems yet to reach!
I stay for what I just begin to see.
    Lur. So that you turn not to the Past!
    Dom.   You trace
Nothing but ill in it—my selfish impulse,
Which sought its ends and disregarded yours?
    Lur. Speak not against your nature: best, each keep
His own—you, yours—most, now, when I keep mine,
—At least, fall by it, having too weakly stood.
God's finger marks distinctions, all so fine,
We would confound—the Lesser has its use,
Which, when it apes the Greater, is foregone.
I, born a Moor, lived half a Florentine;
But, punished properly, can die a Moor.
Beside, there is what makes me understand
Your nature . . . I have seen it—
    Dom.   One like mine?
    Lur. In my own East . . . if you would stoop and help
My barbarous illustration . . . it sounds ill—
Yet there's no wrong at bottom—rather, praise—
    Dom. Well?
    Lur.   We have creatures there, which if you saw
The first time, you would doubtless marvel at,
For their surpassing beauty, craft and strength,
And tho' it were a lively moment's shock
Wherein you found the purpose of those tongues
That seemed innocuous in their lambent play,
Yet, once made know such grace required such guard,
Your reason soon would acquiesce, I think,
In the Wisdom which made all things for the best;
So take them, good with ill, contentedly—
The prominent beauty with the secret sting.
I am glad to have seen you wondrous Florentines,
Yet . . .
    Dom. I am here to listen.
    Lur.   My own East!
How nearer God we were!   He glows above
With scarce an intervention, presses close
And palpitatingly, His soul o'er ours!
We feel Him, nor by painful reason know!

The everlasting minute of creation
Is felt there; *Now* it is, as it was Then;
All changes at His instantaneous will,
Not by the operation of a law
Whose maker is elsewhere at other work!
His soul is still engaged upon his world—
Man's praise can forward it, Man's prayer suspend,
For is not God all-mighty?—To recast
The world, erase old things and make them new,
What costs it Him?   So, man breathes nobly there
And inasmuch as Feeling, the East's gift,
Is quick and transient—comes, and lo, is gone—
While Northern Thought is slow and durable,
Oh, what a mission was reserved for me,
Who, born with a perception of the power
And use of the North's thought for us of the East,
Should have stayed there and turned it to account,
Giving Thought's character and permanence
To the too-transitory Feelings there—
Writing God's messages in mortal words!
Instead of which, I leave my fated field
For this where such a task is needed least,
Where all are born consummate in the art
I just perceive a chance of making mine,—
And then, deserting thus my early post,
I wonder that the men I come among
Mistake me!   There, how all had understood,
Still brought fresh stuff for me to stamp and keep,
Fresh instinct to translate them into law!
Me, who . . .
   Dom.   Who here the greater task achieve,
More needful even: who have brought fresh stuff
For us to mould, interpret and prove right,—
New feelings fresh from God, which, could we know
O' the instant, where had been our need of them?
—Whose life re-teaches us what life should be,
What faith is, loyalty and simpleness,
All, their revealment taught us so long since
That, having mere tradition of the fact,
Truth copied falteringly from copies faint,
The early traits all dropped away,—we said
On sight of faith of yours, " so looks not faith
" We understand, described and taught before."
   II—*F 42

But still, the truth was shown; and tho' at first
It suffer from our haste, yet trace by trace
Old memories reappear, the likeness grows,
Our slow Thought does its work, and all's re-known.
Oh, noble Luria! what you have decreed
I see not, but no animal revenge,
No brute-like punishment of bad by worse—
It cannot be, the gross and vulgar way
Traced for me by convention and mistake,
Has gained that calm approving eye and brow!
Spare Florence after all! Let Luria trust
To his own soul, and I will trust to him!

    Lur. In time!
    Dom.   How, Luria?
    Lur.   It is midnight now—
And they arrive from Florence with my fate.
    Dom. I hear no step . . .
    Lur.   I feel it, as you say!

Enter HUSAIN.

    Hus. The man returned from Florence!
    Lur.   As I knew.
    Hus. He seeks thee.
    Lur.   And I only wait for him.
Aught else?
    Hus.   A movement of the Lucchese troops
Southward—
    Lur. . . . Toward Florence? Have out instantly . . .
Ah, old use clings! Puccio must care henceforth!
In—quick—'tis nearly midnight! Bid him come!

Enter TIBURZIO, BRACCIO, *and* PUCCIO.

    Lur. Tiburzio?—not at Pisa?
    Tib.   I return
From Florence: I serve Pisa, and must think
By such procedure I have served her best.
A people is but the attempt of many
To rise to the completer life of one—
And those who live as models for the mass
Are singly of more value than they all.
Such man are you, and such a time is this
That your sole fate concerns a nation more
Than its apparent welfare; and to prove

Your rectitude, and duly crown the same,
Imports it far beyond the day's event,
Its battle's loss or gain—the mass remains,
Keep but the model safe, new men will rise
To study it, and other days to prove
How great a good was Luria's having lived.
I might go try my fortune as you bade,
And joining Lucca, helped by your disgrace,
Repair our harm—so were to-day's work done;
But where were Luria for our sons to see?
No, I look farther. I have testified
(Declaring my submission to your arms)
Your full success to Florence, making clear
Your probity, as none else could: I spoke—
And it shone clearly!

    Lur.   Ah—till Braccio spoke!

    Brac. Till Braccio told in just a word the whole—
His old great error, and return to knowledge—
Which told . . . Nay, Luria, *I* should droop the head,
I, whom shame rests with, yet I dare look up,
Sure of your pardon now I sue for it,
Knowing you wholly—so let midnight end!
Sunrise will come next! Still you answer not?
The shadow of the night is past away:
Our circling faces here 'mid which it rose
Are all that felt it,—they close round you now
To witness its completest vanishing.
Speak, Luria! Here begins your true career—
Look up to it!—All now is possible—
The glory and the grandeur of each dream—
And every prophecy shall be fulfilled
Save one . . . (nay, now your word must come at last)
—That you would punish Florence!

    Hus. (*pointing to* LURIA's *dead body*.) That is done!—

A SOUL'S TRAGEDY

A SOUL'S TRAGEDY

PART FIRST, BEING WHAT WAS CALLED THE POETRY OF
CHIAPPINO'S LIFE: AND PART SECOND, ITS PROSE.

PART I.

Inside LUITOLFO'S *house at Faenza.* CHIAPPINO, EULALIA.

Eu. What is it keeps Luitolfo? Night's fast falling,
And 'twas scarce sunset . . . had the Ave-bell
Sounded before he sought the Provost's House?
I think not: all he had to say would take
Few minutes, such a very few, to say!
How do you think, Chiappino? If our lord
The Provost were less friendly to your friend
Than everybody here professes him,
I should begin to tremble—should not you?
Why are you silent when so many times
I turn and speak to you?
   Ch.   That's good!
   Eu.   You laugh?
   Ch. Yes. I had fancied nothing that bears price
In the whole world was left to call my own,
And, may be, felt a little pride thereat:
Up to a single man's or woman's love,
Down to the right in my own flesh and blood,
There's nothing mine, I fancied,—till you spoke!
—Counting, you see, as " nothing " the permission
To study this peculiar lot of mine
In silence: well, go silence with the rest
Of the world's good! What can I say, shall serve?
   Eu. This,—lest you, even more than needs, embitter
Our parting: say your wrongs have cast, for once,
A cloud across your spirit!
   Ch.   How a cloud?
   Eu. No man nor woman loves you, did you say?
   Ch. My God, were't not for thee!
   Eu.   Ay, God remains,

Even did Men forsake you.
    Ch.   Oh, not so!
Were't not for God, I mean, what hope of truth—
Speaking truth, hearing truth, would stay with Man?
I, now—the homeless, friendless, penniless,
Proscribed and exiled wretch who speak to you,
Ought to speak truth, yet could not, for my death,
(The thing that tempts me most) help speaking lies
About your friendship, and Luitolfo's courage,
And all our townsfolk's equanimity,—
Through sheer incompetence to rid myself
Of the old miserable lying trick
Caught from the liars I have lived with,—God,
Did I not turn to thee! it is thy prompting
I dare to be ashamed of, and thy counsel
Would die along my coward lip, I know—
But I do turn to thee! This craven tongue,
These features which refuse the soul its way,
Reclaim Thou! Give me truth—truth, power to speak
—And after be sole present to approve
The spoken truth!—or, stay, that spoken truth,
Who knows but you, too, might approve?
    Eu.   Ah, well—
Keep silence, then, Chiappino!
    Ch.   You would hear,
And shall now,—why the thing we're pleased to style
My gratitude to you and all your friends
For service done me, is just gratitude
So much as yours was service—and no more.
I was born here, so was Luitolfo,—both
At one time, much with the same circumstance
Of rank and wealth; and both, up to this night
Of parting company, have side by side
Still fared, he in the sunshine—I, the shadow:
" Why? " asks the world: " Because," replies the world
To its complacent self, " these playfellows,
Who took at church the holy-water drop
One from the other's finger, and so forth,—
Were of two moods: Luitolfo was the proper
Friend-making, everywhere friend-finding soul,
Fit for the sunshine, so it followed him;
A happy-tempered bringer of the best
Out of the worst; who bears with what's past cure,

And puts so good a face on't—wisely passive
Where action's fruitless, while he remedies
In silence what the foolish rail against;
A man to smooth such natures as parade
Of opposition must exasperate—
No general gauntlet-gatherer for the weak
Against the strong, yet over-scrupulous
At lucky junctures; one who won't forego
The after-battle work of binding wounds,
Because, forsooth, he'd have to bring himself
To side with their inflictors for their leave!"
—Why do you gaze, nor help me to repeat
What comes so glibly from the common mouth,
About Luitolfo and his so-styled friend?

    Eu. Because, that friend's sense is obscured . . .
    Ch.   I thought
You would be readier with the other half
Of the world's story,—my half!—Yet, 'tis true,
For all the world does say it! Say your worst!
True, I thank God, I ever said " you sin,"
When a man did sin: if I could not say it,
I glared it at him,—if I could not glare it,
I prayed against him,—then my part seemed over;
God's may begin yet—so it will, I trust!

    Eu. If the world outraged you, did we?
    Ch.   What's " me "
That you use well or ill? It's Man, in me,
All your successes are an outrage to,
You all, whom sunshine follows, as you say!
Here's our Faenza birthplace—they send here
A Provost from Ravenna—how he rules,
You can at times be eloquent about—
" Then, end his rule! " ah yes, one stroke does that!
But patience under wrong works slow and sure:
Must violence still bring peace forth? He, beside,
Returns so blandly one's obeisance—ah—
Some latent virtue may be lingering yet,
Some human sympathy which, once excite,
And all the lump were leavened quietly—
So, no more talk of striking, for this time!
But I, as one of those he rules, won't bear
These pretty takings-up and layings down
Our cause, just as you think occasion suits!

Enough of earnest, is there? You'll play, will you?
Diversify your tactics,—give submission,
Obsequiousness and flattery a turn,
While we die in our misery patient deaths?
We all are outraged then, and I the first!
I, for Mankind, resent each shrug and smirk,
Each beck and bend, each . . . all you do and are,
I hate!

   Eu.   We share a common censure, then!
'Tis well you have not poor Luitolfo's part
Or mine to point out in the wide offence.

   Ch.   Oh, shall I let you so escape me, Lady?
Come, on your own ground, Lady,—from yourself?
(Leaving the people's wrong, which most is mine,)
What have I got to be so grateful for?
These three last fines, no doubt, one on the other
Paid by Luitolfo?

   Eu.   Shame, Chiappino!

   Ch.   Shame
Fall presently on who deserves it most!
Which is to see. He paid my fines—my friend,
Your prosperous smooth husband presently,
Then, scarce your wooer,—now, your lover: well—
I loved you!

   Eu.   Hold!

   Ch.   You knew it, years ago;
When my voice faltered and my eyes grew dim
Because you gave me your silk mask to hold—
My voice that greatens when there's need to curse
The people's Provost to their heart's content,
—My eyes, the Provost, who bears all men's eyes,
Banishes now because he cannot bear!
You knew . . . but you do your parts—my part, I!
So be it! you flourish—I decay! All's well!

   Eu.   I hear this for the first time!

   Ch.   The fault's there?
Then, my days spoke not, and my nights of fire
Were voiceless? Then, the very heart may burst
Yet all prove nought, because no mincing speech
Tells leisurely that thus it is and thus?
Eulalia—truce with toying for this once—
A banished fool, who troubles you to-night
For the last time—Oh, what's to fear from me?

You knew I loved you!
   Eu.   Not so, on my faith!
You were my now-affianced lover's friend—
Came in, went out with him, could speak as he;
All praise your ready parts and pregnant wit;
See how your words come from you in a crowd!
Luitolfo's first to place you o'er himself
In all that challenges respect and love—
Yet you were silent then, who blame me now!
I say all this by fascination, sure—
I am all but wed to one I love, yet listen—
It must be, you are wronged, and that the wrongs
Luitolfo pities . . .
   Ch.   —You too pity? Do!
But hear first what my wrongs are; so began
This talk and so shall end this talk. I say,
Was't not enough that I must strive, I saw,
To grow so far familiar with your charms
As to contrive some way to win them—which
To do, an age seemed far too little—for, see!
We all aspire to Heaven—and there is Heaven
Above us—go there! Dare we go? no, surely!
How dare we go without a reverent pause,
A growing less unfit for Heaven?—Even so,
I dared not speak—the greater fool, it seems!
Was't not enough to struggle with such folly,
But I must have, beside, the very man
Whose slight, free, loose and incapacious soul
Gave his tongue scope to say whate'er he would
—Must have him load me with his benefits
For fortune's fiercest stroke!
   Eu.   Justice to him
That's now entreating, at his risk perhaps,
Justice for you! Did he once call those acts
Of simple friendship—bounties, benefits?
   Ch. No—the straight course had been to call them so—
Then, I had flung them back, and kept myself
Unhampered, free as he to win the prize
We both sought—but " the gold was dross," he said,
" He loved me, and I loved him not—to spurn
" A trifle out of superfluity:
" He had forgotten he had done as much! "
So had not I!—Henceforth, try as I could

To take him at his word, there stood by you
My benefactor—who might speak and laugh
And urge his nothings—even banter me
Before you—but my tongue was tied.   A dream!
Let's wake: your husband . . . how you shake at that!
Good—my revenge!
    Eu.   Why should I shake?   What forced,
Or forces me to be Luitolfo's bride?
    Ch.   There's my revenge, that nothing forces you!
No gratitude, no liking of the eye,
Nor longing of the heart, but the poor bond
Of habit—here so many times he came,
So much he spoke,—all these compose the tie
That pulls you from me!   Well, he paid my fines,
Nor missed a cloak from wardrobe, dish from table—
—He spoke a good word to the Provost here—
Held me up when my fortunes fell away
—It had not looked so well to let me drop—
Men take pains to preserve a tree-stump, even,
Whose boughs they played beneath—much more a friend!
But one grows tired of seeing, after the first,
Pains spent upon impracticable stuff
Like me: I could not change—you know the rest.
I've spoke my mind too fully out, for once,
This morning to our Provost; so ere night
I leave the city on pain of death—and now
On my account there's gallant intercession
Goes forward—that's so graceful!—and anon
He'll noisily come back: the intercession
Was made and fails—all's over for us both—
'Tis vain contending—I had better go:
And I do go—and so to you he turns
Light of a load, and ease of that permits
His visage to repair its natural bland
Œconomy, sore broken late to suit
My discontent: so, all are pleased—you, with him,
He with himself, and all of you with me
—Who, say the citizens, had done far better
In letting people sleep upon their woes,
If not possessed with talent to relieve them
When once they woke;—but then I had, they'll say,
Doubtless some unknown compensating pride
In what I did—and as I seem content

With ruining myself, why so should they be,
And so they are, and so be with his prize
The devil, when he gets them speedily!
Why does not your Luitolfo come?   I long
To don this cloak and take the Lugo path.
It seems you never loved me, then?

    Eu.   Chiappino!
    Ch.   Never?
    Eu.   Never.
    Ch.   That's sad—say what I might,
There was no helping being sure this while
You loved me—love like mine must have return,
I thought—no river starts but to some sea!
And had you loved me, I could soon devise
Some specious reason why you stifled love,
Some fancied self-denial on your part,
Which made you choose Luitolfo; so, excepting
From the wide condemnation of all here,
One woman!   Well, the other dream may break!
If I knew any heart, as mine loved you,
Loved me, tho' in the vilest breast 'twere lodged,
I should, I think, be forced to love again—
Else there's no right nor reason in the world!

    Eu.   " If you knew," say you,—but I did not know—
That's where you're blind, Chiappino!—a disease
Which if I may remove, I'll not repent
The listening to: you cannot, will not, see
How, place you but in every circumstance
Of us, you are just now indignant at,
You'd be as we.

    Ch.   I should be? . . . that, again!
I, to my Friend, my Country and my Love,
Be as Luitolfo and these Faentines?

    Eu.   As we.
    Ch.   Now, I'll say something to remember!
I trust in Nature for the stable laws
Of Beauty and Utility—Spring shall plant,
And Autumn garner to the end of time:
I trust in God—the Right shall be the Right
And other than the Wrong, while He endures—
I trust in my own soul, that can perceive
The outward and the inward, nature's good
And God's—So—seeing these men and myself,

Having a right to speak, thus do I speak:
I'll not curse . . . God bears with them—well may I—
But I—protest against their claiming me!
I simply say, if that's allowable,
I would not . . . broadly . . . do as they have done—
—God curse this townful of born slaves, bred slaves,
Branded into the blood and bone, slaves!   Curse
Whoever loved, above his liberty,
House, land, or life! and . . .   [*A knocking without.*
                                    . . . Bless my hero-friend,

Luitolfo!
   Eu. How he knocks!
   Ch.   The peril, Lady!
" Chiappino, I have run a risk!   My God!
" How when I prayed the Provost—(he's my friend)—
" To grant you a week's respite of his sentence
" That confiscates your goods, and exiles you,
" He shrugged his shoulder . . . I say, shrugged it!   Yes,
" And fright of that drove all else from my head.
" Here's a good purse of *scudi*—off with you!
" Lest of that shrug come—what God only knows!
" The *scudi*—friend, they're trash—no thanks, I beg—
" Take the North gate,—for San Vitale's suburb
" Whose double taxes you appealed against,
" In discomposure at your ill-success
" Is apt to stone you: there, there—only go!
" Beside, Eulalia here looks sleepily—
" Shake . . . oh, you hurt me, so you squeeze my wrist! "
—Is it not thus you'll speak, adventurous friend?
     [*As he opens the door,* LUITOLFO *rushes in, his garments*
      disordered.
   Eu. Luitolfo!   Blood?
   Luit.   There's more—and more of it!
Eulalia—take the garment . . . no . . . you, friend!
You take it and the blood from me—you dare!
   Eu. Oh, who has hurt you?   where's the wound?
   Ch.   " Who," say you?
The man with many a touch of virtue yet!
The Provost's friend has proved too frank of speech
And this comes of it.   Miserable hound!
This comes of temporising, as I said!
Here's fruit of your smooth speeches and fair looks!
Now see my way!   As God lives, I go straight

To the palace and do justice, once for all!

Luit. What says he?

Ch.   I'll do justice on him!

Luit.   Him?

Ch. The Provost.

Luit.   I've just killed him!

Eu.   Oh, my God!

Luit. My friend, they're on my trace — they'll have
        me—now!

They're round him, busy with him: soon they'll find
He's past their help, and then they'll be on me!
Chiappino! save Eulalia . . . I forget . . .
Were you not bound . . . for . . .

Ch.   Lugo!

Luit.   Ah—yes—yes—

That was the point I prayed of him to change.
Well—go—be happy . . . is Eulalia safe?
They're on me!

Ch.   'Tis through me they reach you, then!
Friend, seem the man you are! Lock arms—that's right.
Now tell me what you've done; explain how you
That still professed forbearance, still preached peace,
Could bring yourself . . .

Luit.   What was peace for, Chiappino?
I tried peace—did that say that when peace failed
Strife should not follow? All my peaceful days
Were just the prelude to a day like this,
I cried " You call me ' friend '—save my true friend!
" Save him, or lose me! "

Ch.   But you never said
You meant to tell the Provost thus and thus!

Luit. Why should I say it? What else did I mean?

Ch. Well? He persisted?

Luit.   . . . Would so order it
You should not trouble him too soon again—
I saw a meaning in his eye and lip—
I poured my heart's store of indignant words
Out on him—then—I know not—He retorted—
And I . . . some staff lay there to hand—I think
He bade his servants thrust me out—I struck—
. . . Ah, they come! Fly you, save yourselves, you two!
The dead back-weight of the beheading axe!
The glowing trip-hook, thumbscrews and the gadge!

Eu. They do come! Torches in the Place! Farewell—
Chiappino! You can work no good to us—
Much to yourself; believe not, all the world
Must needs be cursed henceforth!
  Ch.   And you?
  Eu.   I stay.
  Ch. Ha, ha! Now, listen! I am master here!
This was my coarse disguise—this paper shows
My path of flight and place of refuge—see—
Lugo—Argenta—past San Nicolo—
Ferrara, then to Venice and all's safe!
Put on the cloak! His people have to fetch
A compass round about.—There's time enough
Ere they can reach us—so you straightway make
For Lugo . . . Nay, he hears not! On with it—
The cloak, Luitolfo, do you hear me? See—
He obeys he knows not how.—Then, if I must . . .
Answer me! Do you know the Lugo gate?
  Eu. The north-west gate, over the bridge!
  Luit.   I know!
  Ch. Well, there—you are not frightened? All my route
Is traced in that—at Venice you'll escape
Their power! Eulalia—I am master here!
    [*Shouts from without. He pushes out* LUITOLFO, *who
        complies mechanically.*
In time! nay, help me with him—So!—he's gone.
  Eu. What have you done? On you, perchance, all know
The Provost's hater, will men's vengeance fall
As our accomplice . . .
  Ch.   Mere accomplice? See!
                    [*Putting on* LUITOLFO'S *vest.*
Now, Lady, am I true to my profession,
Or one of these?
  Eu.   You take Luitolfo's place?
  Ch. Die for him!
  Eu.   Well done!   [*Shouts increase.*
  Ch.   How the people tarry!
I can't be silent . . . I must speak . . . or sing—
How natural to sing now!
  Eu.   Hush and pray!
We are to die—but even I perceive
'Tis not a very hard thing so to die—
My cousin of the pale-blue tearful eyes,

Poor Cesca, suffers more from one day's life
With the stern husband; Tisbe's heart goes forth
Each evening after that wild son of hers,
To track his thoughtless footstep thro' the streets—
How easy for them both to die like this!
I am not sure that I could live as they.

    Ch. Here they come, crowds! They pass the gate?
           Yes!—No!—
One torch is in the court-yard. Here flock all!

    Eu. A least Luitolfo has escaped!—What cries!

    Ch. If they would drag one to the market-place,
One might speak there!

    Eu.   List, list!

    Ch.   They mount the steps!

Enter the Populace.

    Ch. I killed the Provost!
[*The Populace speaking together.*] 'Twas Chiappino, friends!
Our Saviour.—The best man at last as first!
He who first made us see what chains we wore,
He also strikes the blow that shatters them,
He at last saves us—our best citizen!
—Oh, have you only courage to speak now?
My eldest son was christened a year since
" Cino " to keep Chiappino's name in mind—
Cino, for shortness merely, you observe!
The City's in our hands.—The guards are fled—
Do you, the cause of all, come down—come down—
Come forth to counsel us, our chief, our king,
Whate'er rewards you! Choose your own reward!
The peril over, its reward begins!
Come and harangue us in the market-place!

    Eu. Chiappino!

    Ch.   Yes . . . I understand your eyes!
You think I should have promptlier disowned
This deed with its strange unforeseen success
In favour of Luitolfo—but the peril,
So far from ended, hardly seems begun!
To-morrow, rather, when a calm succeeds,
We easily shall make him full amends:
And meantime . . . if we save them as they pray,
And justify the deed by its effects?

Eu. You would, for worlds, you had denied at once!

Ch. I know my own intention, be assured!
All's well! Precede us, fellow-citizens!

PART II.

The Market-place. LUITOLFO *in disguise mingling with the* Populace *assembled opposite the* Provost's *Palace.*

1st Bystander [*To* LUIT.] You, a friend of Luitolfo's! Then, your friend is vanished,—in all probability killed on the night that his patron the tyrannical Provost was loyally suppressed here, exactly a month ago, by our illustrious fellow-citizen, thrice-noble saviour, and new Provost that is like to be, this very morning,—Chiappino!

Luit. *He* the new Provost?

2nd. Up those steps will he go, and beneath yonder pillar stand, while Ogniben, the Pope's Legate from Ravenna, reads the new dignitary's title to the people, according to established usage.—For which reason, there is the assemblage you inquire about.

Luit. Chiappino — the old Provost's successor? Impossible! But tell me of that presently—What I would know first of all is, wherefore Luitolfo must so necessarily have been killed on that memorable night?

3rd. You were Luitolfo's friend? So was I—Never, if you will credit me, did there exist so poor-spirited a milk-sop! He, with all the opportunities in the world furnished by daily converse with our oppressor, would not stir a finger to help us: so when Chiappino rose in solitary majesty and . . . how does one go on saying? . . . dealt the godlike blow,— this Luitolfo, not unreasonably fearing the indignation of an aroused and liberated people, fled precipitately: he may have got trodden to death in the press at the south-east gate, when the Provost's guards fled thro' it to Ravenna, with their wounded master,—if he did not rather hang himself under some hedge.

Luit. Or why not simply have lain perdue in some quiet corner,—such as San Cassiano, where his estate was,— receiving daily intelligence from some sure friend, meanwhile, as to the turn matters were taking here . . . how, for instance, the Provost, was not dead after all, only wounded . . . or, as to-day's news would seem to prove, how Chiappino

was not Brutus the Elder, after all, only the new Provost . . .
and thus Luitolfo be enabled to watch a favourable opportunity for returning—might it not have been so?

   3rd. Why, he may have taken that care of himself,
certainly, for he came of a cautious stock.—I'll tell you how
his uncle, just such another gingerly treader on tiptoes with
finger on lip,—how he met his death in the great plague-
year: *dico vobis!* Hearing that the seventeenth house in a
certain street was infected, he calculates to pass it in safety
by taking plentiful breath, say, when he shall arrive at the
eleventh house; then scouring by, holding that breath, till
he be got so far on the other side as number twenty-three
and thus elude the danger.—And so did he begin—but, as
he arrived at thirteen, we will say,—thinking to improve on
his precaution by putting up a little prayer to St. Nepomu-
cene of Prague, this exhausted so much of his lungs' reserve,
that at sixteen it was clean spent,—consequently at the
fatal seventeen he inhaled with a vigour and persistence
enough to suck you any latent venom out of the heart of a
stone—ha, ha!

   Luit. [*Aside.*] (If I had not lent that man the money he
wanted last spring, I should fear this bitterness was attribut-
able to me). Luitolfo is dead then, one may conclude!

   3rd. Why, he had a house here, and a woman to whom
he was affianced; and as they both pass naturally to the new
Provost, his friend and heir . . .

   Luit. Ah, I suspected you of imposing on me with your
pleasantry—I know Chiappino better!

   1st. (Our friend has the bile! after all, I do not dislike
finding somebody vary a little this general gape of admiration
at Chiappino's glorious qualities—.) Pray, how much may
you know of what has taken place in Faenza since that
memorable night?

   Luit. It is most to the purpose, that I know Chiappino
to have been by profession a hater of that very office of
Provost, you now charge him with proposing to accept.

   1st. Sir, I'll tell you. That night was indeed memorable
—up we rose, a mass of us, men, women, children—out fled
the guards with the body of the tyrant—we were to defy the
world: but, next grey morning, " What will Rome say,"
began everybody—(you know we are governed by Ravenna,
which is governed by Rome). And quietly into the town, by
the Ravenna road, comes on muleback a portly personage,

Ogniben by name, with the quality of Pontifical Legate—
trots briskly thro' the streets humming a " *Cur fremuêre
gentes,*" and makes directly for the Provost's Palace—there
it faces you—" One Messer Chiappino is your leader?   I
have known three-and-twenty leaders of revolts! " (laughing
gently to himself)—" Give me the help of your arm from my
mule to yonder steps under the pillar—So!   And now, my
revolters and good friends, what do you want?   The guards
burst into Ravenna last night bearing your wounded Provost
—and, having had a little talk with him, I take on myself to
come and try appease the disorderliness, before Rome, hearing
of it, resort to another method; 'tis I come, and not another,
from a certain love I confess to, of composing differences.
So, do you understand, you are about to experience this
unheard-of tyranny from me, that there shall be no heading
nor hanging, no confiscation nor exile,—I insist on your
simply pleasing yourselves,—and now, pray, what does please
you?   To live without any government at all?   Or having
decided for one, to see its minister murdered by the first of
your body that chooses to find himself wronged, or disposed
for reverting to first principles and a Justice anterior to all
institutions,—and so will you carry matters, that the rest
of the world must at length unite and put down such a den
of wild beasts?   As for vengeance on what has just taken
place,—once for all, the wounded man assures me he cannot
conjecture who struck him—and this so earnestly, that one
may be sure he knows perfectly well what intimate acquaintance could find admission to speak with him so late that
evening—I come not for vengeance therefore, but from pure
curiosity to hear what you will do next."—And thus he ran
on, easily and volubly, till he seemed to arrive quite naturally
at the praise of Law, Order and Paternal Government by
somebody from rather a distance: all our citizens were in the
snare, and about to be friends with so congenial an adviser;
but that Chiappino suddenly stood forth, spoke out in-
dignantly, and set things right again . . .

   Luit.   Do you see?—I recognise him there!

   3rd.   Ay, but mark you, at the end of Chiappino's longest
period in praise of a pure Republic.   " And by whom do I
desire such a government should be administered, perhaps,
but by one like yourself? "—returns the Legate—thereupon
speaking, for a quarter of an hour together, on the natural
and only legitimate government by the Best and Wisest—

and it should seem there was soon discovered to be no such
vast discrepancy at bottom between this and Chiappino's
theory, place but each in its proper light—" Oh, are you
there? " quoth Chiappino:—" In that, I agree," returns
Chiappino, and so on.

Luit. But did Chiappino cede at once to this?

1st. Why, not altogether at once—for instance, he said
that the difference between him and all his fellows was, that
they seemed all wishing to be kings in one or another way,—
whereas what right, asked he, has any man to wish to be
superior to another?—whereat, " Ah, Sir," answers the
Legate, " this is the death of me, so often as I expect something is really going to be revealed to us by your clearer-seers,
deeper-thinkers—this—that your right-hand (to speak by a
figure) should be found taking up the weapon it displayed so
ostentatiously, not to destroy any dragon in our path, as
was prophesied, but simply to cut off its own fellow left-hand
—yourself set about attacking yourself—for see now! Here
are you who, I make sure, glory exceedingly in knowing the
noble nature of the soul, its divine impulses, and so forth;
and with such a knowledge you stand, as it were, armed to
encounter the natural doubts and fears as to that same
inherent nobility, that are apt to waylay us, the weaker ones
in the road of Life,—and when we look eagerly to see them
fall before you, lo, round you wheel, only the left hand gets
the blow; one proof of the soul's nobility destroys simply
another proof, quite as good, of the same,—you are found
delivering an opinion like this! Why, what is this perpetual
yearning to exceed, to subdue, to be better than, and a king
over, one's fellows,—all that you so disclaim,—but the very
tendency yourself are most proud of, and under another form,
would oppose to it,—only in a lower stage of manifestation?
You don't want to be vulgarly superior to your fellows after
their poor fashion—to have me hold solemnly up your gown's
tail, or hand you an express of the last importance from the
Pope, with all these bystanders noticing how unconcerned
you look the while—but neither does our gaping friend, the
burgess yonder, want the other kind of kingship, that con-
sists in understanding better than his fellows this and similar
points of human nature, nor to roll under the tongue this
sweeter morsel still, the feeling that, thro' immense philosophy, he does *not* feel, he rather thinks, above you and me! "
—And so chatting, they glided off arm in arm.

Luit. And the result is . . .

1st. Why, that a month having gone by, the indomitable Chiappino, marrying as he will Luitolfo's love—at all events succeeding to Luitolfo's goods,—becomes the first inhabitant of Faenza, and a proper aspirant to the Provostship—which we assemble here to see conferred on him this morning. The Legate's Guard to clear the way! He will follow presently!

Luit. [*withdrawing a little*]. I understand the drift of Eulalia's communication less than ever—yet she surely said, in so many words, that Chiappino was in urgent danger,—wherefore, disregarding her injunctions to continue in my retreat and wait the result of, what she called, some experiment yet in process—I hastened here without her leave or knowledge—what could I else?—Yet if what they say be true . . . if it were for such a purpose, she and Chiappino kept me away . . . Oh, no, no! I must confront him and her before I believe this of them—and at the word, see!

Enter CHIAPPINO *and* EULALIA.

Eu. We art here, then? The change in your principles would seem to be complete!

Ch. Now, why refuse to see that in my present course I change no principles, only re-adapt them and more adroitly? I had despaired of what you may call the material instrumentality of Life; of ever being able to rightly operate on mankind thro' such a deranged machinery as the existing modes of government—but now, if I suddenly discover how to inform these perverted institutions with fresh purpose, bring the functionary limbs once more into immediate communication with, and subjection to the soul I am about to bestow on them . . . do you see? Why should one desire to invent, so long as it remains possible to renew and transform? When all further hope of the old organisation shall be extinct, then, I grant you, it will be time to try and create another.

Eu. And there being discoverable some hope yet in the hitherto much-abused old system of absolute government by a Provost here, you mean to take your time about endeavouring to realise those visions of a perfect State, we once heard of?

Ch. Say, I would fain realise my conception of a Palace, for instance, and that there is, abstractedly, but a single way of erecting one perfectly; here, in the market-place is my allotted building-ground; here I stand without a stone to lay, or a labourer to help me,—stand, too, during a short day of life, close on which the night comes. On the other hand, circumstances suddenly offer me . . . turn and see it . . . the old Provost's House to experiment upon—ruinous, if you please, wrongly constructed at the beginning, and ready to tumble now—but materials abound, a crowd of workmen offer their services; here, exists yet a Hall of Audience of originally noble proportions, there, a Guest-chamber of symmetrical design enough; and I may restore, enlarge, abolish or unite these to heart's content—ought I not rather make the best of such an opportunity, than continue to gaze disconsolately with folded arms on the flat pavement here, while the sun goes slowly down, never to rise again? But you cannot understand this nor me: it is better we should part as you desire.

Eu. So the love breaks away too!

Ch. No, rather my soul's capacity for love widens—needs more than one object to content it,—and, being better instructed, will not persist in seeing all the component parts of love in what is only a single part,—nor in finding the so many and so various loves, united in the love of a woman,— finding all uses in one instrument, as the savage has his sword, sceptre and idol, all in one club-stick. Love is a very compound thing. I shall give the intellectual part of my love to Men, the mighty dead, or illustrious living; and determine to call a mere sensual instinct by as few fine names as possible. What do I lose?

Eu. Nay, I only think, what do I lose! and, one more word—which shall complete my instruction—does Friendship go too?—What of Luitolfo—the author of your present prosperity?

Ch. How the author?—

Eu. That blow now called yours . . .

Ch. Struck without principle or purpose, as by a blind natural operation—and to which all my thoughts and life directly and advisedly tended. I would have struck it, and could not. He would have done his utmost to avoid striking it, yet did so. I dispute his right to that deed of mine—a final action with him, from the first effect of which he fled away—a mere first step with me, on which I base a whole mighty superstructure of good to follow. Could he get good from it?

Eu. So we profess, so we perform!

Enter OGNIBEN. EULALIA *stands apart.*

Ogni. I have seen three-and-twenty leaders of revolts!—
By your leave, Sir! Perform? What does the lady say of
Performing?

Ch. Only the trite saying, that we must not trust Profession, only Performance.

Ogni. She'll not say that, Sir, when she knows you longer;
you'll instruct her better. Ever judge of men by their pro-
fessions! For tho' the bright moment of promising is but
a moment and cannot be prolonged, yet, if sincere in its
moment's extravagant goodness, why, trust it and know the
man by it, I say—not by his performance—which is half the
world's work, interfere as the world needs must with its
accidents and circumstances,—the profession was purely the
man's own! I judge people by what they might be,—not
are, nor will be.

Ch. But have there not been found, too, performing
natures, not merely promising?

Ogni. Plenty: little Bindo of our town, for instance,
promised his friend, great ugly Masaccio, once, " I will repay
you! "—for a favour done him: so when his father came to
die, and Bindo succeeded to the inheritance, he sends straightway for Masaccio and shares all with him; gives him half the
land, half the money, half the kegs of wine in the cellar.
" Good," say you—and it is good: but had little Bindo found
himself possessor of all this wealth—some five years before
on the happy night when Masaccio procured him that inter-
view in the garden with his pretty cousin Lisa—instead of
being the beggar he then was,—I am bound to believe that
in the warm moment of promise he would have given away
all the wine-kegs, and all the money, and all the land, and
only reserved to himself some hut on a hill-top hard by,
whence he might spend his life in looking and seeing his
friend enjoy himself: he meant fully that much, but the
world interfered!—To our business—did I understand you
just now within-doors? You are not going to marry your
old friend's love, after all?

Ch. I must have a woman that can sympathise with,
and appreciate me, I told you.

Ogni. Oh, I remember! you, the greater nature, needs
must have a lesser one (—avowedly lesser—contest with
you on that score would never do!)—such a nature must

comprehend you, as the phrase is, accompany and testify of your greatness from point to point onward: why, that were being not merely as great as yourself, but greater considerably! Meantime, might not the more bounded nature as reasonably count on your appreciation of it, rather?—on your keeping close by it, so far as you both go together, and then going on by yourself as far as you please? So God serves us!

Ch. And yet a woman that could understand the whole of me, to whom I could reveal alike the strength and the weakness—

Ogni. Ah, my friend, wish for nothing so foolish! Worship your love, give her the best of you to see; be to her like the Western Lands (they bring us such strange news of) to the Spanish Court—send her only your lumps of gold, fans of feathers, your spirit-like birds, and fruits and gems—so shall you, what is unseen of you, be supposed altogether a Paradise by her,—as these Western lands by Spain—tho' I warrant there is filth, red baboons, ugly reptiles and squalor enough, which they bring Spain as few samples of as possible. Do you want your mistress to respect your body generally? Offer her your mouth to kiss—don't strip off your boot and put your foot to her lips! You understand my humour by this time? I help men to carry out their own principle: if they please to say two and two make five, I assent, if they will but go on and say, four and four make ten!

Ch. But these are my private affairs—what I desire you to occupy yourself about, is my public appearance presently: for when the people hear that I am appointed Provost, tho' you and I may thoroughly discern—and easily, too—the right principle at bottom of such a movement, and how my republicanism remains thoroughly unaltered, only takes a form of expression hitherto commonly judged . . . and heretofore by myself . . . incompatible with its existence . . . when thus I reconcile myself to an old form of government instead of proposing a new one . . .

Ogni. Why, you must deal with people broadly. Begin at a distance from this matter and say,—new truths, old truths! why, there is nothing new possible to be revealed to us in the moral world—we know all we shall ever know, and it is for simply reminding us, by their various respective expedients, how we *do* know this and the other matter, that men get called prophets, poets and the like. A philosopher's life is spent in discovering that, of the half-dozen truths he knew when a child, such an one is a lie, as the world states it in set terms; and then, after a weary lapse of years, and plenty of hard thinking, it becomes a truth again after all, as he happens to newly consider it and view it in a different relation with the others—and so he restates it, to the confusion of somebody else in good time.—As for adding to the original stock of truths,—impossible!—So you see the expression of them is the grand business:—you have got a truth in your head about the right way of governing people, and you took a mode of expressing it—which now you confess to be imperfect—but what then? There is Truth in Falsehood, Falsehood in Truth.—No man ever told one great truth, that I know, without the help of a good dozen of lies at least, generally unconscious ones: and as when a child comes in breathlessly and relates a strange story, you try to conjecture from the very falsities in it, what the reality was, —do not conclude that he saw nothing in the sky, because he assuredly did not see a flying horse there as he says,—so, thro' the contradictory expression, do you see, men should look painfully for, and trust to arrive eventually at, what you call the true principle at bottom. Ah, what an answer is there! to what will it not prove applicable!—" Contradictions? "—Of course there were, say you!

Ch. Still, the world at large may call it inconsistency, and what shall I say in reply?

Ogni. Why look you, when they tax you with tergiversation or duplicity, you may answer—you begin to perceive that, when all's done and said, both great parties in the state, the advocators of change in the present system of things, and the opponents of it, patriot and anti-patriot, are found working together for the common good, and that in the midst of their efforts for and against its progress, the world somehow or other still advances—to which result they contribute in equal proportions, those who spent their life in pushing it onward as those who gave theirs to the business of pulling it back—now, if you found the world stand still between the opposite forces, and were glad, I should conceive you—but it steadily advances, you rejoice to see! By the side of such a rejoicer, the man who only winks as he keeps cunning and quiet, and says, " Let yonder hot-headed fellow fight out my battle; I, for one, shall win in the end by the blows he gives, and which I ought to be giving "—even he seems graceful in his avowal, when one considers that he might say,

"I shall win quite as much by the blows our antagonist
gives him, and from which he saves me—I thank the antagonist equally!" Moreover, you must enlarge on the loss of
the edge of party-animosity with age and experience—

Ch. And naturally time must wear off such asperities
—the bitterest adversaries get to discover certain points
of similarity between each other, common sympathies—
do they not?

Ogni. Ay, had the young David but sate first to dine on
his cheeses with the Philistine, he had soon discovered an
abundance of such common sympathies—He of Gath, it is
recorded, was born of a father and mother, had brothers
and sisters like another man,—they, no more than the sons
of Jesse, were used to eat each other; but, for the sake of
one broad antipathy that had existed from the beginning,
David slung the stone, cut off the giant's head, made a spoil
of it, and after ate his cheeses alone, with the better appetite,
for all I can learn. My friend, as you, with a quickened
eyesight, go on discovering much good on the worse side,
remember that the same process should proportionably
magnify and demonstrate to you the much more good on the
better side—and when I profess no sympathy for the Goliahs
of our time, and you object that a large nature should sympathise with every form of intelligence, and see the good in it,
however limited—I answer, so I do—but preserve the proportions of my sympathy, however finelier or widelier I may
extend its action. I desire to be able, with a quickened eyesight, to descry beauty in corruption where others see foulness only,—but I hope I shall also continue to see a redoubled
beauty in the higher forms of matter, where already every
body sees no foulness at all. I must retain, too, my old
power of selection, and choice of appropriation, to apply to
such new gifts . . . else they only dazzle instead of enlighten-
ing me. God has his Archangels and consorts with them—
tho' he made too, and intimately sees what is good in, the
worm. Observe, I speak only as you profess to think and so
ought to speak—I do justice to your own principles, that
is all!

Ch. But you very well know that the two parties do, on
occasion, assume each other's characteristics: what more
disgusting, for instance, than to see how promptly the newly
emancipated slave will adopt, in his own favour, the very
measures of precaution, which pressed soreliest on himself as

institutions of the tyranny he has just escaped from.—Do
the classes, hitherto without opinion, get leave to express
it? there is a confederacy immediately, from which—exercise
your individual right and dissent, and woe be to you!

Ogni. And a journey over the sea to you!—That is the
generous way. Say—emancipated slaves, the first excess,
and off I go! The first time a poor devil, who has been
bastinadoed steadily his whole life long, finds himself let
alone and able to legislate, so begins pettishly, while he rubs
his soles, " Woe be to whoever brings anything in the shape
of a stick this way,"—you, rather than give up the very
innocent pleasure of carrying one to switch flies with,—you,
go away to everybody's sorrow! Yet you were quite reconciled to staying at home while the governors used to pass,
every now and then, some such edict as " Let no man indulge
in owning a stick which is not thick enough to chastise our
slaves, if need require." Well — there are pre-ordained
hierarchies among us, and a profane vulgar subjected to a
different law altogether—yet I am rather sorry you should
see it so clearly—for, do you know what is to . . . all but
save you at the Day of Judgment, all you Men of Genius?
It is this—that, while you generally began by pulling down
God, and went on to the end of your life, in one effort at
setting up your own Genius in his place,—still, the last,
bitterest concession wrung with the utmost unwillingness
from the experience of the very loftiest of you, was invariably
—would one think it?—that the rest of mankind, down to the
lowest of the mass, stood not, nor ever could stand, just on
a level and equality with yourselves.—That will be a point
in the favour of all such, I hope and believe!

Ch. Why, men of genius are usually charged, I think,
with doing just the reverse; and at once acknowledging the
natural inequality of mankind, by themselves participating
in the universal craving after, and deference to, the civil
distinctions which represent it. You wonder they pay such
undue respect to titles and badges of superior rank!

Ogni. Not I! (always on your own ground and showing,
be it noted!) Who doubts that, with a weapon to brandish,
a man is the more formidable? Titles and badges are
exercised as such a weapon, to which you and I look up
wistfully.—We could pin lions with it moreover, while in its
present owner's hands it hardly prods rats. Nay, better
than a mere weapon of easy mastery and obvious use, it is a

mysterious divining rod that may serve you in undreamed of ways.—Beauty, Strength, Intellect—men often have none of these and yet conceive pretty accurately what kind of advantages they would bestow on the possessor.— You know at least what it is you make up your mind to forego, and so can apply the fittest substitute in your power; wanting Beauty, you cultivate Good Humour, missing Wit, you get Riches; but the mystic unimaginable operation of that gold collar and string of Latin names which suddenly turned poor stupid little peevish Cecco of our town into natural Lord of the best of us—a Duke, he is now! there indeed is a Virtue to be reverenced!

Ch. Ay, by the vulgar—not by Messere Stiatta the poet, who pays more assiduous court to him than anybody.

Ogni. What else should Stiatta pay court to? He has talent, not honour and riches—men naturally covet what they have not.

Ch. No—or Cecco would covet talent, which he has not, whereas he covets more riches, of which he has plenty already.

Ogni. Because a purse added to a purse makes the holder twice as rich—but just such another talent as Stiatta's, added to what he now possesses, what would that profit him? Give the talent a purse indeed, to do something with! But lo, how we keep the good people waiting. I only desired to do justice to the noble sentiments which animate you, and which you are too modest to duly enforce. Come, to our main business: shall we ascend the steps? I am going to propose you for Provost to the people; they know your antecedents, and will accept you with a joyful unanimity: whereon I confirm their choice. Rouse up! you are nerving yourself to an effort? Beware the disaster of Messere Stiatta we were talking of—who determining to keep an equal mind and constant face on whatever might be the fortune of his last new poem with our townsmen,—heard too plainly " hiss, hiss, hiss," increase every moment, till at last the man fell senseless—not perceiving that the portentous sounds had all the while been issuing from between his own nobly clenched teeth, and nostrils narrowed by resolve!

Ch. Do you begin to throw off the mask? to jest with me, having got me effectually into your trap?

Ogni. Where is the trap, my friend? You hear what I engage to do, for my part—you, for yours, have only to fulfil your promise made just now within doors, of professing

unlimited obedience to Rome's authority in my person—
and I shall authorise no more than the simple re-establish-
ment of the Provostship and the conferment of its privileges
upon yourself—the only novel stipulation being a birth of
the peculiar circumstances of the time.

Ch. And that stipulation?

Ogni. Oh, the obvious one—that in the event of the
discovery of the actual assailant of the late Provost . . .

Ch. Ha!

Ogni. Why, he shall suffer the proper penalty, of course;
what did you expect?

Ch. Who heard of this?

Ogni. Rather, who needed to hear of this?

Ch. Can it be, the popular rumour never reached you . . .

Ogni. Many more such rumours reach me, friend, than
I choose to receive: those which wait longest have best
chance—has the present one sufficiently waited? Now is
its time for entry with effect. See the good people crowding
about yonder palace-steps—which we may not have to ascend
after all!—my good friends—(nay, two or three of you will
answer every purpose)—who was it fell upon and proved
nearly the death of your late Provost?—his successor desires
to hear, that his day of inauguration may be graced by the
act of prompt, bare justice we all anticipate? Who dealt
the blow that night, does anybody know?

Luitolfo [*coming forward.*] I!

All. Luitolfo!

Luit. I avow the deed, justify and approve it, and stand
forth now, to relieve my friend of an unearned responsibility.
—Having taken thought, I am grown stronger—I shall
shrink from nothing that awaits me. Nay, Chiappino—
we are friends still—I dare say there is some proof of your
superior nature in this starting aside, strange as it seems at
first. So, they tell me, my horse is of the right stock, because
a shadow in the path frightens him into a frenzy, makes him
dash my brains out. I understand only the dull mule's way
of standing stockishly, plodding soberly, suffering on occasion
a blow or two with due patience.

Eu. I was determined to justify my choice, Chiappino;
to let Luitolfo's nature vindicate itself. Henceforth we are
undivided, whatever be our fortune.

Ogni. Now, in these last ten minutes of silence, what
have I been doing, deem you? Putting the finishing stroke

to a homily of mine, I have long taken thought to perfect, on the text "Let whoso thinketh he standeth, take heed lest he fall." To your house, Luitolfo!—Still silent, my patriotic friend? Well, that is a good sign, however! And you will go aside for a time? That is better still. I understand—it would be easy for you to die of remorse here on the spot, and shock us all, but you will live and grow worthy of coming back to us one day. There, I will tell everybody; and you only do right to believe you will get better as you get older! All men do so,—they are worst in childhood, improve in manhood, and get ready in old age for another world. Youth, with its Beauty and Grace, would seem bestowed on us for some such reason as to make us partly endurable till we have time for really becoming so of ourselves, without their aid, when they leave us. The sweetest child we all smile on for his pleasant want of the whole world to break up, or suck in his mouth, seeing no other good in it—would be rudely handled by that world's inhabitants, if he retained those angelic infantine desires when he has grown six feet high, black and bearded: but, little by little, he sees fit to forego claim after claim on the world, puts up with a less and less share of its good as his proper portion,—and when the octo-genarian asks barely a sup of gruel and a fire of dry sticks, and thanks you as for his full allowance and right in the common good of life,—hoping nobody may murder him,—he who began by asking and expecting the whole of us to bow down in worship to him,—why, I say he is advanced, far onward, very far, nearly out of sight like our friend Chiappino yonder! And now—(Ay, good-bye to you! He turns round the North-west gate—going to Lugo again? Good-bye!)—And now give thanks to God, the keys of the Provost's Palace to me, and yourselves to profitable meditation at home. I have known *Four*-and-twenty leaders of revolts!—

CHRISTMAS-EVE AND EASTER-DAY

A POEM

CHRISTMAS-EVE AND EASTER-DAY

CHRISTMAS-EVE.

1. OUT of the little chapel I burst
   Into the fresh night air again.
   I had waited a good five minutes first
   In the doorway, to escape the rain
   That drove in gusts down the common's centre,
   At the edge of which the chapel stands,
   Before I plucked up heart to enter:
   Heaven knows how many sorts of hands
   Reached past me, groping for the latch
   Of the inner door that hung on catch,
   More obstinate the more they fumbled,
   Till, giving way at last with a scold
   Of the crazy hinge, in squeezed or tumbled
   One sheep more to the rest in fold,
   And left me irresolute, standing sentry
   In the sheepfold's lath-and-plaster entry,
   Four feet long by two feet wide,
   Partitioned off from the vast inside—
   I blocked up half of it at least.
   No remedy; the rain kept driving:
   They eyed me much as some wild beast,
   The congregation, still arriving,
   Some of them by the mainroad, white
   A long way past me into the night,
   Skirting the common, then diverging;
   Not a few suddenly emerging
   From the common's self thro' the paling-gaps,—
   —They house in the gravel-pits perhaps,
   Where the road stops short with its safeguard border
   Of lamps, as tired of such disorder;—
   But the most turned in yet more abruptly
   From a certain squalid knot of alleys,
   Where the town's bad blood once slept corruptly,
   Which now the little chapel rallies

And leads into day again,—its priestliness
Lending itself to hide their beastliness
So cleverly (thanks in part to the mason),
And putting so cheery a whitewashed face on
Those neophytes too much in lack of it,
That, where you cross the common as I did,
And meet the party thus presided,
" Mount Zion," with Love-lane at the back of it,
They front you as little disconcerted,
As, bound for the hills, her fate averted
And her wicked people made to mind him,
Lot might have marched with Gomorrah behind him.

II. Well, from the road, the lanes or the common,
In came the flock: the fat weary woman,
Panting and bewildered, down-clapping
Her umbrella with a mighty report,
Grounded it by me, wry and flapping,
A wreck of whalebones; then, with a snort,
Like a startled horse, at the interloper
Who humbly knew himself improper,
But could not shrink up small enough,
Round to the door, and in,—the gruff
Hinge's invariable scold
Making your very blood run cold.
Prompt in the wake of her, up-pattered
On broken clogs, the many-tattered
Little old-faced, peaking sister-turned-mother
Of the sickly babe she tried to smother
Somehow up, with its spotted face,
From the cold, on her breast, the one warm place;
She too must stop, wring the poor suds dry
Of a draggled shawl, and add thereby
Her tribute to the door-mat, sopping
Already from my own clothes' dropping,
Which yet she seemed to grudge I should stand on;
Then stooping down to take off her pattens,
She bore them defiantly, in each hand one,
Planted together before her breast
And its babe, as good as a lance in rest.
Close on her heels, the dingy satins
Of a female something, past me flitted,
With lips as much too white, as a streak

Lay far too red on each hollow cheek;
And it seemed the very door-hinge pitied
All that was left of a woman once,
Holding at least its tongue for the nonce.
Then a tall yellow man, like the Penitent Thief,
With his jaw bound up in a handkerchief,
And eyelids screwed together tight,
Led himself in by some inner light.
And, except from him, from each that entered,
I had the same interrogation—
" What, you, the alien, you have ventured
" To take with us, elect, your station?
" A carer for none of it, a Gallio? "—
Thus, plain as print, I read the glance
At a common prey, in each countenance,
As of huntsman giving his hounds the tallyho:
And, when the door's cry drowned their wonder,
The draught, it always sent in shutting,
Made the flame of the single tallow candle
In the cracked square lanthorn I stood under,
Shoot its blue lip at me, rebutting,
As it were, the luckless cause of scandal:
I verily thought the zealous light
(In the chapel's secret, too!) for spite,
Would shudder itself clean off the wick,
With the airs of a St. John's Candlestick.
There was no standing it much longer.
" Good folks," said I, as resolve grew stronger,
" This way you perform the Grand-Inquisitor,
" When the weather sends you a chance visitor?
" You are the men, and wisdom shall die with you,
" And none of the old Seven Churches vie with you!
" But still, despite the pretty perfection
" To which you carry your trick of exclusiveness,
" And, taking God's word under wise protection,
" Correct its tendency to diffusiveness,
" Bidding one reach it over hot ploughshares,—
" Still, as I say, though you've found salvation,
" If I should choose to cry—as now—' Shares! '—
" See if the best of you bars me my ration!
" Because I prefer for my expounder
" Of the laws of the feast, the feast's own Founder:
" Mine's the same right with your poorest and sickliest,

" Supposing I don the marriage-vestment;
" So, shut your mouth, and open your Testament,
" And carve me my portion at your quickliest! "
Accordingly, as a shoemaker's lad
With wizened face in want of soap,
And wet apron wound round his waist like a rope,
After stopping outside, for his cough was bad,
To get the fit over, poor gentle creature,
And so avoid disturbing the preacher,
Passed in, I sent my elbow spikewise
At the shutting door, and entered likewise,—
Received the hinge's accustomed greeting,
Crossed the threshold's magic pentacle,
And found myself in full conventicle,
—To wit, in Zion Chapel Meeting,
On the Christmas-Eve of 'Forty-nine,
Which, calling its flock to their special clover,
Found them assembled and one sheep over,
Whose lot, as the weather pleased, was mine.

III. I very soon had enough of it.
The hot smell and the human noises,
And my neighbour's coat, the greasy cuff of it,
Were a pebble-stone that a child's hand poises,
Compared with the pig-of-lead-like pressure
Of the preaching-man's immense stupidity,
As he poured his doctrine forth, full measure,
To meet his audience's avidity.
You needed not the wit of the Sybil
To guess the cause of it all, in a twinkling—
No sooner had our friend an inkling
Of treasure hid in the Holy Bible,
(Whenever it was the thought first struck him
How Death, at unawares, might duck him
Deeper than the grave, and quench
The gin-shop's light in Hell's grim drench)
Then he handled it so, in fine irreverence,
As to hug the Book of books to pieces:
And, a patchwork of chapters and texts in severance,
Not improved by the private dog's-ears and creases,
Having clothed his own soul with, he'd fain see equipt
      yours,—
So tossed you again your Holy Scriptures.

And you picked them up, in a sense, no doubt:
Nay, had but a single face of my neighbours
Appeared to suspect that the preacher's labours
Were help which the world could be saved without,
'Tis odds but I had borne in quiet
A qualm or two at my spiritual diet;
Or, who can tell? had even mustered
Somewhat to urge in behalf of the sermon:
But the flock sate on, divinely flustered,
Sniffing, methought, its dew of Hermon
With such content in every snuffle,
As the devil inside us loves to ruffle.
My old fat woman purred with pleasure,
And thumb round thumb went twirling faster
While she, to his periods keeping measure,
Maternally devoured the pastor.
The man with the handkerchief, untied it,
Showed us a horrible wen inside it,
Gave his eyelids yet another screwing,
And rocked himself as the woman was doing.
The shoemaker's lad, discreetly choking,
Kept down his cough. 'Twas too provoking!
My gorge rose at the nonsense and stuff of it,
And saying, like Eve when she plucked the apple,
" I wanted a taste, and now there's enough of it,"
I flung out of the little chapel.

IV. There was a lull in the rain, a lull
In the wind too; the moon was risen,
And would have shone out pure and full,
But for the ramparted cloud-prison,
Block on block built up in the west,
For what purpose the wind knows best,
Who changes his mind continually.
And the empty other half of the sky
Seemed in its silence as if it knew
What, any moment, might look through
A chance-gap in that fortress massy:—
Through its fissures you got hints
Of the flying moon, by the shifting tints,
Now, a dull lion-colour, now, brassy
Burning to yellow, and whitest yellow,
Like furnace-smoke just ere the flames bellow,

All a-simmer with intense strain
To let her through,—then blank again,
At the hope of her appearance failing.
Just by the chapel, a break in the railing
Shows a narrow path directly across;
'Tis ever dry walking there, on the moss—
Besides, you go gently all the way uphill:
I stooped under and soon felt better:
My head grew light, my limbs more supple,
As I walked on, glad to have slipt the fetter;
My mind was full of the scene I had left,
That placid flock, that pastor vociferant,
—How this outside was pure and different!
The sermon, now—what a mingled weft
Of good and ill! were either less,
Its fellow had coloured the whole distinctly;
But alas for the excellent earnestness,
And the truths, quite true if stated succinctly,
But as surely false, in their quaint presentment,
However to pastor and flock's contentment!
Say rather, such truths looked false to your eyes,
With his provings and parallels twisted and twined,
Till how could you know them, grown double their size,
In the natural fog of the good man's mind?
Like yonder spots of our roadside lamps,
Haloed about with the common's damps.
Truth remains true, the fault's in the prover;
The zeal was good, and the aspiration;
And yet, and yet, yet, fifty times over,
Pharaoh received no demonstration
By his Baker's dream of Baskets Three,
Of the doctrine of the Trinity,—
Although, as our preacher thus embellished it,
Apparently his hearers relished it
With so unfeigned a gust—who knows if
They did not prefer our friend to Joseph?
But so it is everywhere, one way with all of them!
These people have really felt, no doubt,
A something, the motion they style the Call of them;
And this is their method of bringing about,
By a mechanism of words and tones,
(So many texts in so many groans)
A sort of reviving or reproducing,

More or less perfectly, (who can tell?—)
Of the mood itself, that strengthens by using;
And how it happens, I understand well.
A tune was born in my head last week,
Out of the thump-thump and shriek-shriek
Of the train, as I came by it, up from Manchester;
And when, next week, I take it back again,
My head will sing to the engine's clack again,
While it only makes my neighbour's haunches stir,
—Finding no dormant musical sprout
In him, as in me, to be jolted out.
'Tis the taught already that profit by teaching;
He gets no more from the railway's preaching,
Than, from this preacher who does the rail's office, I,
Whom therefore the flock casts a jealous eye on.
Still, why paint over their door " Mount Zion,"
To which all flesh shall come, saith the prophecy?

v. But wherefore be harsh on a single case?
After how many modes, this Christmas-Eve,
Does the selfsame weary thing take place?
The same endeavour to make you believe,
And much with the same effect, no more:
Each method abundantly convincing,
As I say, to those convinced before,
But scarce to be swallowed without wincing,
By the not-as-yet-convinced.   For me,
I have my own church equally.
And in *this* church my faith sprang first!
(I said, as I reached the rising ground,
And the wind began again, with a burst
Of rain in my face, and a glad rebound
From the heart beneath, as if, God speeding me,
I entered His church-door, Nature leading me)
—In youth I looked to these very skies,
And probing their immensities,
I found God there, His visible power;
Yet felt in my heart, amid all its sense
Of that power, an equal evidence
That His love, there too, was the nobler dower.
For the loving worm within its clod,
Were diviner than a loveless god
Amid his worlds, I will dare to say.
You know what I mean: God's all, man's **nought**:

But also, God, whose pleasure brought
Man into being, stands away
As it were, an handbreadth off, to give
Room for the newly-made to live,
And look at Him from a place of apart,
And use His gifts of brain and heart,
Given, indeed, but to keep for ever.
Who speaks of man, then, must not sever
Man's very elements from man,
Saying, " But all is God's "—whose plan
Was to create man and then leave him
Able, His own word saith, to grieve Him,
But able to glorify Him too,
As a mere machine could never do,
That prayed or praised, all unaware
Of its fitness for aught but praise and prayer,
Made perfect as a thing of course.
Man, therefore, stands on his own stock
Of love and power as a pin-point rock,
And, looking to God who ordained divorce
Of the rock from His boundless continent,
Sees in His Power made evident,
Only excess by a million fold
O'er the power God gave man in the mould.
For, see: Man's hand, first formed to carry
A few pounds' weight, when taught to marry
Its strength with an engine's, lifts a mountain,
—Advancing in power by one degree;
And why count steps through eternity?
But Love is the ever springing fountain:
Man may enlarge or narrow his bed
For the water's play, but the water head—
How can he multiply or reduce it?
As easy create it, as cause it to cease:
He may profit by it, or abuse it;
But 'tis not a thing to bear increase
As power will: be love less or more
In the heart of man, he keeps it shut
Or opes it wide as he pleases, but
Love's sum remains what it was before.
So, gazing up, in my youth, at love
As seen through power, ever above
All modes which make it manifest,

My soul brought all to a single test—
That He, the Eternal First and Last,
Who, in His power, had so surpassed
All man conceives of what is might,—
Whose wisdom, too, showed infinite,
—Would prove as infinitely good;
Would never, my soul understood,
With power to work all love desires,
Bestow e'en less than man requires:
That He who endlessly was teaching,
Above my spirit's utmost reaching,
What love can do in the leaf or stone,
(So that to master this alone,
This done in the stone or leaf for me,
I must go on learning endlessly)
Would never need that I, in turn,
Should point him out a defect unheeded,
And show that God had yet to learn
What the meanest human creature needed,—
—Not life, to wit, for a few short years,
Tracking His way through doubts and fears,
While the stupid earth on which I stay
Suffers no change, but passive adds
Its myriad years to myriads,
Though I, He gave it to, decay,
Seeing death come and choose about me,
And my dearest ones depart without me.
No! love which, on earth, amid all the shows of it,
Has ever been seen the sole good of life in it,
The love, ever growing there, spite of the strife in it,
Shall arise, made perfect, from death's repose of it!
And I shall behold Thee, face to face,
O God, and in Thy light retrace
How in all I loved here, still wast Thou!
Whom pressing to, then, as I fain would now,
I shall find as able to satiate
The love, Thy gift, as my spirit's wonder
Thou art able to quicken and sublimate,
Was this sky of Thine, that I now walk under,
And glory in Thee as thus I gaze,
—Thus, thus! oh, let men keep their ways
Of seeking Thee in a narrow shrine—
Be this my way! And this *is* mine!

vi. For lo, what think you? suddenly
    The rain and the wind ceased, and the sky
    Received at once the full fruition
    Of the moon's consummate apparition.
    The black cloud-barricade was riven,
    Ruined beneath her feet, and driven
    Deep in the west; while, bare and breathless,
    North and south and east lay ready
    For a glorious Thing, that, dauntless, deathless,
    Sprang across them, and stood steady.
    'Twas a moon-rainbow, vast and perfect,
    From heaven to heaven extending, perfect
    As the mother-moon's self, full in face.
    It rose, distinctly at the base
    With its seven proper colours chorded,
    Which still, in the rising, were compressed,
    Until at last they cöalesced,
    And supreme the spectral creature lorded
    In a triumph of whitest white,—
    Above which intervened the night.
    But above night too, like the next,
    The second of a wondrous sequence,
    Reaching in rare and rarer frequence,
    Till the heaven of heavens be circumflext,
    Another rainbow rose, a mightier,
    Fainter, flushier, and flightier,—
    Rapture dying along its verge!
    Oh, whose foot shall I see emerge,
    Whose, from the straining topmost dark,
    On to the keystone of that arc?

vii. This sight was shown me, there and then,—
     Me, one out of a world of men,
     Singled forth, as the chance might hap
     To another, if in a thunderclap
     Where I heard noise, and you saw flame,
     Some one man knew God called his name.
     For me, I think I said, " Appear!
     " Good were it to be ever here.
     " If Thou wilt, let me build to Thee
     " Service-tabernacles Three,
     " Where, for ever in Thy presence,
     " In extatic acquiescence,

" Far alike from thriftless learning
" And ignorance's undiscerning,
" I may worship and remain! "
Thus, at the show above me, gazing
With upturned eyes, I felt my brain
Glutted with the glory, blazing
Throughout its whole mass, over and under,
Until at length it burst asunder,
And out of it bodily there streamed
The too-much glory, as it seemed,
Passing from out me to the ground,
Then palely serpentining round
Into the dark with mazy error.

VIII. All at once I looked up with terror.
He was there.
He Himself with His human air,
On the narrow pathway, just before:
I saw the back of Him, no more—
He had left the chapel, then, as I.
I forgot all about the sky.
No face: only the sight
Of a sweepy Garment, vast and white,
With a hem that I could recognise.
I felt terror, no surprise:
My mind filled with the cataract,
At one bound, of the mighty fact.
I remembered, He did say
Doubtless, that, to this world's end,
Where two or three should meet and pray,
He would be in the midst, their Friend:
Certainly He was there with them.
And my pulses leaped for joy
Of the golden thought without alloy,
That I saw His very Vesture's hem.
Then rushed the blood back, cold and clear
With a fresh enhancing shiver of fear,
And I hastened, cried out while I pressed
To the salvation of the Vest,
" But not so, Lord!   It cannot be
" That Thou, indeed, art leaving me—
" Me, that have despised Thy friends.
" Did my heart make no amends?

" Thou art the Love of God—above
" His Power, didst hear me place His Love,
" And that was leaving the world for Thee!
" Therefore Thou must not turn from me
" As if I had chosen the other part.
" Folly and pride o'ercame my heart.
" Our best is bad, nor bears Thy test;
" Still it should be our very best.
" I thought it best that Thou, the Spirit,
" Be worshipped in spirit and in truth,
" And in beauty, as even we require it—
" Not in the forms burlesque, uncouth,
" I left but now, as scarcely fitted
" For Thee: I knew not what I pitied:
" But, all I felt there, right or wrong,
" What is it to Thee, who curest sinning?
" Am I not weak as Thou art strong?
" I have looked to Thee from the beginning,
" Straight up to Thee through all the world
" Which, like an idle scroll, lay furled
" To nothingness on either side:
" And since the time Thou wast descried,
" Spite of the weak heart, so have I
" Lived ever, and so fain would die,
" Living and dying, Thee before!
" But if Thou leavest me—"

IX.   Less or more,
I suppose that I spoke thus.
When,—have mercy, Lord, on us!
The whole Face turned upon me full.
And I spread myself beneath it,
As when the bleacher spreads, to seethe it
In the cleansing sun, his wool,—
Steeps in the flood of noontide whiteness
Some defiled, discoloured web—
So lay I, saturate with brightness.
And when the flood appeared to ebb,
Lo, I was walking, light and swift,
With my senses settling fast and steadying,
But my body caught up in the whirl and drift
Of the Vesture's amplitude, still eddying
On, just before me, still to be followed,

As it carried me after with its motion:
What shall I say?—as a path were hollowed
And a man went weltering through the ocean,
Sucked along in the flying wake
Of the luminous water-snake.
Darkness and cold were cloven, as through
I passed, upborne yet walking too,
And I turned to myself at intervals,—
" So He said, and so it befals.
" God who registers the cup
" Of mere cold water, for His sake
" To a disciple rendered up,
" Disdains not His own thirst to slake
" At the poorest love was ever offered:
" And because it was my heart I proffered,
" With true love trembling at the brim,
" He suffers me to follow Him
" For ever, my own way,—dispensed
" From seeking to be influenced
" By all the less immediate ways
" That earth, in worships manifold,
" Adopts to reach, by prayer and praise,
" The Garment's hem, which, lo, I hold! "

x. And so we crossed the world and stopped.
For where am I, in city or plain,
Since I am 'ware of the world again?
And what is this that rises propped
With pillars of prodigious girth?
Is it really on the earth,
This miraculous Dome of God?
Has the angel's measuring-rod
Which numbered cubits, gem from gem,
'Twixt the gates of the New Jerusalem,
Meted it out,—and what he meted,
Have the sons of men completed?
—Binding, ever as he bade,
Columns in this colonnade
With arms wide open to embrace
The entry of the human race
To the breast of . . . what is it, yon building,
Ablaze in front, all paint and gilding,
With marble for brick, and stones of price

For garniture of the edifice?
Now I see: it is no dream:
It stands there and it does not seem;
For ever, in pictures, thus it looks,
And thus I have read of it in books,
Often in England, leagues away,
And wondered how those fountains play,
Growing up eternally
Each to a musical water-tree,
Whose blossoms drop, a glittering boon,
Before my eyes, in the light of the moon,
To the granite lavers underneath.
Liar and dreamer in your teeth!
I, the sinner that speak to you,
Was in Rome this night, and stood, and knew
Both this and more!   For see, for see,
The dark is rent, mine eye is free
To pierce the crust of the outer wall,
And I view inside, and all there, all,
As the swarming hollow of a hive,
The whole Basilica alive!
Men in the chancel, body, and nave,
Men on the pillars' architrave,
Men on the statues, men on the tombs
With popes and kings in their porphyry wombs,
All famishing in expectation
Of the main-altar's consummation.
For see, for see, the rapturous moment
Approaches, and earth's best endowment
Blends with heaven's: the taper-fires
Pant up, the winding brazen spires
Heave loftier yet the baldachin;
The incense-gaspings, long kept in,
Suspire in clouds; the organ blatant
Holds his breath and grovels latent,
As if God's hushing finger grazed him,
(Like Behemoth when He praised him)
At the silver bell's shrill tinkling,
Quick cold drops of terror sprinkling
On the sudden pavement strewed
With faces of the multitude.
Earth breaks up, time drops away,
In flows heaven, with its new day

Of endless life, when He who trod,
Very Man and very God,
This earth in weakness, shame and pain,
Dying the death whose signs remain
Up yonder on the accursed tree,—
Shall come again, no more to be
Of captivity the thrall,
But the one God, all in all,
King of kings, and Lord of lords,
As His servant John received the words,
" I died, and live for evermore!"

XI.   Yet I was left outside the door.
Why sate I there on the threshold-stone,
Left till He returns, alone
Save for the Garment's extreme fold
Abandoned still to bless my hold?—
My reason, to my doubt, replied,
As if a book were opened wide,
And at a certain page I traced
Every record undefaced,
Added by successive years,—
The harvestings of truth's stray ears
Singly gleaned, and in one sheaf
Bound together for belief.
Yes, I said—that He will go
And sit with these in turn, I know.
Their faith's heart beats, though her head swims
Too giddily to guide her limbs,
Disabled by their palsy-stroke
From propping me.   Though Rome's gross yoke
Drops off, no more to be endured,
Her teaching is not so obscured
By errors and perversities,
That no truth shines athwart the lies:
And He, whose eye detects a spark
Even where, to man's, the whole seems dark,
May well see flame where each beholder
Acknowledges the embers smoulder.
But I, a mere man, fear to quit
The clue God gave me as most fit
To guide my footsteps through life's maze,
Because Himself discerns all ways

Open to reach Him: I, a man
He gave to mark where faith began
To swerve aside, till from its summit
Judgment drops her damning plummet,
Pronouncing such a fatal space
Departed from the Founder's base;
He will not bid me enter too,
But rather sit, as now I do,
Awaiting His return outside.
—'Twas thus my reason straight replied,
And joyously I turned, and pressed
The Garment's skirt upon my breast,
Until, afresh its light suffusing me,
My heart cried,—what has been abusing me
That I should wait here lonely and coldly,
Instead of rising, entering boldly,
Baring truth's face, and letting drift
Her veils of lies as they choose to shift?
Do these men praise Him?   I will raise
My voice up to their point of praise!
I see the error; but above
The scope of error, see the love.—
Oh, love of those first Christian days!
—Fanned so soon into a blaze,
From the spark preserved by the trampled sect,
That the antique sovereign Intellect
Which then sate ruling in the world,
Like a change in dreams, was hurled
From the throne he reigned upon:
—You looked up, and he was gone!
Gone, his glory of the pen!
—Love, with Greece and Rome in ken,
Bade her scribes abhor the trick
Of poetry and rhetoric,
And exult, with hearts set free,
In blessed imbecility
Scrawled, perchance, on some torn sheet,
Leaving Livy incomplete.
Gone, his pride of sculptor, painter!
—Love, while able to acquaint her
With the thousand statues yet
Fresh from chisel, pictures wet
From brush, she saw on every side,

Chose rather with an infant's pride
To frame those portents which impart
Such unction to true Christian Art.
Gone, Music too!   The air was stirred
By happy wings: Terpander's bird
(That, when the cold came, fled away)
Would tarry not the wintry day,—
As more-enduring sculpture must,
Till a filthy saint rebuked the gust
With which he chanced to get a sight
Of some dear naked Aphrodite
He glanced a thought above the toes of,
By breaking zealously her nose off.
Love, surely, from that music's lingering,
Might have filched her organ-fingering,
Nor chose rather to set prayings
To hog-grunts, praises to horse-neighings.
Love was the startling thing, the new;
Love was the all-sufficient too;
And seeing that, you see the rest.
As a babe can find its mother's breast
As well in darkness as in light,
Love shut our eyes, and all seemed right.
True, the world's eyes are open now:
—Less need for me to disallow
Some few that keep Love's zone unbuckled,
Peevish as ever to be suckled,
Lulled by the same old baby-prattle
With intermixture of the rattle,
When she would have them creep, stand steady
Upon their feet, or walk already,
Not to speak of trying to climb.
I will be wise another time,
And not desire a wall between us,
When next I see a church-roof cover
So many species of one genus,
All with foreheads bearing *Lover*
Written above the earnest eyes of them:
All with breasts that beat for beauty,
Whether sublimed, to the surprise of them,
In noble daring, steadfast duty,
The heroic in passion, or in action,—
Or, lowered for the senses' satisfaction,

To the mere outside of human creatures,
Mere perfect form and faultless features.
What! with all Rome here, whence to levy
Such contributions to their appetite,
With women and men in a gorgeous bevy,
They take, as it were, a padlock, and clap it tight
On their southern eyes, restrained from feeding
On the glories of their ancient reading,
On the beauties of their modern singing,
On the wonders of the builder's bringing,
On the majesties of Art around them,—
And, all these loves, late struggling incessant,
When faith has at last united and bound them,
They offer up to God for a present!
Why, I will, on the whole, be rather proud of it,—
And, only taking the act in reference
To the other recipients who might have allowed of it,
I will rejoice that God had the preference!

XII. So I summed up my new resolves:
Too much love there can never be.
And where the intellect devolves
Its function on love exclusively,
I, as one who possesses both,
Will accept the provision, nothing loth,
—Will feast my love, then depart elsewhere,
That my intellect may find its share.
And ponder, O soul, the while thou departest,
And see thou applaud the great heart of the artist,
Who, examining the capabilities
Of the block of marble he has to fashion
Into a type of thought or passion,—
Not always, using obvious facilities,
Shapes it, as any artist can,
Into a perfect symmetrical man,
Complete from head to foot of the life-size,
Such as old Adam stood in his wife's eyes,—
But, now and then, bravely aspires to consummate
A Colossus by no means so easy to come at,
And uses the whole of his block for the bust,
Leaving the minds of the public to finish it,
Since cut it ruefully short he must:
On the face alone he expends his devotion;

He rather would mar than resolve to diminish it,
Saying, " Applaud me for this grand notion
" Of what a face may be! As for completing it
" In breast and body and limbs, do *that*, you! "
All hail! I fancy how, happily meeting it,
A trunk and legs would perfect the statue,
Could man carve so as to answer volition.
And how much nobler than petty cavils,
A hope to find, in my spirit-travels,
Some artist of another ambition,
Who having a block to carve, no bigger,
Has spent his power on the opposite quest,
And believed to begin at the feet was best—
For so may I see, ere I die, the whole figure!

XIII. No sooner said than out in the night!
And still as we swept through storm and night,
My heart beat lighter and more light:
And lo, as before, I was walking swift,
With my senses settling fast and steadying,
But my body caught up in the whirl and drift
Of the Vesture's amplitude, still eddying
On just before me, still to be followed,
As it carried me after with its motion,
—What shall I say?—as a path were hollowed,
And a man went weltering through the ocean
Sucked along in the flying wake
Of the luminous water-snake.

XIV. Alone! I am left alone once more—
(Save for the Garment's extreme fold
Abandoned still to bless my hold)
Alone, beside the entrance-door
Of a sort of temple,—perhaps a college,
—Like nothing I ever saw before
At home in England, to my knowledge.
The tall, old, quaint, irregular town!
It may be . . though *which*, I can't affirm . . any
Of the famous middle-age towns of Germany;
And this flight of stairs where I sit down,
Is it Halle, Weimar, Cassel, or Frankfort,
Or Göttingen, that I have to thank for't?
It may be Göttingen,—most likely.

Through the open door I catch obliquely
Glimpses of a lecture-hall;
And not a bad assembly neither—
Ranged decent and symmetrical
On benches, waiting what's to see there;
Which, holding still by the Vesture's hem,
I also resolve to see with them,
Cautious this time how I suffer to slip
The chance of joining in fellowship
With any that call themselves His friends,
As these folks do, I have a notion.
But hist—a buzzing and emotion!
All settle themselves, the while ascends
By the creaking rail to the lecture-desk,
Step by step, deliberate
Because of his cranium's over-freight,
Three parts sublime to one grotesque,
If I have proved an accurate guesser,
The hawk-nosed, high-cheek-boned Professor.
I felt at once as if there ran
A shoot of love from my heart to the man—
That sallow, virgin-minded, studious
Martyr to mild enthusiasm,
As he uttered a kind of cough-preludious
That woke my sympathetic spasm,
(Beside some spitting that made me sorry)
And stood, surveying his auditory
With a wan pure look, well nigh celestial,—
Those blue eyes had survived so much!
While, under the foot they could not smutch,
Lay all the fleshly and the bestial.
Over he bowed, and arranged his notes,
Till the auditory's clearing of throats
Was done with, died into silence;
And, when each glance was upward sent,
Each bearded mouth composed intent,
And a pin might be heard drop half a mile hence,—
He pushed back higher his spectacles,
Let the eyes stream out like lamps from cells,
And giving his head of hair—a hake
Of undressed tow, for colour and quantity—
One rapid and impatient shake,
(As our own young England adjusts a jaunty tie

When about to impart, on mature digestion,
Some thrilling view of the surplice-question)
—The Professor's grave voice, sweet though hoarse,
Broke into his Christmas-Eve's discourse.

xv. And he began it by observing
How reason dictated that men
Should rectify the natural swerving,
By a reversion, now and then,
To the well-heads of knowledge, few
And far away, whence rolling grew
The life-stream wide whereat we drink,
Commingled, as we needs must think,
With waters alien to the source:
To do which, aimed this Eve's discourse.
Since, where could be a fitter time
For tracing backward to its prime,
This Christianity, this lake,
This reservoir, whereat we slake,
From one or other bank, our thirst?
So he proposed inquiring first
Into the various sources whence
This myth of Christ is derivable;
Demanding from the evidence,
(Since plainly no such life was liveable)
How these phenomena should class?
Whether 'twere best opine Christ was,
Or never was at all, or whether
He was and was not, both together—
It matters little for the name,
So the Idea be left the same:
Only, for practical purpose' sake,
'Twas obviously as well to take
The popular story,—understanding
How the ineptitude of the time,
And the penman's prejudice, expanding
Fact into fable fit for the clime,
Had, by slow and sure degrees, translated it
Into this myth, this Individuum,—
Which, when reason had strained and abated it
Of foreign matter, gave, for residuum,
A Man!—a right true man, however,
Whose work was worthy a man's endeavour!

Work, that gave warrant almost sufficient
To his disciples, for rather believing
He was just omnipotent and omniscient,
As it gives to us, for as frankly receiving
His word, their tradition,—which, though it meant
Something entirely different
From all that those who only heard it,
In their simplicity thought and averred it,
Had yet a meaning quite as respectable:
For, among other doctrines delectable,
Was he not surely the first to insist on,
The natural sovereignty of our race?—
Here the lecturer came to a pausing-place.
And while his cough, like a drouthy piston,
Tried to dislodge the husk that grew to him,
I seized the occasion of bidding adieu to him,
The Vesture still within my hand.

XVI. I could interpret its command.
This time He would not bid me enter
The exhausted air-bell of the Critic.
Truth's atmosphere may grow mephitic
When Papist struggles with Dissenter,
Impregnating its pristine clarity,
—One, by his daily fare's vulgarity,
Its gust of broken meat and garlic;
—One, by his soul's too-much presuming,
To turn the frankincense's fuming
And vapours of the candle starlike
Into the cloud her wings she buoys on:
And each, that sets the pure air seething,
Poisoning it for healthy breathing—
But the Critic leaves no air to poison;
Pumps out by a ruthless ingenuity
Atom by atom, and leaves you—vacuity.
Thus much of Christ, does he reject?
And what retain?   His intellect?
What is it I must reverence duly?
Poor intellect for worship, truly,
Which tells me simply what was told
(If mere morality, bereft
Of the God in Christ, be all that's left)
Elsewhere by voices manifold;

With this advantage, that the stater
Made nowise the important stumble
Of adding, he, the sage and humble,
Was also one with the Creator.
You urge Christ's followers' simplicity:
But how does shifting blame, evade it?
Have wisdom's words no more felicity?
The stumbling-block, His speech—who laid it?
How comes it that for one found able,
To sift the truth of it from fable,
Millions believe it to the letter?
Christ's goodness, then—does that fare better?
Strange goodness, which upon the score
Of being goodness, the mere due
Of man to fellow-man, much more
To God,—should take another view
Of its possessor's privilege,
And bid him rule his race!   You pledge
Your fealty to such rule?   What, all—
From Heavenly John and Attic Paul,
And that brave weather-battered Peter
Whose stout faith only stood completer
For buffets, sinning to be pardoned,
As the more his hands hauled nets, they hardened,—
All, down to you, the man of men,
Professing here at Göttingen,
Compose Christ's flock!   So, you and I
Are sheep of a good man! and why?
The goodness,—how did he acquire it?
Was it self-gained, did God inspire it?
Choose which; then tell me, on what ground
Should its possessor dare propound
His claim to rise o'er us an inch?
Were goodness all some man's invention,
Who arbitrarily made mention
What we should follow, and where flinch,—
What qualities might take the style
Of right and wrong,—and had such guessing
Met with as general acquiescing
As graced the Alphabet erewhile,
When A got leave an Ox to be,
No Camel (quoth the Jews) like G,—
For thus inventing thing and title

Worship were that man's fit requital.
But if the common conscience must
Be ultimately judge, adjust
Its apt name to each quality
Already known,—I would decree
Worship for such mere demonstration
And simple work of nomenclature,
Only the day I praised, not Nature,
But Harvey, for the circulation.
I would praise such a Christ, with pride
And joy, that he, as none beside,
Had taught us how to keep the mind
God gave him, as God gave his kind,
Freer than they from fleshly taint!
I would call such a Christ our Saint,
As I declare our Poet, him
Whose insight makes all others dim:
A thousand poets pried at life,
And only one amid the strife
Rose to be Shakespeare! Each shall take
His crown, I'd say, for the world's sake—
Though some objected—" Had we seen
" The heart and head of each, what screen
" Was broken there to give them light,
" While in ourselves it shuts the sight,
" We should no more admire, perchance,
" That these found truth out at a glance,
" Than marvel how the bat discerns
" Some pitch-dark cavern's fifty turns,
" Led by a finer tact, a gift
" He boasts, which other birds must shift
" Without, and grope as best they can."
No, freely I would praise the man,—
Nor one whit more, if he contended
That gift of his, from God, descended.
Ah, friend, what gift of man's does not?
No nearer Something, by a jot,
Rise an infinity of Nothings
Than one: take Euclid for your teacher:
Distinguish kinds: do crownings, clothings,
Make that Creator which was creature?
Multiply gifts upon his head,
And what, when all's done, shall be said

But . . . the more gifted he, I ween!
That one's made Christ, another, Pilate,
And This might be all That has been,—
So what is there to frown or smile at?
What is left for us, save, in growth,
Of soul, to rise up, far past both,
From the gift looking to the Giver,
And from the cistern to the River,
And from the finite to Infinity,
And from man's dust to God's divinity?

XVII. Take all in a word: the Truth in God's breast
Lies trace for trace upon ours impressed:
Though He is so bright and we so dim,
We are made in His image to witness Him:
And were no eye in us to tell,
Instructed by no inner sense,
The light of Heaven from the dark of Hell,
That light would want its evidence,—
Though Justice, Good and Truth were still
Divine, if by some demon's will,
Hatred and wrong had been proclaimed
Law through the worlds, and Right misnamed.
No mere exposition of morality
Made or in part or in totality,
Should win you to give it worship, therefore:
And, if no better proof you will care for,
—Whom do you count the worst man upon earth?
Be sure, he knows, in his conscience, more
Of what Right is, than arrives at birth
In the best man's acts that we bow before:
This last *knows* better—true; but my fact is,
'Tis one thing to know, and another to practise;
And thence I conclude that the real God-function
Is to furnish a motive and injunction
For practising what we know already.
And such an injunction and such a motive
As the God in Christ, do you waive, and " heady
High minded," hang your tablet-votive
Outside the fane on a finger-post?
Morality to the uttermost,
Supreme in Christ as we all confess,
Why need *we* prove would avail no jot

To make Him God, if God He were not?
What is the point where Himself lays stress?
Does the precept run " Believe in Good,
" In Justice, Truth, now understood
" For the first time? "—or, " Believe in ME,
" Who lived and died, yet essentially
" Am Lord of Life? "   Whoever can take
The same to his heart and for mere love's sake
Conceive of the love,—that man obtains
A new truth; no conviction gains
Of an old one only, made intense
By a fresh appeal to his faded sense.

XVIII. Can it be that He stays inside?
Is the Vesture left me to commune with?
Could my soul find aught to sing in tune with
Even at this lecture, if she tried?
Oh, let me at lowest sympathise
With the lurking drop of blood that lies
In the desiccated brain's white roots
Without a throb for Christ's attributes,
As the Lecturer makes his special boast!
If love's dead there, it has left a ghost.
Admire we, how from heart to brain
(Though to say so strike the doctors dumb)
One instinct rises and falls again,
Restoring the equilibrium.
And how when the Critic had done his best,
And the Pearl of Price, at reason's test,
Lay dust and ashes levigable
On the Professor's lecture-table;
When we looked for the inference and monition
That our faith, reduced to such a condition,
Be swept forthwith to its natural dust-hole,—
He bids us, when we least expect it,
Take back our faith,—if it be not just whole,
Yet a pearl indeed, as his tests affect it,
Which fact pays the damage done rewardingly,
So, prize we our dust and ashes accordingly!
" Go home and venerate the Myth
" I thus have experimented with—
" This Man, continue to adore him
" Rather than all who went before him,

" And all who ever followed after! "—
Surely for this I may praise you, my brother!
Will you take the praise in tears or laughter?
That's one point gained: can I compass another?
Unlearned love was safe from spurning—
Can't we respect your loveless learning?
Let us at least give Learning honour!
What laurels had we showered upon her,
Girding her loins up to perturb
Our theory of the Middle Verb;
Or Turklike brandishing a scimetar
O'er anapæsts in comic-trimeter;
Or curing the halt and maimed Iketides,
While we lounged on at our indebted ease:
Instead of which, a tricksy demon
Sets her at Titus or Philemon!
When Ignorance wags his ears of leather
And hates God's word, 'tis altogether;
Nor leaves he his congenial thistles
To go and browze on Paul's Epistles.
—And you, the audience, who might ravage
The world wide, enviably savage
Nor heed the cry of the retriever,
More than Herr Heine (before his fever),—
I do not tell a lie so arrant
As say my passion's wings are furled up,
And, without the plainest Heavenly warrant,
I were ready and glad to give this world up—
But still, when you rub the brow meticulous,
And ponder the profit of turning holy
If not for God's, for your own sake solely,
—God forbid I should find you ridiculous!
Deduce from this lecture all that eases you,
Nay, call yourselves, if the calling pleases you,
" Christians,"—abhor the Deist's pravity,—
Go on, you shall no more move my gravity,
Than, when I see boys ride a-cockhorse
I find it in my heart to embarrass them
By hinting that their stick's a mock horse,
And they really carry what they say carries them.

XIX. So sate I talking with my mind.
       I did not long to leave the door

And find a new church, as before,
But rather was quiet and inclined
To prolong and enjoy the gentle resting
From further tracking and trying and testing.
This tolerance is a genial mood!
(Said I, and a little pause ensued).
One trims the bark 'twixt shoal and shelf,
And sees, each side, the good effects of it,
A value for religion's self,
A carelessness about the sects of it.
Let me enjoy my own conviction,
Not watch my neighbour's faith with fretfulness,
Still spying there some dereliction
Of truth, perversity, forgetfulness!
Better a mild indifferentism,
To teach that all our faiths (though duller
His shines through a dull spirit's prism)
Originally had one colour—
Sending me on a pilgrimage
Through ancient and through modern times
To many peoples, various climes,
Where I may see Saint, Savage, Sage
Fuse their respective creeds in one
Before the general Father's throne!

xx. . . . 'Twas the horrible storm began afresh!
The black night caught me in his mesh
Whirled me up, and flung me prone.
I was left on the college-step alone.
I looked, and far there, ever fleeting
Far, far away, the receding gesture,
And looming of the lessening Vesture,
Swept forward from my stupid hand,
While I watched my foolish heart expand
In the lazy glow of benevolence,
O'er the various modes of man's belief.
I sprang up with fear's vehemence.
—Needs must there be one way, our chief
Best way of worship: let me strive
To find it, and when found, contrive
My fellows also take their share.
This constitutes my earthly care:
God's is above it and distinct!

For I, a man, with men am linked,
And not a brute with brutes; no gain
That I experience, must remain
Unshared: but should my best endeavour
To share it, fail—subsisteth ever
God's care above, and I exult
That God, by God's own ways occult,
May—doth, I will believe—bring back
All wanderers to a single track!
Meantime, I can but testify
God's care for me—no more, can I—
It is but for myself I *know*.
The world rolls witnessing around me
Only to leave me as it found me;
Men cry there, but my ear is slow.
Their races flourish or decay
—What boots it, while yon lucid way
Loaded with stars, divides the vault?
How soon my soul repairs its fault
When, sharpening senses' hebetude,
She turns on my own life! So viewed,
No mere mote's-breadth but teems immense
With witnessings of providence:
And woe to me if when I look
Upon that record, the sole book
Unsealed to me, I take no heed
Of any warning that I read!
Have I been sure, this Christmas-Eve,
God's own hand did the rainbow weave,
Whereby the truth from heaven slid
Into my soul?—I cannot bid
The world admit He stooped to heal
My soul, as if in a thunder-peal
Where one heard noise, and one saw flame,
I only knew He named my name.
And what is the world to me, for sorrow
Or joy in its censures, when to-morrow
It drops the remark, with just-turned head
Then, on again—That man is dead?
Yes,—but for me—my name called,—drawn
As a conscript's lot from the lap's black yawn,
He has dipt into on a battle-dawn:
Bid out of life by a nod, a glance,—

Stumbling, mute-mazed, at nature's chance,—
With a rapid finger circled round,
Fixed to the first poor inch of ground,
To fight from, where his foot was found;
Whose ear but a minute since lay free
To the wide camp's buzz and gossipry—
Summoned, a solitary man,
To end his life where his life began,
From the safe glad rear, to the dreadful van!
Soul of mine, hadst thou caught and held
By the hem of the Vesture . . .

XXI.   And I caught
At the flying Robe, and unrepelled
Was lapped again in its folds full-fraught
With warmth and wonder and delight,
God's mercy being infinite.
And scarce had the words escaped my tongue,
When, at a passionate bound, I sprung
Out of the wandering world of rain,
Into the little chapel again.

XXII. How else was I found there, bolt upright
On my bench, as if I had never left it?
—Never flung out on the common at night
Nor met the storm and wedge-like cleft it,
Seen the raree-show of Peter's successor,
Or the laboratory of the Professor!
For the Vision, *that* was true, I wist,
True as that heaven and earth exist.
There sate my friend, the yellow and tall,
With his neck and its wen in the selfsame place;
Yet my nearest neighbour's cheek showed gall,
She had slid away a contemptuous space:
And the old fat woman, late so placable,
Eyed me with symptoms, hardly mistakeable,
Of her milk of kindness turning rancid:
In short a spectator might have fancied
That I had nodded betrayed by a slumber,
Yet kept my seat, a warning ghastly,
Through the heads of the sermon, nine in number,
To wake up now at the tenth and lastly.
But again, could such a disgrace have happened?

Each friend at my elbow had surely nudged it;
And, as for the sermon, where did my nap end?
Unless I heard it, could I have judged it?
Could I report as I do at the close,
First, the preacher speaks through his nose:
Second, his gesture is too emphatic:
Thirdly, to waive what's pedagogic,
The subject-matter itself lacks logic:
Fourthly, the English is ungrammatic.
Great news! the preacher is found no Pascal,
Whom, if I pleased, I might to the task call
Of making square to a finite eye
The circle of infinity,
And find so all-but-just-succeeding!
Great news! the sermon proves no reading
Where bee-like in the flowers I may bury me,
Like Taylor's, the immortal Jeremy!
And now that I know the very worst of him,
What was it I thought to obtain at first of him?
Ha! Is God mocked, as He asks?
Shall I take on me to change His tasks,
And dare, despatched to a river-head
For a simple draught of the element,
Neglect the thing for which He sent,
And return with another thing instead?—
Saying . . . "Because the water found
" Welling up from underground,
" Is mingled with the taints of earth,
" While Thou, I know, dost laugh at dearth,
" And couldest, at a word, convulse
" The world with the leap of its river-pulse,—
" Therefore I turned from the oozings muddy,
" And bring thee a chalice I found, instead:
" See the brave veins in the breccia ruddy!
" One would suppose that the marble bled.
" What matters the water? A hope I have nursed,
" That the waterless cup will quench my thirst."
—Better have knelt at the poorest stream
That trickles in pain from the straitest rift!
For the less or the more is all God's gift,
Who blocks up or breaks wide the granite-seam.
And here, is there water or not, to drink?
I, then, in ignorance and weakness,

Taking God's help, have attained to think
My heart does best to receive in meekness
This mode of worship, as most to His mind,
Where earthly aids being cast behind,
His All in All appears serene,
With the thinnest human veil between,
Letting the mystic Lamps, the Seven,
The many motions of His spirit,
Pass, as they list, to earth from Heaven.
For the preacher's merit or demerit,
It were to be wished the flaws were fewer
In the earthen vessel, holding treasure,
Which lies as safe in a golden ewer;
But the main thing is, does it hold good measure?
Heaven soon sets right all other matters!—
Ask, else, these ruins of humanity,
This flesh worn out to rags and tatters,
This soul at struggle with insanity,
Who thence take comfort, can I doubt,
Which an empire gained, were a loss without.
May it be mine!   And let us hope
That no worse blessing befal the Pope,
Turn'd sick at last of the day's buffoonery,
Of his posturings and his petticoatings,
Beside the Bourbon bully's gloatings
In the bloody orgies of drunk poltroonery!
Nor may the Professor forego its peace
At Göttingen, presently, when, in the dusk
Of his life, if his cough, as I fear, should increase,
Prophesied of by that horrible husk;
And when, thicker and thicker, the darkness fills
The world through his misty spectacles,
And he gropes for something more substantial
Than a fable, myth, or personification,
May Christ do for him, what no mere man shall,
And stand confessed as the God of salvation!
Meantime, in the still recurring fear
Lest myself, at unawares, be found,
While attacking the choice of my neighbours round,
Without my own made—I choose here!
The giving out of the hymn reclaims me;
I have done!—And if any blames me,
Thinking that merely to touch in brevity

The topics I dwell on, were unlawful,—
Or, worse, that I trench, with undue levity,
On the bounds of the Holy and the awful,
I praise the heart, and pity the head of him,
And refer myself to THEE, instead of him;
Who head and heart alike discernest,
Looking below light speech we utter,
When the frothy spume and frequent sputter
Prove that the soul's depths boil in earnest!
May the truth shine out, stand ever before us!
I put up pencil and join chorus
To Hepzibah Tune, without further apology,
The last five verses of the third section
Of the seventeenth hymn in Whitfield's Collection,
To conclude with the doxology.

EASTER-DAY.

1. How very hard it is to be
   A Christian! Hard for you and me,
   —Not the mere task of making real
   That duty up to its ideal,
   Effecting thus, complete and whole,
   A purpose of the human soul—
   For that is always hard to do;
   But hard, I mean, for me and you
   To realise it, more or less,
   With even the moderate success
   Which commonly repays our strife
   To carry out the aims of life.
   " This aim is greater," you may say,
   " And so more arduous every way."
   But the importance of the fruits
   Still proves to man, in all pursuits,
   Proportional encouragement.
   " Then, what if it be God's intent
   " That labour to this one result
   " Shall seem unduly difficult? "
   —Ah, that's a question in the dark—
   And the sole thing that I remark
   Upon the difficulty, this;
   We do not see it where it *is*,

At the beginning of the race:
As we proceed, it shifts its place,
And where we looked for palms to fall,
We find the tug's to come,—that's all.

II. At first you say, " The whole, or chief
" Of difficulties, is Belief.
" Could I believe once thoroughly,
" The rest were simple.   What?   Am I
" An idiot, do you think?   A beast?
" Prove to me only that the least
" Command of God is God's indeed,
" And what injunction shall I need
" To pay obedience?   Death so nigh
" When time must end, eternity
" Begin,—and cannot I compute?
" Weigh loss and gain together? suit
" My actions to the balance drawn,
" And give my body to be sawn
" Asunder, hacked in pieces, tied
" To horses, stoned, burned, crucified,
" Like any martyr of the list?
" How gladly,—if I made acquist,
" Through the brief minutes' fierce annoy,
" Of God's eternity of joy."

III. —And certainly you name the point
Whereon all turns: for could you joint
This flexile finite life once tight
Into the fixed and infinite,
You, safe inside, would spurn what's out,
With carelessness enough, no doubt—
Would spurn mere life: but where time brings
To their next stage your reasonings,
Your eyes, late wide, begin to wink
Nor see the path so well, I think.

IV. You say, " Faith may be, one agrees,
" A touchstone for God's purposes,
" Even as ourselves conceive of them.
" Could He acquit us or condemn
" For holding what no hand can loose,
" Rejecting when we can't but choose?

" As well award the victor's wreath
" To whosoever should take breath
" Duly each minute while he lived—
" Grant Heaven, because a man contrived
" To see the sunlight every day
" He walked forth on the public way.
" You must mix some uncertainty
" With faith, if you would have faith *be*.
" Why, what but faith, do we abhor
" And idolize each other for—
" —Faith in our evil, or our good,
" Which is or is not understood
" Aright by those we love or those
" We hate, thence called our friends or foes?
" Your mistress saw your spirit's grace,
" When, turning from the ugly face,
" I found belief in it too hard;
" And both of us have our reward.
" —Yet here a doubt peeps: well for us
" Weak beings, to go using thus
" A touchstone for our little ends,
" And try with faith the foes and friends;
" —But God, bethink you! I would fain
" Conceive of the Creator's reign
" As based upon exacter laws
" Than creatures build by with applause.
" In all God's acts—(as Plato cries
" He doth)—He *should* geometrise.
" Whence, I desiderate . . ."

v.   I see!
You would grow smoothly as a tree,
Soar heavenward, straightly up like fire—
God bless you—there's your world entire
Needing no faith, if you think fit;
Go there, walk up and down in it!
The whole creation travails, groans—
Contrive your music from its moans,
Without or let or hindrance, friend!
That's an old story, and its end
As old—you come back (be sincere)
With every question you put here
(Here where there once was, and is still,

We think, a living oracle,
Whose answers you stood carping at)
This time flung back unanswered flat,—
Besides, perhaps, as many more
As those that drove you out before,
Now added, where was little need!
Questions impossible, indeed,
To us who sate still, all and each
Persuaded that our earth had speech
Of God's writ down, no matter if
In cursive type or hieroglyph,—
Which one fact frees us from the yoke
Of guessing why He never spoke.
You come back in no better plight
Than when you left us,—am I right?

VI. So the old process, I conclude,
Goes on, the reasoning's pursued
Further. You own, " 'Tis well averred,
" A scientific faith's absurd,
" —Frustrates the very end 'twas meant
" To serve: so I would rest content
" With a mere probability,
" But, probable; the chance must lie
" Clear on one side,—lie all in rough,
" So long as there is just enough
" To pin my faith to, though it hap
" Only at points: from gap to gap
" One hangs up a huge curtain so,
" Grandly, nor seeks to have it go
" Foldless and flat along the wall:
" —What care I that some interval
" Of life less plainly might depend
" On God? I'd hang there to the end;
" And thus I should not find it hard
" To be a Christian and debarred
" From trailing on the earth, till furled
" Away by death!—Renounce the world?
" Were that a mighty hardship? Plan
" A pleasant life, and straight some man
" Beside you, with, if he thought fit,
" Abundant means to compass it,
" Shall turn deliberate aside

" To try and live as, if you tried
" You clearly might, yet most despise.
" One friend of mine wears out his eyes,
" Slighting the stupid joys of sense,
" In patient hope that, ten years hence,
" Somewhat completer he may see
" His list of *lepidopteræ*:
" While just the other who most laughs
" At him, above all epitaphs
" Aspires to have his tomb describe
" Himself as Sole among the tribe
" Of snuffbox-fanciers, who possessed
" A Grignon with the Regent's crest.
" So that, subduing as you want,
" Whatever stands predominant
" Among my earthly appetites
" For tastes, and smells, and sounds, and sights,
" I shall be doing that alone,
" To gain a palm-branch and a throne,
" Which fifty people undertake
" To do, and gladly, for the sake
" Of giving a Semitic guess,
" Or playing pawns at blindfold chess."

VII. Good! and the next thing is,—look round
For evidence enough. 'Tis found,
No doubt: as is your sort of mind,
So is your sort of search—you'll find
What you desire, and that's to be
A Christian: what says History?
How comforting a point it were
To find some mummy-scrap declare
There lived a Moses! Better still,
Prove Jonah's whale translatable
Into some quicksand of the seas,
Isle, cavern, rock, or what you please,
That Faith might clap her wings and crow
From such an eminence! Or, no—
The Human Heart's best; you prefer
Making that prove the minister
To truth; you probe its wants and needs
And hopes and fears, then try what creeds
Meet these most aptly,—resolute

That Faith plucks such substantial fruit
Wherever these two correspond,
She little needs to look beyond,
To puzzle out what Orpheus was,
Or Dionysius Zagrias.
You'll find sufficient, as I say,
To satisfy you either way.
You wanted to believe; your pains
Are crowned—you do: and what remains?
Renounce the world!—Ah, were it done
By merely cutting one by one
Your limbs off, with your wise head last,
How easy were it!—how soon past,
If once in the believing mood!
Such is man's usual gratitude,
Such thanks to God do we return,
For not exacting that we spurn
A single gift of life, forego
One real gain,—only taste them so
With gravity and temperance,
That those mild virtues may enhance
Such pleasures, rather than abstract—
Last spice of which, will be the fact
Of love discerned in every gift;
While, when the scene of life shall shift,
And the gay heart be taught to ache,
As sorrows and privations take
The place of joy,—the thing that seems
Mere misery, under human schemes,
Becomes, regarded by the light
Of Love, as very near, or quite
As good a gift as joy before.
So plain is it that all the more
God's dispensation's merciful,
More pettishly we try and cull
Briars, thistles, from our private plot,
To mar God's ground where thorns are not!

VIII. Do you say this, or I?—Oh, you!
Then, what, my friend,—(so I pursue
Our parley)—you indeed opine
That the Eternal and Divine
Did, eighteen centuries ago,

In very truth . . . Enough! you know
The all-stupendous tale,—that Birth,
That Life, that Death! And all, the earth
Shuddered at,—all, the heavens grew black
Rather than see; all, Nature's rack
And throe at dissolution's brink
Attested,—it took place, you think,
Only to give our joys a zest,
And prove our sorrows for the best?
We differ, then! Were I, still pale
And heartstruck at the dreadful tale,
Waiting to hear God's voice declare
What horror followed for my share,
As implicated in the deed,
Apart from other sins,—concede
That if He blacked out in a blot
My brief life's pleasantness, 'twere not
So very disproportionate!
Or there might be another fate—
I certainly could understand
(If fancies were the thing in hand)
How God might save, at that Day's price,
The impure in their impurities,
Leave formal licence and complete
To choose the fair, and pick the sweet.
But there be certain words, broad, plain,
Uttered again and yet again,
Hard to mistake, to overgloss—
Announcing this world's gain for loss,
And bidding us reject the same:
The whole world lieth (they proclaim)
In wickedness,—come out of it!—
Turn a deaf ear, if you think fit,
But I who thrill through every nerve
At thought of what deaf ears deserve,—
How do you counsel in the case?

IX. " I'd take, by all means, in your place,
" The safe side, since it so appears:
" Deny myself, a few brief years,
" The natural pleasure, leave the fruit
" Or cut the plant up by the root.
" Remember what a martyr said

" On the rude tablet overhead—
" ' I was born sickly, poor and mean,
" ' A slave, no misery could screen
" ' The holders of the pearl of price
" ' From Cæsar's envy ; therefore twice
" ' I fought with beasts, and three times saw
" ' My children suffer by his law—
" ' At last my own release was earned:
" ' I was some time in being burned,
" ' But at the close a Hand came through
" ' The fire above my head, and drew
" ' My soul to Christ, whom now I see.
" ' Sergius, a brother, writes for me
" ' This testimony on the wall—
" ' For me, I have forgot it all.'
" You say right; this were not so hard!
" And since one nowise is debarred
" From this, why not escape some sins
" By such a method? "

x.   —Then begins
To the old point, revulsion new—
(For 'tis just this, I bring you to)
If after all we should mistake,
And so renounce life for the sake
Of death and nothing else?   You hear
Our friends we jeered at, send the jeer
Back to ourselves with good effect—
' There *were* my beetles to collect! '
' My box—a trifle, I confess,
' But here I hold it, ne'ertheless! '
Poor idiots, (let us pluck up heart
And answer) we, the better part
Have chosen, though 'twere only hope,—
Nor envy moles like you that grope
Amid your veritable muck,
More than the grasshoppers would truck,
For yours, their passionate life away,
That spends itself in leaps all day
To reach the sun, you want the eyes
To see, as they the wings to rise
And match the noble hearts of them!
So, the contemner we contemn,—

And, when doubt strikes us, so, we ward
Its stroke off, caught upon our guard,
—Not struck enough to overturn
Our faith, but shake it—make us learn
What I began with, and, I wis,
End, having proved,—how hard it is
To be a Christian!

XI.   " Proved, or not,
      " Howe'er you wis, small thanks, I wot,
      " You get of mine, for taking pains
      " To make it hard to me.   Who gains
      " By that, I wonder?   Here I live
      " In trusting ease; and do you drive
      " At causing me to lose what most
      " Yourself would mourn for when 'twas lost? "

XII. But, do you see, my friend, that thus
      You leave St. Paul for Æschylus?—
      —Who made his Titan's arch-device
      The giving men *blind hopes* to spice
      The meal of life with, else devoured
      In bitter haste, while lo! Death loured
      Before them at the platter's edge!
      If faith should be, as we allege,
      Quite other than a condiment
      To heighten flavors with, or meant
      (Like that brave curry of his Grace)
      To take at need the victuals' place?
      If having dined you would digest
      Besides, and turning to your rest
      Should find instead . . .

XIII.   Now, you shall see
      And judge if a mere foppery
      Pricks on my speaking! I resolve
      To utter . . . yes, it shall devolve
      On you to hear as solemn, strange
      And dread a thing as in the range
      Of facts,—or fancies, if God will—
      E'er happened to our kind! I still
      Stand in the cloud, and while it wraps
      My face, ought not to speak, perhaps;
      Seeing that as I carry through

My purpose, if my words in you
Find veritable listeners,
My story, reason's self avers
Must needs be false—the happy chance!
While, if each human countenance
I meet in London streets all day,
Be what I fear,—my warnings fray
No one, and no one they convert,
And no one helps me to assert
How hard it is to really be
A Christian, and in vacancy
I pour this story!

XIV.   I commence
By trying to inform you, whence
It comes that every Easter-night
As now, I sit up, watch, till light
Shall break, those chimney-stacks and roofs
Give, through my window-pane, grey proofs
That Easter-day is breaking slow.
On such a night, three years ago,
It chanced that I had cause to cross
The common, where the chapel was,
Our friend spoke of, the other day—
You've not forgotten, I dare say.
I fell to musing of the time
So close, the blessed matin-prime
All hearts leap up at, in some guise—
One could not well do otherwise.
Insensibly my thoughts were bent
Toward the main point; I overwent
Much the same ground of reasoning
As you and I just now: one thing
Remained, however—one that tasked
My soul to answer; and I asked,
Fairly and frankly, what might be
That History, that Faith, to me—
—Me there—not me, in some domain
Built up and peopled by my brain,
Weighing its merits as one weighs
Mere theories for blame or praise,
—The Kingcraft of the Lucumons,
Or Fourier's scheme, its pros and cons,—

But as *my* faith, or none at all.
' How were my case, now, should I fall
' Dead here, this minute—do I lie
' Faithful or faithless? '—Note that I
Inclined thus ever!—little prone
For instance, when I slept alone
In childhood, to go calm to sleep
And leave a closet where might keep
His watch perdue some murderer
Waiting till twelve o'clock to stir,
As good, authentic legends tell
He might—' But how improbable!
' How little likely to deserve
' The pains and trial to the nerve
' Of thrusting head into the dark,'—
Urged my old nurse, and bade me mark
Besides, that, should the dreadful scout
Really lie hid there, to leap out
At first turn of the rusty key,
It were small gain that she could see
In being killed upon the floor
And losing one night's sleep the more.
I tell you, I would always burst
The door ope, know my fate at first.—
This time, indeed, the closet penned
No such assassin: but a friend
Rather, peeped out to guard me, fit
For counsel, Common Sense, to-wit,
Who said a good deal that might pass,—
Heartening, impartial too, it was,
Judge else: ' For, soberly now,—who
' Should be a Christian if not you? '
(Hear how he smoothed me down). ' One takes
' A whole life, sees what course it makes
' Mainly, and not by fits and starts—
' In spite of stoppage which imparts
' Fresh value to the general speed:
' A life, with none, would fly indeed:
' Your progressing is slower—right!
' We deal with progressing, not flight.
' Through baffling senses passionate,
' Fancies as restless,—with a freight
' Of knowledge cumbersome enough

' To sink your ship when waves grow rough,
' Not serve as ballast in the hold,
' I find, 'mid dangers manifold,
' The good bark answers to the helm
' Where Faith sits, easier to o'erwhelm
' Than some stout peasant's heavenly guide,
' Whose hard head could not, if it tried,
' Conceive a doubt, or understand
' How senses hornier than his hand
' Should 'tice the Christian off his guard—
' More happy!   But shall we award
' Less honour to the hull, which, dogged
' By storms, a mere wreck, waterlogged,
' Masts by the board, and bulwarks gone,
' And stanchions going, yet bears on,—
' Than to mere life-boats, built to save,
' And triumph o'er the breaking wave?
' Make perfect your good ship as these,
' And what were her performances! '
I added—' Would the ship reached home!
' I wish indeed " God's kingdom come—"
' The day when I shall see appear
' His bidding, as my duty, clear
' From doubt!   And it shall dawn, that day,
' Some future season; Easter may
' Prove, not impossibly, the time—
' Yes, that were striking—fates would chime
' So aptly!   Easter-morn, to bring
' The Judgment!—deeper in the Spring
' Than now, however, when there's snow
' Capping the hills; for earth must show
' All signs of meaning to pursue
' Her tasks as she was wont to do—
' —The lark, as taken by surprise
' As we ourselves, shall recognise
' Sudden the end: for suddenly
' It comes—the dreadfulness must be
' In that—all warrants the belief—
' " At night it cometh like a thief."
' I fancy why the trumpet blows;
' —Plainly, to wake one.   From repose
' We shall start up, at last awake
' From life, that insane dream we take

' For waking now, because it seems.
' And as, when now we wake from dreams,
' We say, while we recall them, " Fool,
' " To let the chance slip, linger cool
' " When such adventure offered!   Just
' " A bridge to cross, a dwarf to thrust
' " Aside, a wicked mage to stab—
' " And, lo ye, I had kissed Queen Mab,"—
' So shall we marvel why we grudged
' Our labours here, and idly judged
' Of Heaven, we might have gained, but lose!
' Lose?   Talk of loss, and I refuse
' To plead at all!   I speak no worse
' Nor better than my ancient nurse
' When she would tell me in my youth
' I well deserved that shapes uncouth
' Should fright and tease me in my sleep—
' Why did I not in memory keep
' Her precept for the evil's cure?
' " Pinch your own arm, boy, and be sure
' " You'll wake forthwith! " '

xv.   And as I said
This nonsense, throwing back my head
With light complacent laugh, I found
Suddenly all the midnight round
One fire.   The dome of Heaven had stood
As made up of a multitude
Of handbreadth cloudlets, one vast rack
Of ripples infinite and black,
From sky to sky.   Sudden there went,
Like horror and astonishment,
A fierce vindictive scribble of red
Quick flame across, as if one said
(The angry scribe of Judgment) ' There—
' Burn it! '   And straight I was aware
That the whole ribwork round, minute
Cloud touching cloud beyond compute,
Was tinted each with its own spot
Of burning at the core, till clot
Jammed against clot, and spilt its fire
Over all heaven, which 'gan suspire
As fanned to measure equable,—

As when great conflagrations kill
Night overhead, and rise and sink,
Reflected. Now the fire would shrink
And wither off the blasted face
Of heaven, and I distinct could trace
The sharp black ridgy outlines left
Unburned like network—then, each cleft
The fire had been sucked back into,
Regorged, and out it surging flew
Furiously, and night writhed inflamed,
Till, tolerating to be tamed
No longer, certain rays world-wide
Shot downwardly, on every side,
Caught past escape; the earth was lit;
As if a dragon's nostril split
And all his famished ire o'erflowed;
Then, as he winced at his Lord's goad,
Back he inhaled: whereat I found
The clouds into vast pillars bound,
Based on the corners of the earth,
Propping the skies at top: a dearth
Of fire i' the violet intervals,
Leaving exposed the utmost walls
Of time, about to tumble in
And end the world.

XVI.   I felt begin
The Judgment-Day: to retrocede
Was too late now.—' In very deed,
(I uttered to myself) ' that Day!'
The intuition burned away
All darkness from my spirit too—
There, stood I, found and fixed, I knew,
Choosing the world. The choice was made—
And naked and disguiseless stayed,
And unevadeable, the fact.
My brain held ne'ertheless compact
Its senses, nor my heart declined
Its office—rather, both combined
To help me in this juncture—I
Lost not a second,—agony
Gave boldness: there, my life had end
And my choice with it—best defend,

Applaud them! I resolved to say,
' So was I framed by Thee, this way
' I put to use Thy senses here!
' It was so beautiful, so near,
' Thy world,—what could I do but choose
' My part there?   Nor did I refuse
' To look above the transient boon
' In time—but it was hard so soon
' As in a short life, to give up
' Such beauty: I had put the cup
' Undrained of half its fullness, by;
' But, to renounce it utterly,
' —That was too hard! Nor did the Cry
' Which bade renounce it, touch my brain
' Authentically deep and plain
' Enough, to make my lips let go.
' But Thou, who knowest all, dost know
' Whether I was not, life's brief while,
' Endeavouring to reconcile
' Those lips—too tardily, alas!
' To letting the dear remnant pass,
' One day,—some drops of earthly good
' Untasted!   Is it for this mood,
' That Thou, whose earth delights so well,
' Hast made its complement a Hell?'

xvii. A final belch of fire like blood,
Overbroke all, next, in one flood
Of doom.   Then fire was sky, and sky
Was fire, and both, one extasy,
Then ashes.   But I heard no noise
(Whatever was) because a Voice
Beside me spoke thus, " All is done,
" Time ends, Eternity's begun,
" And thou art judged for evermore!"

xviii. I looked up; all was as before;
Of that cloud-Tophet overhead,
No trace was left: I saw instead
The common round me, and the sky
Above, stretched drear and emptily
Of life: 'twas the last watch of night,
Except what brings the morning quite,

When the armed angel, conscience-clear
His task nigh done, leans o'er his spear
And gazes on the earth he guards,
Safe one night more through all its wards,
Till God relieve him at his post.
' A dream—a waking dream at most!'
(I spoke out quick that I might shake
The horrid nightmare off, and wake.)
' The world's gone, yet the world is here?
' Are not all things as they appear?
' Is Judgment past for me alone?
' —And where had place the Great White Throne?
' The rising of the Quick and Dead?
' Where stood they, small and great?   Who read
' The sentence from the Opened Book?'
So, by degrees, the blood forsook
My heart, and let it beat afresh:
I knew I should break through the mesh
Of horror, and breathe presently—
When, lo, again, the Voice by me!

xix. I saw . . . Oh, brother, 'mid far sands
The palm-tree-cinctured city stands,—
Bright-white beneath, as Heaven, bright-blue,
Above it, while the years pursue
Their course, unable to abate
Its paradisal laugh at fate:
One morn,—the Arab staggers blind
O'er a new tract of death, calcined
To ashes, silence, nothingness,—
Striving, with dizzy wits, to guess
Whence fell the blow: what if, 'twixt skies
And prostrate earth, he should surprise
The imaged Vapour, head to foot,
Surveying, motionless and mute,
Its work, ere, in a whirlwind rapt,
It vanish up again?—So hapt
My chance.   HE stood there.   Like the smoke
Pillared o'er Sodom, when day broke,—
I saw Him.   One magnific pall
Mantled in massive fold and fall
His Dread, and coiled in snaky swathes
About His feet: night's black, that bathes

All else, broke, grizzled with despair,
Against the soul of blackness there.
A gesture told the mood within—
That wrapped right hand which based the chin,—
That intense meditation fixed
On His procedure,—pity mixed
With the fulfilment of decree.
Motionless, thus, He spoke to me,
Who fell before His feet, a mass,
No man now.

xx.   " All is come to pass.
" Such shows are over for each soul
" They had respect to.   In the roll
" Of Judgment which convinced mankind
" Of sin, stood many, bold and blind,
" Terror must burn the truth into:
" Their fate for them!—thou had'st to do
" With absolute omnipotence,
" Able its judgments to dispense
" To the whole race, as every one
" Were its sole object: that is done:
" God is, thou art,—the rest is hurled
" To nothingness for thee.   This world,
" This finite life, thou hast preferred,
" In disbelief of God's own word,
" To Heaven and to Infinity.
" Here, the probation was for thee,
" To show thy soul the earthly mixed
" With Heavenly, it must choose betwixt.
" The earthly joys lay palpable,—
" A taint, in each, distinct as well;
" The Heavenly flitted, faint and rare,
" Above them, but as truly were
" Taintless, so in their nature, best.
" Thy choice was earth: thou didst attest
" 'Twas fitter spirit should subserve
" The flesh, than flesh refine to nerve
" Beneath the spirit's play.   Advance
" No claim to their inheritance
" Who chose the spirit's fugitive
" Brief gleams, and thought, ' This were to live
" ' Indeed, if rays, completely pure

" ' From flesh that dulls them, should endure,—
" ' Not shoot in meteor-light athwart
" ' Our earth, to show how cold and swart
" ' It lies beneath their fire, but stand
" ' As stars should, destined to expand,
" ' Prove veritable worlds, our home!'
" Thou said'st,—' Let Spirit star the dome
" ' Of sky, that flesh may miss no peak,
" ' No nook of earth,—I shall not seek
" ' Its service further!' Thou art shut
" Out of the Heaven of Spirit; glut
" Thy sense upon the world: 'tis thine
" For ever—take it!"

XXI.   ' How?   Is mine,
' The world?' (I cried, while my soul broke
Out in a transport)   ' Hast thou spoke
' Plainly in that?   Earth's exquisite
' Treasures of wonder and delight,
' For me?'

XXII.   The austere Voice returned,—
" So soon made happy?   Hadst thou learned
" What God accounteth happiness,
" Thou wouldst not find it hard to guess
" What Hell may be His punishment
" For those who doubt if God invent
" Better than they.   Let such men rest
" Content with what they judged the best.
" Let the Unjust usurp at will:
" The Filthy shall be filthy still:
" Miser, there waits the gold for thee!
" Hater, indulge thine enmity!
" And thou, whose heaven, self-ordained,
" Was to enjoy earth unrestrained,
" Do it!   Take all the ancient show!
" The woods shall wave, the rivers flow,
" And men apparently pursue
" Their works, as they were wont to do,
" While living in probation yet:
" I promise not thou shalt forget
" The past, now gone to its account,
" But leave thee with the old amount
" Of faculties, nor less nor more,

" Unvisited, as heretofore,
" By God's free spirit, that makes an end.
" So, once more, take thy world; expend
" Eternity upon its shows,—
" Flung thee as freely as one rose
" Out of a summer's opulence,
" Over the Eden-barrier whence
" Thou art excluded.   Knock in vain! "

XXIII. I sate up.   All was still again.
    I breathed free: to my heart, back fled
    The warmth.   ' But, all the world! ' (I said)
    I stooped and picked a leaf of fern,
    And recollected I might learn
    From books, how many myriad sorts
    Exist, if one may trust reports,
    Each as distinct and beautiful
    As this, the very first I cull.
    Think, from the first leaf to the last!
    Conceive, then, earth's resources!   Vast
    Exhaustless beauty, endless change
    Of wonder! and this foot shall range
    Alps, Andes,—and this eye devour
    The bee-bird and the aloe-flower?

XXIV. And the Voice, " Welcome so to rate
" The arras-folds that variegate
" The earth, God's antechamber, well!
" The wise, who waited there, could tell
" By these, what royalties in store
" Lay one step past the entrance-door.
" For whom, was reckoned, not too much,
" This life's munificence?   For such
" As thou,—a race, whereof not one
" Was able, in a million,
" To feel that any marvel lay
" In objects round his feet all day;
" Nor one, in many millions more,
" Willing, if able, to explore
" The secreter, minuter charm!
" —Brave souls, a fern-leaf could disarm
" Of power to cope with God's intent,—
" Or scared if the South Firmament

" With North-fire did its wings refledge!
" All partial beauty was a pledge
" Of beauty in its plenitude:
" But since the pledge sufficed thy mood,
" Retain it—plenitude be theirs
" Who looked above! "

XXV.   Though sharp despairs
Shot through me, I held up, bore on.
' What is it though my trust is gone
' From natural things?   Henceforth my part
' Be less with Nature than with Art!
' For Art supplants, gives mainly worth
' To Nature; 'tis Man stamps the earth—
' And I will seek his impress, seek
' The statuary of the Greek,
' Italy's painting—there my choice
' Shall fix! '

XXVI.   " Obtain it," said the Voice.
" The one form with its single act,
" Which sculptors laboured to abstract,
" The one face, painters tried to draw,
" With its one look, from throngs they saw!
" And that perfection in their soul,
" These only hinted at?   The whole,
" They were but parts of?   What each laid
" His claim to glory on?—afraid
" His fellow-men should give him rank
" By the poor tentatives he shrank
" Smitten at heart from, all the more,
" That gazers pressed in to adore!
" ' Shall I be judged by only these? '
" If such his soul's capacities,
" Even while he trod the earth,—think, now
" What pomp in Buonarotti's brow,
" With its new palace-brain where dwells
" Superb the soul, unvexed by cells
" That crumbled with the transient clay!
" What visions will his right hand's sway
" Still turn to form, as still they burst
" Upon him?   How will he quench thirst,
" Titanically infantine,
" Laid at the breast of the Divine?

" Does it confound thee,—this first page
" Emblazoning man's heritage?—
" Can this alone absorb thy sight,
" As if they were not infinite,—
" Like the omnipotence which tasks
" Itself, to furnish all that asks
" The soul it means to satiate?
" What was the world, the starry state
" Of the broad skies,—what, all displays
" Of power and beauty intermixed,
" Which now thy soul is chained betwixt,—
" What, else, than needful furniture
" For life's first stage?   God's work, be sure,
" No more spreads wasted, than falls scant:
" He filled, did not exceed, Man's want
" Of beauty in this life.   And pass
" Life's line,—and what has earth to do,
" Its utmost beauty's appanage,
" With the requirements of next stage?
" Did God pronounce earth ' very good '?
" Needs must it be, while understood
" For man's preparatory state;
" Nothing to heighten nor abate:
" But transfer the completeness here,
" To serve a new state's use,—and drear
" Deficiency gapes every side!
" The good, tried once, were bad, retried.
" See the enwrapping rocky niche,
" Sufficient for the sleep, in which
" The lizard breathes for ages safe:
" Split the mould—and as this would chafe
" The creature's new world-widened sense,
" One minute after you dispense
" The thousand sounds and sights that broke
" In, on him, at the chisel's stroke,—
" So, in God's eyes, the earth's first stuff
" Was, neither more nor less, enough
" To house man's soul, man's need fulfil.
" You reckoned it immeasurable:
" So thinks the lizard of his vault!
" Could God be taken in default,
" Short of contrivances, by you,—
" Or reached, ere ready to pursue

" His progress through eternity?
" That chambered rock, the lizard's world,
" Your easy mallet's blow has hurled
" To nothingness for ever; so,
" Has God abolished at a blow
" This world, wherein his saints were pent,—
" Who, though, found grateful and content,
" With the provision there, as thou,
" Yet knew He would not disallow
" Their spirit's hunger, felt as well,—
" Unsated,—not unsatable,
" As Paradise gives proof.   Deride
" Their choice now, thou who sit'st outside ! "

XXVII. I cried in anguish, ' Mind, the mind,
' So miserably cast behind,
' To gain what had been wisely lost !
' Oh, let me strive to make the most
' Of the poor stinted soul, I nipped
' Of budding wings, else well equipt
' For voyage from summer isle to isle !
' And though she needs must reconcile
' Ambition to the life on ground,
' Still, I can profit by late found
' But precious knowledge.   Mind is best—
' I will seize mind, forego the rest
' And try how far my tethered strength
' May crawl in this poor breadth and length.
' —Let me, since I can fly no more,
' At least spin dervish-like about
' (Till giddy rapture almost doubt
' I fly) through circling sciences,
' Philosophies and histories !
' Should the whirl slacken there, then Verse,
' Fining to music, shall asperse
' Fresh and fresh fire-dew, till I strain
' Intoxicate, half-break my chain !
' Not joyless, though more favoured feet
' Stand calm, where I want wings to beat
' The floor?   At least earth's bond is broke ! '

XXVIII. Then, (sickening even while I spoke)
' Let me alone !   No answer, pray,

' To this! I know what Thou wilt say!
' All still is earth's,—to Know, as much
' As Feel its truths, which if we touch
' With sense or apprehend in soul,
' What matter? I have reached the goal—
' " Whereto does Knowledge serve! " will burn
' My eyes, too sure, at every turn!
' I cannot look back now, nor stake
' Bliss on the race, for running's sake.
' The goal's a ruin like the rest! '—
—" And so much worse thy latter quest,
(Added the Voice) " that even on earth
" Whenever, in man's soul, had birth
" Those intuitions, grasps of guess,
" That pull the more into the less,
" Making the finite comprehend
" Infinity, the bard would spend
" Such praise alone, upon his craft,
" As, when wind-lyres obey the waft,
" Goes to the craftsman who arranged
" The seven strings, changed them and rechanged—
" Knowing it was the South that harped.
" He felt his song, in singing, warped,
" Distinguished his and God's part: whence
" A world of spirit as of sense
" Was plain to him, yet not too plain,
" Which he could traverse, not remain
" A guest in:—else were permanent
" Heaven upon earth, its gleams were meant
" To sting with hunger for the light,—
" Made visible in Verse, despite
" The veiling weakness,—truth by means
" Of fable, showing while it screens,—
" Since highest truth, man e'er supplied,
" Was ever fable on outside.
" Such gleams made bright the earth an age;
" Now, the whole sun's his heritage!
" Take up thy world, it is allowed,
" Thou who hast entered in the cloud! "

Then I—' Behold, my spirit bleeds,
' Catches no more at broken reeds,—
' But lilies flower those reeds above—

' I let the world go, and take love!
' Love survives in me, albeit those
' I loved are henceforth masks and shows,
' Not loving men and women: still
' I mind how love repaired all ill,
' Cured wrong, soothed grief, made earth amends
' With parents, brothers, children, friends!
' Some semblance of a woman yet
' With eyes to help me to forget,
' Shall live with me; and I will match
' Departed love with love, attach
' Its fragments to my whole, nor scorn
' The poorest of the grains of corn
' I save from shipwreck on this isle,
' Trusting its barrenness may smile
' With happy foodful green one day,
' More precious for the pains. I pray,
' For love, then, only!'

XXX.   At the word,
The Form, I looked to have been stirred
With pity and approval, rose
O'er me, as when the headsman throws
Axe over shoulder to make end—
I fell prone, letting Him expend
His wrath, while, thus, the inflicting Voice
Smote me. " Is this thy final choice?
" Love is the best? 'Tis somewhat late!
" And all thou dost enumerate
" Of power and beauty in the world,
" The mightiness of love was curled
" Inextricably round about.
" Love lay within it and without,
" To clasp thee,—but in vain! Thy soul
" Still shrunk from Him who made the whole,
" Still set deliberate aside
" His love!—Now take love! Well betide
" Thy tardy conscience! Haste to take
" The show of love for the name's sake,
" Remembering every moment Who
" Beside creating thee unto
" These ends, and these for thee, was said
" To undergo death in thy stead

" In flesh like thine: so ran the tale.
" What doubt in thee could countervail
" Belief in it?   Upon the ground
" ' That in the story had been found
" ' Too much love?   How could God love *so ?* '
" He who in all his works below
" Adapted to the needs of man,
" Made love the basis of the plan,—
" *Did* love, as was demonstrated:
" While man, who was so fit instead,
" To hate, as every day gave proof,—
" You thought man, for his kind's behoof,
" Both could and would invent that scheme
" Of perfect love—'twould well beseem
" Cain's nature thou wast wont to praise,
" Not tally with God's usual ways! "

XXXI. And I cowered deprecatingly—
' Thou Love of God!   Or let me die,
' Or grant what shall seem Heaven almost!
' Let me not know that all is lost,
' Though lost it be—leave me not tied
' To this despair, this corpse-like bride!
' Let that old life seem mine—no more—
' With limitation as before,
' With darkness, hunger, toil, distress:
' Be all the earth a wilderness!
' Only let me go on, go on,
' Still hoping ever and anon
' To reach one eve the Better Land! '

XXXII. Then did the Form expand, expand—
I knew Him through the dread disguise,
As the whole God within his eyes
Embraced me.

XXXIII.   When I lived again,
The day was breaking,—the grey plain
I rose from, silvered thick with dew.
Was this a vision?   False or true?
Since then, three varied years are spent,
And commonly my mind is bent
To think it was a dream—be sure

A mere dream and distemperature—
The last day's watching: then the night,—
The shock of that strange Northern Light
Set my head swimming, bred in me
A dream.   And so I live, you see,
Go through the world, try, prove, reject,
Prefer, still struggling to effect
My warfare; happy that I can
Be crossed and thwarted as a man,
Not left in God's contempt apart,
With ghastly smooth life, dead at heart,
Tame in earth's paddock as her prize.
Thank God she still each method tries
To catch me, who may yet escape,
She knows, the fiend in angel's shape!
Thank God, no paradise stands barred
To entry, and I find it hard
To be a Christian, as I said!
Still every now and then my head
Raised glad, sinks mournful—all grows drear
Spite of the sunshine, while I fear
And think, ' How dreadful to be grudged
' No ease henceforth, as one that's judged,
' Condemned to earth for ever, shut
' From Heaven ' . .
                        But Easter-Day breaks! But
Christ rises!   Mercy every way
Is infinite,—and who can say?

MEN AND WOMEN

MEN AND WOMEN

LOVE AMONG THE RUINS.

I. WHERE the quiet-coloured end of evening smiles
        Miles and miles
  On the solitary pastures where our sheep
        Half-asleep
  Tinkle homeward thro' the twilight, stray or stop
        As they crop—

II. Was the site once of a city great and gay,
        (So they say)
  Of our country's very capital, its prince
        Ages since
  Held his court in, gathered councils, wielding far
        Peace or war.

III. Now—the country does not even boast a tree,
        As you see,
  To distinguish slopes of verdure, certain rills
        From the hills
  Intersect and give a name to (else they run
        Into one)

IV. Where the domed and daring palace shot its spires
        Up like fires
  O'er the hundred-gated circuit of a wall
        Bounding all,
  Made of marble, men might march on nor be prest,
        Twelve abreast.

V. And such plenty and perfection, see, of grass
        Never was!
  Such a carpet as, this summer-time, o'erspreads
        And embeds
  Every vestige of the city, guessed alone,
        Stock or stone—

VI. Where a multitude of men breathed joy and woe
        Long ago;
  Lust of glory pricked their hearts up, dread of shame
        Struck them tame;
  And that glory and that shame alike, the gold
        Bought and sold.

VII. Now,—the single little turret that remains
        On the plains,
  By the caper overrooted, by the gourd
        Overscored,
  While the patching houseleek's head of blossom winks
        Through the chinks—

VIII. Marks the basement whence a tower in ancient time
        Sprang sublime,
  And a burning ring all round, the chariots traced
        As they raced,
  And the monarch and his minions and his dames
        Viewed the games.

IX. And I know, while thus the quiet-coloured eve
        Smiles to leave
  To their folding, all our many-tinkling fleece
        In such peace,
  And the slopes and rills in undistinguished grey
        Melt away—

X. That a girl with eager eyes and yellow hair
        Waits me there
  In the turret, whence the charioteers caught soul
        For the goal,
  When the king looked, where she looks now, breathless,
    dumb
        Till I come.

XI. But he looked upon the city, every side,
        Far and wide,
  All the mountains topped with temples, all the glades'
        Colonnades,
  All the causeys, bridges, aqueducts,—and then,
        All the men!

xii. When I do come, she will speak not, she will stand,
        Either hand
  On my shoulder, give her eyes the first embrace
        Of my face,
  Ere we rush, ere we extinguish sight and speech
        Each on each.

xiii. In one year they sent a million fighters forth
        South and north,
  And they built their gods a brazen pillar high
        As the sky,
  Yet reserved a thousand chariots in full force—
        Gold, of course.

xiv. Oh, heart! oh, blood that freezes, blood that burns!
        Earth's returns
  For whole centuries of folly, noise and sin!
        Shut them in,
  With their triumphs and their glories and the rest.
        Love is best!

A LOVER'S QUARREL.

i. Oh, what a dawn of day!
  How the March sun feels like May!
      All is blue again
      After last night's rain,
  And the south dries the hawthorn-spray.
      Only, my Love's away!
  I'd as lief that the blue were grey.

ii. Runnels, which rillets swell,
  Must be dancing down the dell
      With a foamy head
      On the beryl bed
  Paven smooth as a hermit's cell;
      Each with a tale to tell,
  Could my Love but attend as well.

iii. Dearest, three months ago!
  When we lived blocked-up with snow,—

    When the wind would edge
    In and in his wedge,
In, as far as the point could go—
    Not to our ingle, though,
Where we loved each the other so!

IV. Laughs with so little cause!
    We devised games out of straws.
       We would try and trace
       One another's face
In the ash, as an artist draws;
       Free on each other's flaws,
How we chattered like two church daws!

V. What's in the " Times "?—a scold
    At the emperor deep and cold;
       He has taken a bride
       To his gruesome side,
That's as fair as himself is bold:
       There they sit ermine-stoled,
And she powders her hair with gold.

VI. Fancy the Pampas' sheen!
    Miles and miles of gold and green
       Where the sun-flowers blow
       In a solid glow,
And to break now and then the screen—
       Black neck and eyeballs keen,
Up a wild horse leaps between!

VII. Try, will our table turn?
    Lay your hands there light, and yearn
       Till the yearning slips
       Thro' the finger tips
In a fire which a few discern,
       And a very few feel burn,
And the rest, they may live and learn!

VIII. Then we would up and pace,
    For a change, about the place,
       Each with arm o'er neck.
       'Tis our quarter-deck,
We are seamen in woeful case,
       Help in the ocean-space!
Or, if no help, we'll embrace.

IX. See, how she looks now, drest
In a sledging-cap and vest.
    'Tis a huge fur cloak—
    Like a reindeer's yoke
Falls the lappet along the breast:
    Sleeves for her arms to rest,
Or to hang, as my Love likes best.

X. Teach me to flirt a fan
As the Spanish ladies can,
    Or I tint your lip
    With a burnt stick's tip
And you turn into such a man!
    Just the two spots that span
Half the bill of the young male swan.

XI. Dearest, three months ago
When the mesmeriser Snow
    With his hand's first sweep
    Put the earth to sleep,
'Twas a time when the heart could show
    All—how was earth to know,
'Neath the mute hand's to-and-fro!

XII. Dearest, three months ago
When we loved each other so,
    Lived and loved the same
    Till an evening came
When a shaft from the Devil's bow
    Pierced to our ingle-glow,
And the friends were friend and foe!

XIII. Not from the heart beneath—
'Twas a bubble born of breath
    Neither sneer nor vaunt,
    Nor reproach nor taunt.
See a word, how it severeth!
    Oh, power of life and death
In the tongue, as the Preacher saith!

XIV. Woman, and will you cast
For a word, quite off at last,
    Me, your own, your you,—
    Since, as Truth is true,

I was you all the happy past—
Me do you leave aghast
With the memories we amassed?

xv. Love, if you knew the light
That your soul casts in my sight,
How I look to you
For the pure and true,
And the beauteous and the right,—
Bear with a moment's spite
When a mere mote threats the white!

xvi. What of a hasty word?
Is the fleshly heart not stirred
By a worm's pin-prick
Where its roots are quick?
See the eye, by a fly's foot blurred—
Ear, when a straw is heard
Scratch the brain's coat of curd!

xvii. Foul be the world or fair,
More or less, how can I care?
'Tis the world the same
For my praise or blame,
And endurance is easy there.
Wrong in the one thing rare—
Oh, it is hard to bear!

xviii. Here's the spring back or close,
When the almond-blossom blows;
We shall have the word
In that minor third
There is none but the cuckoo knows—
Heaps of the guelder-rose!
I must bear with it, I suppose.

xix. Could but November come,
Were the noisy birds struck dumb
At the warning slash
Of his driver's-lash—
I would laugh like the valiant Thumb
Facing the castle glum
And the giant's fee-faw-fum!

xx. Then, were the world well stript
  Of the gear wherein equipped
      We can stand apart,
      Heart dispense with heart
  In the sun, with the flowers unnipped,—
      Oh, the world's hangings ripped,
  We were both in a bare-walled crypt!

xxi. Each in the crypt would cry
  " But one freezes here! and why?
      When a heart as chill
      At my own would thrill
  Back to life, and its fires out-fly?
      Heart, shall we live or die?
  The rest, . . . settle it by and by!"

xxii. So, she'd efface the score,
  And forgive me as before.
      Just at twelve o'clock
      I shall hear her knock
  In the worst of a storm's uproar—
      I shall pull her through the door—
  I shall have her for evermore!

EVELYN HOPE.

i. Beautiful Evelyn Hope is dead!
  Sit and watch by her side an hour.
That is her book-shelf, this her bed;
  She plucked that piece of geranium-flower,
Beginning to die too, in the glass.
  Little has yet been changed, I think—
The shutters are shut, no light may pass
  Save two long rays thro' the hinge's chink.

ii. Sixteen years old when she died!
  Perhaps she had scarcely heard my name—
It was not her time to love: beside,
  Her life had many a hope and aim,
Duties enough and little cares,
  And now was quiet, now astir—
Till God's hand beckoned unawares,
  And the sweet white brow is all of her.

III. Is it too late then, Evelyn Hope?
    What, your soul was pure and true,
The good stars met in your horoscope,
    Made you of spirit, fire and dew—
And just because I was thrice as old,
    And our paths in the world diverged so wide,
Each was nought to each, must I be told?
    We were fellow mortals, nought beside?

IV. No, indeed! for God above
    Is great to grant, as mighty to make,
And creates the love to reward the love,—
    I claim you still, for my own love's sake!
Delayed it may be for more lives yet,
    Through worlds I shall traverse, not a few—
Much is to learn and much to forget
    Ere the time be come for taking you.

V. But the time will come,—at last it will,
    When, Evelyn Hope, what meant, I shall say,
In the lower earth, in the years long still,
    That body and soul so pure and gay?
Why your hair was amber, I shall divine,
    And your mouth of your own geranium's red—
And what you would do with me, in fine,
    In the new life come in the old one's stead.

VI. I have lived, I shall say, so much since then,
    Given up myself so many times,
Gained me the gains of various men,
    Ransacked the ages, spoiled the climes;
Yet one thing, one, in my soul's full scope,
    Either I missed or itself missed me—
And I want and find you, Evelyn Hope!
    What is the issue? let us see!

VII. I loved you, Evelyn, all the while;
    My heart seemed full as it could hold—
There was place and to spare for the frank young smile
    And the red young mouth and the hair's young gold.
So, hush,—I will give you this leaf to keep—
    See, I shut it inside the sweet cold hand.
There, that is our secret! go to sleep;
    You will wake, and remember, and understand.

UP AT A VILLA—DOWN IN THE CITY.

(AS DISTINGUISHED BY AN ITALIAN PERSON OF QUALITY.)

I.

HAD I but plenty of money, money enough and to spare,
The house for me, no doubt, were a house in the city-square.
Ah, such a life, such a life, as one leads at the window there!

II.

Something to see, by Bacchus, something to hear, at least!
There, the whole day long, one's life is a perfect feast;
While up at a villa one lives, I maintain it, no more than a
    beast.

III.

Well, now, look at our villa! stuck like the horn of a bull
Just on a mountain's edge as bare as the creature's skull,
Save a mere shag of a bush with hardly a leaf to pull!
—I scratch my own, sometimes, to see if the hair's turned
    wool.

IV.

But the city, oh the city—the square with the houses!
    Why?
They are stone-faced, white as a curd, there's something to
    take the eye!
Houses in four straight lines, not a single front awry!
You watch who crosses and gossips, who saunters, who
    hurries by:
Green blinds, as a matter of course, to draw when the sun
    gets high;
And the shops with fanciful signs which are painted properly.

V.

What of a villa? Though winter be over in March by rights,
'Tis May perhaps ere the snow shall have withered well off
    the heights:
You've the brown ploughed land before, where the oxen
    steam and wheeze,
And the hills over-smoked behind by the faint grey olive trees.

VI.

Is it better in May, I ask you? you've summer all at once;
In a day he leaps complete with a few strong April suns!
'Mid the sharp short emerald wheat, scarce risen three fingers
  well,
The wild tulip, at end of its tube, blows out its great red bell,
Like a thin clear bubble of blood, for the children to pick
  and sell.

VII.

Is it ever hot in the square? There's a fountain to spout
  and splash!
In the shade it sings and springs; in the shine such foam-bows
  flash
On the horses with curling fish-tails, that prance and paddle
  and pash
Round the lady atop in the conch—fifty gazers do not abash,
Though all that she wears is some weeds round her waist in
  a sort of sash!

VIII.

All the year long at the villa, nothing's to see though you
  linger,
Except yon cypress that points like Death's lean lifted fore-
  finger.
Some think fireflies pretty, when they mix in the corn and
  mingle,
Or thrid the stinking hemp till the stalks of it seem a-tingle.
Late August or early September, the stunning cicala is shrill,
And the bees keep their tiresome whine round the resinous
  firs on the hill.
Enough of the seasons,—I spare you the months of the fever
  and chill.

IX.

Ere opening your eyes in the city, the blessed church-bells
  begin:
No sooner the bells leave off, than the diligence rattles in:
You get the pick of the news, and it costs you never a pin.
By and by there's the travelling doctor gives pills, lets blood,
  draws teeth;

Or the Pulcinello-trumpet breaks up the market beneath.

At the post-office such a scene-picture—the new play, piping
    hot!

And a notice how, only this morning, three liberal thieves
    were shot.

Above it, behold the archbishop's most fatherly of rebukes,

And beneath, with his crown and his lion, some little new law
    of the Duke's!

Or a sonnet with flowery marge, to the Reverend Don So-
    and-so

Who is Dante, Boccaccio, Petrarca, Saint Jerome, and Cicero,

" And moreover," (the sonnet goes rhyming,) " the skirts of
    St. Paul has reached,

Having preached us those six Lent-lectures more unctuous
    than ever he preached."

Noon strikes,—here sweeps the procession! our Lady borne
    smiling and smart

With a pink gauze gown all spangles, and seven swords stuck
    in her heart!

Bang, whang, whang, goes the drum, *tootle-te-tootle* the fife;

No keeping one's haunches still: it's the greatest pleasure in
    life.

x.

But bless you, it's dear—it's dear! fowls, wine, at double the
    rate.

They have clapped a new tax upon salt, and what oil pays
    passing the gate

It's a horror to think of.   And so, the villa for me, not the city!

Beggars can scarcely be choosers—but still—ah, the pity,
    the pity!

Look, two and two go the priests, then the monks with cowls
    and sandals,

And the penitents dressed in white shirts, a-holding the
    yellow candles.

One, he carries a flag up straight, and another a cross with
    handles,

And the Duke's guard brings up the rear, for the better
    prevention of scandals.

Bang, whang, whang, goes the drum, *tootle-te-tootle* the fife.

Oh, a day in the city-square, there is no such pleasure in life!

A WOMAN'S LAST WORD.

I. LET'S contend no more, Love,
   Strive nor weep—
   All be as before, Love,
   —Only sleep!

II. What so wild as words are?
    —I and thou
    In debate, as birds are,
    Hawk on bough!

III. See the creature stalking
     While we speak—
     Hush and hide the talking,
     Cheek on cheek!

IV. What so false as truth is,
    False to thee?
    Where the serpent's tooth is,
    Shun the tree—

V. Where the apple reddens
   Never pry—
   Lest we lose our Edens,
   Eve and I!

VI. Be a god and hold me
    With a charm—
    Be a man and fold me
    With thine arm!

VII. Teach me, only teach, Love!
     As I ought
     I will speak thy speech, Love,
     Think thy thought—

VIII. Meet, if thou require it,
      Both demands,
      Laying flesh and spirit
      In thy hands!

    IX. That shall be to-morrow
          Not to-night:
      I must bury sorrow
          Out of sight.

    X. —Must a little weep, Love,
          —Foolish me!
      And so fall asleep, Love,
          Loved by thee.

FRA LIPPO LIPPI

I AM poor brother Lippo, by your leave!
You need not clap your torches to my face.
Zooks, what's to blame? you think you see a monk!
What, it's past midnight, and you go the rounds,
And here you catch me at an alley's end
Where sportive ladies leave their doors ajar.
The Carmine's my cloister: hunt it up,
Do,—harry out, if you must show your zeal,
Whatever rat, there, haps on his wrong hole,
And nip each softling of a wee white mouse,
Weke, weke, that's crept to keep him company!
Aha, you know your betters? Then, you'll take
Your hand away that's fiddling on my throat,
And please to know me likewise. Who am I?
Why, one, sir, who is lodging with a friend
Three streets off—he's a certain . . . how d'ye call?
Master—a . . . Cosimo of the Medici,
In the house that caps the corner. Boh! you were best!
Remember and tell me, the day you're hanged,
How you affected such a gullet's-gripe
But you, sir, it concerns you that your knaves
Pick up a manner nor discredit you.
Zooks, are we pilchards, that they sweep the streets
And count fair prize what comes into their net?
He's Judas to a tittle, that man is!
Just such a face! why, sir, you make amends.
Lord, I'm not angry! Bid your hangdogs go
Drink out this quarter-florin to the health
Of the munificent House that harbours me

(And many more beside, lads! more beside!)
And all's come square again. I'd like his face—
His, elbowing on his comrade in the door
With the pike and lantern,—for the slave that holds
John Baptist's head a-dangle by the hair
With one hand (" look you, now," as who should say)
And his weapon in the other, yet unwiped!
It's not your chance to have a bit of chalk,
A wood-coal or the like? or you should see!
Yes, I'm the painter, since you style me so.
What, brother Lippo's doings, up and down,
You know them and they take you? like enough!
I saw the proper twinkle in your eye—
Tell you I liked your looks at very first.
Let's sit and set things straight now, hip to haunch.
Here's spring come, and the nights one makes up bands
To roam the town and sing out carnival,
And I've been three weeks shut within my mew,
A-painting for the great man, saints and saints
And saints again. I could not paint all night—
Ouf! I leaned out of window for fresh air.
There came a hurry of feet and little feet,
A sweep of lute-strings, laughs, and whiffs of song,—
Flower o' the broom,
Take away love, and our earth is a tomb !
Flower o' the quince,
I let Lisa go, and what good's in life since ?
Flower o' the thyme—and so on. Round they went.
Scarce had they turned the corner when a titter,
Like the skipping of rabbits by moonlight,—three slim
    shapes—
And a face that looked up . . . zooks, sir, flesh and blood,
That's all I'm made of! Into shreds it went,
Curtain and counterpane and coverlet,
All the bed furniture—a dozen knots,
There was a ladder! down I let myself,
Hands and feet, scrambling somehow, and so dropped,
And after them. I came up with the fun
Hard by St. Laurence, hail fellow, well met,—
Flower o' the rose
If I've been merry, what matter who knows ?
And so as I was stealing back again
To get to bed and have a bit of sleep

Ere I rise up to-morrow and go work
On Jerome knocking at his poor old breast
With his great round stone to subdue the flesh,
You snap me of the sudden.   Ah, I see!
Though your eye twinkles still, you shake your head—
Mine's shaved,—a monk, you say—the sting's in that!
If Master Cosimo announced himself,
Mum's the word naturally; but a monk!
Come, what am I a beast for? tell us, now!
I was a baby when my mother died
And father died and left me in the street.
I starved there, God knows how, a year or two
On fig-skins, melon-parings, rinds and shucks,
Refuse and rubbish.   One fine frosty day
My stomach being empty as your hat,
The wind doubled me up and down I went.
Old Aunt Lapaccia trussed me with one hand,
(Its fellow was a stinger as I knew)
And so along the wall, over the bridge,
By the straight cut to the convent.   Six words, there,
While I stood munching my first bread that month:
" So, boy, you're minded," quoth the good fat father
Wiping his own mouth, 'twas refection-time,—
" To quit this very miserable world?
Will you renounce " . . . The mouthful of bread? thought I;
By no means!   Brief, they made a monk of me,
I did renounce the world, its pride and greed,
Palace, farm, villa, shop and banking-house,
Trash, such as these poor devils of Medici
Have given their hearts to—all at eight years old.
Well, sir, I found in time, you may be sure,
'Twas not for nothing—the good bellyful,
The warm serge and the rope that goes all round,
And day-long blessed idleness beside!
" Let's see what the urchin's fit for "—that came next.
Not overmuch their way, I must confess.
Such a to-do!   they tried me with their books.
Lord, they'd have taught me Latin in pure waste!
Flower o' the clove,
All the Latin I construe is, " amo," I love!
But, mind you, when a boy starves in the streets
Eight years together, as my fortune was,
Watching folk's faces to know who will fling

The bit of half-stripped grape-bunch he desires,
And who will curse or kick him for his pains—
Which gentleman processional and fine,
Holding a candle to the Sacrament
Will wink and let him lift a plate and catch
The droppings of the wax to sell again,
Or holla for the Eight and have him whipped,—
How say I?—nay, which dog bites, which lets drop
His bone from the heap of offal in the street!
—The soul and sense of him grow sharp alike,
He learns the look of things, and none the less
For admonitions from the hunger-pinch.
I had a store o' such remarks, be sure,
Which, after I found leisure, turned to use:
I drew men's faces on my copy-books,
Scrawled them within the antiphonary's marge,
Joined legs and arms to the long music-notes,
Found nose and eyes and chin for A.s and B.s,
And made a string of pictures of the world
Betwixt the ins and outs of verb and noun,
On the wall, the bench, the door. The monks looked black.
" Nay," quoth the Prior, " turn him out, d'ye say?
In no wise. Lose a crow and catch a lark.
What if at last we get our man of parts,
We Carmelites, like those Camaldolese
And Preaching Friars, to do our church up fine
And put the front on it that ought to be!"
And hereupon they bade me daub away.
Thank you! my head being crammed, their walls a blank,
Never was such prompt disemburdening.
First, every sort of monk, the black and white,
I drew them, fat and lean: then, folks at church,
From good old gossips waiting to confess
Their cribs of barrel-droppings, candle-ends,—
To the breathless fellow at the altar-foot,
Fresh from his murder, safe and sitting there
With the little children round him in a row
Of admiration, half for his beard and half
For that white anger of his victim's son
Shaking a fist at him with one fierce arm,
Signing himself with the other because of Christ
(Whose sad face on the cross sees only this
After the passion of a thousand years)

Till some poor girl, her apron o'er her head
Which the intense eyes looked through, came at eve
On tip-toe, said a word, dropped in a loaf,
Her pair of ear-rings and a bunch of flowers
The brute took growling, prayed, and then was gone.
I painted all, then cried " 'tis ask and have—
Choose, for more's ready!"—laid the ladder flat,
And showed my covered bit of cloister-wall.
The monks closed in a circle and praised loud
Till checked, (taught what to see and not to see,
Being simple bodies) " that's the very man!
Look at the boy who stoops to pat the dog!
That woman's like the Prior's niece who comes
To care about his asthma: it's the life!"
But there my triumph's straw-fire flared and funked—
Their betters took their turn to see and say:
The Prior and the learned pulled a face
And stopped all that in no time.   " How? what's here?
Quite from the mark of painting, bless us all!
Faces, arms, legs and bodies like the true
As much as pea and pea! it's devil's game!
Your business is not to catch men with show,
With homage to the perishable clay,
But lift them over it, ignore it all,
Make them forget there's such a thing as flesh.
Your business is to paint the souls of men—
Man's soul, and it's a fire, smoke . . . no it's not . . .
It's vapour done up like a new-born babe—
(In that shape when you die it leaves your mouth)
It's . . . well, what matters talking, it's the soul!
Give us no more of body than shows soul.
Here's Giotto, with his Saint a-praising God!
That sets you praising,—why not stop with him?
Why put all thoughts of praise out of our heads
With wonder at lines, colours, and what not?
Paint the soul, never mind the legs and arms!
Rub all out, try at it a second time.
Oh, that white smallish female with the breasts,
She's just my niece . . . Herodias, I would say,—
Who went and danced and got men's heads cut off—
Have it all out!"   Now, is this sense, I ask?
A fine way to paint soul, by painting body
So ill, the eye can't stop there, must go further

And can't fare worse! Thus, yellow does for white
When what you put for yellow's simply black,
And any sort of meaning looks intense
When all beside itself means and looks nought.
Why can't a painter lift each foot in turn,
Left foot and right foot, go a double step,
Make his flesh liker and his soul more like,
Both in their order? Take the prettiest face,
The Prior's niece . . . patron-saint—is it so pretty
You can't discover if it means hope, fear,
Sorrow or joy? won't beauty go with these?
Suppose I've made her eyes all right and blue,
Can't I take breath and try to add life's flash
And then add soul and heighten them threefold?
Or say there's beauty with no soul at all—
(I never saw it—put the case the same—)
If you get simple beauty and nought else,
You get about the best thing God invents,—
That's somewhat. And you'll find the soul you have missed,
Within yourself when you return Him thanks!
" Rub all out! " well, well, there's my life, in short,
And so the thing has gone on ever since.
I'm grown a man no doubt, I've broken bounds—
You should not take a fellow eight years old
And make him swear to never kiss the girls—
I'm my own master, paint now as I please—
Having a friend, you see, in the Corner-house!
Lord, its fast holding by the rings in front—
Those great rings serve more purposes than just
To plant a flag in, or tie up a horse!
And yet the old schooling sticks—the old grave eyes
Are peeping o'er my shoulder as I work,
The heads shake still—" it's Art's decline, my son!
You're not of the true painters, great and old:
Brother Angelico's the man, you'll find:
Brother Lorenzo stands his single peer.
Fag on at flesh, you'll never make the third! "
Flower o' the pine,
You keep your mistr . . . manners, and I'll stick to mine!
I'm not the third, then: bless us, they must know!
Don't you think they're the likeliest to know,
They, with their Latin? so I swallow my rage,
Clench my teeth, suck my lips in tight, and paint

To please them—sometimes do, and sometimes don't,
For, doing most, there's pretty sure to come
A turn—some warm eve finds me at my saints—
A laugh, a cry, the business of the world—
(*Flower o' the peach,*
Death for us all, and his own life for each!)
And my whole soul revolves, the cup runs o'er,
The world and life's too big to pass for a dream,
And I do these wild things in sheer despite,
And play the fooleries you catch me at,
In pure rage! the old mill-horse, out at grass
After hard years, throws up his stiff heels so,
Although the miller does not preach to him
The only good of grass is to make chaff.
What would men have? Do they like grass or no—
May they or mayn't they? all I want's the thing
Settled for ever one way: as it is,
You tell too many lies and hurt yourself.
You don't like what you only like too much,
You do like what, if given you at your word,
You find abundantly detestable.
For me, I think I speak as I was taught—
I always see the Garden and God there
A-making man's wife—and, my lesson learned,
The value and significance of flesh,
I can't unlearn ten minutes afterward.

    You understand me: I'm a beast, I know.
But see, now—why, I see as certainly
As that the morning-star's about to shine,
What will hap some day. We've a youngster here
Comes to our convent, studies what I do,
Slouches and stares and lets no atom drop—
His name is Guidi—he'll not mind the monks—
They call him Hulking Tom, he lets them talk—
He picks my practice up—he'll paint apace,
I hope so—though I never live so long,
I know what's sure to follow. You be judge!
You speak no Latin more than I, belike—
However, you're my man, you've seen the world
—The beauty and the wonder and the power,
The shapes of things, their colours, lights and shades,
Changes, surprises,—and God made it all!
—For what? do you feel thankful, ay or no,

For this fair town's face, yonder river's line,
The mountain round it and the sky above,
Much more the figures of man, woman, child,
These are the frame to? What's it all about?
To be passed o'er, despised? or dwelt upon,
Wondered at? oh, this last of course, you say.
But why not do as well as say,—paint these
Just as they are, careless what comes of it?
God's works—paint any one, and count it crime
To let a truth slip. Don't object, " His works
Are here already—nature is complete:
Suppose you reproduce her—(which you can't)
There's no advantage! you must beat her, then."
For, don't you mark, we're made so that we love
First when we see them painted, things we have passed
Perhaps a hundred times nor cared to see;
And so they are better, painted—better to us,
Which is the same thing. Art was given for that—
God uses us to help each other so,
Lending our minds out. Have you noticed, now,
Your cullion's hanging face? A bit of chalk,
And trust me but you should, though! How much more,
If I drew higher things with the same truth!
That were to take the Prior's pulpit-place,
Interpret God to all of you! oh, oh,
It makes me mad to see what men shall do
And we in our graves! This world's no blot for us,
Nor blank—it means intensely, and means good:
To find its meaning is my meat and drink.
" Ay, but you don't so instigate to prayer,"
Strikes in the Prior! " when your meaning's plain
It does not say to folks—remember matins—
Or, mind you fast next Friday." Why, for this
What need of art at all? A skull and bones,
Two bits of stick nailed cross-wise, or, what's best,
A bell to chime the hour with, does as well.
I painted a St. Laurence six months since
At Prato, splashed the fresco in fine style.
" How looks my painting, now the scaffold's down? "
I ask a brother: " Hugely," he returns—
" Already not one phiz of your three slaves
That turn the Deacon off his toasted side,
But's scratched and prodded to our heart's content,

The pious people have so eased their own
When coming to say prayers there in a rage.
We get on fast to see the bricks beneath.
Expect another job this time next year,
For pity and religion grow i' the crowd—
Your painting serves its purpose!"   Hang the fools!

   —That is—you'll not mistake an idle word
Spoke in a huff by a poor monk, God wot,
Tasting the air this spicy night which turns
The unaccustomed head like Chianti wine!
Oh, the church knows! don't misreport me, now!
It's natural a poor monk out of bounds
Should have his apt word to excuse himself:
And hearken how I plot to make amends.
I have bethought me: I shall paint a piece
. . . There's for you!   Give me six months, then go, see
Something in Sant' Ambrogio's . . . (bless the nuns!
They want a cast of my office) I shall paint
God in the midst, Madonna and her babe,
Ringed by a bowery, flowery angel-brood,
Lilies and vestments and white faces, sweet
As puff on puff of grated orris-root
When ladies crowd to church at midsummer.
And then in the front, of course a saint or two—
Saint John, because he saves the Florentines,
Saint Ambrose, who puts down in black and white
The convent's friends and gives them a long day.
And Job, I must have him there past mistake,
The man of Uz, (and Us without the z,
Painters who need his patience).   Well, all these
Secured at their devotions, up shall come
Out of a corner when you least expect,
As one by a dark stair into a great light,
Music and talking, who but Lippo! I!—
Mazed, motionless and moon-struck—I'm the man!
Back I shrink—what is this I see and hear?
I, caught up with my monk's things by mistake,
My old serge gown and rope that goes all round,
I, in this presence, this pure company!
Where's a hole, where's a corner for escape?
Then steps a sweet angelic slip of a thing
Forward, puts out a soft palm—" Not so fast!"
—Addresses the celestial presence, " nay—

He made you and devised you, after all,
Though he's none of you!   Could Saint John there, draw—
His camel-hair make up a painting-brush?
We come to brother Lippo for all that,
Iste perfecit opus ! "   So, all smile—
I shuffle sideways with my blushing face
Under the cover of a hundred wings
Thrown like a spread of kirtles when you're gay
And play hot cockles, all the doors being shut,
Till, wholly unexpected, in there pops
The hothead husband!   Thus I scuttle off
To some safe bench behind, not letting go
The palm of her, the little lily thing
That spoke the good word for me in the nick,
Like the Prior's niece . . . Saint Lucy, I would say.
And so all's saved for me, and for the church
A pretty picture gained.   Go, six months hence!
Your hand, sir, and good-bye: no lights, no lights!
The street's hushed, and I know my own way back—
Don't fear me!   There's the grey beginning, Zooks!

A TOCCATA OF GALUPPI'S.

I.

OH, Galuppi, Baldassaro, this is very sad to find!
I can hardly misconceive you; it would prove me deaf and
    blind;
But although I give you credit, 'tis with such a heavy mind!

II.

Here you come with your old music, and here's all the good
    it brings.
What, they lived once thus at Venice, where the merchants
    were the kings,
Where St. Marks is, where the Doges used to wed the sea
    with rings?

III.

Ay, because the sea's the street there; and 'tis arched by
    . . . what you call
. . . Shylock's bridge with houses on it, where they kept
    the carnival!
I was never out of England—it's as if I saw it all!

IV.

Did young people take their pleasure when the sea was
    warm in May?
Balls and masks begun at midnight, burning ever to mid-day,
When they made up fresh adventures for the morrow, do
    you say?

V.

Was a lady such a lady, cheeks so round and lips so red,—
On her neck the small face buoyant, like a bell-flower on its
    bed,
O'er the breast's superb abundance where a man might base
    his head?

VI.

Well (and it was graceful of them) they'd break talk off and
    afford
—She, to bite her mask's black velvet, he to finger on his
    sword,
While you sat and played Toccatas, stately at the clavichord?

VII.

What? Those lesser thirds so plaintive, sixths diminished,
    sigh on sigh,
Told them something? Those suspensions, those solutions
    —" Must we die? "
Those commiserating sevenths—" Life might last! we can
    but try! "

VIII.

" Were you happy? "—" Yes."—" And are you still as
    happy? "—" Yes—And you? "
—" Then more kisses "—" Did *I* stop them, when a million
    seemed so few? "
Hark—the dominant's persistence, till it must be answered
    to!

IX.

So an octave struck the answer. Oh, they praised you, I
    dare say!
" Brave Galuppi! that was music! good alike at grave and
    gay!
I can always leave off talking, when I hear a master play."

Then they left you for their pleasure: till in due time, one
    by one,
Some with lives that came to nothing, some with deeds as
    well undone,
Death came tacitly and took them where they never see
    the sun.

But when I sit down to reason,—think to take my stand nor
    swerve
Till I triumph o'er a secret wrung from nature's close reserve,
In you come with your cold music, till I creep thro' every
    nerve,

Yes, you, like a ghostly cricket, creaking where a house
    was burned—
" Dust and ashes, dead and done with, Venice spent what
    Venice earned!
The soul, doubtless, is immortal—where a soul can be dis-
    cerned.

" Yours for instance, you know physics, something of
    geology,
Mathematics are your pastime; souls shall rise in their
    degree;
Butterflies may dread extinction,—you'll not die, it cannot
    be!

" As for Venice and its people, merely born to bloom and
    drop,
Here on earth they bore their fruitage, mirth and folly were
    the crop,
What of soul was left, I wonder, when the kissing had to stop?

" Dust and ashes! " So you creak it, and I want the heart
    to scold.
Dear dead women, with such hair, too—what's become of all
    the gold
Used to hang and brush their bosoms? I feel chilly and
    grown old.

BY THE FIRE-SIDE.

I. How well I know what I mean to do
    When the long dark Autumn evenings come,
And where, my soul, is thy pleasant hue?
    With the music of all thy voices, dumb
In life's November too!

II. I shall be found by the fire, suppose,
    O'er a great wise book as beseemeth age,
While the shutters flap as the cross-wind blows,
    And I turn the page, and I turn the page,
Not verse now, only prose!

III. Till the young ones whisper, finger on lip,
    " There he is at it, deep in Greek—
Now or never, then, out we slip
    To cut from the hazels by the creek
A mainmast for our ship."

IV. I shall be at it indeed, my friends!
    Greek puts already on either side
Such a branch-work forth, as soon extends
    To a vista opening far and wide,
And I pass out where it ends.

V. The outside-frame like your hazel-trees—
    But the inside-archway narrows fast,
And a rarer sort succeeds to these,
    And we slope to Italy at last
And youth, by green degrees.

VI. I follow wherever I am led,
    Knowing so well the leader's hand—
Oh, woman-country, wooed, not wed,
    Loved all the more by earth's male-lands,
Laid to their hearts instead!

VII. Look at the ruined chapel again
    Half way up in the Alpine gorge.
Is that a tower, I point you plain,
    Or is it a mill or an iron forge
Breaks solitude in vain?

VIII. A turn, and we stand in the heart of things;
    The woods are round us, heaped and dim;
From slab to slab how it slips and springs,
    The thread of water single and slim,
Thro' the ravage some torrent brings!

IX. Does it feed the little lake below?
    That speck of white just on its marge
Is Pella; see, in the evening glow
    How sharp the silver spear-heads charge
When Alp meets Heaven in snow.

X. On our other side is the straight-up rock;
    And a path is kept 'twixt the gorge and it
By boulder-stones where lichens mock
    The marks on a moth, and small ferns fit
Their teeth to the polished block.

XI. Oh, the sense of the yellow mountain flowers,
    And the thorny balls, each three in one,
The chestnuts throw on our path in showers,
    For the drop of the woodland fruit's begun
These early November hours—

XII. That crimson the creeper's leaf across
    Like a splash of blood, intense, abrupt,
O'er a shield, else gold from rim to boss,
    And lay it for show on the fairy-cupped
Elf-needled mat of moss,

XIII. By the rose-flesh mushrooms, undivulged
    Last evening—nay, in to-day's first dew
Yon sudden coral nipple bulged
    Where a freaked, fawn-coloured, flaky crew
Of toad-stools peep indulged.

XIV. And yonder, at foot of the fronting ridge
    That takes the turn to a range beyond,
Is the chapel reached by the one-arched bridge
    Where the water is stopped in a stagnant pond
Danced over by the midge.

XV. The chapel and bridge are of stone alike,
    Blackish grey and mostly wet;
Cut hemp-stalks steep in the narrow dyke.
    See here again, how the lichens fret
And the roots of the ivy strike!

XVI. Poor little place, where its one priest comes
　　　　On a festa-day, if he comes at all,
　　To the dozen folk from their scattered homes,
　　　　Gathered within that precinct small
　　By the dozen ways one roams

XVII. To drop from the charcoal-burners' huts,
　　　　Or climb from the hemp-dressers' low shed,
　　Leave the grange where the woodman stores his nuts,
　　　　Or the wattled cote where the fowlers spread
　　Their gear on the rock's bare juts.

XVIII. It has some pretension too, this front,
　　　　With its bit of fresco half-moon-wise
　　Set over the porch, art's early wont—
　　　　'Tis John in the Desert, I surmise,
　　But has borne the weather's brunt—

XIX. Not from the fault of the builder, though,
　　　　For a pent-house properly projects
　　Where three carved beams make a certain show,
　　　　Dating—good thought of our architect's—
　　'Five, six, nine, he lets you know.

XX. And all day long a bird sings there,
　　　　And a stray sheep drinks at the pond at times:
　　The place is silent and aware;
　　　　It has had its scenes, its joys and crimes,
　　But that is its own affair.

XXI. My perfect wife, my Leonor,
　　　　Oh, heart my own, oh, eyes, mine too,
　　Whom else could I dare look backward for,
　　　　With whom beside should I dare pursue
　　The path grey heads abhor?

XXII. For it leads to a crag's sheer edge with them;
　　　　Youth, flowery all the way, there stops—
　　Not they; age threatens and they contemn,
　　　　Till they reach the gulf wherein youth drops,
　　One inch from our life's safe hem!

XXIII. With me, youth led—I will speak now,
　　　　No longer watch you as you sit
　　Reading by fire-light, that great brow
　　　　And the spirit-small hand propping it
　　Mutely—my heart knows how—

XXIV. When, if I think but deep enough,
    You are wont to answer, prompt as rhyme;
And you, too, find without a rebuff
    The response your soul seeks many a time
Piercing its fine flesh-stuff—

XXV. My own, confirm me! If I tread
    This path back, is it not in pride
To think how little I dreamed it led
    To an age so blest that by its side
Youth seems the waste instead!

XXVI. My own, see where the years conduct!
    At first, 'twas something our two souls
Should mix as mists do: each is sucked
    Into each now; on, the new stream rolls,
Whatever rocks obstruct.

XXVII. Think, when our one soul understands
    The great Word which makes all things new—
When earth breaks up and Heaven expands--
    How will the change strike me and you
In the House not made with hands?

XXVIII. Oh, I must feel your brain prompt mine,
    Your heart anticipate my heart,
You must be just before, in fine,
    See and make me see, for your part,
New depths of the Divine!

XXIX. But who could have expected this,
    When we two drew together first
Just for the obvious human bliss,
    To satisfy life's daily thirst
With a thing men seldom miss?

XXX. Come back with me to the first of all,
    Let us lean and love it over again—
Let us now forget and then recall,
    Break the rosary in a pearly rain,
And gather what we let fall!

XXXI. What did I say?—that a small bird sings
    All day long, save when a brown pair
Of hawks from the wood float with wide wings
    Strained to a bell: 'gainst the noon-day glare
You count the streaks and rings.

XXXII. But at afternoon or almost eve
　　　　'Tis better; then the silence grows
To that degree, you half believe
　　　　It must get rid of what it knows,
Its bosom does so heave.

XXXIII. Hither we walked, then, side by side,
　　　　Arm in arm and cheek to cheek,
And still I questioned or replied,
　　　　While my heart, convulsed to really speak,
Lay choking in its pride.

XXXIV. Silent the crumbling bridge we cross,
　　　　And pity and praise the chapel sweet,
And care about the fresco's loss,
　　　　And wish for our souls a like retreat,
And wonder at the moss.

XXXV. Stoop and kneel on the settle under—
　　　　Look through the window's grated square :
Nothing to see! for fear of plunder,
　　　　The cross is down and the altar bare,
As if thieves don't fear thunder.

XXXVI. We stoop and look in through the grate,
　　　　See the little porch and rustic door,
Read duly the dead builder's date,
　　　　Then cross the bridge we crossed before,
Take the path again—but wait!

XXXVII. Oh moment, one and infinite!
　　　　The water slips o'er stock and stone;
The west is tender, hardly bright.
　　　　How grey at once is the evening grown—
One star, the chrysolite!

XXXVIII. We two stood there with never a third,
　　　　But each by each, as each knew well.
The sights we saw and the sounds we heard,
　　　　The lights and the shades made up a spell
Till the trouble grew and stirred.

XXXIX. Oh, the little more, and how much it is!
　　　　And the little less, and what worlds away!
How a sound shall quicken content to bliss,
　　　　Or a breath suspend the blood's best play,
And life be a proof of this!

XL. Had she willed it, still had stood the screen
     So slight, so sure, 'twixt my love and her.
   I could fix her face with a guard between,
     And find her soul as when friends confer,
   Friends—lovers that might have been.

XLI. For my heart had a touch of the woodland time,
      Wanting to sleep now over its best.
    Shake the whole tree in the summer-prime,
      But bring to the last leaf no such test.
    "Hold the last fast!" says the rhyme.

XLII. For a chance to make your little much,
       To gain a lover and lose a friend,
     Venture the tree and a myriad such,
       When nothing you mar but the year can mend!
     But a last leaf—fear to touch.

XLIII. Yet should it unfasten itself and fall
        Eddying down till it find your face
      At some slight wind—(best chance of all!)
        Be your heart henceforth its dwelling-place
      You trembled to forestal!

XLIV. Worth how well, those dark grey eyes,
       —That hair so dark and dear, how worth
     That a man should strive and agonise,
       And taste a very hell on earth
     For the hope of such a prize!

XLV. Oh, you might have turned and tried a man,
      Set him a space to weary and wear,
    And prove which suited more your plan,
      His best of hope or his worst despair,
    Yet end as he began.

XLVI. But you spared me this, like the heart you are,
       And filled my empty heart at a word.
     If you join two lives, there is oft a scar,
       They are one and one, with a shadowy third;
     One near one is too far.

XLVII. A moment after, and hands unseen
        Were hanging the night around us fast.
      But we knew that a bar was broken between
        Life and life; we were mixed at last
      In spite of the mortal screen.

XLVIII. The forests had done it; there they stood--
    We caught for a second the powers at play;
They had mingled us so, for once and for good,
    Their work was done—we might go or stay,
They relapsed to their ancient mood.

XLIX. How the world is made for each of us!
    How all we perceive and know in it
Tends to some moment's product thus,
    When a soul declares itself—to wit,
By its fruit—the thing it does!

L. Be Hate that fruit or Love that fruit,
    It forwards the General Deed of Man,
And each of the Many helps to recruit
    The life of the race by a general plan,
Each living his own, to boot.

LI. I am named and known by that hour's feat,
    There took my station and degree.
So grew my own small life complete
    As nature obtained her best of me—
One born to love you, sweet!

LII. And to watch you sink by the fire-side **now**
    Back again, as you mutely sit
Musing by fire-light, that great brow
    And the spirit-small hand propping it
Yonder, my heart knows how!

LIII. So the earth has gained by one man more,
    And the gain of earth must be Heaven's gain too,
And the whole is well worth thinking o'er
    When the autumn comes: which I mean to do
One day, as I said before.

ANY WIFE TO ANY HUSBAND.

I. My love, this is the bitterest, that thou
    Who art all truth and who dost love me now
      As thine eyes say, as thy voice breaks to say—
Should'st love so truly and could'st love me still
A whole long life through, had but love its will,
    Would death that leads me from thee brook delay!

II. I have but to be by thee, and thy hand
    Would never let mine go, thy heart withstand
       The beating of my heart to reach its place.
    When should I look for thee and feel thee gone?
    When cry for the old comfort and find none?
       Never, I know! Thy soul is in thy face.

III. Oh, I should fade—'tis willed so! might I save,
    Gladly I would, whatever beauty gave
       Joy to thy sense, for that was precious too.
    It is not to be granted. But the soul
    Whence the love comes, all ravage leaves that whole;
       Vainly the flesh fades—soul makes all things new.

IV. And 'twould not be because my eye grew dim
    Thou could'st not find the love there, thanks to Him
       Who never is dishonoured in the spark
    He gave us from his fire of fires, and bade
    Remember whence it sprang nor be afraid
       While that burns on, though all the rest grow dark.

V. So, how thou would'st be perfect, white and clean
    Outside as inside, soul and soul's demesne
       Alike, this body given to show it by!
    Oh, three-parts through the worst of life's abyss,
    What plaudits from the next world after this,
       Could'st thou repeat a stroke and gain the sky!

VI. And is it not the bitterer to think
    That, disengage our hands and thou wilt sink
       Although thy love was love in very deed?
    I know that nature! Pass a festive day
    Thou dost not throw its relic-flower away
       Nor bid its music's loitering echo speed.

VII. Thou let'st the stranger's glove lie where it fell;
    If old things remain old things all is well,
       For thou art grateful as becomes man best:
    And hadst thou only heard me play one tune,
    Or viewed me from a window, not so soon
       With thee would such things fade as with the rest.

VIII. I seem to see! we meet and part: 'tis brief:
    The book I opened keeps a folded leaf,

The very chair I sat on, breaks the rank;
That is a portrait of me on the wall—
Three lines, my face comes at so slight a call;
   And for all this, one little hour's to thank.

IX. But now, because the hour through years was fixed,
Because our inmost beings met and mixed,
   Because thou once hast loved me—wilt thou dare
Say to thy soul and Who may list beside,
"Therefore she is immortally my bride,
   Chance cannot change that love, nor time impair.

X. "So, what if in the dusk of life that's left,
I, a tired traveller, of my sun bereft,
   Look from my path when, mimicking the same,
The fire-fly glimpses past me, come and gone?
—Where was it till the sunset? where anon
   It will be at the sunrise! what's to blame?"

XI. Is it so helpful to thee? canst thou take
The mimic up, nor, for the true thing's sake,
   Put gently by such efforts at a beam?
Is the remainder of the way so long
Thou need'st the little solace, thou the strong?
   Watch out thy watch, let weak ones doze and dream!

XII. "—Ah, but the fresher faces! Is it true,"
Thou'lt ask, "some eyes are beautiful and new?
   Some hair,—how can one choose but grasp such
      wealth?
And if a man would press his lips to lips
Fresh as the wilding hedge-rose-cup there slips
   The dew-drop out of, must it be by stealth?

XIII. "It cannot change the love kept still for Her,
Much more than, such a picture to prefer
   Passing a day with, to a room's bare side.
The painted form takes nothing she possessed,
Yet while the Titian's Venus lies at rest
   A man looks.   Once more, what is there to chide?

XIV. So must I see, from where I sit and watch,
My own self sell myself, my hand attach

Its warrant to the very thefts from me—
Thy singleness of soul that made me proud,
Thy purity of heart I loved aloud,
    Thy man's truth I was bold to bid God see!

xv. Love so, then, if thou wilt! Give all thou canst
Away to the new faces—disentranced—
    (Say it and think it) obdurate no more,
Re-issue looks and words from the old mint—
Pass them afresh, no matter whose the print
    Image and superscription once they bore!

xvi. Re-coin thyself and give it them to spend,—
It all comes to the same thing at the end,
    Since mine thou wast, mine art, and mine shalt be,
Faithful or faithless, sealing up the sum
Or lavish of my treasure, thou must come
    Back to the heart's place here I keep for thee!

xvii. Only, why should it be with stain at all?
Why must I, 'twixt the leaves of coronal,
    Put any kiss of pardon on thy brow?
Why need the other women know so much
And talk together, " Such the look and such
    The smile he used to love with, then as now!"

xviii. Might I die last and shew thee! Should I find
Such hardship in the few years left behind,
    If free to take and light my lamp, and go
Into thy tomb, and shut the door and sit
Seeing thy face on those four sides of it
    The better that they are so blank, I know!

xix. Why, time was what I wanted, to turn o'er
Within my mind each look, get more and more
    By heart each word, too much to learn at first,
And join thee all the fitter for the pause
'Neath the low door-way's lintel. That were cause
    For lingering, though thou calledst, if I durst!

xx. And yet thou art the nobler of us two.
What dare I dream of, that thou canst not do,
    Outstripping my ten small steps with one stride?
I'll say then, here's a trial and a task—
Is it to bear?—if easy, I'll not ask—
    Though love fail, I can trust on in thy pride.

xxi. Pride?—when those eyes forestal the life behind
      The death I have to go through!—when I find,
         Now that I want thy help most, all of thee!
      What did I fear?   Thy love shall hold me fast
      Until the little minute's sleep is past
         And I wake saved.—And yet, it will not be!

AN EPISTLE

CONTAINING THE STRANGE MEDICAL EXPERIENCE OF KARSHISH, THE ARAB PHYSICIAN.

KARSHISH, the picker-up of learning's crumbs,
The not-incurious in God's handiwork
(This man's-flesh He hath admirably made,
Blown like a bubble, kneaded like a paste,
To coop up and keep down on earth a space
That puff of vapour from his mouth, man's soul)
—To Abib, all-sagacious in our art,
Breeder in me of what poor skill I boast,
Like me inquisitive how pricks and cracks
Befall the flesh through too much stress and strain,
Whereby the wily vapour fain would slip
Back and rejoin its source before the term,—
And aptest in contrivance, under God,
To baffle it by deftly stopping such:—
The vagrant Scholar to his Sage at home
Sends greeting (health and knowledge, fame with peace),
Three samples of true snake-stone—rarer still,
One of the other sort, the melon-shaped,
(But fitter, pounded fine, for charms than drugs)
And writeth now the twenty-second time.

   My journeyings were brought to Jericho,
Thus I resume. Who studious in our art
Shall count a little labour unrepaid?
I have shed sweat enough, left flesh and bone
On many a flinty furlong of this land.
Also the country-side is all on fire
With rumours of a marching hitherward—
Some say Vespasian cometh, some, his son.
A black lynx snarled and pricked a tufted ear;

Lust of my blood inflamed his yellow balls:
I cried and threw my staff and he was gone.
Twice have the robbers stripped and beaten me,
And once a town declared me for a spy,
But at the end, I reach Jerusalem,
Since this poor covert where I pass the night,
This Bethany, lies scarce the distance thence
A man with plague-sores at the third degree
Runs till he drops down dead.   Thou laughest here!
'Sooth, it elates me, thus reposed and safe,
To void the stuffing of my travel-scrip
And share with thee whatever Jewry yields.
A viscid choler is observable
In tertians, I was nearly bold to say,
And falling-sickness hath a happier cure
Than our school wots of: there's a spider here
Weaves no web, watches on the ledge of tombs,
Sprinkled with mottles on an ash-grey back;
Take five and drop them . . . but who knows his mind,
The Syrian run-a-gate I trust this to?
His service payeth me a sublimate
Blown up his nose to help the ailing eye.
Best wait: I reach Jerusalem at morn,
There set in order my experiences,
Gather what most deserves and give thee all—
Or I might add, Judea's gum-tragacanth
Scales off in purer flakes, shines clearer-grained,
Cracks 'twixt the pestle and the porphyry,
In fine exceeds our produce.   Scalp-disease
Confounds me, crossing so with leprosy—
Thou hadst admired one sort I gained at Zoar—
But zeal outruns discretion.   Here I end.

   Yet stay: my Syrian blinketh gratefully,
Protesteth his devotion is my price—
Suppose I write what harms not, though he steal?
I half resolve to tell thee, yet I blush,
What set me off a-writing first of all.
An itch I had, a sting to write, a tang!
For, be it this town's barrenness—or else
The Man had something in the look of him—
His case has struck me far more than 'tis worth.
So, pardon if—(lest presently I lose

In the great press of novelty at hand
The care and pains this somehow stole from me)
I bid thee take the thing while fresh in mind,
Almost in sight—for, wilt thou have the truth?
The very man is gone from me but now,
Whose ailment is the subject of discourse.
Thus then, and let thy better wit help all.

    'Tis but a case of mania—subinduced
By epilepsy, at the turning-point
Of trance prolonged unduly some three days,
When by the exhibition of some drug
Or spell, exorcisation, stroke of art
Unknown to me and which 'twere well to know,
The evil thing out-breaking all at once
Left the man whole and sound of body indeed,—
But, flinging, so to speak, life's gates too wide,
Making a clear house of it too suddenly,
The first conceit that entered pleased to write
Whatever it was minded on the wall
So plainly at that vantage, as it were,
(First come, first served) that nothing subsequent
Attaineth to erase the fancy-scrawls
Which the returned and new-established soul
Hath gotten now so thoroughly by heart
That henceforth she will read or these or none.
And first—the man's own firm conviction rests
That he was dead (in fact they buried him)
That he was dead and then restored to life
By a Nazarene physician of his tribe:
—'Sayeth, the same bade " Rise," and he did rise.
" Such cases are diurnal," thou wilt cry.
Not so this figment!—not, that such a fume,
Instead of giving way to time and health,
Should eat itself into the life of life,
As saffron tingeth flesh, blood, bones and all!
For see, how he takes up the after-life.
The man—it is one Lazarus a Jew,
Sanguine, proportioned, fifty years of age,
The body's habit wholly laudable,
As much, indeed, beyond the common health
As he were made and put aside to show.
Think, could we penetrate by any drug

And bathe the wearied soul and worried flesh,
And bring it clear and fair, by three days sleep!
Whence has the man the balm that brightens all?
This grown man eyes the world now like a child.
Some elders of his tribe, I should premise,
Led in their friend, obedient as a sheep,
To bear my inquisition.   While they spoke,
Now sharply, now with sorrow,—told the case,—
He listened not except I spoke to him,
But folded his two hands and let them talk,
Watching the flies that buzzed: and yet no fool.
And that's a sample how his years must go.
Look if a beggar, in fixed middle-life,
Should find a treasure, can he use the same
With straightened habits and with tastes starved small,
And take at once to his impoverished brain
The sudden element that changes things,
—That sets the undreamed-of rapture at his hand,
And puts the cheap old joy in the scorned dust?
Is he not such an one as moves to mirth—
Warily parsimonious, when's no need,
Wasteful as drunkenness at undue times?
All prudent counsel as to what befits
The golden mean, is lost on such an one.
The man's fantastic will is the man's law.
So here—we'll call the treasure knowledge, say—
Increased beyond the fleshy faculty—
Heaven opened to a soul while yet on earth,
Earth forced on a soul's use while seeing Heaven.
The man is witless of the size, the sum,
The value in proportion of all things,
Or whether it be little or be much.
Discourse to him of prodigious armaments
Assembled to besiege his city now,
And of the passing of a mule with gourds—
'Tis one!   Then take it on the other side,
Speak of some trifling fact—he will gaze rapt
With stupor at its very littleness—
(Far as I see) as if in that indeed
He caught prodigious import, whole results;
And so will turn to us the bystanders
In ever the same stupor (note this point)
That we too see not with his opened eyes!
II—*K 42

Wonder and doubt come wrongly into play,
Preposterously, at cross purposes.
Should his child sicken unto death,—why, look
For scarce abatement of his cheerfulness,
Or pretermission of his daily craft—
While a word, gesture, glance, from that same child
At play or in the school or laid asleep,
Will start him to an agony of fear,
Exasperation, just as like! demand
The reason why—"'tis but a word," object—
" A gesture "—he regards thee as our lord
Who lived there in the pyramid alone,
Looked at us, dost thou mind, when being young
We both would unadvisedly recite
Some charm's beginning, from that book of his,
Able to bid the sun throb wide and burst
All into stars, as suns grown old are wont.
Thou and the child have each a veil alike
Thrown o'er your heads from under which ye both
Stretch your blind hands and trifle with a match
Over a mine of Greek fire, did ye know!
He holds on firmly to some thread of life—
(It is the life to lead perforcedly)
Which runs across some vast distracting orb
Of glory on either side that meagre thread,
Which, conscious of, he must not enter yet—
The spiritual life around the earthly life!
The law of that is known to him as this—
His heart and brain move there, his feet stay here.
So is the man perplext with impulses
Sudden to start off crosswise, not straight on,
Proclaiming what is Right and Wrong across—
And not along—this black thread through the blaze—
" It should be " balked by " here it cannot be."
And oft the man's soul springs into his face
As if he saw again and heard again
His sage that bade him " Rise " and he did rise.
Something—a word, a tick of the blood within
Admonishes—then back he sinks at once
To ashes, that was very fire before,
In sedulous recurrence to his trade
Whereby he earneth him the daily bread—
And studiously the humbler for that pride,

Professedly the faultier that he knows
God's secret, while he holds the thread of life.
Indeed the especial marking of the man
Is prone submission to the Heavenly will—
Seeing it, what it is, and why it is.
'Sayeth, he will wait patient to the last
For that same death which will restore his being
To equilibrium, body loosening soul
Divorced even now by premature full growth:
He will live, nay, it pleaseth him to live
So long as God please, and just how God please.
He even seeketh not to please God more
(Which meaneth, otherwise) than as God please.
Hence I perceive not he affects to preach
The doctrine of his sect whate'er it be—
Make proselytes as madmen thirst to do.
How can he give his neighbour the real ground,
His own conviction? ardent as he is—
Call his great truth a lie, why still the old
" Be it as God please " reassureth him.
I probed the sore as thy disciple should—
" How, beast," said I, " this stolid carelessness
Sufficeth thee, when Rome is on her march
To stamp out like a little spark thy town,
Thy tribe, thy crazy tale and thee at once? "
He merely looked with his large eyes on me.
The man is apathetic, you deduce?
Contrariwise he loves both old and young,
Able and weak—affects the very brutes
And birds—how say I? flowers of the field—
As a wise workman recognises tools
In a master's workshop, loving what they make.
Thus is the man as harmless as a lamb:
Only impatient, let him do his best,
At ignorance and carelessness and sin—
An indignation which is promptly curbed.
As when in certain travels I have feigned
To be an ignoramus in our art
According to some preconceived design,
And happed to hear the land's practitioners
Steeped in conceit sublimed by ignorance,
Prattle fantastically on disease,
Its cause and cure—and I must hold my peace!

Thou wilt object—why have I not ere this
Sought out the sage himself, the Nazarene
Who wrought this cure, enquiring at the source,
Conferring with the frankness that befits?
Alas! it grieveth me, the learned leech
Perished in a tumult many years ago,
Accused,—our learning's fate,—of wizardry.
Rebellion, to the setting up a rule
And creed prodigious as described to me.
His death which happened when the earthquake fell
(Prefiguring, as soon appeared, the loss
To occult learning in our lord the sage
That lived there in the pyramid alone)
Was wrought by the mad people—that's their wont—
On vain recourse, as I conjecture it,
To his tried virtue, for miraculous help—
How could he stop the earthquake?   That's their way!
The other imputations must be lies:
But take one—though I loathe to give it thee,
In mere respect to any good man's fame!
(And after all our patient Lazarus
Is stark mad—should we count on what he says?
Perhaps not—though in writing to a leech
'Tis well to keep back nothing of a case.)
This man so cured regards the curer then,
As—God forgive me—who but God himself,
Creater and Sustainer of the world,
That came and dwelt in flesh on it awhile!
—'Sayeth that such an One was born and lived,
Taught, healed the sick, broke bread at his own house,
Then died, with Lazarus by, for ought I know,
And yet was . . . what I said nor choose repeat,
And must have so avouched himself, in fact,
In hearing of this very Lazarus
Who saith—but why all this of what he saith?
Why write of trivial matters, things of price
Calling at every moment for remark?
I noticed on the margin of a pool
Blue-flowering borage, the Aleppo sort,
Aboundeth, very nitrous.   It is strange!

Thy pardon for this long and tedious case,
Which, now that I review it, needs must seem

Unduly dwelt on, prolixly set forth.
Nor I myself discern in what is writ
Good cause for the peculiar interest
And awe indeed this man has touched me with.
Perhaps the journey's end, the weariness
Had wrought upon me first.   I met him thus—
I crossed a ridge of short sharp broken hills
Like an old lion's cheek-teeth.   Out there came
A moon made like a face with certain spots
Multiform, manifold, and menacing:
Then a wind rose behind me.   So we met
In this old sleepy town at unaware,
The man and I.   I send thee what is writ.
Regard it as a chance, a matter risked
To this ambiguous Syrian—he may lose,
Or steal, or give it thee with equal good.
Jerusalem's repose shall make amends
For time this letter wastes, thy time and mine,
Till when, once more thy pardon and farewell!

The very God! think, Abib; dost thou think?
So, the All-Great, were the All-Loving too—
So, through the thunder comes a human voice
Saying, "O heart I made, a heart beats here!
Face, my hands fashioned, see it in myself.
Thou hast no power nor may'st conceive of mine,
But love I gave thee, with Myself to love,
And thou must love me who have died for thee!"
The madman saith He said so: it is strange.

MESMERISM.

    I. ALL I believed is true!
        I am able yet
        All I want to get
      By a method as strange as new:
      Dare I trust the same to you?

    II. If at night, when the doors are shut,
        And the wood-worm picks,
        And the death-watch ticks,
      And the bar has a flag of smut,
      And a cat's in the water-butt—

III. And the socket floats and flares,
    And the house-beams groan,
    And a foot unknown
Is surmised on the garret-stairs,
And the locks slip unawares—

IV. And the spider, to serve his ends,
    By a sudden thread,
    Arms and legs outspread,
On the table's midst descends,
Comes to find, God knows what friends!—

V. If since eve drew in, I say,
    I have sate and brought
    (So to speak) my thought
To bear on the woman away,
Till I felt my hair turn grey—

VI. Till I seemed to have and hold
    In the vacancy
    'Twixt the wall and me,
From the hair-plait's chestnut gold
To the foot in its muslin fold—

VII. Have and hold, then and there,
    Her, from head to foot,
    Breathing and mute,
Passive and yet aware,
In the grasp of my steady stare—

VIII. Hold and have, there and then,
    All her body and soul
    That completes my Whole,
All that women add to men,
In the clutch of my steady ken—

IX. Having and holding, till
    I imprint her fast
    On the void at last
As the sun does whom he will
By the calotypist's skill—

X. Then,—if my heart's strength serve,
    And through all and each
    Of the veils I reach
To her soul and never swerve,
Knitting an iron nerve—

XI. Commanding that to advance
      And inform the shape
       Which has made escape
   And before my countenance
  Answers me glance for glance—

XII. I, still with a gesture fit
      Of my hands that best
       Do my soul's behest,
   Pointing the power from it,
  While myself do steadfast sit—

XIII. Steadfast and still the same
      On my object bent
       While the hands give vent
   To my ardour and my aim
  And break into very flame—

XIV. Then, I reach, I must believe,
      Not her soul in vain,
       For to me again
   It reaches, and past retrieve
  Is wound in the toils I weave—

XV. And must follow as I require
      As befits a thrall,
       Bringing flesh and all,
   Essence and earth-attire,
  To the source of the tractile fire—

XVI. Till the house called hers, not mine,
      With a growing weight
       Seems to suffocate
   If she break not its leaden line
  And escape from its close confine—

XVII. Out of doors into the night!
      On to the maze
       Of the wild wood-ways,
   Not turning to left or right
  From the pathway, blind with sight—

XVIII. Making thro' rain and wind
      O'er the broken shrubs,
       'Twixt the stems and stubs,
   With a still composed strong mind,
  Not a care for the world behind—

XIX. Swifter and still more swift,
　　　As the crowding peace
　　　Doth to joy increase
　　In the wide blind eyes uplift,
　　Thro' the darkness and the drift!

XX. While I—to the shape, I too
　　　Feel my soul dilate
　　　Nor a whit abate
　　And relax not a gesture due
　　As I see my belief come true—

XXI. For there! have I drawn or no
　　　Life to that lip?
　　　Do my fingers dip
　　In a flame which again they throw
　　On the cheek that breaks a-glow?

XXII. Ha! was the hair so first?
　　　What, unfilleted,
　　　Made alive and spread
　　Through the void with a rich outburst,
　　Chestnut gold-interspersed!

XXIII. Like the doors of a casket-shrine,
　　　See, on either side,
　　　Her two arms divide
　　Till the heart betwixt makes sign,
　　Take me, for I am thine!

XXIV. Now—now—the door is heard
　　　Hark! the stairs and near—
　　　Nearer—and here—
　　Now! and at call the third
　　She enters without a word.

XXV. On doth she march and on
　　　To the fancied shape—
　　　It is past escape
　　Herself, now—the dream is done
　　And the shadow and she are one.

XXVI. First I will pray. Do Thou
　　　That ownest the soul,
　　　Yet wilt grant controul
　　To another nor disallow
　　For a time, restrain me now!

XXVII. I admonish me while I may,
    Not to squander guilt,
    Since require Thou wilt
At my hand its price one day!
What the price is, who can say?

A SERENADE AT THE VILLA.

I. THAT was I, you heard last night
    When there rose no moon at all,
Nor, to pierce the strained and tight
    Tent of heaven, a planet small:
Life was dead, and so was light.

II. Not a twinkle from the fly,
    Not a glimmer from the worm.
When the crickets stopped their cry,
    When the owls forbore a term,
You heard music; that was I.

III. Earth turned in her sleep with pain,
    Sultrily suspired for proof:
In at heaven, and out again,
    Lightning!—where it broke the roof,
Bloodlike, some few drops of rain.

IV. What they could my words expressed,
    O my love, my all, my one!
Singing helped the verses best,
    And when singing's best was done,
To my lute I left the rest.

V. So wore night; the east was grey,
    White the broad-faced hemlock flowers;
Soon would come another day;
    Ere its first of heavy hours
Found me, I had past away.

VI. What became of all the hopes,
    Words and song and lute as well?
Say, this struck you—" When life gropes
    Feebly for the path where fell
Light last on the evening slopes,

VII. " One friend in that path shall be
    To secure my steps from wrong;
One to count night day for me,
    Patient through the watches long,
Serving most with none to see."

VIII. Never say—as something bodes—
    " So the worst has yet a worse!
When life halts 'neath double loads,
    Better the task-master's curse
Than such music on the roads!

IX. " When no moon succeeds the sun,
    Nor can pierce the midnight's tent
Any star, the smallest one,
    While some drops, where lightning went,
Show the final storm begun—

X. " When the fire-fly hides its spot,
    When the garden-voices fail
In the darkness thick and hot,—
    Shall another voice avail,
That shape be where those are not?

XI. " Has some plague a longer lease
    Proffering its help uncouth?
Can't one even die in peace?
    As one shuts one's eyes on youth,
Is that face the last one sees? "

XII. Oh, how dark your villa was,
    Windows fast and obdurate!
How the garden grudged me grass
    Where I stood—the iron gate
Ground its teeth to let me pass!

MY STAR.

ALL that I know
    Of a certain star,
Is, it can throw
    (Like the angled spar)
Now a dart of red,
    Now a dart of blue,
Till my friends have said
    They would fain see, too,

My star that dartles the red and the blue!
Then it stops like a bird,—like a flower, hangs furled;
  They must solace themselves with the Saturn above it.
What matter to me if their star is a world?
  Mine has opened its soul to me; therefore I love it.

INSTANS TYRANNUS.

I. Of the million or two, more or less,
  I rule and possess,
One man, for some cause undefined,
  Was least to my mind.

II. I struck him, he grovelled of course—
  For, what was his force?
I pinned him to earth with my weight
  And persistence of hate—
And he lay, would not moan, would not curse,
  As if lots might be worse.

III. " Were the object less mean, would he stand
  At the swing of my hand!
For obscurity helps him and blots
  The hole where he squats."
So I set my five wits on the stretch
  To inveigle the wretch.
All in vain! gold and jewels I threw,
  Still he couched there perdue.
I tempted his blood and his flesh,
  Hid in roses my mesh,
Choicest cates and the flagon's best spilth—
  Still he kept to his filth!

IV. Had he kith now or kin, were access
  To his heart, if I press—
Just a son or a mother to seize—
  No such booty as these!
Were it simply a friend to pursue
  'Mid my million or two,
Who could pay me in person or pelf
  What he owes me himself.
No! I could not but smile through my chafe—
  For the fellow lay safe

As his mates do, the midge and the nit,
—Through minuteness, to wit.
Then a humour more great took its place
At the thought of his face,
The droop, the low cares of the mouth,
The trouble uncouth

v. 'Twixt the brows, all that air one is fain
To put out of its pain—
And, no, I admonished myself,
" Is one mocked by an elf,
Is one baffled by toad or by rat?
The gravamen's in that!
How the lion, who crouches to suit
His back to my foot,
Would admire that I stand in debate!
But the Small is the Great
If it vexes you,—that is the thing!
Toad or rat vex the King?
Though I waste half my realm to unearth
Toad or rat, 'tis well worth! "

vi. So I soberly laid my last plan
To extinguish the man.
Round his creep-hole,—with never a break
Ran my fires for his sake;
Over-head, did my thunders combine
With my under-ground mine:
Till I looked from my labour content
To enjoy the event.

vii. When sudden . . . how think ye, the end?
Did I say " without friend? "
Say rather, from marge to blue marge
The whole sky grew his targe
With the sun's self for visible boss,
While an Arm ran across
Which the earth heaved beneath like a breast
Where the wretch was safe prest!
Do you see? just my vengeance complete,
The man sprang to his feet,
Stood erect, caught at God's skirts and prayed!
—So, I was afraid!

A PRETTY WOMAN.

I. THAT fawn-skin-dappled hair of hers,
      And the blue eye
      Dear and dewy,
And that infantine fresh air of hers!

II. To think men cannot take you, Sweet,
      And enfold you,
      Ay, and hold you,
And so keep you what they make you, Sweet!

III. You like us for a glance, you know—
      For a word's sake,
      Or a sword's sake,
All's the same, whate'er the chance, you know.

IV. And in turn we make you ours, we say—
      You and youth too,
      Eyes and mouth too,
All the face composed of flowers, we say.

V. All's our own, to make the most of, Sweet—
      Sing and say for,
      Watch and pray for,
Keep a secret or go boast of, Sweet.

VI. But for loving, why, you would not, Sweet,
      Though we prayed you,
      Paid you, brayed you
In a mortar—for you could not, Sweet.

VII. So, we leave the sweet face fondly there—
      Be its beauty
      Its sole duty!
Let all hope of grace beyond, lie there!

VIII. And while the face lies quiet there,
      Who shall wonder
      That I ponder
A conclusion?   I will try it there.

IX. As,—why must one, for the love forgone,
    Scout mere liking?
    Thunder-striking
Earth,—the heaven, we looked above for, gone!

X. Why with beauty, needs there money be—
    Love with liking?
    Crush the fly-king
In his gauze, because no honey bee?

XI. May not liking be so simple-sweet,
    If love grew there
    'Twould undo there
All that breaks the cheek to dimples sweet?

XII. Is the creature too imperfect, say?
    Would you mend it
    And so end it?
Since not all addition perfects aye!

XIII. Or is it of its kind, perhaps,
    Just perfection—
    Whence, rejection
Of a grace not to its mind, perhaps?

XIV. Shall we burn up, tread that face at once
    Into tinder,
    And so hinder
Sparks from kindling all the place at once?

XV. Or else kiss away one's soul on her?
    Your love-fancies!—
    A sick man sees
Truer, when his hot eyes roll on her!

XVI. Thus the craftsman thinks to grace the rose,—
    Plucks a mould-flower
    For his gold flower,
Uses fine things that efface the rose.

XVII. Rosy rubies make its cup more rose,
    Precious metals
    Ape the petals,—
Last, some old king locks it up, morose!

XVIII. Then, how grace a rose?   I know a way!
Leave it rather.
Must you gather?
Smell, kiss, wear it—at last, throw away!

"CHILDE ROLAND TO THE DARK TOWER CAME."
(See Edgar's Song in " LEAR.")

I.

My first thought was, he lied in every word,
That hoary cripple, with malicious eye
Askance to watch the working of his lie
On mine, and mouth scarce able to afford
Suppression of the glee that pursed and scored
Its edge at one more victim gained thereby.

II.

What else should he be set for, with his staff?
What, save to waylay with his lies, ensnare
All travellers that might find him posted there,
And ask the road?   I guessed what skull-like laugh
Would break, what crutch 'gin write my epitaph
For pastime in the dusty thoroughfare,

III.

If at his counsel I should turn aside
Into that ominous tract which, all agree,
Hides the Dark Tower.   Yet acquiescingly
I did turn as he pointed; neither pride
Nor hope rekindling at the end descried,
So much as gladness that some end should be.

IV.

For, what with my whole world-wide wandering,
What with my search drawn out thro' years, my hope
Dwindled into a ghost not fit to cope
With that obstreperous joy success would bring,—
I hardly tried now to rebuke the spring
My heart made, finding failure in its scope.

V.

As when a sick man very near to death
Seems dead indeed, and feels begin and end
The tears and takes the farewell of each friend,

And hears one bid the other go, draw breath
Freelier outside, (" since all is o'er," he saith,
    " And the blow fall'n no grieving can amend ")

VI.

While some discuss if near the other graves
    Be room enough for this, and when a day
    Suits best for carrying the corpse away,
With care about the banners, scarves and staves,—
And still the man hears all, and only craves
    He may not shame such tender love and stay.

VII.

Thus, I had so long suffered in this quest,
    Heard failure prophesied so oft, been writ
    So many times among " The Band "—to wit,
The knights who to the Dark Tower's search addressed
Their steps—that just to fail as they, seemed best,
    And all the doubt was now—should I be fit.

VIII.

So, quiet as despair, I turned from him,
    That hateful cripple, out of his highway
    Into the path he pointed.   All the day
Had been a dreary one at best, and dim
Was settling to its close, yet shot one grim
    Red leer to see the plain catch its estray.

IX.

For mark! no sooner was I fairly found
    Pledged to the plain, after a pace or two,
    Than pausing to throw backward a last view
To the safe road, 'twas gone! grey plain all round!
Nothing but plain to the horizon's bound.
    I might go on; nought else remained to do.

X.

So on I went.   I think I never saw
    Such starved ignoble nature; nothing throve:
    For flowers—as well expect a cedar grove!
But cockle, spurge, according to their law
Might propagate their kind, with none to awe,
    You'd think: a burr had been a treasure-trove.

XI.

No! penury, inertness, and grimace,
  In some strange sort, were the land's portion. "See
  Or shut your eyes"—said Nature peevishly—
" It nothing skills: I cannot help my case:
The Judgment's fire alone can cure this place,
  Calcine its clods and set my prisoners free."

XII.

If there pushed any ragged thistle-stalk
  Above its mates, the head was chopped—the bents
  Were jealous else. What made those holes and rents
In the dock's harsh swarth leaves—bruised as to baulk
All hope of greenness? 'tis a brute must walk
  Pashing their life out, with a brute's intents.

XIII.

As for the grass, it grew as scant as hair
  In leprosy—thin dry blades pricked the mud
  Which underneath looked kneaded up with blood,
One stiff blind horse, his every bone a-stare,
Stood stupified, however he came there—
  Thrust out past service from the devil's stud!

XIV.

Alive? he might be dead for all I know,
  With that red gaunt and colloped neck a-strain,
  And shut eyes underneath the rusty mane.
Seldom went such grotesqueness with such woe:
I never saw a brute I hated so—
  He must be wicked to deserve such pain.

XV.

I shut my eyes and turned them on my heart.
  As a man calls for wine before he fights,
  I asked one draught of earlier, happier sights
Ere fitly I could hope to play my part.
Think first, fight afterwards—the soldier's art:
  One taste of the old times sets all to rights!

XVI.

Not it! I fancied Cuthbert's reddening face
  Beneath its garniture of curly gold,
  Dear fellow, till I almost felt him fold

An arm in mine to fix me to the place,
That way he used.   Alas! one night's disgrace!
  Out went my heart's new fire and left it cold.

XVII.

Giles, then, the soul of honour—there he stands
   Frank as ten years ago when knighted first.
   What honest men should dare (he said) he durst.
Good—but the scene shifts—faugh! what hangman's hands
Pin to his breast a parchment? his own bands
   Read it.   Poor traitor, spit upon and curst!

XVIII.

Better this present than a past like that—
   Back therefore to my darkening path again.
   No sound, no sight as far as eye could strain.
Will the night send a howlet or a bat?
I asked: when something on the dismal flat
   Came to arrest my thoughts and change their train.

XIX.

A sudden little river crossed my path
   As unexpected as a serpent comes.
   No sluggish tide congenial to the glooms—
This, as it frothed by, might have been a bath
For the fiend's glowing hoof—to see the wrath
   Of its black eddy bespate with flakes and spumes.

XX.

So petty yet so spiteful! all along,
   Low scrubby alders kneeled down over it;
   Drenched willows flung them headlong in a fit
Of mute despair, a suicidal throng:
The river which had done them all the wrong,
   Whate'er that was, rolled by, deterred no whit.

XXI.

Which, while I forded,—good saints, how I feared
   To set my foot upon a dead man's cheek,
   Each step, or feel the spear I thrust to seek
For hollows, tangled in his hair or beard!
—It may have been a water-rat I speared,
   But, ugh; it sounded like a baby's shriek.

XXII.

Glad was I when I reached the other bank.
  Now for a better country.   Vain presage!
  Who were the strugglers, what war did they wage
Whose savage trample thus could pad the dank
Soil to a plash? toads in a poisoned tank,
  Or wild cats in a red-hot iron cage—

XXIII.

The fight must so have seemed in that fell cirque.
  What kept them there, with all the plain to choose?
  No foot-print leading to that horrid mews,
None out of it: mad brewage set to work
Their brains, no doubt, like galley-slaves the Turk
  Pits for his pastime, Christians against Jews.

XXIV.

And more than that—a furlong on—why, there!
  What bad use was that engine for, that wheel,
  Or brake, not wheel—that harrow fit to reel
Men's bodies out like silk? with all the air
Of Tophet's tool, on earth left unaware,
  Or brought to sharpen its rusty teeth of steel.

XXV.

Then came a bit of stubbed ground, once a wood,
  Next a marsh, it would seem, and now mere earth
  Desperate and done with; (so a fool finds mirth,
Makes a thing and then mars it, till his mood
Changes and off he goes!) within a rood
  Bog, clay and rubble, sand and stark black dearth.

XXVI.

Now blotches rankling, coloured gay and grim,
  Now patches where some leanness of the soil's
  Broke into moss or substances like boils;
Then came some palsied oak, a cleft in him
Like a distorted mouth that splits its rim
  Gaping at death, and dies while it recoils.

XXVII.

And just as far as ever from the end!
  Nought in the distance but the evening, nought
  To point my footstep further!   At the thought,

A great black bird, Apollyon's bosom-friend,
Sailed past, nor beat his wide wing dragon-penned
   That brushed my cap—perchance the guide I sought.

XXVIII.

For looking up, aware I somehow grew,
   'Spite of the dusk, the plain had given place
   All round to mountains—with such name to grace
Mere ugly heights and heaps now stol'n in view.
How thus they had surprised me,—solve it, you!
   How to get from them was no plainer case.

XXIX.

Yet half I seemed to recognise some trick
   Of mischief happened to me, God knows when—
   In a bad dream perhaps.   Here ended, then,
Progress this way.   When, in the very nick
Of giving up, one time more, came a click
   As when a trap shuts—you're inside the den!

XXX.

Burningly it came on me all at once,
   This was the place! those two hills on the right
   Crouched like two bulls locked horn in horn in fight—
While to the left, a tall scalped mountain . . . Dunce,
Fool, to be dozing at the very nonce,
   After a life spent training for the sight!

XXXI.

What in the midst lay but the Tower itself?
   The round squat turret, blind as the fool's heart,
   Built of brown stone, without a counterpart
In the whole world.   The tempest's mocking elf
Points to the shipman thus the unseen shelf
   He strikes on, only when the timbers start.

XXXII.

Not see? because of night perhaps?—Why, day
   Came back again for that! before it left,
   The dying sunset kindled through a cleft:
The hills, like giants at a hunting, lay—
Chin upon hand, to see the game at bay,—
   " Now stab and end the creature—to the heft!"

XXXIII.

Not hear? when noise was everywhere? it tolled
  Increasing like a bell. Names in my ears,
  Of all the lost adventurers my peers,—
How such a one was strong, and such was bold,
And such was fortunate, yet each of old
  Lost, lost! one moment knelled the woe of years.

XXXIV.

There they stood, ranged along the hill-sides—met
  To view the last of me, a living frame
  For one more picture; in a sheet of flame
I saw them and I knew them all. And yet
Dauntless the slug-horn to my lips I set
  And blew. "*Childe Roland to the Dark Tower came.*"

RESPECTABILITY.

I. DEAR, had the world in its caprice
      Deigned to proclaim " I know you both,
      Have recognised your plighted troth,
    Am sponsor for you—live in peace ! "—
    How many precious months and years
      Of youth had passed, that speed so fast,
      Before we found it out at last,
    The world, and what it fears?

II. How much of priceless life were spent
      With men that every virtue decks,
      And women models of their sex,
    Society's true ornament,—
    Ere we dared wander, nights like this,
      Thro' wind and rain, and watch the Seine,
      And feel the Boulevart break again
    To warmth and light and bliss?

III. I know! the world proscribes not love;
      Allows my finger to caress
      Your lip's contour and downiness,
    Provided it supply a glove.
    The world's good word!—the Institute!
      Guizot receives Montalembert!
      Eh? down the court three lampions flare—
    Put forward your best foot!

A LIGHT WOMAN.

I. So far as our story approaches the end,
    Which do you pity the most of us three?—
My friend, or the mistress of my friend
    With her wanton eyes, or me?

II. My friend was already too good to lose,
    And seemed in the way of improvement yet,
When she crossed his path with her hunting-noose
    And over him drew her net.

III. When I saw him tangled in her toils,
    A shame, said I, if she adds just him
To her nine-and-ninety other spoils,
    The hundredth, for a whim!

IV. And before my friend be wholly hers,
    How easy to prove to him, I said,
An eagle's the game her pride prefers,
    Though she snaps at the wren instead!

V. So I gave her eyes my own eyes to take,
    My hand sought her as in earnest need,
And round she turned for my noble sake,
    And gave me herself indeed.

VI. The eagle am I, with my fame in the world,
    The wren is he, with his maiden face.
—You look away and your lip is curled?
    Patience, a moment's space!

VII. For see—my friend goes shaking and white;
    He eyes me as the basilisk:
I have turned, it appears, his day to night,
    Eclipsing his sun's disc.

VIII. And I did it, he thinks, as a very thief:
    " Though I love her—that he comprehends—
One should master one's passions, (love, in chief)
    And be loyal to one's friends!"

IX. And she,—she lies in my hand as tame
  As a pear hung basking over a wall;
 Just a touch to try and off it came;
  'Tis mine,—can I let it fall?

X. With no mind to eat it, that's the worst!
  Were it thrown in the road, would the case assist?
 'Twas quenching a dozen blue-flies' thirst
  When I gave its stalk a twist.

XI. And I,—what I seem to my friend, you see—
  What I soon shall seem to his love, you guess.
 What I seem to myself, do you ask of me?
  No hero, I confess.

XII. 'Tis an awkward thing to play with souls,
  And matter enough to save one's own.
 Yet think of my friend, and the burning coals
  He played with for bits of stone!

XIII. One likes to show the truth for the truth;
  That the woman was light is very true:
 But suppose she says,—never mind that youth—
  What wrong have I done to you?

XIV. Well, any how, here the story stays,
  So far at least as I understand;
 And, Robert Browning, you writer of plays,
  Here's a subject made to your hand!

THE STATUE AND THE BUST.

THERE's a palace in Florence, the world knows well,
And a statue watches it from the square,
And this story of both do the townsmen tell.

Ages ago, a lady there,
At the farthest window facing the east
Asked, " Who rides by with the royal air? "

The brides-maids' prattle around her ceased;
She leaned forth, one on either hand;
They saw how the blush of the bride increased—

They felt by its beats her heart expand—
As one at each ear and both in a breath
Whispered, " The Great-Duke Ferdinand."

That selfsame instant, underneath,
The Duke rode past in his idle way,
Empty and fine like a swordless sheath.

Gay he rode, with a friend as gay,
Till he threw his head back—" Who is she? "
—" A Bride the Riccardi brings home to-day."

Hair in heaps laid heavily
Over a pale brow spirit-pure—
Carved like the heart of the coal-black tree,

Crisped like a war-steed's encolure—
Which vainly sought to dissemble her eyes
Of the blackest black our eyes endure.

And lo, a blade for a knight's emprise
Filled the fine empty sheath of a man,—
The Duke grew straightway brave and wise.

He looked at her, as a lover can;
She looked at him, as one who awakes,—
The past was a sleep, and her life began.

As love so ordered for both their sakes,
A feast was held that selfsame night
In the pile which the mighty shadow makes,

(For Via Larga is three-parts light,
But the Palace overshadows one,
Because of a crime which may God requite!

To Florence and God the wrong was done,
Through the first republic's murder there
By Cosimo and his cursed son.)

The Duke (with the statue's face in the square)
Turned in the midst of his multitude
At the bright approach of the bridal pair.

Face to face the lovers stood
A single minute and no more,
While the bridegroom bent as a man subdued—

Bowed till his bonnet brushed the floor—
For the Duke on the lady a kiss conferred,
As the courtly custom was of yore.

In a minute can lovers exchange a word?
If a word did pass, which I do not think,
Only one out of the thousand heard.

That was the bridegroom.   At day's brink
He and his bride were alone at last
In a bed-chamber by a taper's blink.

Calmly he said that her lot was cast,
That the door she had passed was shut on her
Till the final catafalk repassed.

The world meanwhile, its noise and stir,
Through a certain window facing the east
She might watch like a convent's chronicler.

Since passing the door might lead to a feast,
And a feast might lead to so much beside,
He, of many evils, chose the least.

" Freely I choose too," said the bride—
" Your window and its world suffice."
So replied the tongue, while the heart replied—

" If I spend the night with that devil twice,
May his window serve as my loop of hell
Whence a damned soul looks on Paradise!

" I fly to the Duke who loves me well,
Sit by his side and laugh at sorrow
Ere I count another ave-bell.

" 'Tis only the coat of a page to borrow,
And tie my hair in a horse-boy's trim,
And I save my soul—but not to-morrow "—

(She checked herself and her eye grew dim)—
" My father tarries to bless my state:
I must keep it one day more for him.

" Is one day more so long to wait?
Moreover the Duke rides past, I know—
We shall see each other, sure as fate."

She turned on her side and slept.   Just so!
So we resolve on a thing and sleep.
So did the lady, ages ago.

That night the Duke said, " Dear or cheap
As the cost of this cup of bliss may prove
To body or soul, I will drain it deep."

And on the morrow, bold with love,
He beckoned the bridegroom (close on call,
As his duty bade, by the Duke's alcove)

And smiled " 'Twas a very funeral
Your lady will think, this feast of ours,—
A shame to efface, whate'er befall!

" What if we break from the Arno bowers,
And let Petraja, cool and green,
Cure last night's fault with this morning's flowers? "

The bridegroom, not a thought to be seen
On his steady brow and quiet mouth,
Said, " Too much favour for me so mean!

" Alas! my lady leaves the south.
Each wind that comes from the Apennine
Is a menace to her tender youth.

" No way exists, the wise opine,
If she quits her palace twice this year,
To avert the flower of life's decline."

Quoth the Duke, " A sage and a kindly fear.
Moreover Petraja is cold this spring—
Be our feast to-night as usual here! "

And then to himself—" Which night shall bring
Thy bride to her lover's embraces, fool—
Or I am the fool, and thou art his king!

" Yet my passion must wait a night, nor cool—
For to-night the Envoy arrives from France,
Whose heart I unlock with thyself, my tool.

" I need thee still and might miss perchance.
To-day is not wholly lost, beside,
With its hope of my lady's countenance—

" For I ride—what should I do but ride?
And passing her palace, if I list,
May glance at its window—well betide! "

So said, so done: nor the lady missed
One ray that broke from the ardent brow,
Nor a curl of the lips where the spirit kissed.

Be sure that each renewed the vow,
No morrow's sun should arise and set
And leave them then as it left them now.

But next day passed, and next day yet,
With still fresh cause to wait one more
Ere each leaped over the parapet.

And still, as love's brief morning wore,
With a gentle start, half smile, half sigh,
They found love not as it seemed before.

They thought it would work infallibly,
But not in despite of heaven and earth—
The rose would blow when the storm passed by.

Meantime they could profit in winter's dearth
By winter's fruits that supplant the rose:
The world and its ways have a certain worth!

And to press a point while these oppose
Were a simple policy—best wait,
And lose no friends and gain no foes.

Meanwhile, worse fates than a lover's fate,
Who daily may ride and lean and look
Where his lady watches behind the grate!

And she—she watched the square like a book
Holding one picture and only one,
Which daily to find she undertook.

When the picture was reached the book was done,
And she turned from it all night to scheme
Of tearing it out for herself next sun.

Weeks grew months, years—gleam by gleam
The glory dropped from youth and love,
And both perceived they had dreamed a dream,

Which hovered as dreams do, still above,—
But who can take a dream for truth?
Oh, hide our eyes from the next remove!

One day as the lady saw her youth
Depart, and the silver thread that streaked
Her hair, and, worn by the serpent's tooth,

The brow so puckered, the chin so peaked,—
And wondered who the woman was,
So hollow-eyed and haggard-cheeked,

Fronting her silent in the glass—
" Summon here," she suddenly said,
" Before the rest of my old self pass,

" Him, the Carver, a hand to aid,
Who moulds the clay no love will change,
And fixes a beauty never to fade.

" Let Robbia's craft so apt and strange
Arrest the remains of young and fair,
And rivet them while the seasons range.

" Make me a face on the window there
Waiting as ever, mute the while,
My love to pass below in the square!

" And let me think that it may beguile
Dreary days which the dead must spend
Down in their darkness under the aisle—

" To say,—' What matters at the end?
I did no more while my heart was warm,
Than does that image, my pale-faced friend.'

" Where is the use of the lip's red charm,
The heaven of hair, the pride of the brow,
And the blood that blues the inside arm—

" Unless we turn, as the soul knows how,
The earthly gift to an end divine?
A lady of clay is as good, I trow."

But long ere Robbia's cornice, fine
With flowers and fruits which leaves enlace,
Was set where now is the empty shrine—

(With, leaning out of a bright blue space,
As a ghost might from a chink of sky,
The passionate pale lady's face—

Eyeing ever with earnest eye
And quick-turned neck at its breathless stretch,
Some one who ever passes by—)

The Duke sighed like the simplest wretch
In Florence, " So, my dream escapes!
Will its record stay?" And he bade them fetch

Some subtle fashioner of shapes—
" Can the soul, the will, die out of a man
Ere his body find the grave that gapes?

" John of Douay shall work my plan,
Mould me on horseback here aloft,
Alive—(the subtle artisan!)

" In the very square I cross so oft!
That men may admire, when future suns
Shall touch the eyes to a purpose soft.

" While the mouth and the brow are brave in bronze—
Admire and say, ' When he was alive,
How he would take his pleasure once ! '

" And it shall go hard but I contrive
To listen meanwhile and laugh in my tomb
At indolence which aspires to strive."

———

So! while these wait the trump of doom,
How do their spirits pass, I wonder,
Nights and days in the narrow room?

Still, I suppose, they sit and ponder
What a gift life was, ages ago,
Six steps out of the chapel yonder.

Surely they see not God, I know,
Nor all that chivalry of His,
The soldier-saints who, row on row,

Burn upward each to his point of bliss—
Since, the end of life being manifest,
He had cut his way thro' the world to this.

I hear your reproach—" But delay was best,
For their end was a crime ! "—Oh, a crime will do
As well, I reply, to serve for a test,

As a virtue golden through and through,
Sufficient to vindicate itself
And prove its worth at a moment's view.

Must a game be played for the sake of pelf?
Where a button goes, 'twere an epigram
To offer the stamp of the very Guelph.

The true has no value beyond the sham.
As well the counter as coin, I submit,
When your table's a hat, and your prize, a dram.

Stake your counter as boldly every whit,
Venture as truly, use the same skill,
Do your best, whether winning or losing it,

If you choose to play—is my principle!
Let a man contend to the uttermost
For his life's set prize, be what it will!

The counter our lovers staked was lost
As surely as if it were lawful coin:
And the sin I impute to each frustrate ghost

Was, the unlit lamp and the ungirt loin,
Though the end in sight was a crime I say.
You of the virtue (we issue join)
How strive you? *De te, fabula!*

LOVE IN A LIFE.

I. ROOM after room,
  I hunt the house through
  We inhabit together.
  Heart, fear nothing, for, heart, thou shalt find her,
  Next time, herself!—not the trouble behind her
  Left in the curtain, the couch's perfume!
  As she brushed it, the cornice-wreath blossomed anew,—
  Yon looking-glass gleamed at the wave of her feather.

II. Yet the day wears,
  And door succeeds door;
  I try the fresh fortune—
  Range the wide house from the wing to the centre,
  Still the same chance! she goes out as I enter.
  Spend my whole day in the quest,—who cares?
  But 'tis twilight, you see,—with such suites to explore,
  Such closets to search, such alcoves to importune!

LIFE IN A LOVE.

ESCAPE me?
Never—
Beloved!
While I am I, and you are you,
  So long as the world contains us both,
  Me the loving and you the loth,
While the one eludes, must the other pursue.

My life is a fault at last, I fear—
    It seems too much like a fate, indeed!
    Though I do my best I shall scarce succeed—
But what if I fail of my purpose here?
It is but to keep the nerves at strain,
    To dry one's eyes and laugh at a fall,
And baffled, get up to begin again,—
    So the chace takes up one's life, that's all.
While, look but once from your farthest bound,
    At me so deep in the dust and dark,
No sooner the old hope drops to ground
    Than a new one, straight to the self-same mark,
        I shape me—
        Ever
        Removed!

HOW IT STRIKES A CONTEMPORARY.

I ONLY knew one poet in my life:
And this, or something like it, was his way.

    You saw go up and down Valladolid,
A man of mark, to know next time you saw.
His very serviceable suit of black
Was courtly once and conscientious still,
And many might have worn it, though none did:
The cloak that somewhat shone and shewed the threads
Had purpose, and the ruff, significance.
He walked and tapped the pavement with his cane,
Scenting the world, looking it full in face,
An old dog, bald and blindish, at his heels.
They turned up, now, the alley by the church,
That leads no whither; now, they breathed themselves
On the main promenade just at the wrong time.
You'd come upon his scrutinising hat,
Making a peaked shade blacker than itself
Against the single window spared some house
Intact yet with its mouldered Moorish work,—
Or else surprise the ferrel of his stick
Trying the mortar's temper 'tween the chinks
Of some new shop a-building, French and fine.
He stood and watched the cobbler at his trade,

The man who slices lemons into drink,
The coffee-roaster's brazier, and the boys
That volunteer to help him turn its winch.
He glanced o'er books on stalls with half an eye,
And fly-leaf ballads on the vendor's string,
And broad-edge bold-print posters by the wall.
He took such cognisance of men and things,
If any beat a horse, you felt he saw;
If any cursed a woman, he took note;
Yet stared at nobody,—they stared at him,
And found, less to their pleasure than surprise,
He seemed to know them and expect as much.
So, next time that a neighbour's tongue was loosed,
It marked the shameful and notorious fact,
We had among us, not so much a spy,
As a recording chief-inquisitor,
The town's true master if the town but knew!
We merely kept a Governor for form,
While this man walked about and took account
Of all thought, said, and acted, then went home,
And wrote it fully to our Lord the King
Who has an itch to know things, He knows why,
And reads them in His bed-room of a night.
Oh, you might smile! there wanted not a touch,
A tang of . . . well, it was not wholly ease
As back into your mind the man's look came—
Stricken in years a little,—such a brow
His eyes had to live under!—clear as flint
On either side the formidable nose
Curved, cut, and coloured, like an eagle's claw.
Had he to do with A.'s surprising fate?
When altogether old B. disappeared
And young C. got his mistress,—was't our friend,
His letter to the King, that did it all?
What paid the bloodless man for so much pains?
Our Lord the King has favourites manifold,
And shifts his ministry some once a month;
Our city gets new Governors at whiles,—
But never word or sign, that I could hear,
Notified to this man about the streets
The King's approval of those letters conned
The last thing duly at the dead of night.
Did the man love his office? frowned our Lord,

Exhorting when none heard—" Beseech me not!
Too far above my people,—beneath Me!
I set the watch,—how should the people know?
Forget them, keep Me all the more in mind!"
Was some such understanding 'twixt the Two?

I found no truth in one report at least—
That if you tracked him to his home, down lanes
Beyond the Jewry, and as clean to pace,
You found he ate his supper in a room
Blazing with lights, four Titians on the wall,
And twenty naked girls to change his plate!
Poor man, he lived another kind of life
In that new, stuccoed, third house by the bridge,
Fresh-painted, rather smart than otherwise!
The whole street might o'erlook him as he sat,
Leg crossing leg, one foot on the dog's back,
Playing a decent cribbage with his maid
(Jacynth, you're sure her name was) o'er the cheese
And fruit, three red halves of starved winter-pears,
Or treat of radishes in April! nine—
Ten, struck the church clock, straight to bed went he.

My father, like the man of sense he was,
Would point him out to me a dozen times;
" St—St," he'd whisper, " the Corregidor!"
I had been used to think that personage
Was one with lacquered breeches, lustrous belt,
And feathers like a forest in his hat,
Who blew a trumpet and proclaimed the news,
Announced the bull-fights, gave each church its turn,
And memorized the miracle in vogue!
He had a great observance from us boys—
I was in error; that was not the man.

I'd like now, yet had haply been afraid,
To have just looked, when this man came to die,
And seen who lined the clean gay garret's sides
And stood about the neat low truckle-bed,
With the heavenly manner of relieving guard.
Here had been, mark, the general-in-chief,
Thro' a whole campaign of the world's life and death,
Doing the King's work all the dim day long,

In his old coat, and up to his knees in mud,
Smoked like a herring, dining on a crust,—
And now the day was won, relieved at once!
No further show or need for that old coat,
You are sure, for one thing!   Bless us, all the while
How sprucely we are dressed out, you and I!
A second, and the angels alter that.
Well, I could never write a verse,—could you?
Let's to the Prado and make the most of time.

THE LAST RIDE TOGETHER.

I. I SAID—Then, dearest, since 'tis so,
   Since now at length my fate I know,
   Since nothing all my love avails,
   Since all my life seemed meant for, fails,
     Since this was written and needs must be—
   My whole heart rises up to bless
   Your name in pride and thankfulness!
   Take back the hope you gave,—I claim
   Only a memory of the same,
   —And this beside, if you will not blame,
     Your leave for one more last ride with me.

II. My mistress bent that brow of hers,
   Those deep dark eyes where pride demurs
   When pity would be softening through,
   Fixed me a breathing-while or two
     With life or death in the balance—Right!
   The blood replenished me again:
   My last thought was at least not vain.
   I and my mistress, side by side
   Shall be together, breathe and ride,
   So one day more am I deified.
     Who knows but the world may end to-night?

III. Hush! if you saw some western cloud
   All billowy-bosomed, over-bowed
   By many benedictions—sun's
   And moon's and evening star's at once—
     And so, you, looking and loving best,
   Conscious grew, your passion drew
   Cloud, sunset, moonrise, star-shine too

Down on you, near and yet more near,
Till flesh must fade for heaven was here!—
Thus leant she and lingered—joy and fear!
    Thus lay she a moment on my breast.

IV. Then we began to ride. My soul
Smoothed itself out, a long-cramped scroll
Freshening and fluttering in the wind.
Past hopes already lay behind.
    What need to strive with a life awry?
Had I said that, had I done this,
So might I gain, so might I miss.
Might she have loved me? just as well
She might have hated,—who can tell?
Where had I been now if the worst befell?
    And here we are riding, she and I.

V. Fail I alone, in words and deeds?
Why, all men strive and who succeeds?
We rode; it seemed my spirit flew,
Saw other regions, cities new,
    As the world rushed by on either side.
I thought, All labour, yet no less
Bear up beneath their unsuccess.
Look at the end of work, contrast
The petty Done, the Undone vast,
This present of theirs with the hopeful past!
    I hoped she would love me. Here we ride.

VI. What hand and brain went ever paired?
What heart alike conceived and dared?
What act proved all its thought had been?
What will but felt the fleshly screen?
    We ride and I see her bosom heave.
There's many a crown for who can reach.
Ten lines, a statesman's life in each!
The flag stuck on a heap of bones,
A soldier's doing! what atones?
They scratch his name on the Abbey-stones.
    My riding is better, by their leave.

VII. What does it all mean, poet? well,
Your brain's beat into rhythm—you tell
What we felt only; you expressed

The Last Ride Together x

You hold things beautiful the best,
   And pace them in rhyme so, side by side.
'Tis something, nay 'tis much—but then,
Have you yourself what's best for men?
Are you—poor, sick, old ere your time—
Nearer one whit your own sublime
Than we who never have turned a rhyme?
   Sing, riding's a joy! For me, I ride.

VIII. And you, great sculptor—so you gave
A score of years to art, her slave,
And that's your Venus—whence we turn
To yonder girl that fords the burn!
   You acquiesce and shall I repine?
What, man of music, you, grown grey
With notes and nothing else to say,
Is this your sole praise from a friend,
" Greatly his opera's strains intend,
But in music we know how fashions end!"
   I gave my youth—but we ride, in fine.

IX. Who knows what's fit for us? Had fate
Proposed bliss here should sublimate
My being; had I signed the bond—
Still one must lead some life beyond,
   —Have a bliss to die with, dim-descried.
This foot once planted on the goal,
This glory-garland round my soul,
Could I descry such? Try and test!
I sink back shuddering from the quest—
Earth being so good, would Heaven seem best?
   Now, Heaven and she are beyond this ride.

X. And yet—she has not spoke so long!
What if Heaven be, that, fair and strong
At life's best, with our eyes upturned
Whither life's flower is first discerned,
   We, fixed so, ever should so abide?
What if we still ride on, we two,
With life for ever old yet new,
Changed not in kind but in degree,
The instant made eternity,—
And Heaven just prove that I and she
   Ride, ride together, for ever ride?

THE PATRIOT.

AN OLD STORY.

I. It was roses, roses, all the way,
　　With myrtle mixed in my path like mad.
　The house-roofs seemed to heave and sway
　　The church-spires flamed, such flags they had,
　A year ago on this very day!

II. The air broke into a mist with bells,
　　The old walls rocked with the crowds and cries.
　Had I said, " Good folks, mere noise repels—
　　But give me your sun from yonder skies! "
　They had answered, " And afterward, what else? "

III. Alack, it was I who leaped at the sun,
　　To give it my loving friends to keep.
　Nought man could do, have I left undone
　　And you see my harvest, what I reap
　This very day, now a year is run.

IV. There's nobody on the house-tops now—
　　Just a palsied few at the windows set—
　For the best of the sight is, all allow,
　　At the Shambles' Gate—or, better yet,
　By the very scaffold's foot, I trow.

V. I go in the rain, and, more than needs,
　　A rope cuts both my wrists behind,
　And I think, by the feel, my forehead bleeds,
　　For they fling, whoever has a mind,
　Stones at me for my year's misdeeds.

VI. Thus I entered Brescia, and thus I go!
　　In such triumphs, people have dropped down dead.
　" Thou, paid by the World,—what dost thou owe
　　Me? "　God might have questioned: but now instead
　'Tis God shall requite! I am safer so.

MASTER HUGUES OF SAXE-GOTHA.

AN UNKNOWN MUSICIAN.

I. HIST, but a word, fair and soft!
   Forth and be judged, Master Hugues!
   Answer the question I've put you so oft—
      What do you mean by your mountainous fugues?
   See, we're alone in the loft,

II. I, the poor organist here,
    Hugues, the composer of note—
    Dead, though, and done with, this many a year—
       Let's have a colloquy, something to quote,
    Make the world prick up its ear!

III. See, the church empties a-pace.
     Fast they extinguish the lights—
     Hallo, there, sacristan! five minutes' grace!
        Here's a crank pedal wants setting to rights,
     Baulks one of holding the base.

IV. See, our huge house of the sounds
    Hushing its hundreds at once,
    Bids the last loiterer back to his bounds
       —Oh, you may challenge them, not a response
    Get the church saints on their rounds!

V. (Saints go their rounds, who shall doubt?
      —March, with the moon to admire,
    Up nave, down chancel, turn transept about,
       Supervise all betwixt pavement and spire,
    Put rats and mice to the rout—

VI. Aloys and Jurien and Just—
       Order things back to their place,
    Have a sharp eye lest the candlesticks rust,
       Rub the church plate, darn the sacrament lace,
    Clear the desk velvet of dust.)

VII. Here's your book, younger folks shelve!
        Played I not off-hand and runningly,
     Just now, your masterpiece, hard number twelve?
        Here's what should strike,—could one handle it
           cunningly.
     Help the axe, give it a helve!

VIII. Page after page as I played,
  Every bar's rest where one wipes
Sweat from one's brow, I looked up and surveyed
  O'er my three claviers, yon forest of pipes
Whence you still peeped in the shade.

IX. Sure you were wishful to speak,
  You, with brow ruled like a score,
Yes, and eyes buried in pits on each cheek.
  Like two great breves as they wrote them of yore
Each side that bar, your straight beak!

X. Sure you said—" Good, the mere notes!
  Still, couldst thou take my intent,
Know what procured me our Company's votes—
  Masters being lauded and sciolists shent,
Parted the sheep from the goats!"

XI. Well then, speak up, never flinch!
  Quick, ere my candle's a snuff
—Burnt, do you see? to its uttermost inch—
  I believe in you, but that's not enough.
Give my conviction a clinch!

XII. First you deliver your phrase
  —Nothing propound, that I see,
Fit in itself for much blame or much praise—
  Answered no less, where no answer needs be:
Off start the Two on their ways!

XIII. Straight must a Third interpose,
  Volunteer needlessly help—
In strikes a Fourth, a Fifth thrusts in his nose,
  So the cry's open, the kennel's a-yelp,
Argument's hot to the close!

XIV. One dissertates, he is candid—
  Two must discept,—has distinguished!
Three helps the couple, if ever yet man did:
  Four protests, Five makes a dart at the thing
    wished—
Back to One, goes the case bandied!

XV. One says his say with a difference—
  More of expounding, explaining!
All now is wrangle, abuse, and vociferance—

      Now there's a truce, all's subdued, self-restrain-
           ing—
Five, though, stands out all the stiffer hence.

XVI. One is incisive, corrosive—
      Two retorts, nettled, curt, crepitant—
Three makes rejoinder, expansive, explosive—
      Four overbears them all, strident and strepitant—
Five . . . O Danaides, O Sieve!

XVII. Now, they ply axes and crowbars—
      Now, they prick pins at a tissue
Fine as a skein of the casuist Escobar's
      Worked on the bone of a lie.   To what issue?
Where is our gain at the Two-bars?

XVIII. *Est fuga, volvitur rota!*
      On we drift.   Where looms the dim port?
One, Two, Three, Four, Five, contribute their quota—
      Something is gained, if one caught but the import—
Show it us, Hugues of Saxe-Gotha!

XIX. What with affirming, denying,
      Holding, risposting, subjoining,
All's like . . . it's like . . . for an instance I'm
      trying . . .
      There! See our roof, its gilt moulding and groining
Under those spider-webs lying!

XX. So your fugue broadens and thickens,
      Greatens and deepens and lengthens,
Till one exclaims—" But where's music, the dickens?
      Blot ye the gold, while your spider-web strengthens,
Blacked to the stoutest of tickens? "

XXI. I for man's effort am zealous.
      Prove me such censure's unfounded!
Seems it surprising a lover grows jealous—
      Hopes 'twas for something his organ-pipes sounded,
Tiring three boys at the bellows?

XXII. Is it your moral of Life?
      Such a web, simple and subtle,
Weave we on earth here in impotent strife,
      Backward and forward each throwing his shuttle,
Death ending all with a knife?

XXIII. Over our heads Truth and Nature—
    Still our life's zigzags and dodges,
Ins and outs weaving a new legislature—
    God's gold just shining its last where that lodges,
Palled beneath Man's usurpature!

XXIV. So we o'ershroud stars and roses,
    Cherub and trophy and garland.
Nothings grow something which quietly closes
    Heaven's earnest eye,—not a glimpse of the far
    land
Gets through our comments and glozes.

XXV. Ah, but traditions, inventions,
    (Say we and make up a visage)
So many men with such various intentions
    Down the past ages must know more than this age!
Leave the web all its dimensions!

XXVI. Who thinks Hugues wrote for the deaf?
    Proved a mere mountain in labour?
Better submit—try again—what's the clef?
    'Faith, it's no trifle for pipe and for tabor—
Four flats—the minor in F.

XXVII. Friend, your fugue taxes the finger.
    Learning it once, who would lose it?
Yet all the while a misgiving will linger—
    Truth's golden o'er us although we refuse it—
Nature, thro' dust-clouds we fling her!

XXVIII. Hugues! I advise *meâ pœnâ*
    (Counterpoint glares like a Gorgon)
Bid One, Two, Three, Four, Five, clear the arena!
    Say the word, straight I unstop the Full-Organ,
Blare out the *mode Palestrina*.

XXIX. While in the roof, if I'm right there—
    . . . Lo, you, the wick in the socket!
Hallo, you sacristan, show us a light there!
    Down it dips, gone like a rocket!
What, you want, do you, to come unawares,
Sweeping the church up for first morning-prayers,
And find a poor devil at end of his cares
    At the foot of your rotten-planked rat-riddled stairs?
    Do I carry the moon in my pocket?

BISHOP BLOUGRAM'S APOLOGY.

No more wine?   Then we'll push back chairs and talk.
A final glass for me, tho'; cool, i'faith!
We ought to have our Abbey back, you see.
It's different, preaching in basilicas,
And doing duty in some masterpiece
Like this of brother Pugin's, bless his heart!
I doubt if they're half baked, those chalk rosettes,
Ciphers and stucco-twiddlings everywhere;
It's just like breathing in a lime-kiln: eh?
These hot long ceremonies of our church
Cost us a little—oh, they pay the price,
You take me—amply pay it!   Now, we'll talk.

So, you despise me, Mr. Gigadibs.
No deprecation,—nay, I beg you, sir!
Beside 'tis our engagement: don't you know,
I promised, if you'd watch a dinner out,
We'd see truth dawn together?—truth that peeps
Over the glass's edge when dinner's done,
And body gets its sop and holds its noise
And leaves soul free a little.   Now's the time—
'Tis break of day!   You do despise me then.
And if I say, " despise me,"—never fear—
I know you do not in a certain sense—
Not in my arm-chair for example: here,
I well imagine you respect my place
(Status, *entourage*, worldly circumstance)
Quite to its value—very much indeed
—Are up to the protesting eyes of you
In pride at being seated here for once—
You'll turn it to such capital account!
When somebody, through years and years to come,
Hints of the bishop,—names me—that's enough—
" Blougram?   I knew him "—(into it you slide)
" Dined with him once, a Corpus Christi Day,
All alone, we two—he's a clever man—
And after dinner,—why, the wine you know,—
Oh, there was wine, and good!—what with the wine . . .
'Faith, we began upon all sorts of talk!

He's no bad fellow, Blougram—he had seen
Something of mine he relished—some review—
He's quite above their humbug in his heart,
Half-said as much, indeed—the thing's his trade—
I warrant, Blougram's sceptical at times—
How otherwise? I liked him, I confess!"
Che ch'è, my dear sir, as we say at Rome,
Don't you protest now! It's fair give and take;
You have had your turn and spoken your home-truths—
The hand's mine now, and here you follow suit.

Thus much conceded, still the first fact stays—
You do despise me; your ideal of life
Is not the bishop's—you would not be I—
You would like better to be Goethe, now,
Or Buonaparte—or, bless me, lower still,
Count D'Orsay,—so you did what you preferred,
Spoke as you thought, and, as you cannot help,
Believed or disbelieved, no matter what,
So long as on that point, whate'er it was,
You loosed your mind, were whole and sole yourself.
—That, my ideal never can include,
Upon that element of truth and worth
Never be based! for say they make me Pope
(They can't—suppose it for our argument)
Why, there I'm at my tether's end—I've reached
My height, and not a height which pleases you.
An unbelieving Pope won't do, you say.
It's like those eerie stories nurses tell,
Of how some actor played Death on a stage
With pasteboard crown, sham orb, and tinselled dart,
And called himself the monarch of the world,
Then going in the tire-room afterward
Because the play was done, to shift himself,
Got touched upon the sleeve familiarly
The moment he had shut the closet door
By Death himself. Thus God might touch a Pope
At unawares, ask what his baubles mean,
And whose part he presumed to play just now?
Best be yourself, imperial, plain and true!

So, drawing comfortable breath again,
You weigh and find whatever more or less

I boast of my ideal realised
Is nothing in the balance when opposed
To your ideal, your grand simple life,
Of which you will not realise one jot.
I am much, you are nothing; you would be all,
I would be merely much—you beat me there.

No, friend, you do not beat me,—hearken why.
The common problem, yours, mine, every one's,
Is not to fancy what were fair in life
Provided it could be,—but, finding first
What may be, then find how to make it fair
Up to our means—a very different thing!
No abstract intellectual plan of life
Quite irrespective of life's plainest laws,
But one, a man, who is man and nothing more,
May lead within a world which (by your leave)
Is Rome or London—not Fool's-paradise.
Embellish Rome, idealise away,
Make Paradise of London if you can,
You're welcome, nay, you're wise.

                                        A simile!
We mortals cross the ocean of this world
Each in his average cabin of a life—
The best's not big, the worst yields elbow-room.
Now for our six months' voyage—how prepare?
You come on shipboard with a landsman's list
Of things he calls convenient—so they are!
An India screen is pretty furniture,
A piano-forte is a fine resource,
All Balzac's novels occupy one shelf,
The new edition fifty volumes long;
And little Greek books with the funny type
They get up well at Leipsic fill the next—
Go on! slabbed marble, what a bath it makes!
And Parma's pride, the Jerome, let us add!
'Twere pleasant could Correggio's fleeting glow
Hang full in face of one where'er one roams,
Since he more than the others brings with him
Italy's self,—the marvellous Modenese!
Yet 'twas not on your list before, perhaps.
—Alas! friend, here's the agent . . . is't the name?

The captain, or whoever's master here—
You see him screw his face up; what's his cry
Ere you set foot on shipboard? " Six feet square!"
If you won't understand what six feet mean,
Compute and purchase stores accordingly—
And if in pique because he overhauls
Your Jerome, piano and bath, you come on board
Bare—why you cut a figure at the first
While sympathetic landsmen see you off;
Not afterwards, when, long ere half seas o'er,
You peep up from your utterly naked boards
Into some snug and well-appointed berth
Like mine, for instance (try the cooler jug—
Put back the other, but don't jog the ice)
And mortified you mutter " Well and good—
He sits enjoying his sea-furniture—
'Tis stout and proper, and there's store of it,
Though I've the better notion, all agree,
Of fitting rooms up! hang the carpenter,
Neat ship-shape fixings and contrivances—
I would have brought my Jerome, frame and all!"
And meantime you bring nothing: never mind—
You've proved your artist-nature: what you don't,
You might bring, so despise me, as I say.

　　Now come, let's backward to the starting place.
See my way: we're two college friends, suppose—
Prepare together for our voyage, then,
Each note and check the other in his work,—
Here's mine, a bishop's outfit; criticise!
What's wrong? why won't you be a bishop too?

　　Why, first, you don't believe, you don't and can't,
(Not statedly, that is, and fixedly
And absolutely and exclusively)
In any revelation called divine.
No dogmas nail your faith—and what remains
But say so, like the honest man you are?
First, therefore, overhaul theology!
Nay, I too, not a fool, you please to think,
Must find believing every whit as hard,
And if I do not frankly say as much,
The ugly consequence is clear enough.

Now, wait, my friend: well, I do not believe—
If you'll accept no faith that is not fixed,
Absolute and exclusive, as you say.
(You're wrong—I mean to prove it in due time)
Meanwhile, I know where difficulties lie
I could not, cannot solve, nor ever shall,
So give up hope accordingly to solve—
(To you, and over the wine).   Our dogmas then
With both of us, tho' in unlike degree,
Missing full credence—overboard with them!
I mean to meet you on your own premise—
Good, there go mine in company with yours!

And now what are we? unbelievers both,
Calm and complete, determinately fixed
To-day, to-morrow, and for ever, pray?
You'll guarantee me that?   Not so, I think.
In no-wise! all we've gained is, that belief,
As unbelief before, shakes us by fits,
Confounds us like its predecessor.   Where's
The gain? how can we guard our unbelief,
Make it bear fruit to us?—the problem here.
Just when we are safest, there's a sunset-touch,
A fancy from a flower-bell, some one's death,
A chorus-ending from Euripides,—
And that's enough for fifty hopes and fears
As old and new at once as Nature's self,
To rap and knock and enter in our soul,
Take hands and dance there, a fantastic ring,
Round the ancient idol, on his base again,—
The grand Perhaps! we look on helplessly,—
There the old misgivings, crooked questions are—
This good God,—what he could do, if he would,
Would, if he could—then must have done long since:
If so, when, where, and how? some way must be,—
Once feel about, and soon or late you hit
Some sense, in which it might be, after all.
Why not, " The Way, the Truth, the Life? "

                                        —That way

Over the mountain, which who stands upon
Is apt to doubt if it's indeed a road;
While if he views it from the waste itself,

Up goes the line there, plain from base to brow,
Not vague, mistakeable! what's a break or two
Seen from the unbroken desert either side?
And then (to bring in fresh philosophy)
What if the breaks themselves should prove at last
The most consummate of contrivances
To train a man's eye, teach him what is faith,—
And so we stumble at truth's very test?
What have we gained then by our unbelief
But a life of doubt diversified by faith,
For one of faith diversified by doubt?
We called the chess-board white,—we call it black.

" Well," you rejoin, " the end's no worse, at least,
We've reason for both colours on the board.
Why not confess, then, where I drop the faith
And you the doubt, that I'm as right as you? "

Because, friend, in the next place, this being so,
And both things even,—faith and unbelief
Left to a man's choice,—we'll proceed a step,
Returning to our image, which I like.

A man's choice, yes—but a cabin-passenger's—
The man made for the special life of the world—
Do you forget him?   I remember though!
Consult our ship's conditions and you find
One and but one choice suitable to all,
The choice that you unluckily prefer
Turning things topsy-turvy—they or it
Going to the ground.   Belief or unbelief
Bears upon life, determines its whole course,
Begins at its beginning.   See the world
Such as it is,—you made it not, nor I;
I mean to take it as it is,—and you
Not so you'll take it,—though you get nought else.
I know the special kind of life I like,
What suits the most my idiosyncrasy,
Brings out the best of me and bears me fruit
In power, peace, pleasantness, and length of days.
I find that positive belief does this
For me, and unbelief, no whit of this.
—For you, it does, however—that we'll try!

'Tis clear, I cannot lead my life, at least
Induce the world to let me peaceably,
Without declaring at the outset, " Friends,
I absolutely and peremptorily
Believe! "—I say faith is my waking life.
One sleeps, indeed, and dreams at intervals,
We know, but waking's the main point with us,
And my provision's for life's waking part.
Accordingly, I use heart, head and hands
All day, I build, scheme, study and make friends;
And when night overtakes me, down I lie,
Sleep, dream a little, and get done with it,
The sooner the better, to begin afresh.
What's midnight's doubt before the dayspring's faith?
You, the philosopher, that disbelieve,
That recognise the night, give dreams their weight—
To be consistent you should keep your bed,
Abstain from healthy acts that prove you a man,
For fear you drowse perhaps at unawares!
And certainly at night you'll sleep and dream,
Live through the day and bustle as you please.
And so you live to sleep as I to wake,
To unbelieve as I to still believe?
Well, and the common sense of the world calls you
Bed-ridden,—and its good things come to me.
Its estimation, which is half the fight,
That's the first cabin-comfort I secure—
The next . . . but you perceive with half an eye!
Come, come, it's best believing, if we can—
You can't but own that.

                              Next, concede again—
If once we choose belief, on all accounts
We can't be too decisive in our faith,
Conclusive and exclusive in its terms,
To suit the world which gives us the good things.
In every man's career are certain points
Whereon he dares not be indifferent;
The world detects him clearly, if he is,
As baffled at the game, and losing life.
He may care little or he may care much
For riches, honour, pleasure, work, repose,
Since various theories of life and life's

Success are extant which might easily
Comport with either estimate of these,
And whoso chooses wealth or poverty,
Labour or quiet, is not judged a fool
Because his fellows would choose otherwise.
We let him choose upon his own account
So long as he's consistent with his choice.
But certain points, left wholly to himself,
When once a man has arbitrated on,
We say he must succeed there or go hang.
Thus, he should wed the woman he loves most
Or needs most, whatsoe'er the love or need—
For he can't wed twice.   Then, he must avouch
Or follow, at the least, sufficiently,
The form of faith his conscience holds the best,
Whate'er the process of conviction was.
For nothing can compensate his mistake
On such a point, the man himself being judge—
He cannot wed twice, nor twice lose his soul.

    Well now—there's one great form of Christian faith
I happened to be born in—which to teach
Was given me as I grew up, on all hands,
As best and readiest means of living by;
The same on examination being proved
The most pronounced moreover, fixed, precise
And absolute form of faith in the whole world—
Accordingly, most potent of all forms
For working on the world.   Observe, my friend,
Such as you know me, I am free to say,
In these hard latter days which hamper one,
Myself, by no immoderate exercise
Of intellect and learning, and the tact
To let external forces work for me,
Bid the street's stones be bread and they are bread,
Bid Peter's creed, or, rather, Hildebrand's,
Exalt me o'er my fellows in the world
And make my life an ease and joy and pride,
It does so,—which for me's a great point gained,
Who have a soul and body that exact
A comfortable care in many ways.
There's power in me and will to dominate
Which I must exercise, they hurt me else:

In many ways I need mankind's respect,
Obedience, and the love that's born of fear:
While at the same time, there's a taste I have,
A toy of soul, a titillating thing,
Refuses to digest these dainties crude.
The naked life is gross till clothed upon:
I must take what men offer, with a grace
As though I would not, could I help it, take!
A uniform to wear though over-rich—
Something imposed on me, no choice of mine;
No fancy-dress worn for pure fashion's sake
And despicable therefore! now men kneel
And kiss my hand—of course the Church's hand.
Thus I am made, thus life is best for me,
And thus that it should be I have procured;
And thus it could not be another way,
I venture to imagine.

                                    You'll reply—
So far my choice, no doubt, is a success;
But were I made of better elements,
With nobler instincts, purer tastes, like you,
I hardly would account the thing success
Though it do all for me I say.

                                    But, friend,
We speak of what is—not of what might be,
And how 'twere better if 'twere otherwise.
I am the man you see here plain enough—
Grant I'm a beast, why beasts must lead beasts' lives '
Suppose I own at once to tail and claws—
The tailless man exceeds me; but being tailed
I'll lash out lion-fashion, and leave apes
To dock their stump and dress their haunches up.
My business is not to remake myself,
But make the absolute best of what God made.
Or—our first simile—though you proved me doomed
To a viler berth still, to the steerage-hole,
The sheep-pen or the pig-stye, I should strive
To make what use of each were possible;
And as this cabin gets upholstery,
That hutch should rustle with sufficient straw.

  But, friend, I don't acknowledge quite so fast
I fail of all your manhood's lofty tastes

Enumerated so complacently,
On the mere ground that you forsooth can find
In this particular life I choose to lead
No fit provision for them. Can you not?
Say you, my fault is I address myself
To grosser estimators than I need,
And that's no way of holding up the soul—
Which, nobler, needs men's praise perhaps, yet knows
One wise man's verdict outweighs all the fools',—
Would like the two, but, forced to choose, takes that?
I pine among my million imbeciles
(You think) aware some dozen men of sense
Eye me and know me, whether I believe
In the last winking Virgin, as I vow,
And am a fool, or disbelieve in her
And am a knave,—approve in neither case,
Withhold their voices though I look their way:
Like Verdi when, at his worst opera's end
(The thing they gave at Florence,—what's its name?)
While the mad houseful's plaudits near out-bang
His orchestra of salt-box, tongs and bones,
He looks through all the roaring and the wreaths
Where sits Rossini patient in his stall.

    Nay, friend, I meet you with an answer here—
For even your prime men who appraise their kind
Are men still, catch a thing within a thing,
See more in a truth than the truth's simple self,
Confuse themselves. You see lads walk the street
Sixty the minute; what's to note in that?
You see one lad o'erstride a chimney-stack;
Him you must watch—he's sure to fall, yet stands!
Our interest's on the dangerous edge of things.
The honest thief, the tender murderer,
The superstitious atheist, demireps
That love and save their souls in new French books—
We watch while these in equilibrium keep
The giddy line midway: one step aside,
They're classed and done with. I, then, keep the line
Before your sages,—just the men to shrink
From the gross weights, coarse scales, and labels broad
You offer their refinement. Fool or knave?
Why needs a bishop be a fool or knave

When there's a thousand diamond weights between?
So I enlist them.   Your picked Twelve, you'll find,
Profess themselves indignant, scandalised
At thus being held unable to explain
How a superior man who disbelieves
May not believe as well: that's Schelling's way!
It's through my coming in the tail of time,
Nicking the minute with a happy tact.
Had I been born three hundred years ago
They'd say, " What's strange? Blougram of course believes; "
And, seventy years since, " disbelieves of course."
But now, " He may believe; and yet, and yet
How can he? "—All eyes turn with interest.
Whereas, step off the line on either side—
You, for example, clever to a fault,
The rough and ready man that write apace,
Read somewhat seldomer, think perhaps even less—
You disbelieve!   Who wonders and who cares?
Lord So-and-So—his coat bedropt with wax,
All Peter's chains about his waist, his back
Brave with the needlework of Noodledom,
Believes!   Again, who wonders and who cares?
But I, the man of sense and learning too,
The able to think yet act, the this, the that,
I, to believe at this late time of day!
Enough; you see, I need not fear contempt.

—Except it's yours! admire me as these may,
You don't.   But what at least do you admire?
Present your own perfections, your ideal,
Your pattern man for a minute—oh, make haste!
Is it Napoleon you would have us grow?
Concede the means; allow his head and hand,
(A large concession, clever as you are)
Good!—In our common primal element
Of unbelief (we can't believe, you know—
We're still at that admission, recollect)
Where do you find—apart from, towering-o'er
The secondary temporary aims
Which satisfy the gross tastes you despise—
Where do you find his star?—his crazy trust
God knows through what or in what? it's alive
And shines and leads him and that's all we want.

Have we ought in our sober night shall point
Such ends as his were, and direct the means
Of working out our purpose straight as his,
Nor bring a moment's trouble on success,
With after-care to justify the same?
—Be a Napoleon and yet disbelieve!
Why, the man's mad, friend, take his light away.
What's the vague good of the world for which you'd dare
With comfort to yourself blow millions up?
We neither of us see it! we do see
The blown-up millions—spatter of their brains
And writhing of their bowels and so forth,
In that bewildering entanglement
Of horrible eventualities
Past calculation to the end of time!
Can I mistake for some clear word of God
(Which were my ample warrant for it all)
His puff of hazy instincts, idle talk,
" The state, that's I," quack-nonsense about kings,
And (when one beats the man to his last hold)
The vague idea of setting things to rights,
Policing people efficaciously,
More to their profit, most of all to his own;
The whole to end that dismallest of ends
By an Austrian marriage, cant to us the church,
And resurrection of the old *régime*.
Would I, who hope to live a dozen years,
Fight Austerlitz for reasons such and such?
No: for, concede me but the merest chance
Doubt may be wrong—there's judgment, life to come!
With just that chance, I dare not.   Doubt proves right?
This present life is all? you offer me
Its dozen noisy years with not a chance
That wedding an Arch-Duchess, wearing lace,
And getting called by divers new-coined names,
Will drive off ugly thoughts and let me dine,
Sleep, read and chat in quiet as I like!
Therefore, I will not.
                                 Take another case;
Fit up the cabin yet another way.
What say you to the poet's? shall we write
Hamlets, Othellos—make the world our own,
Without a risk to run of either sort?

I can't!—to put the strongest reason first.
" But try," you urge, " the trying shall suffice:
The aim, if reached or not, makes great the life.
Try to be Shakspeare, leave the rest to fate!"
Spare my self-knowledge—there's no fooling me!
If I prefer remaining my poor self,
I say so not in self-dispraise but praise.
If I'm a Shakspeare, let the well alone—
Why should I try to be what now I am?
If I'm no Shakspeare, as too probable,—
His power and consciousness and self-delight
And all we want in common, shall I find—
Trying for ever? while on points of taste
Wherewith, to speak it humbly, he and I
Are dowered alike—I'll ask you, I or he,
Which in our two lives realises most?
Much, he imagined—somewhat, I possess.
He had the imagination; stick to that!
Let him say " In the face of my soul's works
Your world is worthless and I touch it not
Lest I should wrong them "—I withdraw my plea.
But does he say so? look upon his life!
Himself, who only can, gives judgment there.
He leaves his towers and gorgeous palaces
To build the trimmest house in Stratford town;
Saves money, spends it, owns the worth of things,
Giulio Romano's pictures, Dowland's lute;
Enjoys a show, respects the puppets, too,
And none more, had he seen its entry once,
Than " Pandulph, of fair Milan cardinal."
Why then should I who play that personage,
The very Pandulph Shakspeare's fancy made,
Be told that had the poet chanced to start
From where I stand now (some degree like mine
Being just the goal he ran his race to reach)
He would have run the whole race back, forsooth,
And left being Pandulph, to begin write plays?
Ah, the earth's best can be but the earth's best!
Did Shakspeare live, he could but sit at home
And get himself in dreams the Vatican,
Greek busts, Venetian paintings, Roman walls,
And English books, none equal to his own,
Which I read, bound in gold, (he never did).

—Terni and Naples' bay and Gothard's top—
Eh, friend?   I could not fancy one of these—
But, as I pour this claret, there they are—
I've gained them—crossed St. Gothard last July
With ten mules to the carriage and a bed
Slung inside; is my hap the worse for that?
We want the same things, Shakspeare and myself,
And what I want, I have: he, gifted more,
Could fancy he too had it when he liked,
But not so thoroughly that if fate allowed
He would not have it also in my sense.
We play one game.   I send the ball aloft
No less adroitly that of fifty strokes
Scarce five go o'er the wall so wide and high
Which sends them back to me: I wish and get.
He struck balls higher and with better skill,
But at a poor fence level with his head,
And hit—his Stratford house, a coat of arms,
Successful dealings in his grain and wool,—
While I receive heaven's incense in my nose
And style myself the cousin of Queen Bess.
Ask him, if this life's all, who wins the game?

Believe—and our whole argument breaks up.
Enthusiasm's the best thing, I repeat;
Only, we can't command it; fire and life
Are all, dead matter's nothing; we agree:
And be it a mad dream or God's very breath,
The fact's the same,—belief's fire once in us,
Makes of all else mere stuff to show itself.
We penetrate our life with such a glow
As fire lends wood and iron—this turns steel,
That burns to ash—all's one, fire proves its power
For good or ill, since men call flare success.
But paint a fire, it will not therefore burn.
Light one in me, I'll find it food enough!
Why, to be Luther—that's a life to lead,
Incomparably better than my own.
He comes, reclaims God's earth for God, he says,
Sets up God's rule again by simple means,
Re-opens a shut book, and all is done.
He flared out in the flaring of mankind;
Such Luther's luck was—how shall such be mine?

If he succeeded, nothing's left to do:
And if he did not altogether—well,
Strauss is the next advance.   All Strauss should be
I might be also.   But to what result?
He looks upon no future: Luther did.
What can I gain on the denying side?
Ice makes no conflagration.   State the facts,
Read the text right, emancipate the world—
The emancipated world enjoys itself
With scarce a thank-you—Blougram told it first
It could not owe a farthing,—not to him
More than St. Paul! 'twould press its pay, you think?
Then add there's still that plaguey hundredth chance
Strauss may be wrong.   And so a risk is run—
For what gain? not for Luther's, who secured
A real heaven in his heart throughout his life,
Supposing death a little altered things!

   " Ay, but since really I lack faith," you cry,
" I run the same risk really on all sides,
In cool indifference as bold unbelief.
As well be Strauss as swing 'twixt Paul and him.
It's not worth having, such imperfect faith,
Nor more available to do faith's work
Than unbelief like yours.   Whole faith, or none! "

   Softly, my friend!   I must dispute that point.
Once own the use of faith, I'll find you faith.
We're back on Christian ground.   You call for faith;
I show you doubt, to prove that faith exists.
The more of doubt, the stronger faith, I say,
If faith o'ercomes doubt.   How I know it does?
By life and man's free will, God gave for that!
To mould life as we choose it, shows our choice:
That's our one act, the previous work's His own.
You criticise the soil? it reared this tree—
This broad life and whatever fruit it bears!
What matter though I doubt at every pore,
Head-doubts, heart-doubts, doubts at my fingers' ends,
Doubts in the trivial work of every day,
Doubts at the very bases of my soul
In the grand moments when she probes herself—
If finally I have a life to show,

The thing I did, brought out in evidence
Against the thing done to me underground
By Hell and all its brood, for ought I know?
I say, whence sprang this? shows it faith or doubt?
All's doubt in me; where's break of faith in this?
It is the idea, the feeling and the love
God means mankind should strive for and show forth,
Whatever be the process to that end,—
And not historic knowledge, logic sound,
And metaphysical acumen, sure!
" What think ye of Christ," friend? when all's done and said,
You like this Christianity or not?
It may be false, but will you wish it true?
Has it your vote to be so if it can?
Trust you an instinct silenced long ago
That will break silence and enjoin you love
What mortified philosophy is hoarse,
And all in vain, with bidding you despise?
If you desire faith—then you've faith enough.
What else seeks God—nay, what else seek ourselves?
You form a notion of me, we'll suppose,
On hearsay; it's a favourable one:
" But still " (you add), " there was no such good man,
Because of contradictions in the facts.
One proves, for instance, he was born in Rome,
This Blougram—yet throughout the tales of him
I see he figures as an Englishman."
Well, the two things are reconcileable.
But would I rather you discovered that
Subjoining—" Still, what matter though they be?
Blougram—concerns me nought, born here or there."

Pure faith indeed—you know not what you ask!
Naked belief in God the Omnipotent,
Omniscient, Omnipresent, sears too much
The sense of conscious creatures to be borne.
It were the seeing him, no flesh shall dare.
Some think, Creation's meant to show him forth:
I say, it's meant to hide him all it can,
And that's what all the blessed Evil's for.
Its use in time is to environ us,
Our breath, our drop of dew, with shield enough
Against that sight till we can bear its stress.

Under a vertical sun, the exposed brain
And lidless eye and disemprisoned heart
Less certainly would wither up at once
Than mind, confronted with the truth of Him.
But time and earth case-harden us to live;
The feeblest sense is trusted most; the child
Feels God a moment, ichors o'er the place,
Plays on and grows to be a man like us.
With me, faith means perpetual unbelief
Kept quiet like the snake 'neath Michael's foot
Who stands calm just because he feels it writhe.
Or, if that's too ambitious,—here's my box—
I need the excitation of a pinch
Threatening the torpor of the inside-nose
Nigh on the imminent sneeze that never comes.
" Leave it in peace " advise the simple folk—
Make it aware of peace by itching-fits,
Say I—let doubt occasion still more faith!

You'll say, once all believed, man, woman, child,
In that dear middle-age these noodles praise.
How you'd exult if I could put you back
Six hundred years, blot out cosmogony,
Geology, ethnology, what not,
(Greek endings, each the little passing-bell
That signifies some faith's about to die)
And set you square with Genesis again,—
When such a traveller told you his last news,
He saw the ark a-top of Ararat
But did not climb there since 'twas getting dusk
And robber-bands infest the mountain's foot!
How should you feel, I ask, in such an age,
How act? As other people felt and did;
With soul more blank than this decanter's knob,
Believe—and yet lie, kill, rob, fornicate
Full in belief's face, like the beast you'd be!

No, when the fight begins within himself,
A man's worth something. God stoops o'er his head,
Satan looks up between his feet—both tug—
He's left, himself, in the middle: the soul wakes
And grows. Prolong that battle through his life!
Never leave growing till the life to come!

Here, we've got callous to the Virgin's winks
That used to puzzle people wholesomely—
Men have outgrown the shame of being fools.
What are the laws of Nature, not to bend
If the Church bid them, brother Newman asks.
Up with the Immaculate Conception, then—
On to the rack with faith—is my advice!
Will not that hurry us upon our knees
Knocking our breasts, "It can't be—yet it shall!
Who am I, the worm, to argue with my Pope?
Low things confound the high things!" and so forth.
That's better than acquitting God with grace
As some folks do. He's tried—no case is proved,
Philosophy is lenient—He may go!

You'll say—the old system's not so obsolete
But men believe still: ay, but who and where?
King Bomba's lazzaroni foster yet
The sacred flame, so Antonelli writes;
But even of these, what ragamuffin-saint
Believes God watches him continually,
As he believes in fire that it will burn,
Or rain that it will drench him? Break fire's law,
Sin against rain, although the penalty
Be just singe or soaking? No, he smiles;
Those laws are laws that can enforce themselves.

The sum of all is—yes, my doubt is great,
My faith's the greater—then my faith's enough.
I have read much, thought much, experienced much,
Yet would die rather than avow my fear
The Naples' liquefaction may be false,
When set to happen by the palace-clock
According to the clouds or dinner-time.
I hear you recommend, I might at least
Eliminate, decrassify my faith
Since I adopt it; keeping what I must
And leaving what I can—such points as this!
I won't—that is, I can't throw one away.
Supposing there's no truth in what I said
About the need of trials to man's faith,
Still, when you bid me purify the same,
To such a process I discern no end,
Clearing off one excrescence to see two;

There's ever a next in size, now grown as big,
That meets the knife—I cut and cut again!
First cut the Liquefaction, what comes last
But Fichte's clever cut at God himself?
Experimentalize on sacred things?
I trust nor hand nor eye nor heart nor brain
To stop betimes: they all get drunk alike.
The first step, I am master not to take.

You'd find the cutting-process to your taste
As much as leaving growths of lies unpruned,
Nor see more danger in it, you retort.
Your taste's worth mine; but my taste proves more wise
When we consider that the steadfast hold
On the extreme end of the chain of faith
Gives all the advantage, makes the difference,
With the rough purblind mass we seek to rule.
We are their lords, or they are free of us
Just as we tighten or relax that hold.
So, other matters equal, we'll revert
To the first problem—which if solved my way
And thrown into the balance turns the scale—
How we may lead a comfortable life,
How suit our luggage to the cabin's size.

Of course you are remarking all this time
How narrowly and grossly I view life,
Respect the creature-comforts, care to rule
The masses, and regard complacently
" The cabin," in our old phrase! Well, I do.
I act for, talk for, live for this world now,
As this world calls for action, life and talk—
No prejudice to what next world may prove,
Whose new laws and requirements my best pledge
To observe them, is that I observe these now,
Doing hereafter what I do meanwhile.
Let us concede (gratuitously though)
Next life relieves the soul of body, yields
Pure spiritual enjoyments: well, my friend,
Why lose this life in the meantime, since its use
May be to make the next life more intense?

Do you know, I have often had a dream
(Work it up in your next month's article)

Of man's poor spirit in its progress still
Losing true life for ever and a day
Through ever trying to be and ever being
In the evolution of successive spheres,
Before its actual sphere and place of life,
Halfway into the next, which having reached,
It shoots with corresponding foolery
Halfway into the next still, on and off!
As when a traveller, bound from north to south,
Scouts fur in Russia—what's its use in France?
In France spurns flannel—where's its need in Spain?
In Spain drops cloth—too cumbrous for Algiers!
Linen goes next, and last the skin itself,
A superfluity at Timbuctoo.
When, through his journey, was the fool at ease?
I'm at ease now, friend—worldly in this world
I take and like its way of life; I think
My brothers who administer the means
Live better for my comfort—that's good too;
And God, if he pronounce upon it all,
Approves my service, which is better still.
If He keep silence,—why for you or me
Or that brute-beast pulled-up in to-day's " Times,"
What odds is't, save to ourselves, what life we lead?

You meet me at this issue—you declare,
All special pleading done with, truth is truth,
And justifies itself by undreamed ways.
You don't fear but it's better, if we doubt,
To say so, acting up to our truth perceived
However feebly.   Do then,—act away!
'Tis there I'm on the watch for you!   How one acts
Is, both of us agree, our chief concern:
And how you'll act is what I fain would see
If, like the candid person you appear,
You dare to make the most of your life's scheme
As I of mine, live up to its full law
Since there's no higher law that counterchecks.
Put natural religion to the test
You've just demolished the revealed with—quick,
Down to the root of all that checks your will,
All prohibition to lie, kill, and thieve
Or even to be an atheistic priest!

Suppose a pricking to incontinence—
Philosophers deduce you chastity
Or shame, from just the fact that at the first
Whoso embraced a woman in the plain,
Threw club down, and forewent his brains beside,
So stood a ready victim in the reach
Of any brother-savage club in hand—
Hence saw the use of going out of sight
In wood or cave to prosecute his loves—
I read this in a French book t'other day.
Does law so analyzed coerce you much?
Oh, men spin clouds of fuzz where matters end,
But you who reach where the first thread begins,
You'll soon cut that!—which means you can, but won't
Through certain instincts, blind, unreasoned-out,
You dare not set aside, you can't tell why,
But there they are, and so you let them rule.
Then, friend, you seem as much a slave as I,
A liar, conscious coward and hypocrite,
Without the good the slave expects to get,
Suppose he has a master after all!
You own your instincts—why what else do I,
Who want, am made for, and must have a God
Ere I can be ought, do ought?—no mere name
Want, but the true thing with what proves its truth,
To wit, a relation from that thing to me,
Touching from head to foot—which touch I feel,
And with it take the rest, this life of ours!
I live my life here; yours you dare not live.

Not as I state it, who (you please subjoin)
Disfigure such a life and call it names,
While, in your mind, remains another way
For simple men: knowledge and power have rights,
But ignorance and weakness have rights too.
There needs no crucial effort to find truth
If here or there or anywhere about—
We ought to turn each side, try hard and see,
And if we can't, be glad we've earned at least
The right, by one laborious proof the more,
To graze in peace earth's pleasant pasturage.
Men are not gods, but, properly, are brutes.
Something we may see, all we cannot see—

What need of lying? I say, I see all,
And swear to each detail the most minute,
In what I think a man's face—you, mere cloud:
I swear I hear him speak and see him wink,
For fear, if once I drop the emphasis,
Mankind may doubt if there's a cloud at all.
You take the simpler life—ready to see,
Willing to see—for no cloud's worth a face—
And leaving quiet what no strength can move,
And which, who bids you move? who has the right?
I bid you; but you are God's sheep, not mine—
" *Pastor est tui Dominus.*" You find
In these the pleasant pastures of this life
Much you may eat without the least offence,
Much you don't eat because your maw objects,
Much you would eat but that your fellow-flock
Open great eyes at you and even butt,
And thereupon you like your friends so much
You cannot please yourself, offending them—
Though when they seem exorbitantly sheep,
You weigh your pleasure with their butts and kicks
And strike the balance. Sometimes certain fears
Restrain you—real checks since you find them so—
Sometimes you please yourself and nothing checks;
And thus you graze through life with not one lie,
And like it best.

              But do you, in truth's name?
If so, you beat—which means—you are not I—
Who needs must make earth mine and feed my fill
Not simply unbutted at, unbickered with,
But motioned to the velvet of the sward
By those obsequious wethers' very selves.
Look at me, sir; my age is double yours.
At yours, I knew beforehand, so enjoyed,
What now I should be—as, permit the word,
I pretty well imagine your whole range
And stretch of tether twenty years to come.
We both have minds and bodies much alike.
In truth's name, don't you want my bishopric,
My daily bread, my influence and my state?
You're young, I'm old, you must be old one day;
Will you find then, as I do hour by hour,

Women their lovers kneel to, that cut curls
From your fat lap-dog's ears to grace a brooch—
Dukes, that petition just to kiss your ring—
With much beside you know or may conceive?
Suppose we die to-night: well, here am I,
Such were my gains, life bore this fruit to me,
While writing all the same my articles
On music, poetry, the fictile vase
Found at Albano, or Anacreon's Greek.
But you—the highest honour in your life,
The thing you'll crown yourself with, all your days,
Is—dining here and drinking this last glass
I pour you out in sign of amity
Before we part for ever.   Of your power
And social influence, worldly worth in short,
Judge what's my estimation by the fact—
I do not condescend to enjoin, beseech,
Hint secresy on one of all these words!
You're shrewd and know that should you publish it
The world would brand the lie—my enemies first,
" Who'd sneer—the bishop's an arch-hypocrite,
And knave perhaps, but not so frank a fool,"
Whereas I should not dare for both my ears
Breathe one such syllable, smile one such smile,
Before my chaplain who reflects myself—
My shade's so much more potent than your flesh.
What's your reward, self-abnegating friend?
Stood you confessed of those exceptional
And privileged great natures that dwarf mine—
A zealot with a mad ideal in reach,
A poet just about to print his ode,
A statesman with a scheme to stop this war,
An artist whose religion is his art,
I should have nothing to object! such men
Carry the fire, all things grow warm to them,
Their drugget's worth my purple, they beat me.
But you,—you're just as little those as I—
You, Gigadibs, who, thirty years of age,
Write stately for Blackwood's Magazine,
Believe you see two points in Hamlet's soul
Unseized by the Germans yet—which view you'll print—
Meantime the best you have to show being still
That lively lightsome article we took

Almost for the true Dickens,—what's the name?
" The Slum and Cellar—or Whitechapel life
Limned after dark! " it made me laugh, I know,
And pleased a month and brought you in ten pounds.
—Success I recognise and compliment,
And therefore give you, if you please, three words
(The card and pencil-scratch is quite enough)
Which whether here, in Dublin, or New York,
Will get you, prompt as at my eyebrow's wink,
Such terms as never you aspired to get
In all our own reviews and some not ours.
Go write your lively sketches—be the first
" Blougram, or The Eccentric Confidence "—
Or better simply say, " The Outward-bound."
Why, men as soon would throw it in my teeth
As copy and quote the infamy chalked broad
About me on the church-door opposite.
You will not wait for that experience though,
I fancy, howsoever you decide,
To discontinue—not detesting, not
Defaming, but at least—despising me!

Over his wine so smiled and talked his hour
Sylvester Blougram, styled *in partibus*
Episcopus, nec non—(the deuce knows what
It's changed to by our novel hierarchy)
With Gigadibs the literary man,
Who played with spoons, explored his plate's design,
And ranged the olive stones about its edge,
While the great bishop rolled him out his mind.

For Blougram, he believed, say, half he spoke.
The other portion, as he shaped it thus
For argumentatory purposes,
He felt his foe was foolish to dispute.
Some arbitrary accidental thoughts
That crossed his mind, amusing because new,
He chose to represent as fixtures there,
Invariable convictions (such they seemed
Beside his interlocutor's loose cards
Flung daily down, and not the same way twice)
While certain hell-deep instincts, man's weak tongue
Is never bold to utter in their truth
Because styled hell-deep ('tis an old mistake

To place hell at the bottom of the earth)
He ignored these,—not having in readiness
Their nomenclature and philosophy:
He said true things, but called them by wrong names.
" On the whole," he thought, " I justify myself
On every point where cavillers like this
Oppugn my life: he tries one kind of fence—
I close—he's worsted, that's enough for him;
He's on the ground! if the ground should break away
I take my stand on, there's a firmer yet
Beneath it, both of us may sink and reach.
His ground was over mine and broke the first.
So let him sit with me this many a year! "

He did not sit five minutes.   Just a week
Sufficed his sudden healthy vehemence.
(Something had struck him in the " Outward-bound "
Another way than Blougram's purpose was)
And having bought, not cabin-furniture
But settler's-implements (enough for three)
And started for Australia—there, I hope,
By this time he has tested his first plough,
And studied his last chapter of St. John.

MEMORABILIA.

I. Ah, did you once see Shelley plain,
    And did he stop and speak to you?
And did you speak to him again?
    How strange it seems, and new!

II. But you were living before that,
    And you are living after,
And the memory I started at—
    My starting moves your laughter!

III. I crossed a moor with a name of its own
    And a use in the world no doubt,
Yet a hand's-breadth of it shines alone
    'Mid the blank miles round about—

IV. For there I picked up on the heather
    And there I put inside my breast
A moulted feather, an eagle-feather—
    Well, I forget the rest.

ANDREA DEL SARTO.

(CALLED THE " FAULTLESS PAINTER.")

BUT do not let us quarrel any more,
No, my Lucrezia; bear with me for once:
Sit down and all shall happen as you wish.
You turn your face, but does it bring your heart?
I'll work then for your friend's friend, never fear,
Treat his own subject after his own way,
Fix his own time, accept too his own price
And shut the money into this small hand
When next it takes mine. Will it? tenderly?
Oh, I'll content him,—but to-morrow, Love!
I often am much wearier than you think,
This evening more than usual, and it seems
As if—forgive now—should you let me sit
Here by the window with your hand in mine
And look a half hour forth on Fiesole,
Both of one mind, as married people use,
Quietly, quietly, the evening through,
I might get up to-morrow to my work
Cheerful and fresh as ever. Let us try.
To-morrow how you shall be glad for this!
Your soft hand is a woman of itself,
And mine the man's bared breast she curls inside.
Don't count the time lost, either; you must serve
For each of the five pictures we require—
It saves a model. So! keep looking so—
My serpentining beauty, rounds on rounds!
—How could you ever prick those perfect ears,
Even to put the pearl there! oh, so sweet—
My face, my moon, my everybody's moon,
Which everybody looks on and calls his,
And, I suppose, is looked on by in turn,
While she looks—no one's: very dear, no less!
You smile? why, there's my picture ready made.
There's what we painters call our harmony!
A common greyness silvers everything,—
All in a twilight, you and I alike
—You, at the point of your first pride in me
(That's gone you know),—but I, at every point;

My youth, my hope, my art, being all toned down
To yonder sober pleasant Fiesole.
There's the bell clinking from the chapel-top;
That length of convent-wall across the way
Holds the trees safer, huddled more inside;
The last monk leaves the garden; days decrease
And autumn grows, autumn in everything.
Eh? the whole seems to fall into a shape
As if I saw alike my work and self
And all that I was born to be and do,
A twilight-piece.   Love, we are in God's hand.
How strange now, looks the life he makes us lead!
So free we seem, so fettered fast we are:
I feel he laid the fetter: let it lie!
This chamber for example—turn your head—
All that's behind us! you don't understand
Nor care to understand about my art,
But you can hear at least when people speak;
And that cartoon, the second from the door
—It is the thing, Love! so such things should be—
Behold Madonna, I am bold to say.
I can do with my pencil what I know,
What I see, what at bottom of my heart
I wish for, if I ever wish so deep—
Do easily, too—when I say perfectly
I do not boast, perhaps: yourself are judge
Who listened to the Legate's talk last week,
And just as much they used to say in France.
At any rate, 'tis easy, all of it,
No sketches first, no studies, that's long past—
I do what many dream of all their lives
—Dream? strive to do, and agonise to do,
And fail in doing.   I could count twenty such
On twice your fingers, and not leave this town,
Who strive—you don't know how the others strive
To paint a little thing like that you smeared
Carelessly passing with your robes afloat,
Yet do much less, so much less, some one says,
(I know his name, no matter) so much less!
Well, less is more, Lucrezia! I am judged.
There burns a truer light in them,
In their vexed, beating, stuffed and stopped-up brain,
Heart, or whate'er else, than goes on to prompt

This low-pulsed forthright craftsman's hand of mine.
Their works drop groundward, but themselves, I know,
Reach many a time a heaven that's shut to me,
Enter and take their place there sure enough,
Though they come back and cannot tell the world.
My works are nearer heaven, but I sit here.
The sudden blood of these men! at a word—
Praise them, it boils, or blame them, it boils too.
I, painting from myself and to myself,
Know what I do, am unmoved by men's blame
Or their praise either.   Somebody remarks
Morello's outline there is wrongly traced,
His hue mistaken—what of that?   or else,
Rightly traced and well ordered—what of that?
Ah, but a man's reach should exceed his grasp,
Or what's a Heaven for? all is silver-grey
Placid and perfect with my art—the worse!
I know both what I want and what might gain—
And yet how profitless to know, to sigh
" Had I been two, another and myself,
Our head would have o'erlooked the world!"   No doubt.
Yonder's a work, now, of that famous youth
The Urbinate who died five years ago.
('Tis copied, George Vasari sent it me.)
Well, I can fancy how he did it all,
Pouring his soul, with kings and popes to see,
Reaching, that Heaven might so replenish him,
Above and through his art—for it gives way;
That arm is wrongly put—and there again—
A fault to pardon in the drawing's lines,
Its body, so to speak! its soul is right,
He means right—that, a child may understand.
Still, what an arm! and I could alter it.
But all the play, the insight and the stretch—
Out of me! out of me! And wherefore out?
Had you enjoined them on me, given me soul,
We might have risen to Rafael, I and you.
Nay, Love, you did give all I asked, I think—
More than I merit, yes, by many times.
But had you—oh, with the same perfect brow,
And perfect eyes, and more than perfect mouth,
And the low voice my soul hears, as a bird
The fowler's pipe, and follows to the snare—

Had you, with these the same, but brought a mind!
Some women do so.   Had the mouth there urged
" God and the glory! never care for gain.
The present by the future, what is that?
Live for fame, side by side with Angelo—
Rafael is waiting. Up to God all three! "
I might have done it for you. So it seems—
Perhaps not. All is as God over-rules.
Beside, incentives come from the soul's self;
The rest avail not. Why do I need you?
What wife had Rafael, or has Angelo?
In this world, who can do a thing, will not—
And who would do it, cannot, I perceive:
Yet the will's somewhat—somewhat, too, the power—
And thus we half-men struggle. At the end,
God, I conclude, compensates, punishes.
'Tis safer for me, if the award be strict,
That I am something underrated here,
Poor this long while, despised, to speak the truth.
I dared not, do you know, leave home all day,
For fear of chancing on the Paris lords.
The best is when they pass and look aside;
But they speak sometimes; I must bear it all.
Well may they speak! That Francis, that first time,
And that long festal year at Fontainebleau!
I surely then could sometimes leave the ground,
Put on the glory, Rafael's daily wear,
In that humane great monarch's golden look,—
One finger in his beard or twisted curl
Over his mouth's good mark that made the smile,
One arm about my shoulder, round my neck,
The jingle of his gold chain in my ear,
[I] painting proudly with his breath on me,
All his court round him, seeing with her eyes,
Such frank French eyes, and such a fire of souls
Profuse, my hand kept plying by those hearts,—
And, best of all, this, this, this face beyond,
This in the back-ground, waiting on my work,
To crown the issue with a last reward!
A good time, was it not, my kingly days?
And had you not grown restless—but I know—
'Tis done and past; 'twas right, my instinct said;
Too live the life grew, golden and not grey—

And I'm the weak-eyed bat no sun should tempt
Out of the grange whose four walls make his world.
How could it end in any other way?
You called me, and I came home to your heart.
The triumph was to have ended there—then if
I reached it ere the triumph, what is lost?
Let my hands frame your face in your hair's gold,
You beautiful Lucrezia that are mine!
" Rafael did this, Andrea painted that—
The Roman's is the better when you pray,
But still the other's Virgin was his wife—"
Men will excuse me.   I am glad to judge
Both pictures in your presence; clearer grows
My better fortune, I resolve to think.
For, do you know, Lucrezia, as God lives,
Said one day Angelo, his very self,
To Rafael . . . I have known it all these years . . .
(When the young man was flaming out his thoughts
Upon a palace-wall for Rome to see,
Too lifted up in heart because of it)
" Friend, there's a certain sorry little scrub
Goes up and down our Florence, none cares how,
Who, were he set to plan and execute
As you are pricked on by your popes and kings,
Would bring the sweat into that brow of yours! "
To Rafael's!—And indeed the arm is wrong.
I hardly dare—yet, only you to see,
Give the chalk here—quick, thus the line should go!
Ay, but the soul! he's Rafael! rub it out!
Still, all I care for, if he spoke the truth,
(What he? why, who but Michael Angelo?
Do you forget already words like those?)
If really there was such a chance, so lost,
Is, whether you're—not grateful—but more pleased.
Well, let me think so.   And you smile indeed!
This hour has been an hour!   Another smile?
If you would sit thus by me every night
I should work better, do you comprehend?
I mean that I should earn more, give you more.
See, it is settled dusk now; there's a star;
Morello's gone, the watch-lights shew the wall,
The cue-owls speak the name we call them by.
Come from the window, Love,—come in, at last,

Inside the melancholy little house
We built to be so gay with. God is just.
King Francis may forgive me. Oft at nights
When I look up from painting, eyes tired out,
The walls become illumined, brick from brick
Distinct, instead of mortar fierce bright gold,
That gold of his I did cement them with!
Let us but love each other. Must you go?
That Cousin here again? he waits outside?
Must see you—you, and not with me? Those loans!
More gaming debts to pay? you smiled for that?
Well, let smiles buy me! have you more to spend?
While hand and eye and something of a heart
Are left me, work's my ware, and what's it worth?
I'll pay my fancy. Only let me sit
The grey remainder of the evening out,
Idle, you call it, and muse perfectly
How I could paint were I but back in France,
One picture, just one more—the Virgin's face,
Not yours this time! I want you at my side
To hear them—that is, Michael Angelo—
Judge all I do and tell you of its worth.
Will you? To-morrow, satisfy your friend.
I take the subjects for his corridor,
Finish the portrait out of hand—there, there,
And throw him in another thing or two
If he demurs; the whole should prove enough
To pay for this same Cousin's freak. Beside,
What's better and what's all I care about,
Get you the thirteen scudi for the ruff.
Love, does that please you? Ah, but what does he,
The Cousin! what does he to please you more?

I am grown peaceful as old age to-night.
I regret little, I would change still less.
Since there my past life lies, why alter it?
The very wrong to Francis! it is true
I took his coin, was tempted and complied,
And built this house and sinned, and all is said.
My father and my mother died of want.
Well, had I riches of my own? you see
How one gets rich! Let each one bear his lot.
They were born poor, lived poor, and poor they died:

And I have laboured somewhat in my time
And not been paid profusely.   Some good son
Paint my two hundred pictures—let him try!
No doubt, there's something strikes a balance.   Yes,
You loved me quite enough, it seems to-night.
This must suffice me here.   What would one have?
In heaven, perhaps, new chances, one more chance—
Four great walls in the New Jerusalem
Meted on each side by the angel's reed,
For Leonard, Rafael, Angelo and me
To cover—the three first without a wife,
While I have mine!   So—still they overcome
Because there's still Lucrezia,—as I choose.

Again the Cousin's whistle!   Go, my Love.

BEFORE.

I.

Let them fight it out, friend! things have gone too far.
God must judge the couple! leave them as they are
—Whichever one's the guiltless, to his glory,
And whichever one the guilt's with, to my story.

II.

Why, you would not bid men, sunk in such a slough,
Strike no arm out further, stick and stink as now,
Leaving right and wrong to settle the embroilment,
Heaven with snaky Hell, in torture and entoilment?

III.

Which of them's the culprit, how must he conceive
God's the queen he caps to, laughing in his sleeve!
'Tis but decent to profess oneself beneath her.
Still, one must not be too much in earnest either.

IV.

Better sin the whole sin, sure that God observes,
Then go live his life out! life will try his nerves,
When the sky which noticed all, makes no disclosure,
And the earth keeps up her terrible composure.

v.

Let him pace at pleasure, past the walls of rose,
Pluck their fruits when grape-trees graze him as he goes.
For he 'gins to guess the purpose of the garden,
With the sly mute thing beside there for a warden.

vi.

What's the leopard-dog-thing, constant to his side,
A leer and lie in every eye on its obsequious hide?
When will come an end of all the mock obeisance,
And the price appear that pays for the misfeasance?

vii.

So much for the culprit.   Who's the martyred man?
Let him bear one stroke more, for be sure he can.
He that strove thus evil's lump with good to leaven,
Let him give his blood at last and get his heaven.

viii.

All or nothing, stake it! trusts he God or no?
Thus far and no farther? farther? be it so.
Now, enough of your chicane of prudent pauses,
Sage provisos, sub-intents, and saving-clauses.

ix.

Ah, " forgive " you bid him?   While God's champion lives,
Wrong shall be resisted: dead, why he forgives.
But you must not end my friend ere you begin him;
Evil stands not crowned on earth, while breath is in him.

x.

Once more—Will the wronger, at this last of all,
Dare to say " I did wrong," rising in his fall?
No?—Let go, then—both the fighters to their places—
While I count three, step you back as many paces.

AFTER.

Take the cloak from his face, and at first
  Let the corpse do its worst.
How he lies in his rights of a man!
  Death has done all death can.

And absorbed in the new life he leads,
    He recks not, he heeds
Nor his wrong nor my vengeance—both strike
    On his senses alike,
And are lost in the solemn and strange
    Surprise of the change.
Ha, what avails death to erase
    His offence, my disgrace?
I would we were boys as of old
    In the field, by the fold—
His outrage, God's patience, man's scorn
    Were so easily borne.

I stand here now, he lies in his place—
    Cover the face.

IN THREE DAYS.

I. So, I shall see her in three days
    And just one night, but nights are short,
    Then two long hours, and that is morn.
    See how I come, unchanged, unworn—
    Feel, where my life broke off from thine,
    How fresh the splinters keep and fine,—
    Only a touch and we combine!

II. Too long, this time of year, the days!
    But nights—at least the nights are short.
    As night shows where her one moon is,
    A hand's-breadth of pure light and bliss,
    So, life's night gives my lady birth
    And my eyes hold her! what is worth
    The rest of heaven, the rest of earth?

III. O loaded curls, release your store
    Of warmth and scent as once before
    The tingling hair did, lights and darks
    Out-breaking into fairy sparks
    When under curl and curl I pried
    After the warmth and scent inside
    Thro' lights and darks how manifold—
    The dark inspired, the light controlled!
    As early Art embrowned the gold.

IV. What great fear—should one say, " Three days
    That change the world, might change as well
    Your fortune; and if joy delays,
    Be happy that no worse befell."
    What small fear—if another says,
    " Three days and one short night beside
    May throw no shadow on your ways;
    But years must teem with change untried,
    With chance not easily defied,
    With an end somewhere undescried."
    No fear!—or if a fear be born
    This minute, it dies out in scorn.
    Fear? I shall see her in three days
    And one night, now the nights are short,
    Then just two hours, and that is morn.

IN A YEAR.

I. NEVER any more
    While I live,
    Need I hope to see his face
    As before.
    Once his love grown chill,
    Mine may strive—
    Bitterly we re-embrace,
    Single still.

II. Was it something said,
    Something done,
    Vexed him? was it touch of hand,
    Turn of head?
    Strange! that very way
    Love begun.
    I as little understand
    Love's decay.

III. When I sewed or drew,
    I recall
    How he looked as if I sang,
    —Sweetly too.
    If I spoke a word,
    First of all
    Up his cheek the colour sprang,
    Then he heard.

IV. Sitting by my side,
      At my feet,
  So he breathed the air I breathed,
      Satisfied!
  I, too, at love's brim
      Touched the sweet:
  I would die if death bequeathed
      Sweet to him.

V. "Speak, I love thee best!"
      He exclaimed,
  "Let my love thy own foretell,—"
      I confessed:
  "Clasp my heart on thine
      Now unblamed,
  Since upon thy soul as well
      Hangeth mine!"

VI. Was it wrong to own,
      Being truth?
  Why should all the giving prove
      His alone?
  I had wealth and ease,
      Beauty, youth—
  Since my lover gave me love,
      I gave these.

VII. That was all I meant,
      —To be just.
  And the passion I had raised
      To content.
  Since he chose to change
      Gold for dust,
  If I gave him what he praised
      Was it strange?

VIII. Would he love me yet,
      On and on,
  While I found some way undreamed
      —Paid my debt!
  Gave more life and more,
      Till, all gone,
  He should smile "She never seemed
      Mine before.

IX. " What—she felt the while,
       Must I think?
   Love's so different with us men,"
       He should smile.
   " Dying for my sake—
       White and pink!
   Can't we touch these bubbles then
       But they break? "

X. Dear, the pang is brief.
       Do thy part,
   Have thy pleasure.   How perplext
       Grows belief!
   Well, this cold clay clod
       Was man's heart.
   Crumble it—and what comes next?
       Is it God?

OLD PICTURES IN FLORENCE.

I. THE morn when first it thunders in March,
       The eel in the pond gives a leap, they say.
   As I leaned and looked over the aloed arch
       Of the villa-gate, this warm March day,
   No flash snapt, no dumb thunder rolled
       In the valley beneath, where, white and wide,
   Washed by the morning's water-gold,
       Florence lay out on the mountain-side.

II. River and bridge and street and square
       Lay mine, as much at my beck and call,
   Through the live translucent bath of air,
       As the sights in a magic crystal ball.
   And of all I saw and of all I praised,
       The most to praise and the best to see,
   Was the startling bell-tower Giotto raised:
       But why did it more than startle me?

III. Giotto, how, with that soul of yours,
       Could you play me false who loved you so?
   Some slights if a certain heart endures
       It feels, I would have your fellows know!

Faith—I perceive not why I should care
    To break a silence that suits them best,
But the thing grows somewhat hard to bear
    When I find a Giotto join the rest.

IV. On the arch where olives overhead
    Print the blue sky with twig and leaf,
(That sharp-curled leaf they never shed)
    'Twixt the aloes I used to lean in chief,
And mark through the winter afternoons,
    By a gift God grants me now and then,
In the mild decline of those suns like moons,
    Who walked in Florence, besides her men.

V. They might chirp and chaffer, come and go
    For pleasure or profit, her men alive—
My business was hardly with them, I trow,
    But with empty cells of the human hive;
—With the chapter-room, the cloister-porch,
    The church's apsis, aisle or nave,
Its crypt, one fingers along with a torch—
    Its face, set full for the sun to shave.

VI. Wherever a fresco peels and drops,
    Wherever an outline weakens and wanes
Till the latest life in the painting stops,
    Stands One whom each fainter pulse-tick pains!
One, wishful each scrap should clutch its brick,
    Each tinge not wholly escape the plaster,
—A lion who dies of an ass's kick,
    The wronged great soul of an ancient Master.

VII. For oh, this world and the wrong it does!
    They are safe in heaven with their backs to it,
The Michaels and Rafaels, you hum and buzz
    Round the works of, you of the little wit!
Do their eyes contract to the earth's old scope,
    Now that they see God face to face,
And have all attained to be poets, I hope?
    'Tis their holiday now, in any case.

VIII. Much they reck of your praise and you!
    But the wronged great souls—can they be quit
Of a world where all their work is to do,
    Where you style them, you of the little wit,

Old Master this and Early the other,
  Not dreaming that Old and New are fellows,
That a younger succeeds to an elder brother,
  Da Vincis derive in good time from Dellos.

IX. And here where your praise would yield returns
  And a handsome word or two give help,
Here, after your kind, the mastiff girns
  And the puppy pack of poodles yelp.
What, not a word for Stefano there
  —Of brow once prominent and starry,
Called Nature's ape and the world's despair
  For his peerless painting (see Vasari)?

X. There he stands now. Study, my friends,
  What a man's work comes to! so he plans it,
Performs it, perfects it, makes amends
  For the toiling and moiling, and there's its transit!
Happier the thrifty blind-folk labour,
  With upturned eye while the hand is busy,
Not sidling a glance at the coin of their neighbour!
  'Tis looking downward makes one dizzy.

XI. If you knew their work you would deal your dole.
  May I take upon me to instruct you?
When Greek Art ran and reached the goal,
  Thus much had the world to boast *in fructu*—
The truth of Man, as by God first spoken,
  Which the actual generations garble,
Was re-uttered,—and Soul (which Limbs betoken)
  And Limbs (Soul informs) were made new in marble.

XII. So you saw yourself as you wished you were,
  As you might have been, as you cannot be;
And bringing your own shortcomings there.
  You grew content in your poor degree
With your little power, by those statues' godhead,
  And your little scope, by their eyes' full sway,
And your little grace, by their grace embodied,
  And your little date, by their forms that stay.

XIII. You would fain be kinglier, say than I am?
  Even so, you would not sit like Theseus.
You'd fain be a model? the Son of Priam
  Has yet the advantage in arms' and knees' use.

You're wroth—can you slay your snake like Apollo?
    You're grieved—still Niobe's the grander!
You live—there's the Racer's frieze to follow—
    You die—there's the dying Alexander.

xiv. So, testing your weakness by their strength,
    Your meagre charms by their rounded beauty,
Measured by Art in your breadth and length,
    You learn—to submit is the worsted's duty.
—When I say " you " 'tis the common soul,
    The collective, I mean—the race of Man
That receives life in parts to live in a whole,
    And grow here according to God's own plan.

xv. Growth came when, looking your last on them all,
    You turned your eyes inwardly one fine day
And cried with a start—What if we so small
    Are greater, ay, greater the while than they!
Are they perfect of lineament, perfect of stature?
    In both, of such lower types are we
Precisely because of our wider nature;
    For time, theirs—ours, for eternity.

xvi. To-day's brief passion limits their range,
    It seethes with the morrow for us and more.
They are perfect—how else? they shall never change:
    We are faulty—why not? we have time in store.
The Artificer's hand is not arrested
    With us—we are rough-hewn, no-wise polished:
They stand for our copy, and, once invested
    With all they can teach, we shall see them abolished.

xvii. 'Tis a life-long toil till our lump be leaven—
    The better! what's come to perfection perishes.
Things learned on earth, we shall practise in heaven.
    Works done least rapidly, Art most cherishes.
Thyself shall afford the example, Giotto!
    Thy one work, not to decrease or diminish,
Done at a stroke, was just (was it not?) " O! "
    Thy great Campanile is still to finish.

xviii. Is it true, we are now, and shall be hereafter,
    And what—is depending on life's one minute?
Hails heavenly cheer or infernal laughter
    Our first step out of the gulf or in it?

And Man, this step within his endeavour,
  His face, have no more play and action
Than joy which is crystallized for ever,
  Or grief, an eternal petrifaction!

XIX. On which I conclude, that the early painters,
      To cries of " Greek Art and what more wish
          you? "—
    Replied, " Become now self-acquainters,
      And paint man, man,—whatever the issue!
    Make the hopes shine through the flesh they fray,
      New fears aggrandise the rags and tatters.
    So bring the invisible full into play,
      Let the visible go to the dogs—what matters? "

XX. Give these, I say, full honour and glory
      For daring so much, before they well did it.
    The first of the new, in our race's story,
      Beats the last of the old, 'tis no idle quiddit.
    The worthies began a revolution
      Which if on the earth we intend to acknowledge
    Honour them now—(ends my allocution)
      Nor confer our degree when the folks leave college.

XXI. There's a fancy some lean to and others hate—
      That, when this life is ended, begins
    New work for the soul in another state,
      Where it strives and gets weary, loses and wins—
    Where the strong and the weak, this world's
          congeries,
      Repeat in large what they practised in small.
    Through life after life in unlimited series;
      Only the scale's to be changed, that's all.

XXII. Yet I hardly know.   When a soul has seen
      By the means of Evil that Good is best,
    And through earth and its noise, what is heaven's
          serene,—
      When its faith in the same has stood the test—
    Why, the child grown man, you burn the rod,
      The uses of labour are surely done.
    There remaineth a rest for the people of God,
      And I have had troubles enough for one.

XXIII. But at any rate I have loved the season
    Of Art's spring-birth so dim and dewy,
My sculptor is Nicolo the Pisan;
    My painter—who but Cimabue?
Nor ever was man of them all indeed,
    From these to Ghiberti and Ghirlandajo,
Could say that he missed my critic-meed.
    So now to my special grievance—heigh ho!

XXIV. Their ghosts now stand, as I said before,
    Watching each fresco flaked and rasped,
Blocked up, knocked out, or whitewashed o'er
    —No getting again what the church has grasped!
The works on the wall must take their chance,
    " Works never conceded to England's thick clime!"
(I hope they prefer their inheritance
    Of a bucketful of Italian quick-lime.)

XXV. When they go at length, with such a shaking
    Of heads o'er the old delusions, sadly
Each master his way through the black streets taking,
    Where many a lost work breathes though badly—
Why don't they bethink them of who has merited?
    Why not reveal, while their pictures dree
Such doom, that a captive's to be out-ferreted?
    Why do they never remember me?

XXVI. Not that I expect the great Bigordi
    Nor Sandro to hear me, chivalric, bellicose;
Nor wronged Lippino—and not a word I
    Say of a scrap of Fra Angelico's.
But are you too fine, Taddeo Gaddi,
    To grant me a taste of your intonaco—
Some Jerome that seeks the heaven with a sad eye?
    No churlish saint, Lorenzo Monaco?

XXVII. Could not the ghost with the close red cap,
    My Pollajolo, the twice a craftsman,
Save me a sample, give me the hap
    Of a muscular Christ that shows the draughtsman?
No Virgin by him, the somewhat petty,
    Of finical touch and tempera crumbly—
Could not Alesso Baldovinetti
    Contribute so much, I ask him humbly?

XXVIII. Margheritone of Arezzo,
   With the grave-clothes garb and swaddling barret.
  (Why purse up mouth and beak in a pet so,
   You bald, saturnine, poll-clawed parrot?)
  No poor glimmering Crucifixion,
   Where in the foreground kneels the donor?
  If such remain, as in my conviction,
   The hoarding does you but little honour.

XXIX. They pass: for them the panels may thrill,
   The tempera grow alive and tinglish—
  Rot or are left to the mercies still
   Of dealers and stealers, Jews and the English!
  Seeing mere money's worth in their prize,
   Who sell it to some one calm as Zeno
  At naked Art, and in ecstacies
   Before some clay-cold, vile Carlino!

XXX. No matter for these! But Giotto, you,
   Have you allowed, as the town-tongues babble it,
  Never! it shall not be counted true—
   That a certain precious little tablet
  Which Buonarroti eyed like a lover,—
   Buried so long in oblivion's womb,
  Was left for another than I to discover,—
   Turns up at last, and to whom?—to whom?

XXXI. I, that have haunted the dim San Spirito,
   (Or was it rather the Ognissanti?)
  Stood on the altar-steps, patient and weary too!
   Nay, I shall have it yet, *detur amanti!*
  My Koh-i-noor—or (if that's a platitude)
   Jewel of Giamschid, the Persian Sofi's eye!
  So, in anticipative gratitude,
   What if I take up my hope and prophesy?

XXXII. When the hour is ripe, and a certain dotard
   Pitched, no parcel that needs invoicing,
  To the worse side of the Mont St. Gothard,
   Have, to begin by way of rejoicing,
  None of that shooting the sky (blank cartridge),
   No civic guards, all plumes and lacquer,
  Hunting Radetsky's soul like a partridge
   Over Morello with squib and cracker.

XXXIII. We'll shoot this time better game and bag 'em hot—
     No display at the stone of Dante,
But a kind of [sober] Witan-agemot
     (" Casa Guidi," quod videas ante)
To ponder Freedom restored to Florence,
     How Art may return that departed with her.
Go, hated house, go each trace of the Lorraine's!
     And bring us the days of Orgagna hither.

XXXIV. How we shall prologuise, how we shall perorate,
     Say fit things upon art and history—
Set truth at blood-heat and the false at a zero rate,
     Make of the want of the age no mystery!
Contrast the fructuous and sterile eras,
     Show, monarchy its uncouth cub licks
Out of the bear's shape to the chimæra's—
     Pure Art's birth being still the republic's!

XXXV. Then one shall propose (in a speech, curt Tuscan,
     Sober, expurgate, spare of an " *issimo*,")
Ending our half-told tale of Cambuscan,
     Turning the Bell-tower's alt altissimo.
And fine as the beak of a young beccaccia
     The Campanile, the Duomo's fit ally,
Soars up in gold its full fifty braccia,
     Completing Florence, as Florence, Italy.

XXXVI. Shall I be alive that morning the scaffold
     Is broken away, and the long-pent fire
Like the golden hope of the world unbaffled
     Springs from its sleep, and up goes the spire—
As, " God and the People " plain for its motto,
     Thence the new tricolor flaps at the sky?
Foreseeing the day that vindicates Giotto
     And Florence together, the first am I!

IN A BALCONY.

FIRST PART.

CONSTANCE *and* NORBERT.

NORBERT.

Now.

CONSTANCE.

Not now.

NORBERT.

    Give me them again, those hands—
Put them upon my forehead, how it throbs!
Press them before my eyes, the fire comes through.
You cruellest, you dearest in the world,
Let me! the Queen must grant whate'er I ask—
How can I gain you and not ask the Queen?
There she stays waiting for me, here stand you.
Some time or other this was to be asked,
Now is the one time—what I ask, I gain—
Let me ask now, Love!

CONSTANCE.

  Do, and ruin us.

NORBERT.

Let it be now, Love! All my soul breaks forth.
How I do love you! give my love its way!
A man can have but one life and one death,
One heaven, one hell. Let me fulfil my fate—
Grant me my heaven now. Let me know you mine,
Prove you mine, write my name upon your brow,
Hold you and have you, and then die away
If God please, with completion in my soul.

CONSTANCE.

I am not yours then? how content this man?
I am not his, who change into himself,
Have passed into his heart and beat its beats,
Who give my hands to him, my eyes, my hair,

Give all that was of me away to him
So well, that now, my spirit turned his own,
Takes part with him against the woman here,
Bids him not stumble at so mere a straw
As caring that the world be cognisant
How he loves her and how she worships him.
You have this woman, not as yet that world.
Go on, I bid, nor stop to care for me
By saving what I cease to care about,
The courtly name and pride of circumstance—
The name you'll pick up and be cumbered with
Just for the poor parade's sake, nothing more;
Just that the world may slip from under you—
Just that the world may cry " So much for him
The man predestined to the heap of crowns!
There goes his chance of winning one, at least."

NORBERT.

The world!

CONSTANCE.

          You love it. Love me quite as well,
And see if I shall pray for this in vain!
Why must you ponder what it knows or thinks?

NORBERT.

You pray for—what, in vain?

CONSTANCE.

          Oh my heart's heart,
How I do love you, Norbert!—that is right!
But listen, or I take my hands away.
You say, " let it be now "—you would go now
And tell the Queen, perhaps six steps from us,
You love me—so you do, thank God!

NORBERT.

          Thank God!

CONSTANCE.

Yes, Norbert,—but you fain would tell your love,
And, what succeeds the telling, ask of her
My hand. Now take this rose and look at it,
Listening to me. You are the minister,

The Queen's first favourite, nor without a cause.
To-night completes your wonderful year's-work
(This palace-feast is held to celebrate)
Made memorable by her life's success,
That junction of two crowns on her sole head
Her house had only dreamed of anciently.
That this mere dream is grown a stable truth
To-night's feast makes authentic.   Whose the praise?
Whose genius, patience, energy, achieved
What turned the many heads and broke the hearts?
You are the fate—your minute's in the heaven.
Next comes the Queen's turn.   Name your own reward!
With leave to clench the past, chain the to-come,
Put out an arm and touch and take the sun
And fix it ever full-faced on your earth,
Possess yourself supremely of her life,
You choose the single thing she will not grant—
The very declaration of which choice
Will turn the scale and neutralise your work.
At best she will forgive you, if she can.
You think I'll let you choose—her cousin's hand?

NORBERT.

Wait.   First, do you retain your old belief
The Queen is generous,—nay is just?

CONSTANCE.

There, there!
So men make women love them, while they know
No more of women's hearts than . . . look you here,
You that are just and generous beside,
Make it your own case.   For example now,
I'll say—I let you kiss me and hold my hands—
Why? do you know why? I'll instruct you, then—
The kiss, because you have a name at court,
This hand and this, that you may shut in each
A jewel, if you please to pick up such.
That's horrible!   Apply it to the Queen—
Suppose, I am the Queen to whom you speak.
" I was a nameless man: you needed me:
Why did I proffer you my aid? there stood
A certain pretty Cousin by your side.
Why did I make such common cause with you?

Access to her had not been easy else.
You give my labours here abundant praise:
'Faith, labour, while she overlooked, grew play,
How shall your gratitude discharge itself?
Give me her hand!"

NORBERT.

                    And still I urge the same.
Is the Queen just? just—generous or no!

CONSTANCE.

Yes, just.   You love a rose—no harm in that—
But was it for the rose's sake or mine
You put it in your bosom? mine, you said—
Then mine you still must say or else be false.
You told the Queen you served her for herself:
If so, to serve her was to serve yourself
She thinks, for all your unbelieving face!
I know her.   In the hall, six steps from us,
One sees the twenty pictures—there's a life
Better than life—and yet no life at all;
Conceive her born in such a magic dome,
Pictures all round her! why, she sees the world
Can recognise its given things and facts,
The fight of giants or the feast of gods,
Sages in senate, beauties at the bath,
Chaces and battles, the whole earth's display,
Landscape and sea-piece, down to flowers and fruit—
And who shall question that she knows them all
In better semblance than the things outside?
Yet bring into the silent gallery
Some live thing to contrast in breath and blood,
Some lion, with the painted lion there—
You think she'll understand composedly?
—Say, " that's his fellow in the hunting-piece
Yonder, I've turned to praise a hundred times? "
Not so.   Her knowledge of our actual earth,
Its hopes and fears, concerns and sympathies,
Must be too far, too mediate, too unreal.
The real exists for us outside, not her—
How should it, with that life in these four walls,
That father and that mother, first to last
No father and no mother—friends, a heap,

Lovers, no lack—a husband in due time,
And everyone of them alike a lie!
Things painted by a Rubens out of nought
Into what kindness, friendship, love should be;
All better, all more grandiose than life,
Only no life; mere cloth and surface-paint
You feel while you admire.   How should she feel?
And now that she has stood thus fifty years
The sole spectator in that gallery,
You think to bring this warm real struggling love
In to her of a sudden, and suppose
She'll peep her state untroubled?   Here's the truth—
She'll apprehend its value at a glance,
Prefer it to the pictured loyalty!
You only have to say " so men are made,
For this they act, the thing has many names
But this the right one—and now, Queen, be just!"
And life slips back—you lose her at the word—
You do not even for amends gain me.
He will not understand! oh, Norbert, Norbert,
Do you not understand?

NORBERT.

           The Queen's the Queen,
I am myself—no picture, but alive
In every nerve and every muscle, here
At the palace-window or in the people's street,
As she in the gallery where the pictures glow.
The good of life is precious to us both.
She cannot love—what do I want with rule?
When first I saw your face a year ago
I knew my life's good—my soul heard one voice
" The woman yonder, there's no use of life
But just to obtain her! heap earth's woes in one
And bear them—make a pile of all earth's joys
And spurn them, as they help or help not here;
Only, obtain her!"—How was it to be?
I found she was the cousin of the Queen;
I must then serve the Queen to get to her—
No other way.   Suppose there had been one,
And I by saying prayers to some white star
With promise of my body and my soul
Might gain you,—should I pray the star or no?

Instead, there was the Queen to serve! I served,
And did what other servants failed to do.
Neither she sought nor I declared my end.
Her good is hers, my recompense be mine,
And let me name you as that recompense.
She dreamed that such a thing could never be?
Let her wake now.   She thinks there was some cause—
The love of power, of fame, pure loyalty?
—Perhaps she fancies men wear out their lives
Chasing such shades.   Then I've a fancy too.
I worked because I want you with my soul—
I therefore ask your hand.   Let it be now.

CONSTANCE.

Had I not loved you from the very first,
Were I not yours, could we not steal out thus
So wickedly, so wildly, and so well,
You might be thus impatient.   What's conceived
Of us without here, by the folks within?
Where are you now? immersed in cares of state—
Where am I now?—intent on festal robes—
We two, embracing under death's spread hand!
What was this thought for, what this scruple of yours
Which broke the council up, to bring about
One minute's meeting in the corridor?
And then the sudden sleights, long secresies
The plots inscrutable, deep telegraphs,
Long-planned chance-meetings, hazards of a look,
" Does she know? does she not know? saved or lost?"
A year of this compression's ecstasy
All goes for nothing? you would give this up
For the old way, the open way, the world's,
His way who beats, and his who sells his wife?
What tempts you? their notorious happiness,
That you're ashamed of ours?   The best you'll get
Will be, the Queen grants all that you require,
Concedes the cousin, and gets rid of you
And her at once, and gives us ample leave
To live as our five hundred happy friends.
The world will show us with officious hand
Our chamber-entry and stand sentinel,
When we so oft have stolen across her traps!
Get the world's warrant, ring the falcon's foot,

And make it duty to be bold and swift,
When long ago 'twas nature.   Have it so!
He never hawked by rights till flung from fist?
Oh, the man's thought!—no woman's such a fool.

NORBERT.

Yes, the man's thought and my thought, which is more—
One made to love you, let the world take note.
Have I done worthy work? be love's the praise,
Though hampered by restrictions, barred against
By set forms, blinded by forced secresies.
Set free my love, and see what love will do
Shown in my life—what work will spring from that!
The world is used to have its business done
On other grounds, find great effects produced
For power's sake, fame's sake, motives you have named.
So good.   But let my low ground shame their high.
Truth is the strong thing.   Let man's life be true!
And love's the truth of mine.   Time prove the rest!
I choose to have you stamped all over me,
Your name upon my forehead and my breast,
You, from the sword's blade to the ribbon's edge,
That men may see, all over, you in me—
That pale loves may die out of their pretence
In face of mine, shames thrown on love fall off—
Permit this, Constance!   Love has been so long
Subdued in me, eating me through and through,
That now it's all of me and must have way.
Think of my work, that chaos of intrigues,
Those hopes and fears, surprises and delays,
That long endeavour, earnest, patient, slow,
Trembling at last to its assured result—
Then think of this revulsion.   I resume
Life, after death, (it is no less than life
After such long unlovely labouring days)
And liberate to beauty life's great need
Of the beautiful, which, while it prompted work,
Supprest itself erewhile.   This eve's the time—
This eve intense with yon first trembling star
We seem to pant and reach; scarce ought between
The earth that rises and the heaven that bends—
All nature self-abandoned—every tree
Flung as it will, pursuing its own thoughts

And fixed so, every flower and every weed,
No pride, no shame, no victory, no defeat:
All under God, each measured by itself!
These statues round us, each abrupt, distinct,
The strong in strength, the weak in weakness fixed,
The Muse for ever wedded to her lyre,
The Nymph to her fawn, the Silence to her rose,
And God's approval on his universe!
Let us do so—aspire to live as these
In harmony with truth, ourselves being true.
Take the first way, and let the second come,
My first is to possess myself of you;
The music sets the march-step—forward then!
And there's the Queen, I go to claim you of,
The world to witness, wonder and applaud.
Our flower of life breaks open.   No delay!

CONSTANCE.

And so shall we be ruined, both of us.
Norbert, I know her to the skin and bone—
You do not know her, were not born to it,
To feel what she can see or cannot see.
Love, she is generous,—ay, despite your Smile,
Generous as you are.   For, in that thin frame
Pain-twisted, punctured through and through with cares,
There lived a lavish soul until it starved
Debarred all healthy food.   Look to the soul—
Pity that, stoop to that, ere you begin
(The true man's way) on justice and your rights,
Exactions and acquittance of the past.
Begin so—see what justice she will deal!
We women hate a debt as men a gift.
Suppose her some poor keeper of a school
Whose business is to sit thro' summer-months
And dole out children's leave to go and play,
Herself superior to such lightness—she
In the arm-chair's state and pædagogic pomp,
To the life, the laughter, sun and youth outside—
We wonder such an one looks black on us?
I do not bid you wake her tenderness,
—That were vain truly—none is left to wake—
But, let her think her justice is engaged
To take the shape of tenderness, and mark

If she'll not coldly do its warmest deed!
Does she love me, I ask you? not a whit.
Yet, thinking that her justice was engaged
To help a kinswoman, she took me up—
Did more on that bare ground than other loves
Would do on greater argument. For me,
I have no equivalent of that cold kind
To pay her with; my love alone to give
If I give anything. I give her love.
I feel I ought to help her, and I will.
So for her sake, as yours, I tell you twice
That women hate a debt as men a gift.
If I were you, I could obtain this grace—
Would lay the whole I did to love's account,
Nor yet be very false as courtiers go—
Declare that my success was recompense;
It would be so, in fact: what were it else?
And then, once loosed her generosity
As you will mark it—then,—were I but you
To turn it, let it seem to move itself,
And make it give the thing I really take,
Accepting so, in the poor cousin's hand,
All value as the next thing to the queen—
Since none loves her directly, none dares that!
A shadow of a thing, a name's mere echo
Suffices those who miss the name and thing;
You pick up just a ribbon she has worn
To keep in proof how near her breath you came.
Say I'm so near I seem a piece of her—
Ask for me that way—(oh, you understand)
And find the same gift yielded with a grace,
Which if you make the least show to extort
—You'll see! and when you have ruined both of us,
Dis[s]ertate on the Queen's ingratitude!

NORBERT.

Then, if I turn it that way, you consent?
'Tis not my way; I have more hope in truth.
Still if you won't have truth—why, this indeed,
Is scarcely false, I'll so express the sense.
Will you remain here?

CONSTANCE.

O best heart of mine,
How I have loved you! then, you take my way?
Are mine as you have been her minister,
Work out my thought, give it effect for me,
Paint plain my poor conceit and make it serve?
I owe that withered woman everything—
Life, fortune, you, remember! Take my part—
Help me to pay her! Stand upon your rights?
You, with my rose, my hands, my heart on you?
Your rights are mine—you have no rights but mine.

NORBERT.

Remain here. How you know me!

CONSTANCE.

Ah, but still——

[*He breaks from her; she remains. Dance-
music from within.*

SECOND PART.

Enter the QUEEN.

QUEEN.

Constance!—She is here as he said. Speak! quick!
Is it so? is it true—or false? One word!

CONSTANCE.

True.

QUEEN.

Mercifullest Mother, thanks to thee!

CONSTANCE.

Madam!

QUEEN.

I love you, Constance, from my soul.
Now say once more, with any words you will,
'Tis true—all true—as true as that I speak.

CONSTANCE.

Why should you doubt it?

QUEEN.

Ah, why doubt? why doubt?
Dear, make me see it. Do you see it so?
None see themselves—another sees them best.
You say " why doubt it? "—you see him and me.
It is because the Mother has such grace
That if we had but faith—wherein we fail—
Whate'er we yearn for would be granted us;
Howbeit we let our whims prescribe despair,
Our very fancies thwart and cramp our will,
And so accepting life, abjure ourselves!
Constance, I had abjured the hope of love
And of being loved, as truly as yon palm
The hope of seeing Egypt from that turf.

CONSTANCE.

Heaven!

QUEEN.

But it was so, Constance, it was so.
Men say—or do men say it? fancies say—
" Stop here, your life is set, you are grown old.
Too late—no love for you, too late for love—
Leave love to girls. Be queen—let Constance love! "
One takes the hint—half meets it like a child,
Ashamed at any feelings that oppose.
" Oh, love, true, never think of love again!
I am a queen—I rule, not love, indeed."
So it goes on; so a face grows like this,
Hair like this hair, poor arms as lean as these,
Till,—nay, it does not end so, I thank God!

CONSTANCE.

I cannot understand——

QUEEN.

The happier you!
Constance, I know not how it is with men.
For women, (I am a woman now like you)
There is no good of life but love—but love!
What else looks good, is some shade flung from love—
Love gilds it, gives it worth. Be warned by me,
Never you cheat yourself one instant. Love,
Give love, ask only love, and leave the rest!
O Constance, how I love you!

CONSTANCE.

                     I love you.

QUEEN.

I do believe that all is come through you.
I took you to my heart to keep it warm
When the last chance of love seemed dead in me;
I thought your fresh youth warmed my withered heart.
Oh, I am very old now, am I not?
Not so! it is true and it shall be true!

CONSTANCE.

Tell it me! let me judge if true or false.

QUEEN.

Ah, but I fear you—you will look at me
And say " she's old, she's grown unlovely quite
Who ne'er was beauteous! men want beauty still."
Well, so I feared—the curse! so I felt sure.

CONSTANCE.

Be calm. And now you feel not sure, you say?

QUEEN.

Constance, he came, the coming was not strange—
Do not I stand and see men come and go?
I turned a half look from my pedestal
Where I grow marble—" one young man the more!
He will love some one,—that is nought to me—
What would he with my marble stateliness? "
Yet this seemed somewhat worse than heretofore;
The man more gracious, youthful, like a god,
And I still older, with less flesh to change—
We two those dear extremes that long to touch.
It seemed still harder when he first began
Absorbed to labour at the state-affairs
The old way for the old end, interest.
Oh, to live with a thousand beating hearts
Around you, swift eyes, serviceable hands,
Professing they've no care but for your cause,
Thought but to help you, love but for yourself,

And you the marble statue all the time
They praise and point at as preferred to life,
Yet leave for the first breathing woman's cheek,
First dancer's, gypsy's, or street baladine's!
Why, how I have ground my teeth to hear men's speech
Stifled for fear it should alarm my ear,
Their gait subdued lest step should startle me,
Their eyes declined, such queendom to respect,
Their hands alert, such treasure to preserve,
While not a man of these broke rank and spoke,
Or wrote me a vulgar letter all of love,
Or caught my hand and pressed it like a hand.
There have been moments, if the sentinel
Lowering his halbert to salute the queen,
Had flung it brutally and clasped my knees,
I would have stooped and kissed him with my soul.

CONSTANCE.

Who could have comprehended!

QUEEN.

                Ay, who—who?
Why, no one, Constance, but this one who did.
Not they, not you, not I.   Even now perhaps
It comes too late—would you but tell the truth.

CONSTANCE.

I wait to tell it.

QUEEN.

            Well, you see, he came,
Outfaced the others, did a work this year
Exceeds in value all was ever done
You know—it is not I who say it—all
Say it.   And so (a second pang and worse)
I grew aware not only of what he did,
But why so wondrously.   Oh, never work
Like his was done for work's ignoble sake—
It must have finer aims to spur it on!
I felt, I saw he loved—loved somebody.
And Constance, my dear Constance, do you know,
I did believe this while 'twas you he loved.

CONSTANCE.

Me, madam?

QUEEN.

　　　　It did seem to me your face
Met him where'er he looked: and whom but you
Was such a man to love? it seemed to me
You saw he loved you, and approved the love,
And that you both were in intelligence.
You could not loiter in the garden, step
Into this balcony, but I straight was stung
And forced to understand.　It seemed so true,
So right, so beautiful, so like you both
That all this work should have been done by him
Not for the vulgar hope of recompense,
But that at last—suppose some night like this—
Borne on to claim his due reward of me
He might say, " Give her hand and pay me so."
And I (O Constance, you shall love me now)
I thought, surmounting all the bitterness,
—" And he shall have it.　I will make her blest,
My flower of youth, my woman's self that was,
My happiest woman's self that might have been!
These two shall have their joy and leave me here."
Yes—yes—

CONSTANCE.

　　　Thanks!

QUEEN.

　　　　And the word was on my lips
When he burst in upon me.　I looked to hear
A mere calm statement of his just desire
In payment of his labour.　When, O Heaven,
How can I tell you? cloud was on my eyes
And thunder in my ears at that first word
Which told 'twas love of me, of me, did all—
He loved me—from the first step to the last,
Loved me!

CONSTANCE.

　　　You did not hear . . . you thought he spoke
Of love? what if you should mistake?

QUEEN.

No, no—
No mistake! Ha, there shall be no mistake!
He had not dared to hint the love he felt—
You were my reflex—how I understood!
He said you were the ribbon I had worn,
He kissed my hand, he looked into my eyes,
And love, love was the end of every phrase.
Love is begun—this much is come to pass,
The rest is easy. Constance, I am yours—
I will learn, I will place my life on you,
But teach me how to keep what I have won.
Am I so old? this hair was early grey;
But joy ere now has brought hair brown again,
And joy will bring the cheek's red back, I feel.
I could sing once too; that was in my youth.
Still, when men paint me, they declare me . . . yes,
Beautiful—for the last French Painter did!
I know they flatter somewhat; you are frank—
I trust you. How I loved you from the first!
Some queens would hardly seek a cousin out
And set her by their side to take the eye:
I must have felt that good would come from you.
I am not generous—like him—like you!
But he is not your lover after all—
It was not you he looked at. Saw you him?
You have not been mistaking words or looks?
He said you were the reflex of myself—
And yet he is not such a paragon
To you, to younger women who may choose
Among a thousand Norberts. Speak the truth!
You know you never named his name to me—
You know, I cannot give him up—ah God,
Not up now, even to you!

CONSTANCE.

Then calm yourself.

QUEEN.

See, I am old—look here, you happy girl,
I will not play the fool, deceive myself;
'Tis all gone—put your cheek beside my cheek—
Ah, what a contrast does the moon behold!

But then I set my life upon one chance,
The last chance and the best—am *I* not left,
My soul, myself? All women love great men
If young or old—it is in all the tales—
Young beauties love old poets who can love—
Why should not he the poems in my soul,
The love, the passionate faith, the sacrifice,
The constancy? I throw them at his feet.
Who cares to see the fountain's very shape
And whether it be a Triton's or a Nymph's
That pours the foam, makes rainbows all around?
You could not praise indeed the empty conch;
But I'll pour floods of love and hide myself.
How I will love him! cannot men love love?
Who was a queen and loved a poet once
Humpbacked, a dwarf? ah, women can do that!
Well, but men too! at least, they tell you so.
They love so many women in their youth,
And even in age they all love whom they please;
And yet the best of them confide to friends
That 'tis not beauty makes the lasting love—
They spend a day with such and tire the next;
They like soul,—well then, they like phantasy,
Novelty even. Let us confess the truth
Horrible though it be—that prejudice,
Prescription . . . Curses! they will love a queen.
They will—they do. And will not, does not—he?

CONSTANCE.

How can he? You are wedded—'tis a name
We know, but still a bond. Your rank remains,
His rank remains. How can he, nobly souled
As you believe and I incline to think,
Aspire to be your favourite, shame and all?

QUEEN.

Hear her! there, there now—could she love like me?
What did I say of smooth-cheeked youth and grace?
See all it does or could do! so, youth loves!
Oh, tell him, Constance, you could never do
What I will—you, it was not born in! I
Will drive these difficulties far and fast
As yonder mists curdling before the moon.

I'll use my light too, gloriously retrieve
My youth from its enforced calamity,
Dissolve that hateful marriage, and be his,
His own in the eyes alike of God and man.

CONSTANCE.

You will do—dare do—Pause on what you say!

QUEEN.

Hear her! I thank you, Sweet, for that surprise.
You have the fair face: for the soul, see mine!
I have the strong soul: let me teach you, here.
I think I have borne enough and long enough,
And patiently enough, the world remarks,
To have my own way now, unblamed by all.
It does so happen, I rejoice for it,
This most unhoped-for issue cuts the knot.
There's not a better way of settling claims
Than this; God sends the accident express;
And were it for my subjects' good, no more,
'Twere best thus ordered. I am thankful now,
Mute, passive, acquiescent. I receive,
And bless God simply, or should almost fear
To walk so smoothly to my ends at last.
Why, how I baffle obstacles, spurn fate!
How strong I am! could Norbert see me now!

CONSTANCE.

Let me consider. It is all too strange.

QUEEN.

You, Constance, learn of me; do you, like me.
You are young, beautiful: my own, best girl,
You will have many lovers, and love one—
Light hair, not hair like Norbert's, to suit yours,
And taller than he is, for you are tall.
Love him like me! give all away to him;
Think never of yourself; throw by your pride,
Hope, fear,—your own good as you saw it once,
And love him simply for his very self.
Remember, I (and what am I to you?)
Would give up all for one, leave throne, lose life,
Do all but just unlove him! he loves me.

CONSTANCE.

He shall.

QUEEN.

You, step inside my inmost heart.
Give me your own heart—let us have one heart—
I'll come to you for counsel; " This he says,
This he does, what should this amount to, pray?
Beseech you, change it into current coin.
Is that worth kisses? shall I please him there? "
And then we'll speak in turn of you—what else?
Your love (according to your beauty's worth)
For you shall have some noble love, all gold—
Whom choose you? we will get him at your choice.
—Constance, I leave you.   Just a minute since
I felt as I must die or be alone
Breathing my soul into an ear like yours.
Now, I would face the world with my new life,
With my new crown.   I'll walk around the rooms,
And then come back and tell you how it feels.
How soon a smile of God can change the world!
How we are all made for happiness—how work
Grows play, adversity a winning fight!
True, I have lost so many years.   What then?
Many remain—God has been very good.
You, stay here.   'Tis as different from dreams,—
From the mind's cold calm estimate of bliss,
As these stone statues from the flesh and blood.
The comfort thou hast caused mankind, God's moon!
                    [*She goes out.   Dance-music from within.*

PART THIRD.

NORBERT *enters.*

NORBERT.

Well! we have but one minute and one word—

CONSTANCE.

I am yours, Norbert!

NORBERT.

Yes, mine.

CONSTANCE.

Not till now!
You were mine.   Now I give myself to you.

NORBERT.

Constance!

CONSTANCE.

Your own!   I know the thriftier way
Of giving—haply, 'tis the wiser way.
Meaning to give a treasure, I might dole
Coin after coin out (each, as that were all,
With a new largess still at each despair)
And force you keep in sight the deed, reserve
Exhaustless till the end my part and yours,
My giving and your taking, both our joys
Dying together.   Is it the wiser way?
I choose the simpler; I give all at once.
Know what you have to trust to, trade upon.
Use it, abuse it,—anything but say
Hereafter, " Had I known she loved me so,
And what my means, I might have thriven with it."
This is your means.   I give you all myself.

NORBERT.

I take you and thank God.

CONSTANCE.

Look on through years!
We cannot kiss a second day like this,
Else were this earth, no earth.

NORBERT.

With this day's heat
We shall go on through years of cold.

CONSTANCE.

So best.
I try to see those years—I think I see.
You walk quick and new warmth comes; you look back
And lay all to the first glow—not sit down
For ever brooding on a day like this
While seeing the embers whiten and love die.

Yes, love lives best in its effect; and mine,
Full in its own life, yearns to live in yours.

NORBERT.

Just so.   I take and know you all at once.
Your soul is disengaged so easily,
Your face is there, I know you; give me time,
Let me be proud and think you shall know me.
My soul is slower; in a life I roll
The minute out in which you condense yours—
The whole slow circle round you I must move,
To be just you.   I look to a long life
To decompose this minute, prove its worth.
'Tis the sparks' long succession one by one
Shall show you in the end what fire was crammed
In that mere stone you struck: you could not know,
If it lay ever unproved in your sight,
As now my heart lies? your own warmth would hide
Its coldness, were it cold.

CONSTANCE.

But how prove, how?

NORBERT.

Prove in my life, you ask?

CONSTANCE.

Quick, Norbert—how?

NORBERT.

That's easy told.   I count life just a stuff
To try the soul's strength on, educe the man.
Who keeps one end in view makes all things serve.
As with the body—he who hurls a lance
Or heaps up stone on stone, shows strength alike,
So I will seize and use all means to prove
And show this soul of mine you crown as yours,
And justify us both.

CONSTANCE.

Could you write books,
Paint pictures! one sits down in poverty
And writes or paints, with pity for the rich.

NORBERT.

And loves one's painting and one's writing too,
And not one's mistress! All is best, believe,
And we best as no other than we are.
We live, and they experiment on life
Those poets, painters, all who stand aloof
To overlook the farther. Let us be
The thing they look at! I might take that face
And write of it and paint it—to what end?
For whom? what pale dictatress in the air
Feeds, smiling sadly, her fine ghost-like form
With earth's real blood and breath, the beauteous life
She makes despised for ever? You are mine,
Made for me, not for others in the world,
Nor yet for that which I should call my art,
That cold calm power to see how fair you look.
I come to you—I leave you not, to write
Or paint. You are, I am. Let Rubens there
Paint us.

CONSTANCE.
So best!

NORBERT.
I understand your soul.
You live, and rightly sympathise with life,
With action, power, success: this way is straight.
And days were short beside, to let me change
The craft my childhood learnt; my craft shall serve.
Men set me here to subjugate, enclose,
Manure their barren lives and force the fruit
First for themselves, and afterward for me
In the due tithe; the task of some one man,
By ways of work appointed by themselves.
I am not bid create, they see no star
Transfiguring my brow to warrant that—
But bind in one and carry out their wills.
So I began: to-night sees how I end.
What if it see, too, my first outbreak here
Amid the warmth, surprise and sympathy,
The instincts of the heart that teach the head?
What if the people have discerned in me
The dawn of the next nature, the new man
Whose will they venture in the place of theirs,

And whom they trust to find them out new ways
To the new heights which yet he only sees?
I felt it when you kissed me.   See this Queen,
This people—in our phrase, this mass of men—
See how the mass lies passive to my hand
And how my hand is plastic, and you by
To make the muscles iron!   Oh, an end
Shall crown this issue as this crowns the first.
My will be on this people! then, the strain,
The grappling of the potter with his clay,
The long uncertain struggle,—the success
In that uprising of the spirit-work,
The vase shaped to the curl of the god's lip,
While rounded fair for lower men to see
The Graces in a dance they recognise
With turbulent applause and laughs of heart!
So triumph ever shall renew itself;
Ever to end in efforts higher yet,
Ever begun——

CONSTANCE.

I ever helping?

NORBERT.

Thus!
[*As he embraces her, enter the* QUEEN.

CONSTANCE.

Hist, madam,—so I have performed my part.
You see your gratitude's true decency,
Norbert? a little slow in seeing it!
Begun to end the sooner.   What's a kiss?

NORBERT.

Constance!

CONSTANCE.

Why, must I teach it you again?
You want a witness to your dullness, sir?
What was I saying these ten minutes long?
Then I repeat—when some young handsome man
Like you has acted out a part like yours,
Is pleased to fall in love with one beyond,
So very far beyond him, as he says—
So hopelessly in love, that but to speak

Would prove him mad, he thinks judiciously,
And makes some insignificant good soul
Like me, his friend, adviser, confidant
And very stalking-horse to cover him
In following after what he dares not face—
When his end's gained—(sir, do you understand?)
When she, he dares not face, has loved him first,
—May I not say so, madam?—tops his hope,
And overpasses so his wildest dream,
With glad consent of all, and most of her
The confidant who brought the same about—
Why, in the moment when such joy explodes,
I do say that the merest gentleman
Will not start rudely from the stalking-horse,
Dismiss it with a " There, enough of you ! "
Forget it, show his back unmannerly;
But like a liberal heart will rather turn
And say, " A tingling time of hope was ours—
Betwixt the fears and falterings—we two lived
A chanceful time in waiting for the prize.
The confidant, the Constance, served not ill;
And though I shall forget her in due time,
Her use being answered now, as reason bids,
Nay as herself bids from her heart of hearts,
Still, she has rights, the first thanks go to her,
The first good praise goes to the prosperous tool,
And the first—which is the last—thankful kiss."

NORBERT.

—Constance? it is a dream—ah see you smile!

CONSTANCE.

So, now his part being properly performed,
Madam, I turn to you and finish mine
As duly—I do justice in my turn.
Yes, madam, he has loved you—long and well—
He could not hope to tell you so—'twas I
Who served to prove your soul accessible.
I led his thoughts on, drew them to their place,
When oft they had wandered out into despair,
And kept love constant toward its natural aim.
Enough—my part is played; you stoop half-way
And meet us royally and spare our fears—

'Tis like yourself—he thanks you, so do I.
Take him—with my full heart! my work is praised
By what comes of it.   Be you happy, both!
Yourself—the only one on earth who can—
Do all for him, much more than a mere heart
Which though warm is not useful in its warmth
As the silk vesture of a queen! fold that
Around him gently, tenderly.   For him—
For him,—he knows his own part.

NORBERT.

Have you done?
I take the jest at last.   Should I speak now?
Was yours the wager, Constance, foolish child,
Or did you but accept it?   Well—at least,
You lose by it.

CONSTANCE.

Now madam, 'tis your turn.
Restrain him still from speech a little more
And make him happier and more confident!
Pity him, madam, he is timid yet.
Mark, Norbert! do not shrink now!   Here I yield
My whole right in you to the Queen, observe!
With her go put in practice the great schemes
You teem with, follow the career else closed—
Be all you cannot be except by her!
Behold her.—Madam, say for pity's sake
Anything—frankly say you love him.   Else
He'll not believe it: there's more earnest in
His fear than you conceive—I know the man.

NORBERT.

I know the woman somewhat, and confess
I thought she had jested better—she begins
To overcharge her part.   I gravely wait
Your pleasure, madam: where is my reward?

QUEEN.

Norbert, this wild girl (whom I recognise
Scarce more than you do, in her fancy-fit,
Eccentric speech and variable mirth,
Not very wise perhaps and somewhat bold

Yet suitable, the whole night's work being strange)
—May still be right: I may do well to speak
And make authentic what appears a dream
To even myself.   For, what she says, is true—
Yes, Norbert—what you spoke but now of love,
Devotion, stirred no novel sense in me,
But justified a warmth felt long before.
Yes, from the first—I loved you, I shall say,—
Strange! but I do grow stronger, now 'tis said,
Your courage helps mine: you did well to speak
To-night, the night that crowns your twelvemonths' toil—
But still I had not waited to discern
Your heart so long, believe me!   From the first
The source of so much zeal was almost plain,
In absence even of your own words just now
Which opened out the truth.   'Tis very strange,
But takes a happy ending—in your love
Which mine meets: be it so—as you choose me,
So I choose you.

NORBERT.

                    And worthily you choose!
I will not be unworthy your esteem,
No, madam.   I do love you; I will meet
Your nature, now I know it; this was well,
I see,—you dare and you are justified:
But none had ventured such experiment,
Less versed than you in nobleness of heart,
Less confident of finding it in me.
I like that thus you test me ere you grant
The dearest, richest, beauteousest and best
Of women to my arms! 'tis like yourself!
So—back again into my part's set words—
Devotion to the uttermost is yours,
But no, you cannot, madam, even you,
Create in me the love our Constance does.
Or—something truer to the tragic phrase—
Not yon magnolia-bell superb with scent
Invites a certain insect—that's myself—
But the small eye-flower nearer to the ground:
I take this lady!

CONSTANCE.

                    Stay—not hers, the trap—
Stay, Norbert—that mistake were worst of all.

(He is too cunning, madam!) it was I,
I, Norbert, who . . .

NORBERT.

         You, was it, Constance?   Then,
But for the grace of this divinest hour
Which gives me you, I should not pardon here.
I am the Queen's: she only knows my brain—
She may experiment therefore on my heart
And I instruct her too by the result;
But you, sweet, you who know me, who so long
Have told my heart-beats over, held my life
In those white hands of yours,—it is not well!

CONSTANCE.

Tush! I have said it, did I not say it all?
The life, for her—the heart-beats, for her sake!

NORBERT.

Enough! my cheek grows red, I think.   Your test!
There's not the meanest woman in the world,
Not she I least could love in all the world,
Whom, did she love me, did love prove itself,
I dared insult as you insult me now.
Constance, I could say, if it must be said,
" Take back the soul you offer—I keep mine "
But—" Take the soul still quivering on your hand,
The soul so offered, which I cannot use,
And, please you, give it to some friend of mine,
For—what's the trifle he requites me with? "
I, tempt a woman, to amuse a man,
That two may mock her heart if it succumb?
No! fearing God and standing 'neath his heaven,
I would not dare insult a woman so,
Were she the meanest woman in the world,
And he, I cared to please, ten emperors!

CONSTANCE.

Norbert!

NORBERT.

        I love once as I live but once.
What case is this to think or talk about?
I love you.   Would it mend the case at all

Should such a step as this kill love in me?
Your part were done: account to God for it.
But mine—could murdered love get up again,
And kneel to whom you pleased to designate
And make you mirth? It is too horrible.
You did not know this, Constance? now you know
That body and soul have each one life, but one:
And here's my love, here, living, at your feet.

CONSTANCE.

See the Queen! Norbert—this one more last word—
If thus you have taken jest for earnest—thus
Loved me in earnest . . .

NORBERT.

           Ah, no jest holds here!
Where is the laughter in which jests break up?
And what this horror that grows palpable?
Madam—why grasp you thus the balcony?
Have I done ill? Have I not spoken the truth?
How could I other? Was it not your test,
To try me, and what my love for Constance meant?
Madam, your royal soul itself approves,
The first, that I should choose thus! so one takes
A beggar—asks him what would buy his child,
And then approves the expected laugh of scorn
Returned as something noble from the rags.
Speak, Constance, I'm the beggar! Ha, what's this?
You two glare each at each like panthers now.
Constance—the world fades; only you stand there!
You did not in to-night's wild whirl of things
Sell me—your soul of souls for any price?
No—no—'tis easy to believe in you.
Was it your love's mad trial to o'ertop
Mine by this vain self-sacrifice? well, still—
Though I should curse, I love you. I am love
And cannot change! love's self is at your feet.

[QUEEN *goes out.*

CONSTANCE.

Feel my heart; let it die against your own.

NORBERT.

Against my own! explain not; let this be.
This is life's height.

CONSTANCE.

Yours! Yours! Yours!

NORBERT.

You and I—
Why care by what meanders we are here
In the centre of the labyrinth? men have died
Trying to find this place out, which we have found.

CONSTANCE.

Found, found!

NORBERT.

Sweet, never fear what she can do—
We are past harm now.

CONSTANCE.

On the breast of God.
I thought of men—as if you were a man.
Tempting him with a crown!

NORBERT.

This must end here—
It is too perfect!

CONSTANCE.

There's the music stopped.
What measured heavy tread? it is one blaze
About me and within me.

NORBERT.

Oh, some death
Will run its sudden finger round this spark,
And sever us from the rest—

CONSTANCE.

And so do well.
Now the doors open—

NORBERT.

'Tis the guard comes.

CONSTANCE.

Kiss!

SAUL.

I.

SAID Abner, " At last thou are come!   Ere I tell, ere thou
      speak,
Kiss my cheek, wish me well!"   Then I wished it, and did
      kiss his cheek.
And he, " Since the King, O my friend, for thy countenance
      sent,
Neither drunken nor eaten have we; nor until from his tent
Thou return with the joyful assurance the King liveth yet,
Shall our lip with the honey be bright, with the water be wet.
For out of the black mid-tent's silence, a space of three days,
Not a sound hath escaped to thy servants, of prayer or of
      praise
To betoken that Saul and the Spirit have ended their strife,
And that, faint in his triumph, the monarch sinks back upon
      life.

II.

Yet now my heart leaps, O beloved! God's child, with his
      dew
On thy gracious gold hair, and those lilies still living and blue
Just broken to twine round thy harp-strings, as if no wild
      heat
Were now raging to torture the desert!"

III.

                                        Then I, as was meet,
Knelt down to the God of my fathers, and rose on my feet,
And ran o'er the sand burnt to powder.   The tent was
      unlooped;
I pulled up the spear that obstructed, and under I stooped;
Hands and knees on the slippery grass-patch, all withered
      and gone,
That extends to the second enclosure, I groped my way on
Till I felt where the foldskirts fly open.   Then once more I
      prayed,
And opened the foldskirts and entered, and was not afraid,
But spoke, " Here is David, thy servant!"   And no voice
      replied.

At the first I saw nought but the blackness; but soon I
    descried
A something more black than the blackness—the vast the
    upright
Main prop which sustains the pavilion: and slow into sight
Grew a figure against it, gigantic and blackest of all;—
Then a sunbeam, that burst thro' the tent-roof,—showed
    Saul.

IV.

He stood as erect as that tent-prop; both arms stretched
    out wide
On the great cross-support in the centre, that goes to each
    side:
He relaxed not a muscle, but hung there,—as, caught in his
    pangs
And waiting his change the king-serpent all heavily hangs,
Far away from his kind, in the pine, till deliverance come
With the spring-time,—so agonized Saul, drear and stark,
    blind and dumb.

V.

Then I tuned my harp,—took off the lilies we twine round its
    chords
Lest they snap 'neath the stress of the noontide—those sun-
    beams like swords!
And I first played the tune all our sheep know, as, one after
    one,
So docile they come to the pen-door, till folding be done.
They are white and untorn by the bushes, for lo, they have
    fed
Where the long grasses stifle the water within the stream's
    bed:
And now one after one seeks its lodging, as star follows star
Into eve and the blue far above us,—so blue and so far!

VI.

—Then the tune, for which quails on the cornland will each
    leave his mate
To fly after the player; then, what makes the crickets elate,
Till for boldness they fight one another; and then, what has
    weight
To set the quick jerboa a-musing outside his sand house—

There are none such as he for a wonder, half bird and half
    mouse!—
God made all the creatures and gave them our love and our
    fear,
To give sign, we and they are his children, one family here.

VII.

Then I played the help-tune of our reapers, their wine-song,
    when hand
Grasps at hand, eye lights eye in good friendship, and great
    hearts expand
And grow one in the sense of this world's life.—And then, the
    last song
When the dead man is praised on his journey—" Bear, bear
    him along
With his few faults shut up like dead flowerets! are balm-
    seeds not here
To console us? The land has none left, such as he on the
    bier.
Oh, would we might keep thee, my brother!"—And then,
    the glad chaunt
Of the marriage,—first go the young maidens, next, she
    whom we vaunt
As the beauty, the pride of our dwelling.—And then, the
    great march
Wherein man runs to man to assist him and buttress an arch
Nought can break; who shall harm them, our friends?—
    Then, the chorus intoned
As the Levites go up to the altar in glory enthroned . . .
But I stopped here—for here in the darkness, Saul groaned.

VIII.

And I paused, held my breath in such silence, and listened
    apart;
And the tent shook, for mighty Saul shuddered,—and
    sparkles 'gan dart
From the jewels that woke in his turban at once with a start—
All its lordly male-sapphires, and rubies courageous at heart.
So the head—but the body still moved not, still hung there
    erect.
And I bent once again to my playing, pursued it unchecked,
As I sang,—

IX.

"Oh, our manhood's prime vigour! no
spirit feels waste,
Not a muscle is stopped in its playing, nor sinew unbraced.
Oh, the wild joys of living! the leaping from rock up to rock—
The strong rending of boughs from the fir-tree,—the cool
silver shock
Of the plunge in a pool's living water,—the hunt of the bear,
And the sultriness showing the lion is couched in his lair.
And the meal—the rich dates—yellowed over with gold dust
divine,
And the locust's-flesh steeped in the pitcher; the full draught
of wine,
And the sleep in the dried river-channel where bulrushes tell
That the water was wont to go warbling so softly and well.
How good is man's life, the mere living! how fit to employ
All the heart and the soul and the senses, for ever in joy!
Hast thou loved the white locks of thy father, whose sword
thou didst guard
When he trusted thee forth with the armies, for glorious
reward?
Didst thou see the thin hands of thy mother, held up as men
sung
The low song of the nearly-departed, and heard her faint
tongue
Joining in while it could to the witness, 'Let one more
attest,
I have lived, seen God's hand thro' a lifetime, and all was
for best . . .'
Then they sung thro' their tears in strong triumph, not much,
—but the rest.
And thy brothers, the help and the contest, the working
whence grew
Such result as from seething grape-bundles, the spirit strained
true!
And the friends of thy boyhood—that boyhood of wonder
and hope,
Present promise, and wealth of the future beyond the eye's
scope,—
Till lo, thou art grown to a monarch; a people is thine;
And all gifts which the world offers singly, on one head
combine!

On one head, all the beauty and strength, love and rage,
    like the throe
That, a-work in the rock, helps its labour, and lets the gold
    go:
High ambition and deeds which surpass it, fame crowning
    it,—all
Brought to blaze on the head of one creature—King Saul!"

X.

And lo, with that leap of my spirit, heart, hand, harp and
    voice,
Each lifting Saul's name out of sorrow, each bidding rejoice
Saul's fame in the light it was made for—as when, dare I say,
The Lord's army in rapture of service, strains through its
    array,
And upsoareth the cherubim-chariot—" Saul!" cried I, and
    stopped,
And waited the thing that should follow. Then Saul, who
    hung propt
By the tent's cross-support in the centre, was struck by his
    name.
Have ye seen when Spring's arrowy summons goes right to
    the aim,
And some mountain, the last to withstand her, that held, (he
    alone,
While the vale laughed in freedom and flowers) on a broad
    bust of stone
A year's snow bound about for a breastplate,—leaves grasp
    of the sheet?
Fold on fold all at once it crowds thunderously down to his
    feet,
And there fronts you, stark, black but alive yet, your moun-
    tain of old,
With his rents, the successive bequeathings of ages untold—
Yea, each harm got in fighting your battles, each furrow and
    scar
Of his head thrust 'twixt you and the tempest—all hail, there
    they are!
Now again to be softened with verdure, again hold the nest
Of the dove, tempt the goat and its young to the green on
    its crest
For their food in the ardours of summer! One long shudder
    thrilled

All the tent till the very air tingled, then sank and was
    stilled,
At the King's self left standing before me, released and
    aware.
What was gone, what remained? all to traverse 'twixt hope
    and despair—
Death was past, life not come—so he waited. Awhile his
    right hand
Held the brow, helped the eyes left too vacant forthwith to
    remand
To their place what new object should enter: 'twas Saul as
    before.
I looked up and dared gaze at those eyes, nor was hurt any
    more
Than by slow pallid sunsets in autumn, ye watch from the
    shore
At their sad level gaze o'er the ocean—a sun's slow decline
Over hills which, resolved in stern silence, o'erlap and en-
    twine
Base with base to knit strength more intense: so, arm folded
    in arm
O'er the chest whose slow heavings subsided.

XI.

                    What spell or what charm,
(For, awhile there was trouble within me) what next should
    I urge
To sustain him where song had restored him?—Song filled
    to the verge
His cup with the wine of this life, pressing all that it yields
Of mere fruitage, the strength and the beauty! Beyond, on
    what fields,
Glean a vintage more potent and perfect to brighten the eye
And bring blood to the lip, and commend them the cup they
    put by?
He saith, " It is good; " still he drinks not—he lets me praise
    life,
Gives assent, yet would die for his own part.

XII.

                   Then fancies grew rife
Which had come long ago on the pastures, when round me
    the sheep

Fed in silence—above, the one eagle wheeled slow as in sleep,
And I lay in my hollow, and mused on the world that might
lie
'Neath his ken, though I saw but the strip 'twixt the hill and
the sky:
And I laughed—" Since my days are ordained to be passed
with my flocks,
Let me people at least with my fancies, the plains and the
rocks,
Dream the life I am never to mix with, and image the show
Of mankind as they live in those fashions I hardly shall know!
Schemes of life, its best rules and right uses, the courage
that gains,
And the prudence that keeps what men strive for." And
now these old trains
Of vague thought came again; I grew surer; so once more
the string
Of my harp made response to my spirit, as thus—

XIII.

" Yea, my king,"
I began—" thou dost well in rejecting mere comforts that
spring
From the mere mortal life held in common by man and by
brute:
In our flesh grows the branch of this life, in our soul it bears
fruit.
Thou hast marked the slow rise of the tree,—how its stem
trembled first
Till it passed the kid's lip, the stag's antler; then safely
outburst
The fan-branches all round; and thou mindest when these
too, in turn
Broke a-bloom and the palm-tree seemed perfect; yet more
was to learn,
Ev'n the good that comes in with the palm-fruit. Our
dates shall we slight,
When their juice brings a cure for all sorrow? or care for the
plight
Of the palm's self whose slow growth produced them? Not
so! stem and branch
Shall decay, nor be known in their place, while the palm-
wine shall staunch

Every wound of man's spirit in winter. I pour thee such
    wine.

Leave the flesh to the fate it was fit for: the spirit be
    thine!

By the spirit, when age shall o'ercome thee, thou still shalt
    enjoy

More indeed, than at first when inconscious, the life of a boy.

Crush that life, and behold its wine running! each deed thou
    hast done

Dies, revives, goes to work in the world; until e'en as
    the sun

Looking down on the earth, though clouds spoil him, though
    tempests efface,

Can find nothing his own deed produced not, must every
    where trace

The results of his past summer-prime,—so, each ray of thy
    will,

Every flash of thy passion and prowess, long over, shall thrill

Thy whole people the countless, with ardour, till they too
    give forth

A like cheer to their sons, who in turn, fill the south and the
    north

With the radiance thy deed was the germ of. Carouse in the
    past.

But the license of age has its limit; thou diest at last.

As the lion when age dims his eye-ball, the rose at her
    height,

So with man—so his power and his beauty for ever take
    flight.

No! again a long draught of my soul-wine! look forth o'er
    the years—

Thou hast done now with eyes for the actual; begin with the
    seer's!

Is Saul dead? in the depth of the vale make his tomb—bid
    arise

A grey mountain of marble heaped four-square, till built to
    the skies.

Let it mark where the great First King slumbers—whose
    fame would ye know?

Up above see the rock's naked face, where the record shall go

In great characters cut by the scribe,—Such was Saul, so he
    did,

With the sages directing the work, by the populace chid,—

For not half, they'll affirm, is comprised there! Which fault to amend,
In the grove with his kind grows the cedar, whereon they shall spend
(See, in tablets 'tis level before them) their praise, and record
With the gold of the graver, Saul's story,—the statesman's great word
Side by side with the poet's sweet comment. The river's a-wave
With smooth paper-reeds grazing each other when prophet winds rave:
So the pen gives unborn generations their due and their part
In thy being! Then, first of the mighty, thank God that thou art."

XIV.

And behold while I sang . . . But O Thou who didst grant me that day,
And before it not seldom hast granted, thy help to essay
Carry on and complete an adventure,—my Shield and my Sword
In that act where my soul was thy servant, thy word was my word,—
Still be with me, who then at the summit of human endeavour
And scaling the highest man's thought could, gazed hopeless as ever
On the new stretch of Heaven above me—till, Mighty to save,
Just one lift of thy hand cleared that distance—God's throne from man's grave!
Let me tell out my tale to its ending—my voice to my heart,
Which can scarce dare believe in what marvels that night I took part,
As this morning I gather the fragments, alone with my sheep,
And still fear lest the terrible glory evanish like sleep!
For I wake in the grey dewy covert, while Hebron upheaves
The dawn struggling with night on his shoulder, and Kidron retrieves
Slow the damage of yesterday's sunshine.

XV.

I say then,—my song
While I sang thus, assuring the monarch, and ever more strong

Made a proffer of good to console him—he slowly resumed

His old motions and habitudes kingly. The right hand replumed

His black locks to their wonted composure, adjusted the swathes

Of his turban, and see—the huge sweat that his countenance bathes,

He wipes off with the robe; and he girds now his loins as of yore,

And feels slow for the armlets of price, with the clasp set before.

He is Saul, ye remember in glory,—ere error had bent

The broad brow from the daily communion; and still, though much spent

Be the life and the bearing that front you, the same God did choose,

To receive what a man may waste, desecrate, never quite lose.

So sank he along by the tent-prop, till, stayed by the pile

Of his armour and war-cloak and garments, he leaned there awhile,

And so sat out my singing,—one arm round the tent-prop, to raise

His bent head, and the other hung slack—till I touched on the praise

I foresaw from all men in all times, to the man patient there,

And thus ended, the harp falling forward. Then first I was 'ware

That he sat, as I say, with my head just above his vast knees

Which were thrust out on each side around me, like oak-roots which please

To encircle a lamb when it slumbers. I looked up to know

If the best I could do had brought solace: he spoke not, but slow

Lifted up the hand slack at his side, till he laid it with care

Soft and grave, but in mild settled will, on my brow: thro' my hair

The large fingers were pushed, and he bent back my head, with kind power—

All my face back, intent to peruse it, as men do a flower.

Thus held he me there with his great eyes that scrutinised mine—

And oh, all my heart how it loved him! but where was the sign?

I yearned—" Could I help thee, my father, inventing a bliss,
I would add to that life of the past, both the future and this,
I would give thee new life altogether, as good, ages hence,
As this moment,—had love but the warrant, love's heart to
   dispense!"

XVI.

Then the truth came upon me. No harp more—no song
   more! out-broke—

XVII.

" I have gone the whole round of Creation: I saw and I spoke!
I, a work of God's hand for that purpose, received in my
   brain
And pronounced on the rest of his handwork—returned him
   again
His creation's approval or censure: I spoke as I saw.
I report, as a man may of God's work—all's love, yet all's law!
Now I lay down the judgeship he lent me. Each faculty
   tasked
To perceive him, has gained an abyss, where a dewdrop was
   asked.
Have I knowledge? confounded it shrivels at wisdom laid
   bare.
Have I forethought? how purblind, how blank, to the
   Infinite care!
Do I task any faculty highest, to image success?
I but open my eyes,—and perfection, no more and no less,
In the kind I imagined, full-fronts me, and God is seen God
In the star, in the stone, in the flesh, in the soul and the clod.
And thus looking within and around me, I ever renew
(With that stoop of the soul which in bending upraises it too)
The submission of Man's nothing-perfect to God's All-
   Complete,
As by each new obeisance in spirit, I climb to his feet!
Yet with all this abounding experience, this Deity known,
I shall dare to discover some province, some gift of my own.
There's one faculty pleasant to exercise, hard to hoodwink,
I am fain to keep still in abeyance, (I laugh as I think)
Lest, insisting to claim and parade in it, wot ye, I worst
E'en the Giver in one gift. Behold! I could love if I durst!
But I sink the pretension as fearing a man may o'ertake
God's own speed in the one way of love: I abstain, for love's
   sake!

—What, my soul? see thus far and no farther? when door
    great and small,
Nine-and-ninety flew ope at our touch, should the hundredth
    appal?
In the least things, have faith, yet distrust in the greatest
    of all?
Do I find love so full in my nature, God's ultimate gift,
That I doubt his own love can compete with it? here, the
    parts shift?
Here, the creature surpass the Creator, the end, what Began?—
Would I fain in my impotent yearning do all for this man,
And dare doubt He alone shall not help him, who yet alone
    can?
Would it ever have entered my mind, the bare will, much less
    power,
To bestow on this Saul what I sang of, the marvellous dower
Of the life he was gifted and filled with? to make such a soul,
Such a body, and then such an earth for insphering the whole?
And doth it not enter my mind (as my warm tears attest)
These good things being given, to go on, and give one more,
    the best?
Ay, to save and redeem and restore him, maintain at the
    height
This perfection,—succeed with life's dayspring, death's
    minute of night?
Interpose at the difficult minute, snatch Saul, the mistake,
Saul, the failure, the ruin he seems now,—and bid him awake
From the dream, the probation, the prelude, to find himself
    set
Clear and safe in new light and new life,—a new harmony yet
To be run, and continued, and ended—who knows?—or
    endure!
The man taught enough by life's dream, of the rest to make
    sure.
By the pain-throb, triumphantly winning intensified bliss,
And the next world's reward and repose, by the struggle in
    this.

XVIII.

" I believe it! 'tis Thou, God, that givest, 'tis I who receive:
In the first is the last, in thy will is my power to believe.
All's one gift: thou canst grant it moreover, as prompt to
    my prayer

As I breathe out this breath, as I open these arms to the air.
From thy will, stream the worlds, life and nature, thy dread
  Sabaoth:
I will?—the mere atoms despise me! and why am I loth
To look that, even that in the face too? why is it I dare
Think but lightly of such impuissance? what stops my
  despair?
This:—'tis not what man Does which exalts him, but what
  man Would do!
See the king—I would help him but cannot, the wishes fall
  through.
Could I wrestle to raise him from sorrow, grow poor to enrich,
To fill up his life, starve my own out, I would—knowing
  which,
I know that my service is perfect.—Oh, speak through me
  now!
Would I suffer for him that I love? So wilt Thou—so wilt
  Thou!
So shall crown thee the topmost, ineffablest, uttermost
  Crown—
And thy love fill infinitude wholly, nor leave up nor down
One spot for the creature to stand in! It is by no breath,
Turn of eye, wave of hand, that Salvation joins issue with
  death!
As thy Love is discovered almighty, almighty be proved
Thy power, that exists with and for it, of Being beloved!
He who did most, shall bear most; the strongest shall stand
  the most weak.
'Tis the weakness in strength that I cry for! my flesh, that
  I seek
In the Godhead! I seek and I find it. O Saul, it shall be
A Face like my face that receives thee: a Man like to me,
Thou shalt love and be loved by, for ever! a Hand like this
  hand
Shall throw open the gates of new life to thee! See the
  Christ stand!"

XIX.

I know not too well how I found my way home in the night.
There were witnesses, cohorts about me, to left and to right,
Angels, powers, the unuttered, unseen, the alive—the aware—
I repressed, I got through them as hardly, as strugglingly
  there,

As a runner beset by the populace famished for news—
Life or death. The whole earth was awakened, hell loosed
   with her crews;
And the stars of night beat with emotion, and tingled and
   shot
Out in fire the strong pain of pent knowledge: but I fainted
   not.
For the Hand still impelled me at once and supported—
   suppressed
All the tumult, and quenched it with quiet, and holy behest,
Till the rapture was shut in itself, and the earth sank to rest.
Anon at the dawn, all that trouble had withered from earth—
Not so much, but I saw it die out in the day's tender birth;
In the gathered intensity brought to the grey of the hills;
In the shuddering forests' new awe; in the sudden wind-
   thrills;
In the startled wild beasts that bore off, each with eye
   sidling still
Tho' averted, in wonder and dread; and the birds stiff and
   chill
That rose heavily, as I approached them, made stupid with
   awe!
E'en the serpent that slid away silent,—he felt the new Law.
The same stared in the white humid faces upturned by the
   flowers;
The same worked in the heart of the cedar, and moved the
   vine-bowers.
And the little brooks witnessing murmured, persistent and
   low,
With their obstinate, all but hushed voices—E'en so! it is so.

" DE GUSTIBUS—"

1. YOUR ghost will walk, you lover of trees,
     (If loves remain)
     In an English lane,
  By a cornfield-side a-flutter with poppies.
  Hark, those two in the hazel coppice—
  A boy and a girl, if the good fates please,
     Making love, say,—
     The happier they!

Draw yourself up from the light of the moon,
And let them pass, as they will too soon,
  With the beanflowers' boon,
  And the blackbird's tune,
  And May, and June!

II. What I love best in all the world,
 Is, a castle, precipice-encurled,
 In a gash of the wind-grieved Apennine.
 Or look for me, old fellow of mine,
 (If I get my head from out the mouth
 O' the grave, and loose my spirit's bands,
 And come again to the land of lands)—
 In a sea-side house to the farther south,
 Where the baked cicalas die of drouth,
 And one sharp tree ('tis a cypress) stands,
 By the many hundred years red-rusted,
 Rough iron-spiked, ripe fruit-o'ercrusted,
 My sentinel to guard the sands
 To the water's edge. For, what expands
 Without the house, but the great opaque
 Blue breadth of sea, and not a break?
 While, in the house, for ever crumbles
 Some fragment of the frescoed walls,
 From blisters where a scorpion sprawls.
 A girl bare-footed brings and tumbles
 Down on the pavement, green-flesh melons,
 And says there's news to-day—the king
 Was shot at, touched in the liver-wing,
 Goes with his Bourbon arm in a sling.
 —She hopes they have not caught the felons.
  Italy, my Italy!
 Queen Mary's saying serves for me—
  (When fortune's malice
  Lost her, Calais.)
 Open my heart and you will see
 Graved inside of it, " Italy."
 Such lovers old are I and she;
 So it always was, so it still shall be!

WOMEN AND ROSES.

I. I DREAM of a red-rose tree.
   And which of its roses three
   Is the dearest rose to me?

II. Round and round, like a dance of snow
    In a dazzling drift, as its guardians, go
    Floating the women faded for ages,
    Sculptured in stone, on the poet's pages.
    Then follow the women fresh and gay,
    Living and loving and loved to-day.
    Last, in the rear, flee the multitude of maidens,
    Beauties unborn.   And all, to one cadence,
    They circle their rose on my rose tree.

   III. Dear rose, thy turn is reached,
        Thy leaf hangs loose and bleached:
        Bees pass it unimpeached.

IV. Stay then, stoop, since I cannot climb,
    You, great shapes of the antique time!
    How shall I fix you, fire you, freeze you,
    Break my heart at your feet to please you?
    Oh! to possess, and be possessed!
    Hearts that beat 'neath each pallid breast!
    But once of love, the poesy, the passion,
    Drink once and die!—In vain, the same fashion,
    They circle their rose on my rose tree.

   V. Dear rose, thy joy's undimmed;
      Thy cup is ruby-rimmed,
      Thy cup's heart nectar-brimmed.

VI. Deep as drops from a statue's plinth
    The bee sucked in by the hyacinth,
    So will I bury me while burning,
    Quench like him at a plunge my yearning,
    Eyes in your eyes, lips on your lips!
    Fold me fast where the cincture slips,
    Prison all my soul in eternities of pleasure!
    Girdle me once!   But no—in their old measure
    They circle their rose on my rose tree.

VII. Dear rose without a thorn,
    Thy bud's the babe unborn:
    First streak of a new morn.

VIII. Wings, lend wings for the cold, the clear!
    What's far conquers what is near.
    Roses will bloom nor want beholders,
    Sprung from the dust where our own flesh moulders.
    What shall arrive with the cycle's change?
    A novel grace and a beauty strange.
    I will make an Eve, be the artist that began her,
    Shaped her to his mind!—Alas! in like manner
    They circle their rose on my rose tree.

PROTUS

AMONG these latter busts we count by scores,
Half-emperors and quarter-emperors,
Each with his bay-leaf fillet, loose-thonged vest,
Loric and low-browed Gorgon on the breast
One loves a baby face, with violets there,
Violets instead of laurel in the hair,
As those were all the little locks could bear.

Now read here.   " Protus ends a period
Of empery beginning with a god:
Born in the porphyry chamber at Byzant;
Queens by his cradle, proud and ministrant.
And if he quickened breath there, 'twould like fire
Pantingly through the dim vast realm transpire.
A fame that he was missing, spread afar—
The world, from its four corners, rose in war,
Till he was borne out on a balcony
To pacify the world when it should see.
The captains ranged before him, one, his hand
Made baby points at, gained the chief command.
And day by day more beautiful he grew
In shape, all said, in feature and in hue,
While young Greek sculptors gazing on the child
Were, so, with old Greek sculpture, reconciled.
Already sages laboured to condense

In easy tomes a life's experience:
And artists took grave counsel to impart
In one breath and one hand-sweep, all their art—
To make his graces prompt as blossoming
Of plentifully-watered palms in spring:
Since well beseems it, whoso mounts the throne,
For beauty, knowledge, strength, should stand alone,
And mortals love the letters of his name."

—Stop! have you turned two pages?   Still the same.
New reign, same date.   The scribe goes on to say
How that same year, on such a month and day,
" John the Pannonian, groundedly believed
A blacksmith's bastard, whose hard hand reprieved
The Empire from its fate the year before,—
Came, had a mind to take the crown, and wore
The same for six years, (during which the Huns
Kept off their fingers from us) till his sons
Put something in his liquor "—and so forth.
Then a new reign.   Stay—" Take at its just worth "
(Subjoins an annotator) " what I give
As hearsay.   Some think John let Protus live
And slip away.   'Tis said, he reached man's age
At some blind northern court; made first a page,
Then, tutor to the children—last, of use
About the hunting-stables.   I deduce
He wrote the little tract ' On worming dogs,'
Whereof the name in sundry catalogues
Is extant yet.   A Protus of the Race
Is rumoured to have died a monk in Thrace,—
And if the same, he reached senility."

Here's John the Smith's rough-hammered head.   Great eye,
Gross jaw and griped lips do what granite can
To give you the crown-grasper.   What a man!

HOLY-CROSS DAY,

ON WHICH THE JEWS WERE FORCED TO ATTEND AN ANNUAL
CHRISTIAN SERMON IN ROME.

Though what the Jews really said, on thus being driven to church,
was rather to this effect:

I. FEE, faw, fum! bubble and squeak!
Blessedest Thursday's the fat of the week.
Rumble and tumble, sleek and rough,
Stinking and savoury, smug and gruff,
Take the church-road, for the bell's due chime
Gives us the summons—'tis sermon-time.

II. Boh, here's Barnabas! Job, that's you?
Up stumps Solomon—bustling too?
Shame, man! greedy beyond your years
To handsel the bishop's shaving-shears?
Fair play's a jewel! leave friends in the lurch?
Stand on a line ere you start for the church.

III. Higgledy piggledy, packed we lie,
Rats in a hamper, swine in a sty,
Wasps in a bottle, frogs in a sieve,
Worms in a carcase, fleas in a sleeve.
Hist! square shoulders, settle your thumbs
And buzz for the bishop—here he comes.

IV. Bow, wow, wow—a bone for the dog!
I liken his Grace to an acorned hog.
What, a boy at his side, with the bloom of a lass,
To help and handle my lord's hour-glass!
Didst ever behold so lithe a chine?
His cheek hath laps like a fresh-singed swine.

V. Aaron's asleep—shove hip to haunch,
Or somebody deal him a dig in the paunch!
Look at the purse with the tassel and knob,
And the gown with the angel and thingumbob.
What's he at, quotha? reading his text!
Now you've his curtsey—and what comes next?

vi. See to our converts—you doomed black dozen—
No stealing away—nor cog nor cozen!
You five that were thieves, deserve it fairly;
You seven that were beggars, will live less sparely
You took your turn and dipped in the hat,
Got fortune—and fortune gets you; mind that!

vii. Give your first groan—compunction's at work;
And soft! from a Jew you mount to a Turk.
Lo, Micah,—the self-same beard on chin
He was four times already converted in!
Here's a knife, clip quick—it's a sign of grace—
Or he ruins us all with his hanging-face.

viii. Whom now is the bishop a-leering at?
I know a point where his text falls pat.
I'll tell him to-morrow, a word just now
Went to my heart and made me vow
I meddle no more with the worst of trades—
Let somebody else pay his serenades.

ix. Groan all together now, whee—hee—hee!
It's a-work, it's a-work, ah, woe is me!
It began, when a herd of us, picked and placed,
Were spurred through the Corso, stripped to the waist;
Jew-brutes, with sweat and blood well spent
To usher in worthily Christian Lent.

x. It grew, when the hangman entered our bounds,
Yelled, pricked us out to this church like hounds.
It got to a pitch, when the hand indeed
Which gutted my purse, would throttle my creed.
And it overflows, when, to even the odd,
Men I helped to their sins, help me to their God.

xi. But now, while the scapegoats leave our flock,
And the rest sit silent and count the clock,
Since forced to muse the appointed time
On these precious facts and truths sublime,—
Let us fitly employ it, under our breath,
In saying Ben Ezra's Song of Death.

xii. For Rabbi Ben Ezra, the night he died,
Called sons and sons' sons to his side,
And spoke, " This world has been harsh and strange,

Something is wrong, there needeth a change.
But what, or where? at the last, or first?
In one point only we sinned, at worst.

XIII. " The Lord will have mercy on Jacob yet,
And again in his border see Israel set.
When Judah beholds Jerusalem,
The stranger-seed shall be joined to them:
To Jacob's House shall the Gentiles cleave.
So the prophet saith and his sons believe.

XIV. " Ay, the children of the chosen race
Shall carry and bring them to their place;
In the land of the Lord shall lead the same,
Bondsmen and handmaids. Who shall blame,
When the slaves enslave, the oppressed ones o'er
The oppressor triumph for evermore?

XV. " God spoke, and gave us the word to keep:
Bade never fold the hands nor sleep
'Mid a faithless world,—at watch and ward,
Till the Christ at the end relieve our guard.
By his servant Moses the watch was set:
Though near upon cock-crow—we keep it yet.

XVI. " Thou! if thou wast He, who at mid-watch came,
By the starlight naming a dubious Name!
And if we were too heavy with sleep—too rash
With fear—O thou, if that martyr-gash
Fell on thee coming to take thine own,
And we gave the Cross, when we owed the Throne—

XVII. " Thou art the Judge. We are bruised thus.
But, the judgment over, join sides with us!
Thine too is the cause! and not more thine
Than ours, is the work of these dogs and swine,
Whose life laughs through and spits at their creed,
Who maintain thee in word, and defy thee in deed!

XVIII. " We withstood Christ then? be mindful how
At least we withstand Barabbas now!
Was our outrage sore? but the worst we spared,
To have called these—Christians,—had we dared!
Let defiance to them, pay mistrust of thee,
And Rome make amends for Calvary!

XIX. "By the torture, prolonged from age to age,
　　By the infamy, Israel's heritage,
　　By the Ghetto's plague, by the garb's disgrace,
　　By the badge of shame, by the felon's place,
　　By the branding-tool, the bloody whip,
　　And the summons to Christian fellowship,

XX. "We boast our proofs, that at least the Jew
　　Would wrest Christ's name from the Devil's crew.
　　Thy face took never so deep a shade
　　But we fought them in it, God our aid!
　　A trophy to bear, as we march, a band
　　South, east, and on to the Pleasant Land!"

THE GUARDIAN-ANGEL:

A PICTURE AT FANO.

I. DEAR and great Angel, wouldst thou only leave
　　That child, when thou hast done with him, for me!
Let me sit all the day here, that when eve
　　Shall find performed thy special ministry
And time come for departure, thou, suspending
Thy flight, mayst see another child for tending,
　　Another still, to quiet and retrieve.

II. Then I shall feel thee step one step, no more,
　　From where thou standest now, to where I gaze,
And suddenly my head be covered o'er
　　With those wings, white above the child who prays
Now on that tomb—and I shall feel thee guarding
Me, out of all the world! for me, discarding
　　Yon heaven thy home, that waits and opes its door!

III. I would not look up thither past thy head
　　Because the door opes, like that child, I know,
For I should have thy gracious face instead,
　　Thou bird of God! And wilt thou bend me low
Like him, and lay, like his, my hands together,
And lift them up to pray, and gently tether
　　Me, as thy lamb there, with thy garment's spread?

IV. If this was ever granted, I would rest
  My head beneath thine, while thy healing hands
Close-covered both my eyes beside thy breast,
  Pressing the brain, which too much thought expands
Back to its proper size again, and smoothing
Distortion down till every nerve had soothing,
  And all lay quiet, happy and supprest.

V. How soon all worldly wrong would be repaired!
  I think how I should view the earth and skies
And sea, when once again my brow was bared
  After thy healing, with such different eyes.
O, world, as God has made it! all is beauty:
And knowing this, is love, and love is duty.
  What further may be sought for or declared?

VI. Guercino drew this angel I saw teach
  (Alfred, dear friend)—that little child to pray,
Holding the little hands up, each to each
  Pressed gently,—with his own head turned away
Over the earth where so much lay before him
Of work to do, though heaven was opening o'er him,
  And he was left at Fano by the beach.

VII. We were at Fano, and three times we went
  To sit and see him in his chapel there,
And drink his beauty to our soul's content
  —My angel with me too: and since I care
For dear Guercino's fame, (to which in power
And glory comes this picture for a dower,
  Fraught with a pathos so magnificent)

VIII. And since he did not work so earnestly
  At all times, and has else endured some wrong,—
I took one thought his picture struck from me,
  And spread it out, translating it to song.
My love is here. Where are you, dear old friend?
How rolls the Wairoa at your world's far end?
  This is Ancona, yonder is the sea.

CLEON.

"As certain also of your own poets have said."—

CLEON the poet, (from the sprinkled isles,
Lily on lily, that o'erlace the sea,
And laugh their pride when the light wave lisps "Greece")—
To Protos in his Tyranny: much health!

They give thy letter to me, even now:
I read and seem as if I heard thee speak.
The master of thy galley still unlades
Gift after gift; they block my court at last
And pile themselves along its portico
Royal with sunset, like a thought of thee:
And one white she-slave from the group dispersed
Of black and white slaves, (like the chequer-work
Pavement, at once my nation's work and gift,
Now covered with this settle-down of doves)
One lyric woman, in her crocus vest
Woven of sea-wools, with her two white hands
Commends to me the strainer and the cup
Thy lip hath bettered ere it blesses mine.

Well-counselled, king, in thy munificence!
For so shall men remark, in such an act
Of love for him whose song gives life its joy,
Thy recognition of the use of life;
Nor call thy spirit barely adequate
To help on life in straight ways, broad enough
For vulgar souls, by ruling and the rest.
Thou, in the daily building of thy tower,
Whether in fierce and sudden spasms of toil,
Or through dim lulls of unapparent growth,
Or when the general work 'mid good acclaim
Climbed with the eye to cheer the architect,
Didst ne'er engage in work for mere work's sake—
Hadst ever in thy heart the luring hope
Of some eventual rest a-top of it,
Whence, all the tumult of the building hushed,
Thou first of men mightst look out to the east.
The vulgar saw thy tower; thou sawest the sun.

For this, I promise on thy festival
To pour libation, looking o'er the sea,
Making this slave narrate thy fortunes, speak
Thy great words, and describe thy royal face—
Wishing thee wholly where Zeus lives the most
Within the eventual element of calm.

Thy letter's first requirement meets me here.
It is as thou hast heard: in one short life
I, Cleon, have effected all those things
Thou wonderingly dost enumerate.
That epos on thy hundred plates of gold
Is mine,—and also mine the little chant,
So sure to rise from every fishing-bark
When, lights at prow, the seamen haul their nets.
The image of the sun-god on the phare
Men turn from the sun's self to see, is mine;
The Pœcile, o'er-storied its whole length,
As thou didst hear, with painting, is mine too.
I know the true proportions of a man
And woman also, not observed before; .
And I have written three books on the soul,
Proving absurd all written hitherto,
And putting us to ignorance again.
For music,—why, I have combined the moods,
Inventing one. In brief, all arts are mine;
Thus much the people know and recognise,
Throughout our seventeen islands. Marvel not.
We of these latter days, with greater mind
Than our forerunners, since more composite,
Look not so great (beside their simple way)
To a judge who only sees one way at once,
One mind-point, and no other at a time,—
Compares the small part of a man of us
With some whole man of the heroic age,
Great in his way,—not ours, nor meant for ours,
And ours is greater, had we skill to know.
Yet, what we call this life of men on earth,
This sequence of the soul's achievements here,
Being, as I find much reason to conceive,
Intended to be viewed eventually
As a great whole, not analysed to parts,
But each part having reference to all,—

How shall a certain part, pronounced complete,
Endure effacement by another part?
Was the thing done?—Then what's to do again?
See, in the chequered pavement opposite,
Suppose the artist made a perfect rhomb,
And next a lozenge, then a trapezoid—
He did not overlay them, superimpose
The new upon the old and blot it out,
But laid them on a level in his work,
Making at last a picture; there it lies.
So, first the perfect separate forms were made,
The portions of mankind—and after, so,
Occurred the combination of the same.
Or where had been a progress, or otherwise?
Mankind, made up of all the single men,—
In such a synthesis the labour ends.
Now, mark me—those divine men of old time
Have reached, thou sayest well, each at one point
The outside verge that rounds our faculty;
And where they reached, who can do more than reach?
It takes but little water just to touch
At some one point the inside of a sphere,
And, as we turn the sphere, touch all the rest
In due succession; but the finer air
Which not so palpably nor obviously,
Though no less universally, can touch
The whole circumference of that emptied sphere,
Fills it more fully than the water did;
Holds thrice the weight of water in itself
Resolved into a subtler element.
And yet the vulgar call the sphere first full
Up to the visible height—and after, void;
Not knowing air's more hidden properties.
And thus our soul, misknown, cries out to Zeus
To vindicate his purpose in its life—
Why stay we on the earth unless to grow?
Long since, I imaged, wrote the fiction out,
That he or other God, descended here
And, once for all, showed simultaneously
What, in its nature, never can be shown
Piecemeal or in succession;—showed, I say,
The worth both absolute and relative
Of all his children from the birth of time,

His instruments for all appointed work.
I now go on to image,—might we hear
The judgment which should give the due to each,
Show where the labour lay and where the ease,
And prove Zeus' self, the latent, everywhere!
This is a dream. But no dream, let us hope,
That years and days, the summers and the springs
Follow each other with unwaning powers—
The grapes which dye thy wine, are richer far
Through culture, than the wild wealth of the rock;
The suave plum than the savage-tasted drupe;
The pastured honey-bee drops choicer sweet!
The flowers turn double, and the leaves turn flowers;
That young and tender crescent-moon, thy slave,
Sleeping upon her robe as if on clouds,
Refines upon the women of my youth.
What, and the soul alone deteriorates?
I have not chanted verse like Homer's, no—
Nor swept string like Terpander, no—nor carved
And painted men like Phidias and his friend:
I am not great as they are, point by point:
But I have entered into sympathy
With these four, running these into one soul,
Who, separate, ignored each others' arts.
Say, is it nothing that I know them all?
The wild flower was the larger—I have dashed
Rose-blood upon its petals, pricked its cup's
Honey with wine, and driven its seed to fruit,
And show a better flower if not so large.
I stand, myself. Refer this to the gods
Whose gift alone it is! which, shall I dare
(All pride apart) upon the absurd pretext
That such a gift by chance lay in my hand,
Discourse of lightly or depreciate?
It might have fallen to another's hand—what then?
I pass too surely—let at least truth stay!

And next, of what thou followest on to ask.
This being with me as I declare, O king,
My works, in all these varicoloured kinds,
So done by me, accepted so by men—
Thou askest if (my soul thus in men's hearts)
I must not be accounted to attain

The very crown and proper end of life.
Inquiring thence how, now life closeth up,
I face death with success in my right hand:
Whether I fear death less than dost thyself
The fortunate of men.   " For " (writest thou)
" Thou leavest much behind, while I leave nought:
Thy life stays in the poems men shall sing,
The pictures men shall study; while my life,
Complete and whole now in its power and joy,
Dies altogether with my brain and arm,
Is lost indeed; since,—what survives myself?
The brazen statue that o'erlooks my grave,
Set on the promontory which I named.
And that—some supple courtier of my heir
Shall use its robed and sceptred arm, perhaps,
To fix the rope to, which best drags it down.
I go, then: triumph thou, who dost not go! "

   Nay, thou art worthy of hearing my whole mind.
Is this apparent, when thou turn'st to muse
Upon the scheme of earth and man in chief,
That admiration grows as knowledge grows?
That imperfection means perfection hid,
Reserved in part, to grace the after-time?
If, in the morning of philosophy,
Ere ought had been recorded, ought perceived,
Thou, with the light now in thee, could'st have looked
On all earth's tenantry, from worm to bird,
Ere man had yet appeared upon the stage—
Thou wouldst have seen them perfect, and deduced
The perfectness of others yet unseen.
Conceding which,—had Zeus then questioned thee
" Wilt thou go on a step, improve on this,
Do more for visible creatures than is done? "
Thou wouldst have answered, " Ay, by making each
Grow conscious in himself—by that alone.
All's perfect else: the shell sucks fast the rock,
The fish strikes through the sea, the snake both swims
And slides; the birds take flight, forth range the beasts,
Till life's mechanics can no further go—
And all this joy in natural life, is put,
Like fire from off Thy finger into each,
So exquisitely perfect is the same.

Cleon 427

But 'tis pure fire—and they mere matter are;
It has them, not they it: and so I choose,
For man, Thy last premeditated work
(If I might add a glory to this scheme)
That a third thing should stand apart from both,
A quality arise within the soul,
Which, intro-active, made to supervise
And feel the force it has, may view itself,
And so be happy." Man might live at first
The animal life: but is there nothing more?
In due time, let him critically learn
How he lives; and, the more he gets to know
Of his own life's adaptabilities,
The more joy-giving will his life become.
The man who hath this quality, is best.

But thou, king, hadst more reasonably said:
" Let progress end at once,—man make no step
Beyond the natural man, the better beast,
Using his senses, not the sense of sense."
In man there's failure, only since he left
The lower and inconscious forms of life.
We called it an advance, the rendering plain
A spirit might grow conscious of that life,
And, by new lore so added to the old,
Take each step higher over the brute's head.
This grew the only life, the pleasure-house,
Watch-tower and treasure-fortress of the soul,
Which whole surrounding flats of natural life
Seemed only fit to yield subsistence to;
A tower that crowns a country. But alas!
The soul now climbs it just to perish there,
For thence we have discovered ('tis no dream—
We know this, which we had not else perceived)
That there's a world of capability
For joy, spread round about us, meant for us,
Inviting us; and still the soul craves all,
And still the flesh replies, " Take no jot more
Than ere you climbed the tower to look abroad!
Nay, so much less, as that fatigue has brought
Deduction to it." We struggle—fain to enlarge
Our bounded physical recipiency,
Increase our power, supply fresh oil to life,

Repair the waste of age and sickness. No,
It skills not: life's inadequate to joy,
As the soul sees joy, tempting life to take.
They praise a fountain in my garden here
Wherein a Naiad sends the water-spurt
Thin from her tube; she smiles to see it rise.
What if I told her, it is just a thread
From that great river which the hills shut up,
And mock her with my leave to take the same?
The artificer has given her one small tube
Past power to widen or exchange—what boots
To know she might spout oceans if she could?
She cannot lift beyond her first straight thread.
And so a man can use but a man's joy
While he sees God's. Is it, for Zeus to boast
" See, man, how happy I live, and despair—
That I may be still happier—for thy use!"
If this were so, we could not thank our Lord,
As hearts beat on to doing: 'tis not so—
Malice it is not. Is it carelessness?
Still, no. If care—where is the sign, I ask—
And get no answer: and agree in sum,
O king, with thy profound discouragement,
Who seest the wider but to sigh the more.
Most progress is most failure! thou sayest well.

The last point now:—thou dost except a case—
Holding joy not impossible to one
With artist-gifts—to such a man as I—
Who leave behind me living works indeed;
For, such a poem, such a painting lives.
What? dost thou verily trip upon a word,
Confound the accurate view of what joy is
(Caught somewhat clearer by my eyes than thine)
With feeling joy? confound the knowing how
And showing how to live (my faculty)
With actually living?—Otherwise
Where is the artist's vantage o'er the king?
Because in my great epos I display
How divers men young, strong, fair, wise, can act—
Is this as though I acted? if I paint,
Carve the young Phœbus, am I therefore young?
Methinks I'm older that I bowed myself

The many years of pain that taught me art!
Indeed, to know is something, and to prove
How all this beauty might be enjoyed, is more:
But, knowing nought, to enjoy is something too.
Yon rower with the moulded muscles there
Lowering the sail, is nearer it than I.
I can write love-odes—thy fair slave's an ode.
I get to sing of love, when grown too grey
For being beloved: she turns to that young man
The muscles all a-ripple on his back.
I know the joy of kingship: well—thou art king!

" But," sayest thou—(and I marvel, I repeat,
To find thee tripping on a mere word) " what
Thou writest, paintest, stays: that does not die:
Sappho survives, because we sing her songs,
And Æschylus, because we read his plays! "
Why, if they live still, let them come and take
Thy slave in my despite—drink from thy cup—
Speak in my place. Thou diest while I survive?
Say rather that my fate is deadlier still,—
In this, that every day my sense of joy
Grows more acute, my soul (intensified
In power and insight) more enlarged, more keen;
While every day my hairs fall more and more,
My hand shakes, and the heavy years increase—
The horror quickening still from year to year,
The consummation coming past escape
When I shall know most, and yet least enjoy—
When all my works wherein I prove my worth,
Being present still to mock me in men's mouths,
Alive still, in the phrase of such as thou,
I, I, the feeling, thinking, acting man,
The man who loved his life so over much,
Shall sleep in my urn. It is so horrible,
I dare at times imagine to my need
Some future state revealed to us by Zeus,
Unlimited in capability
For joy, as this is in desire for joy,
To seek which, the joy-hunger forces us.
That, stung by straitness of our life, made strait
On purpose to make sweet the life at large—
Freed by the throbbing impulse we call death

We burst there as the worm into the fly,
Who, while a worm still, wants his wings.   But, no!
Zeus has not yet revealed it; and, alas!
He must have done so—were it possible!

Live long and happy, and in that thought die,
Glad for what was.   Farewell.   And for the rest,
I cannot tell thy messenger aright
Where to deliver what he bears of thine
To one called Paulus—we have heard his fame
Indeed, if Christus be not one with him—
I know not, nor am troubled much to know,
Thou canst not think a mere barbarian Jew,
As Paulus proves to be, one circumcised,
Hath access to a secret shut from us?
Thou wrongest our philosophy, O king,
In stooping to inquire of such an one,
As if his answer could impose at all.
He writeth, doth he? well, and he may write.
Oh, the Jew findeth scholars! certain slaves
Who touched on this same isle, preached him and Christ;
And (as I gathered from a bystander)
Their doctrines could be held by no sane man.

THE TWINS.

" Give " and " It-shall-be-given-unto-you."

I. GRAND rough old Martin Luther
        Bloomed fables—flowers on furze,
    The better the uncouther:
        Do roses stick like burrs?

II. A beggar asked an alms
        One day at an abbey-door,
    Said Luther; but, seized with qualms,
        The Abbot replied, " We're poor! "

III. " Poor, who had plenty once,
        " When gifts fell thick as rain:
    " But they give us nought, for the nonce,
        " And how should we give again? "

IV. Then the beggar, " See your sins!
    " Of old, unless I err,
  " Ye had brothers for inmates, twins,
    " Date and Dabitur."

V. " While Date was in good case
    " Dabitur flourished too:
  " For Dabitur's lenten face,
    " No wonder if Date rue."

VI. " Would ye retrieve the one?
    " Try and make plump the other!
  " When Date's penance is done,
    " Dabitur helps his brother."

VII. " Only, beware relapse! "
    The abbot hung his head.
  This beggar might be, perhaps,
    An angel, Luther said.

POPULARITY.

I. STAND still, true poet that you are,
    I know you; let me try and draw you.
  Some night you'll fail us.   When afar
    You rise, remember one man saw you,
  Knew you, and named a star.

II. My star, God's glow-worm!   Why extend
    That loving hand of His which leads you,
  Yet locks you safe from end to end
    Of this dark world, unless He needs you—
  Just saves your light to spend?

III. His clenched Hand shall unclose at last
    I know, and let out all the beauty.
  My poet holds the future fast,
    Accepts the coming ages' duty,
  Their present for this past.

IV. That day, the earth's feast-master's brow
    Shall clear, to God the chalice raising;
  " Others give best at first, but Thou
    For ever set'st our table praising,—
  Keep'st the good wine till now."

  v. Meantime, I'll draw you as you stand,
     With few or none to watch and wonder,
  I'll say—a fisher (on the sand
     By Tyre the Old) his ocean-plunder,
  A netful, brought to land.

  vi. Who has not heard how Tyrian shells
     Enclosed the blue, that dye of dyes
  Whereof one drop worked miracles,
     And coloured like Astarte's eyes
  Raw silk the merchant sells?

  vii. And each bystander of them all
     Could criticise, and quote tradition
  How depths of blue sublimed some pall,
     To get which, pricked a king's ambition;
  Worth sceptre, crown and ball.

  viii. Yet there's the dye,—in that rough mesh,
     The sea has only just o'er-whispered!
  Live whelks, the lip's-beard dripping fresh,
     As if they still the water's lisp heard
  Through foam the rock-weeds thresh.

  ix. Enough to furnish Solomon
     Such hangings for his cedar-house,
  That when gold-robed he took the throne
     In that abyss of blue, the Spouse
  Might swear his presence shone

  x. Most like the centre-spike of gold
     Which burns deep in the blue-bell's womb,
  What time, with ardours manifold,
     The bee goes singing to her groom,
  Drunken and overbold.

  xi. Mere conchs! not fit for warp or woof!
     Till art comes,—comes to pound and squeeze
  And clarify,—refines to proof
     The liquor filtered by degrees,
  While the world stands aloof.

  xii. And there's the extract, flasked and fine,
     And priced, and saleable at last!
  And Hobbs, Nobbs, Stokes and Nokes combine
     To paint the future from the past,
  Put blue into their line.

XIII. Hobbs hints blue,—straight he turtle eats.
    Nobbs prints blue,—claret crowns his cup.
Nokes outdares Stokes in azure feats,—
    Both gorge.   Who fished the murex up?
What porridge had John Keats?

THE HERETIC'S TRAGEDY.

A MIDDLE-AGE INTERLUDE.

I.

PREADMONISHETH THE ABBOT DEODAET.

THE Lord, we look to once for all,
    Is the Lord we should look at, all at once:
He knows not to vary, saith St. Paul,
    Nor the shadow of turning, for the nonce.
See him no other than as he is;
    Give both the Infinites their due—
Infinite mercy, but, I wis,
    As infinite a justice too.   *[Organ : plagal-cadence.*
    As infinite a justice too.

II.

ONE SINGETH.

John, Master of the Temple of God,
    Falling to sin the Unknown Sin,
What he bought of Emperor Aldabrod,
    He sold it to Sultan Saladin—
Till, caught by Pope Clement, a-buzzing there,
    Hornet-prince of the mad wasps' hive,
And clipt of his wings in Paris square,
    They bring him now to be burned alive.

    [And wanteth there grace of lute or clavicithern, ye
      shall say to confirm him who singeth—

We bring John now to be burned alive.

III.

In the midst is a goodly gallows built;
    'Twixt fork and fork a stake is stuck;
But first they set divers tumbrils a-tilt,
    Make a trench all round with the city muck,

Inside they pile log upon log, good store;
  Faggots not few, blocks great and small,
Reached a man's mid-thigh, no less, no more,—
  For they mean he should roast in the sight of all.

CHORUS.

We mean he should roast in the sight of all.

IV.

Good sappy bavins that kindle forthwith;
  Billets that blaze substantial and slow;
Pine-stump split deftly, dry as pith;
  Larch-heart that chars to a chalk-white glow:
Then up they hoist me John in a chafe,
  Sling him fast like a hog to scorch,
Spit in his face, then leap back safe,
  Sing " Laudes " and bid clap-to the torch.

CHORUS.

Laus Deo—who bids clap-to the torch.

V.

John of the Temple, whose fame so bragged,
  Is burning alive in Paris square!
How can he curse, if his mouth is gagged?
  Or wriggle his neck, with a collar there?
Or heave his chest, while a band goes round?
  Or threat with his fist, since his arms are spliced?
Or kick with his feet, now his legs are bound?
  —Thinks John—I will call upon Jesus Christ.
                    [*Here one crosseth himself.*

VI.

Jesus Christ—John had bought and sold,
  Jesus Christ—John had eaten and drunk;
To him, the Flesh meant silver and gold.
  (*Salvâ reverentiâ.*)
Now it was, " Saviour, bountiful lamb,
  I have roasted thee Turks, though men roast me.
See thy servant, the plight wherein I am!
  Art thou a Saviour? Save thou me! "

CHORUS.

'Tis John the mocker cries, Save thou me!

VII.

Who maketh God's menace an idle word?
   —Saith, it no more means what it proclaims,
Than a damsel's threat to her wanton bird?—
   For she too prattles of ugly names.
—Saith, he knoweth but one thing,—what he knows?
   That God is good and the rest is breath;
Why else is the same styled, Sharon's rose?
   Once a rose, ever a rose, he saith.

CHORUS.

O, John shall yet find a rose, he saith!

VIII.

Alack, there be roses and roses, John!
   Some honied of taste like your leman's tongue.
Some, bitter—for why? (roast gaily on!)
   Their tree struck root in devil's dung!
When Paul once reasoned of righteousness
   And of temperance and of judgment to come,
Good Felix trembled, he could no less—
   John, snickering, crook'd his wicked thumb.

CHORUS.

What cometh to John of the wicked thumb?

IX.

Ha ha, John plucks now at his rose
   To rid himself of a sorrow at heart!
Lo,—petal on petal, fierce rays unclose;
   Anther on anther, sharp spikes outstart;
And with blood for dew, the bosom boils;
   And a gust of sulphur is all its smell;
And lo, he is horribly in the toils
   Of a coal-black giant flower of Hell!

CHORUS.

What maketh Heaven, that maketh Hell.

x.

So, as John called now, through the fire amain,
  On the Name, he had cursed with, all his life—
To the Person, he bought and sold again—
  For the Face, with his daily buffets rife—
Feature by feature It took its place!
  And his voice like a mad dog's choking bark
At the steady Whole of the Judge's Face—
  Died.   Forth John's soul flared into the dark.

SUBJOINETH THE ABBOT DEODAET.

God help all poor souls lost in the dark!

TWO IN THE CAMPAGNA.

I. I WONDER do you feel to-day
    As I have felt, since, hand in hand,
  We sat down on the grass, to stray
    In spirit better through the land,
  This morn of Rome and May?

II. For me, I touched a thought, I know,
    Has tantalised me many times,
  (Like turns of thread the spiders throw
    Mocking across our path) for rhymes
  To catch at and let go.

III. Help me to hold it: first it left
    The yellowing fennel, run to seed
  There, branching from the brickwork's cleft,
    Some old tomb's ruin: yonder weed
  Took up the floating weft,

IV. Where one small orange cup amassed
    Five beetles,—blind and green they grope
  Among the honey-meal,—and last
    Everywhere on the grassy slope
  I traced it.   Hold it fast!

V. The champaign with its endless fleece
    Of feathery grasses everywhere!
  Silence and passion, joy and peace,
    An everlasting wash of air—
  Rome's ghost since her decease.

VI. Such life there, through such lengths of hours,
    Such miracles performed in play,
Such primal naked forms of flowers,
    Such letting Nature have her way
While Heaven looks from its towers.

VII. How say you?   Let us, O my dove,
    Let us be unashamed of soul,
As earth lies bare to heaven above.
    How is it under our control
To love or not to love?

VIII. I would that you were all to me,
    You that are just so much, no more—
Nor yours, nor mine,—nor slave nor free!
    Where does the fault lie? what the core
Of the wound, since wound must be?

IX. I would I could adopt your will,
    See with your eyes, and set my heart
Beating by yours, and drink my fill
    At your soul's springs,—your part, my part
In life, for good and ill.

X. No.   I yearn upward—touch you close,
    Then stand away.   I kiss your cheek,
Catch your soul's warmth,—I pluck the rose
    And love it more than tongue can speak—
Then the good minute goes.

XI. Already how am I so far
    Out of that minute?   Must I go
Still like the thistle-ball, no bar,
    Onward, whenever light winds blow,
Fixed by no friendly star?

XII. Just when I seemed about to learn!
    Where is the thread now?   Off again!
The old trick!   Only I discern—
    Infinite passion and the pain
Of finite hearts that yearn.

A GRAMMARIAN'S FUNERAL.

LET us begin and carry up this corpse,
    Singing together.
Leave we the common crofts, the vulgar thorpes,
    Each in its tether
Sleeping safe on the bosom of the plain,
    Cared-for till cock-crow.
Look out if yonder's not the day again
    Rimming the rock-row!
That's the appropriate country—there, man's thought,
    Rarer, intenser,
Self-gathered for an outbreak, as it ought,
    Chafes in the censer!
Leave we the unlettered plain its herd and crop;
    Seek we sepulture
On a tall mountain, citied to the top,
    Crowded with culture!
All the peaks soar, but one the rest excels;
    Clouds overcome it;
No, yonder sparkle is the citadel's
    Circling its summit!
Thither our path lies—wind we up the heights—
    Wait ye the warning?
Our low life was the level's and the night's;
    He's for the morning!
Step to a tune, square chests, erect the head,
    'Ware the beholders!
This is our master, famous, calm, and dead,
    Borne on our shoulders.
Sleep, crop and herd! sleep, darkling thorpe and croft,
    Safe from the weather!
He, whom we convey to his grave aloft,
    Singing together,
He was a man born with thy face and throat,
    Lyric Apollo!
Long he lived nameless: how should spring take note
    Winter would follow?
Till lo, the little touch, and youth was gone!
    Cramped and diminished,

Moaned he, " New measures, other feet anon!
    My dance is finished? "
No, that's the world's way! (keep the mountain-side,
    Make for the city.)
He knew the signal, and stepped on with pride
    Over men's pity;
Left play for work, and grappled with the world
    Bent on escaping:
" What's in the scroll," quoth he, " thou keepest furled?
    Show me their shaping,
Theirs, who most studied man, the bard and sage,—
    Give! "—So he gowned him,
Straight got by heart that book to its last page:
    Learned, we found him!
Yea, but we found him bald too—eyes like lead,
    Accents uncertain:
" Time to taste life," another would have said,
    " Up with the curtain!"
This man said rather, " Actual life comes next?
    Patience a moment!
Grant I have mastered learning's crabbed text,
    Still, there's the comment.
Let me know all.   Prate not of most or least,
    Painful or easy:
Even to the crumbs I'd fain eat up the feast,
    Ay, nor feel queasy!"
Oh, such a life as he resolved to live,
    When he had learned it,
When he had gathered all books had to give;
    Sooner, he spurned it!
Image the whole, then execute the parts—
    Fancy the fabric
Quite, ere you build, ere steel strike fire from quartz,
    Ere mortar dab brick!

(Here's the town-gate reached: there's the market-place
    Gaping before us.)
Yea, this in him was the peculiar grace
    (Hearten our chorus)
Still before living he'd learn how to live—
    No end to learning.
Earn the means first—God surely will contrive
    Use for our earning.

Others mistrust and say—" But time escapes,—
 Live now or never!"
He said, "What's Time? leave Now for dogs and apes!
 Man has For ever."
Back to his book then: deeper drooped his head;
 Calculus racked him:
Leaden before, his eyes grew dross of lead;
 Tussis attacked him.
"Now, Master, take a little rest!"—not he!
 (Caution redoubled!
Step two a-breast, the way winds narrowly.)
 Not a whit troubled,
Back to his studies, fresher than at first,
 Fierce as a dragon
He, (soul-hydroptic with a sacred thirst)
 Sucked at the flagon.
Oh, if we draw a circle premature,
 Heedless of far gain,
Greedy for quick returns of profit, sure,
 Bad is our bargain!
Was it not great? did not he throw on God,
 (He loves the burthen)—
God's task to make the heavenly period
 Perfect the earthen?
Did not he magnify the mind, shew clear
 Just what it all meant?
He would not discount life, as fools do here,
 Paid by instalment!
He ventured neck or nothing—heaven's success
 Found, or earth's failure:
"Wilt thou trust death or not?" he answered "Yes.
 Hence with life's pale lure!"
That low man seeks a little thing to do,
 Sees it and does it:
This high man, with a great thing to pursue,
 Dies ere he knows it.
That low man goes on adding one to one,
 His hundred's soon hit:
This high man, aiming at a million,
 Misses an unit.
That, has the world here—should he need the next,
 Let the world mind him!
This, throws himself on God, and unperplext

Seeking shall find Him.
So, with the throttling hands of Death at strife,
  Ground he at grammar;
Still, thro' the rattle, parts of speech were rife.
  While he could stammer
He settled *Hoti's* business—let it be!—
  Properly based *Oun*—
Gave us the doctrine of the enclitic *De*,
  Dead from the waist down.
Well, here's the platform, here's the proper place.
  Hail to your purlieus
All ye highfliers of the feathered race,
  Swallows and curlews!
Here's the top-peak! the multitude below
  Live, for they can there.
This man decided not to Live but Know—
  Bury this man there?
Here—here's his place, where meteors shoot, clouds form,
  Lightnings are loosened,
Stars come and go! let joy break with the storm—
  Peace let the dew send!
Lofty designs must close in like effects:
  Loftily lying,
Leave him—still loftier than the world suspects,
  Living and dying.

ONE WAY OF LOVE.

I. ALL June I bound the rose in sheaves.
  Now, rose by rose, I strip the leaves,
  And strew them where Pauline may pass.
  She will not turn aside?   Alas!
  Let them lie.   Suppose they die?
  The chance was they might take her eye.

II. How many a month I strove to suit
  These stubborn fingers to the lute!
  To-day I venture all I know.
  She will not hear my music?   So!
  Break the string—fold music's wing.
  Suppose Pauline had bade me sing!

III. My whole life long I learned to love.
This hour my utmost art I prove
And speak my passion.—Heaven or hell?
She will not give me heaven?   'Tis well!
Lose who may—I still can say,
Those who win heaven, blest are they.

ANOTHER WAY OF LOVE.

I. JUNE was not over,
    Though past the full,
And the best of her roses
    Had yet to blow,
    When a man I know
(But shall not discover,
    Since ears are dull,
    And time discloses)
Turned him and said with a man's true air,
Half sighing a smile in a yawn, as 'twere,—
" If I tire of your June, will she greatly care? "

II. Well, Dear, in-doors with you!
    True, serene deadness
Tries a man's temper.
    What's in the blossom
    June wears on her bosom?
Can it clear scores with you?
    Sweetness and redness,
    Eadem semper !
Go, let me care for it greatly or slightly!
If June mends her bowers now, your hand left unsightly
By plucking their roses,—my June will do rightly.

III. And after, for pastime,
    If June be refulgent
With flowers in completeness,
    All petals, no prickles,
    Delicious as trickles
Of wine poured at mass-time,—
    And choose One indulgent
To redness and sweetness:
Or if, with experience of man and of spider,
She use my June-lightning, the strong insect-ridder,
To stop the fresh spinning,—why, June will consider.

" TRANSCENDENTALISM: "

A POEM IN TWELVE BOOKS.

Stop playing, poet! may a brother speak?
'Tis you speak, that's your error.   Song's our art:
Whereas you please to speak these naked thoughts
Instead of draping them in sights and sounds.
—True thoughts, good thoughts, thoughts fit to treasure up!
But why such long prolusion and display,
Such turning and adjustment of the harp,
And taking it upon your breast at length,
Only to speak dry words across its strings?
Stark-naked thought is in request enough—
Speak prose and holloa it till Europe hears!
The six-foot Swiss tube, braced about with bark,
Which helps the hunter's voice from Alp to Alp—
Exchange our harp for that,—who hinders you?

   But here's your fault; grown men want thought, you think;
Thought's what they mean by verse, and seek in verse:
Boys seek for images and melody,
Men must have reason—so you aim at men.
Quite otherwise!   Objects throng our youth, 'tis true,
We see and hear and do not wonder much.
If you could tell us what they mean, indeed!
As Swedish Bœhme never cared for plants
Until it happed, a-walking in the fields,
He noticed all at once that plants could speak,
Nay, turned with loosened tongue to talk with him.
That day the daisy had an eye indeed—
Colloquised with the cowslip on such themes!
We find them extant yet in Jacob's prose.
But by the time youth slips a stage or two
While reading prose in that tough book he wrote,
(Collating, and amendating the same
And settling on the sense most to our mind)
We shut the clasps and find life's summer past.
Then, who helps more, pray, to repair our loss—
Another Bœhme with a tougher book
And subtler meanings of what roses say,—

Or some stout Mage like him of Halberstadt,
John, who made things Bœhme wrote thoughts about?
He with a " look you ! " vents a brace of rhymes,
And in there breaks the sudden rose herself,
Over us, under, round us every side,
Nay, in and out the tables and the chairs
And musty volumes, Bœhme's book and all,—
Buries us with a glory, young once more,
Pouring heaven into this shut house of life.

So come, the harp back to your heart again!
You are a poem, though your poem's naught.
The best of all you did before, believe,
Was your own boy's face o'er the finer chords
Bent, following the cherub at the top
That points to God with his paired half-moon wings.

MISCONCEPTIONS.

I. THIS is a spray the Bird clung to,
　　Making it blossom with pleasure,
　Ere the high tree-top she sprung to,
　　Fit for her nest and her treasure.
　　Oh, what a hope beyond measure
　Was the poor spray's, which the flying feet hung to,—
　So to be singled out, built in, and sung to!

II. This is a heart the Queen leant on,
　　Thrilled in a minute erratic,
　Ere the true bosom she bent on,
　　Meet for love's regal dalmatic.
　　Oh, what a fancy ecstatic
　Was the poor heart's, ere the wanderer went on—
　Love to be saved for it, proffered to, spent on!

ONE WORD MORE.

TO E. B. B.

I. THERE they are, my fifty men and women
   Naming me the fifty poems finished!
   Take them, Love, the book and me together.
   Where the heart lies, let the brain lie also.

II. Rafael made a century of sonnets,
    Made and wrote them in a certain volume
    Dinted with the silver-pointed pencil
    Else he only used to draw Madonnas:
    These, the world might view—but One, the volume.
    Who that one, you ask?   Your heart instructs you.
    Did she live and love it all her life-time?
    Did she drop, his lady of the sonnets,
    Die, and let it drop beside her pillow
    Where it lay in place of Rafael's glory,
    Rafael's cheek so duteous and so loving—
    Cheek, the world was wont to hail a painter's,
    Rafael's cheek, her love had turned a poet's?

III. You and I would rather read that volume,
     (Take to his beating bosom by it)
     Lean and list the bosom-beats of Rafael,
     Would we not? than wonder at Madonnas—
     Her, San Sisto names, and Her, Foligno,
     Her, that visits Florence in a vision,
     Her, that's left with lilies in the Louvre—
     Seen by us and all the world in circle.

IV. You and I will never read that volume.
    Guido Reni, like his own eye's apple
    Guarded long the treasure-book and loved it.
    Guido Reni dying, all Bologna
    Cried, and the world with it, " Ours—the treasure!"
    Suddenly, as rare things will, it vanished.

V. Dante once prepared to paint an angel:
   Whom to please?   You whisper " Beatrice."
   While he mused and traced it and retraced it,
   (Peradventure with a pen corroded

Still by drops of that hot ink he dipped for,
When, his left hand i' the hair o' the wicked,
Back he held the brow and pricked its stigma,
Bit into the live man's flesh for parchment,
Loosed him, laughed to see the writing rankle,
Let the wretch go festering thro' Florence)—
Dante, who loved well because he hated,
Hated wickedness that hinders loving,
Dante standing, studying his angel,—
In there broke the folk of his Inferno.
Says he—" Certain people of importance "
(Such he gave his daily, dreadful line to)
Entered and would seize, forsooth, the poet.
Says the poet—" Then I stopped my painting."

VI. You and I would rather see that angel,
Painted by the tenderness of Dante,
Would we not?—than read a fresh Inferno.

VII. You and I will never see that picture.
While he mused on love and Beatrice,
While he softened o'er his outlined angel,
In they broke, those " people of importance: "
We and Bice bear the loss forever.

VIII. What of Rafael's sonnets, Dante's picture?

IX. This: no artist lives and loves that longs not
Once, and only once, and for One only,
(Ah, the prize!) to find his love a language
Fit and fair and simple and sufficient—
Using nature that's an art to others,
Not, this one time, art that's turned his nature.
Ay, of all the artists living, loving,
None but would forego his proper dowry,—
Does he paint? he fain would write a poem,—
Does he write? he fain would paint a picture,
Put to proof art alien to the artist's,
Once, and only once, and for One only,
So to be the man and leave the artist,
Save the man's joy, miss the artist's sorrow.

X. Wherefore? Heaven's gift takes earth's abatement!
He who smites the rock and spreads the water,
Bidding drink and live a crowd beneath him,

Even he, the minute makes immortal,
Proves, perchance, his mortal in the minute,
Desecrates, belike, the deed in doing.
While he smites, how can he but remember,
So he smote before, in such a peril,
When they stood and mocked—" Shall smiting help
   us? "
When they drank and sneered—" A stroke is easy! "
When they wiped their mouths and went their journey,
Throwing him for thanks—" But drought was pleas-
   ant."
Thus old memories mar the actual triumph;
Thus the doing savours of disrelish;
Thus achievement lacks a gracious somewhat;
O'er importuned brows becloud the mandate,
Carelessness or consciousness, the gesture.
For he bears an ancient wrong about him,
Sees and knows again those phalanxed faces,
Hears, yet one time more, the 'customed prelude—
" How should'st thou, of all men, smite, and save
   us? "
Guesses what is like to prove the sequel—
" Egypt's flesh-pots—nay, the drought was better."

XI. Oh, the crowd must have emphatic warrant!
   Theirs, the Sinai-forehead's cloven brilliance,
   Right-arm's rod-sweep, tongue's imperial fiat.
   Never dares the man put off the prophet.

XII. Did he love one face from out the thousands,
   (Were she Jethro's daughter, white and wifely,
   Were she but the Æthiopian bondslave,)
   He would envy yon dumb patient camel,
   Keeping a reserve of scanty water
   Meant to save his own life in the desert;
   Ready in the desert to deliver
   (Kneeling down to let his breast be opened)
   Hoard and life together for his mistress.

XIII. I shall never, in the years remaining,
   Paint you pictures, no, nor carve you statues,
   Make you music that should all-express me;
   So it seems: I stand on my attainment.

This of verse alone, one life allows me;
Verse and nothing else have I to give you.
Other heights in other lives, God willing—
All the gifts from all the heights, your own, Love!

xiv. Yet a semblance of resource avails us—
Shade so finely touched, love's sense must seize it.
Take these lines, look lovingly and nearly,
Lines I write the first time and the last time.
He who works in fresco, steals a hair-brush.
Curbs the liberal hand, subservient proudly,
Cramps his spirit, crowds its all in little,
Makes a strange art of an art familiar,
Fills his lady's missal-marge with flowerets.
He who blows thro' bronze, may breathe thro' silver
Fitly serenade a slumbrous princess.
He who writes, may write for once, as I do.

xv. Love, you saw me gather men and women,
Live or dead or fashioned by my fancy,
Enter each and all, and use their service,
Speak from every mouth,—the speech, a poem.
Hardly shall I tell my joys and sorrows,
Hopes and fears, belief and disbelieving:
I am mine and yours—the rest be all men's,
Karshook, Cleon, Norbert and the fifty.
Let me speak this once in my true person,
Not as Lippo, Roland or Andrea,
Though the fruit of speech be just this sentence—
Pray you, look on these my men and women,
Take and keep my fifty poems finished;
Where my heart lies, let my brain lie also!
Poor the speech; be how I speak, for all things.

xvi. Not but that you know me! Lo, the moon's self!
Here in London, yonder late in Florence,
Still we find her face, the thrice-transfigured.
Curving on a sky imbrued with colour,
Drifted over Fiesole by twilight,
Came she, our new crescent of a hair's-breadth.
Full she flared it, lamping Samminiato,
Rounder 'twixt the cypresses and rounder,
Perfect till the nightingales applauded.

Now, a piece of her old self, impoverished,
Hard to greet, she traverses the houseroofs,
Hurries with unhandsome thrift of silver,
Goes dispiritedly,—glad to finish.

XVII. What, there's nothing in the moon note-worthy?
Nay—for if that moon could love a mortal,
Use, to charm him (so to fit a fancy)
All her magic ('tis the old sweet mythos)
She would turn a new side to her mortal,
Side unseen of herdsman, huntsman, steersman—
Blank to Zoroaster on his terrace,
Blind to Galileo on his turret,
Dumb to Homer, dumb to Keats—him, even!
Think, the wonder of the moonstruck mortal—
When she turns round, comes again in heaven,
Opens out anew for worse or better?
Proves she like some portent of an ice-berg
Swimming full upon the ship it founders,
Hungry with huge teeth of splintered chrystals?
Proves she as the paved-work of a sapphire
Seen by Moses when he climbed the mountain?
Moses, Aaron, Nadab and Abihu
Climbed and saw the very God, the Highest,
Stand upon the paved-work of a sapphire.
Like the bodied heaven in his clearness
Shone the stone, the sapphire of that paved-work,
When they ate and drank and saw God also!

XVIII. What were seen? None knows, none ever shall
        know.
Only this is sure—the sight were other,
Not the moon's same side, born late in Florence,
Dying now impoverished here in London.
God be thanked, the meanest of his creatures
Boasts two soul-sides, one to face the world with,
One to show a woman when he loves her.

XIX. This I say of me, but think of you, Love!
This to you—yourself my moon of poets!
Ah, but that's the world's side—there's the wonder—
Thus they see you, praise you, think they know you.
There, in turn I stand with them and praise you,

Out of my own self, I dare to phrase it.
But the best is when I glide from out them,
Cross a step or two of dubious twilight,
Come out on the other side, the novel
Silent silver lights and darks undreamed of,
Where I hush and bless myself with silence.

xx. Oh, their Rafael of the dear Madonnas,
Oh, their Dante of the dread Inferno,
Wrote one song—and in my brain I sing it,
Drew one angel—borne, see, on my bosom!

DRAMATIS PERSONÆ

DRAMATIS PERSONÆ

1864

JAMES LEE'S WIFE.

I.—JAMES LEE'S WIFE SPEAKS AT THE WINDOW.

I. Ah, Love, but a day
    And the world has changed!
The sun's away,
    And the bird estranged;
The wind has dropped,
    And the sky's deranged:
Summer has stopped.

II. Look in my eyes!
    Wilt thou change too?
Should I fear surprise?
    Shall I find aught new
In the old and dear,
    In the good and true,
With the changing year?

III. Thou art a man,
    But I am thy love.
For the lake, its swan;
    For the dell, its dove;
And for thee—(oh, haste!)
    Me, to bend above,
Me, to hold embraced.

II.—BY THE FIRESIDE.

I. Is all our fire of shipwreck wood,
        Oak and pine?
Oh, for the ills half-understood,
        The dim dead woe
        Long ago

452

Befallen this bitter coast of France!
Well, poor sailors took their chance;
    I take mine.

II. A ruddy shaft our fire must shoot
    O'er the sea:
Do sailors eye the casement—mute,
    Drenched and stark,
    From their bark—
And envy, gnash their teeth for hate
O' the warm safe house and happy freight
    —Thee and me?

III. God help you, sailors, at your need!
    Spare the curse!
For some ships, safe in port indeed,
    Rot and rust,
    Run to dust,
All through worms i' the wood, which crept,
Gnawed our hearts out while we slept:
    That is worse.

IV. Who lived here before us two?
    Old-world pairs.
Did a woman ever—would I knew!—
    Watch the man
    With whom began
Love's voyage full-sail,—(now, gnash your teeth!)
When planks start, open hell beneath
    Unawares?

III.—IN THE DOORWAY.

I.

THE swallow has set her six young on the rail,
    And looks sea-ward:
The water's in stripes like a snake, olive-pale
    To the leeward,—
On the weather-side, black, spotted white with the wind.
" Good fortune departs, and disaster's behind,"—
Hark, the wind with its wants and its infinite wail!

II.

Our fig-tree, that leaned for the saltness, has furled
  Her five fingers,
Each leaf like a hand opened wide to the world
  Where there lingers
No glint of the gold, Summer sent for her sake:
How the vines writhe in rows, each impaled on its stake!
My heart shrivels up and my spirit shrinks curled.

III.

Yet here are we two; we have love, house enough,
  With the field there,
This house of four rooms, that field red and rough,
  Though it yield there,
For the rabbit that robs, scarce a blade or a bent;
If a magpie alight now, it seems an event;
And they both will be gone at November's rebuff.

IV.

But why must cold spread? but wherefore bring change
  To the spirit,
God meant should mate his with an infinite range,
  And inherit
His power to put life in the darkness and cold?
Oh, live and love worthily, bear and be bold!
Whom Summer made friends of, let Winter estrange!

IV.—ALONG THE BEACH.

I. I will be quiet and talk with you,
    And reason why you are wrong,
  You wanted my love—is that much true?
  And so I did love, so I do:
    What has come of it all along?

II. I took you—how could I otherwise?
    For a world to me, and more;
  For all, love greatens and glorifies
  Till God's a-glow, to the loving eyes,
    In what was mere earth before.

III. Yes, earth—yes, mere ignoble earth!
    Now do I mis-state, mistake?
Do I wrong your weakness and call it worth?
Expect all harvest, dread no dearth,
    Seal my sense up for your sake?

IV. Oh, Love, Love, no, Love! not so, indeed!
    You were just weak earth, I knew:
With much in you waste, with many a weed,
And plenty of passions run to seed,
    But a little good grain too.

V. And such as you were, I took you for mine:
    Did not you find me yours,
To watch the olive and wait the vine,
And wonder when rivers of oil and wine
    Would flow, as the Book assures?

VI. Well, and if none of these good things came,
    What did the failure prove?
The man was my whole world, all the same,
With his flowers to praise or his weeds to blame,
    And, either or both, to love.

VII. Yet this turns now to a fault—there! there!
    That I do love, watch too long,
And wait too well, and weary and wear;
And 'tis all an old story, and my despair
    Fit subject for some new song:

VIII. " How the light, light love, he has wings to fly
    " At suspicion of a bond:
" My wisdom has bidden your pleasure good-bye,
" Which will turn up next in a laughing eye,
    " And why should you look beyond? "

V.—ON THE CLIFF.

I. I LEANED on the turf,
I looked at a rock
Left dry by the surf;
For the turf, to call it grass were to mock:
Dead to the roots, so deep was done
The work of the summer sun.

II. And the rock lay flat
     As an anvil's face:
     No iron like that!
     Baked dry; of a weed, of a shell, no trace;
     Sunshine outside, but ice at the core,
     Death's altar by the lone shore.

III. On the turf, sprang gay
      With his films of blue,
      No cricket, I'll say,
      But a warhorse, barded and chanfroned too,
      The gift of a quixote-mage to his knight,
      Real fairy, with wings all right.

IV. On the rock, they scorch
     Like a drop of fire
     From a brandished torch,
     Fall two red fans of a butterfly:
     No turf, no rock: in their ugly stead,
     See, wonderful blue and red!

V. Is it not so
    With the minds of men?
    The level and low,
    The burnt and bare, in themselves; but then
    With such a blue and red grace, not theirs,—
    Love settling unawares!

VI.—READING A BOOK, UNDER THE CLIFF.

I.

" STILL ailing, Wind?   Wilt be appeased or no?
  " Which needs the other's office, thou or I?
" Dost want to be disburthened of a woe,
  " And can, in truth, my voice untie
" Its links, and let it go?

II.

" Art thou a dumb wronged thing that would be righted,
  " Entrusting thus thy cause to me?   Forbear!
" No tongue can mend such pleadings; faith, requited
  " With falsehood,—love, at last aware
" Of scorn,—hopes, early blighted,—

III.

" We have them; but I know not any tone
  " So fit as thine to falter forth a sorrow:
" Dost think men would go mad without a moan,
  " If they knew any way to borrow
" A pathos like my own?

IV.

" Which sigh wouldst mock, of all the sighs?   The one
  " So long escaping from lips starved and blue,
" That lasts while on her pallet-bed the nun
  " Stretches her length; her foot comes through
" The straw she shivers on;

V.

" You had not thought she was so tall: and spent,
  " Her shrunk lids open, her lean fingers shut
" Close, close, their sharp and livid nails indent
  " Their clammy palm; then all is mute:
" That way, the spirit went.

VI.

" Or wouldst thou rather that I understand
  " Thy will to help me?—like the dog I found
" Once, pacing sad this solitary strand,
  " Who would not take my food, poor hound,
" But whined and licked my hand."

VII.

All this, and more, comes from some young man's pride
  Of power to see,—in failure and mistake,
Relinquishment, disgrace, on every side,—
  Merely examples for his sake,
Helps to his path untried:

VIII.

Instances he must—simply recognize?
  Oh, more than so!—must, with a learner's zeal,
Make doubly prominent, twice emphasize,
  By added touches that reveal
The god in babe's disguise.

IX.

Oh, he knows what defeat means, and the rest!
  Himself the undefeated that shall be:
Failure, disgrace, he flings them you to test,—
  His triumph, in eternity
Too plainly manifest!

X.

Whence, judge if he learn forthwith what the wind
  Means in its moaning—by the happy prompt
Instinctive way of youth, I mean; for kind
  Calm years, exacting their accompt
Of pain, mature the mind:

XI.

And some midsummer morning, at the lull
  Just about daybreak, as he looks across
A sparkling foreign country, wonderful
  To the sea's edge for gloom and gloss,
Next minute must annul.—

XII.

Then, when the wind begins among the vines,
  So low, so low, what shall it say but this?
" Here is the change beginning, here the lines
  " Circumscribe beauty, set to bliss
" The limit time assigns."

XIII.

Nothing can be as it has been before;
  Better, so call it, only not the same.
To draw one beauty into our hearts' core,
  And keep it changeless! such our claim;
So answered,—Never more!

XIV.

Simple? Why this is the old woe o' the world;
  Tune, to whose rise and fall we live and die.
Rise with it, then! Rejoice that man is hurled
  From change to change unceasingly,
His soul's wings never furled!

XV.

That's a new question; still replies the fact,
    Nothing endures: the wind moans, saying so;
We moan in acquiescence: there's life's pact.
    Perhaps probation—do *I* know?
God does; endure his act!

XVI.

Only, for man, how bitter not to grave
    On his soul's hands' palms one fair good wise thing
Just as he grasped it! For himself, death's wave;
    While time first washes—ah, the sting!—
O'er all he'd sink to save.

VII.—AMONG THE ROCKS.

I.

OH, good gigantic smile o' the brown old earth,
    This autumn morning! How he sets his bones
To bask i' the sun, and thrusts out knees and feet
For the ripple to run over in its mirth;
    Listening the while, where on the heap of stones
The white breast of the sea-lark twitters sweet.

II.

That is the doctrine, simple, ancient, true;
    Such is life's trial, as old earth smiles and knows.
If you loved only what were worth your love,
Love were clear gain, and wholly well for you:
    Make the low nature better by your throes!
Give earth yourself, go up for gain above.

VIII.—BESIDE THE DRAWING BOARD.

1. " As like as a Hand to another Hand! "
        Whoever said that foolish thing,
    Could not have studied to understand
        The counsels of God in fashioning,
    Out of the infinite love of his heart,
    This Hand, whose beauty I praise, apart

From the world of wonder left to praise,
If I tried to learn the other ways
Of love in its skill, or love in its power.
   " As like as a Hand to another Hand ":
   Who said that, never took his stand,
Found and followed, like me, an hour,
The beauty in this,—how free, how fine
To fear, almost,—of the limit-line!
As I looked at this, and learned and drew,
   Drew and learned, and looked again,
While fast the happy minutes flew,
   Its beauty mounted into my brain,
   And a fancy seized me; I was fain
To efface my work, begin anew,
Kiss what before I only drew;
Ay, laying the red chalk 'twixt my lips,
   With soul to help if the mere lips failed,
   I kissed all right where the drawing ailed,
Kissed fast the grace that somehow slips
Still from one's soulless finger-tips.

II. 'Tis a clay cast, the perfect thing,
   From Hand live once, dead long ago:
Princess-like it wears the ring
   To fancy's eye, by which we know
That here at length a master found
   His match, a proud lone soul its mate,
As soaring genius sank to ground,
   And pencil could not emulate
The beauty in this,—how free, how fine
To fear almost!—of the limit-line.
Long ago the god, like me
The worm, learned, each in our degree:
Looked and loved, learned and drew,
   Drew and learned and loved again,
While fast the happy minutes flew,
   Till beauty mounted into his brain
And on the finger which outvied
   His art he placed the ring that's there,
Still by fancy's eye descried,
   In token of a marriage rare:
   For him on earth, his art's despair,
For him in heaven, his soul's fit bride.

III. Little girl with the poor coarse hand
    I turned from to a cold clay cast—
I have my lesson, understand
    The world of flesh and blood at last.
Nothing but beauty in a Hand?
    Because he could not change the hue,
    Mend the lines and make them true
To this which met his soul's demand,—
    Would Da Vinci turn from you?
I hear him laugh my woes to scorn—
" The fool forsooth is all forlorn
" Because the beauty, she thinks best,
" Lived long ago or was never born,—
" Because no beauty bears the test
" In this rough peasant Hand! Confessed!
" ' Art is null and study void!'
    " So sayest thou? So said not I,
    " Who threw the faulty pencil by,
" And years instead of hours employed,
" Learning the veritable use
    " Of flesh and bone and nerve beneath
    " Lines and hue of the outer sheath,
" If haply I might reproduce
" One motive of the powers profuse,
" Flesh and bone and nerve that make
    " The poorest coarsest human hand
    " An object worthy to be scanned
" A whole life long for their sole sake.
" Shall earth and the cramped moment-space
" Yield the heavenly crowning grace?
" Now the parts and then the whole!
" Who art thou, with stinted soul
    " And stunted body, thus to cry
" ' I love,—shall that be life's strait dole?
    " ' I must live beloved or die!'
" This peasant hand that spins the wool
    " And bakes the bread, why lives it on,
    " Poor and coarse with beauty gone,—
" What use survives the beauty?" Fool!

Go, little girl with the poor coarse hand!
I have my lesson, shall understand.

IX.—ON DECK.

I. THERE is nothing to remember in me,
   Nothing I ever said with a grace,
Nothing I did that you care to see,
   Nothing I was that deserves a place
In your mind, now I leave you, set you free.

II. Conceded!   In turn, concede to me,
   Such things have been as a mutual flame.
Your soul's locked fast; but, love for a key,
   You might let it loose, till I grew the same
In your eyes, as in mine you stand: strange plea!

III. For then, then, what would it matter to me
   That I was the harsh ill-favoured one?
We both should be like as pea and pea;
   It was ever so since the world begun:
So, let me proceed with my reverie.

IV. How strange it were if you had all me,
   As I have all you in my heart and brain,
You, whose least word brought gloom or glee,
   Who never lifted the hand in vain—
Will hold mine yet, from over the sea!

V. Strange, if a face, when you thought of me,
   Rose like your own face present now,
With eyes as dear in their due degree,
   Much such a mouth, and as bright a brow,
Till you saw yourself, while you cried " 'Tis She!"

VI. Well, you may, you must, set down to me
   Love that was life, life that was love;
A tenure of breath at your lips' decree,
   A passion to stand as your thoughts approve,
A rapture to fall where your foot might be.

VII. But did one touch of such love for me
   Come in a word or a look of yours,
Whose words and looks will, circling, flee
   Round me and round while life endures,—
Could I fancy " As I feel, thus feels he ";

VIII. Why, fade you might to a thing like me,
    And your hair grow these coarse hanks of hair,
Your skin, this bark of a gnarled tree,—
    You might turn myself!—should I know or care
When I should be dead of joy, James Lee?

GOLD HAIR:

A STORY OF PORNIC.

I. OH, the beautiful girl, too white,
    Who lived at Pornic, down by the sea,
Just where the sea and the Loire unite!
    And a boasted name in Brittany
She bore, which I will not write.

II. Too white, for the flower of life is red;
    Her flesh was the soft seraphic screen
Of a soul that is meant (her parents said)
    To just see earth, and hardly be seen,
And blossom in heaven instead.

III. Yet earth saw one thing, one how fair!
    One grace that grew to its full on earth:
Smiles might be sparse on her cheek so spare,
    And her waist want half a girdle's girth,
But she had her great gold hair.

IV. Hair, such a wonder of flix and floss,
    Freshness and fragrance—floods of it, too!
Gold, did I say? Nay, gold's mere dross:
    Here, Life smiled, "Think what I meant to do!"
And Love sighed, "Fancy my loss!"

V. So, when she died, it was scarce more strange
    Than that, when delicate evening dies,
And you follow its spent sun's pallid range,
    There's a shoot of colour startles the skies
With sudden, violent change,—

VI. That, while the breath was nearly to seek,
    As they put the little cross to her lips,
She changed; a spot came out on her cheek,
    A spark from her eye in mid-eclipse,
And she broke forth, "I must speak!"

vii. " Not my hair!" made the girl her moan—
    " All the rest is gone or to go;
" But the last, last grace, my all, my own,
    " Let it stay in the grave, that the ghost may know!
" Leave my poor gold hair alone!"

viii. The passion thus vented, dead lay she;
    Her parents sobbed their worst on that;
All friends joined in, nor observed degree:
    For indeed the hair was to wonder at,
As it spread—not flowing free,

ix. But curled around her brow, like a crown,
    And coiled beside her cheeks, like a cap,
And calmed about her neck—ay, down
    To her breast, pressed flat, without a gap
I' the gold, it reached her gown.

x. All kissed that face, like a silver wedge
    Mid the yellow wealth, nor disturbed its hair:
E'en the priest allowed death's privilege,
    As he planted the crucifix with care
On her breast, 'twixt edge and edge.

xi. And thus was she buried, inviolate
    Of body and soul, in the very space
By the altar; keeping saintly state
    In Pornic church, for her pride of race,
Pure life and piteous fate.

xii. And in after-time would your fresh tear fall,
    Though your mouth might twitch with a dubious smile,
As they told you of gold, both robe and pall,
    How she prayed them leave it alone awhile,
So it never was touched at all.

xiii. Years flew; this legend grew at last
    The life of the lady; all she had done,
All been, in the memories fading fast
    Of lover and friend, was summed in one
Sentence survivors passed:

xiv. To wit, she was meant for heaven, not earth;
    Had turned an angel before the time:
Yet since she was mortal, in such dearth
    Of frailty, all you could count a crime
Was—she knew her gold hair's worth.

xv. At little pleasant Pornic church,
    It chanced, the pavement wanted repair,
Was taken to pieces: left in the lurch,
    A certain sacred space lay bare,
And the boys began research.

xvi. 'Twas the space where our sires would lay a saint,
    A benefactor,—a bishop, suppose,
A baron with armour-adornments quaint,
    Dame with chased ring and jewelled rose,
Things sanctity saves from taint;

xvii. So we come to find them in after-days
    When the corpse is presumed to have done with
        gauds
Of use to the living, in many ways:
    For the boys get pelf, and the town applauds,
And the church deserves the praise.

xviii. They grubbed with a will: and at length—*O cor
Humanum, pectora cœca*, and the rest!—
They found—no gaud they were prying for,
    No ring, no rose, but—who would have guessed?—
A double Louis-d'or!

xix. Here was a case for the priest: he heard,
    Marked, inwardly digested, laid
Finger on nose, smiled, " There's a bird
    " Chirps in my ear ": then, " Bring a spade,
Dig deeper! "—he gave the word.

xx. And lo, when they came to the coffin-lid,
    Or rotten planks which composed it once,
Why, there lay the girl's skull wedged amid
    A mint of money, it served for the nonce
To hold in its hair-heaps hid!

xxi. Hid there? Why? Could the girl be wont
    (She the stainless soul) to treasure up
Money, earth's trash and heaven's affront?
    Had a spider found out the communion-cup,
Was a toad in the christening-font?

xxii. Truth is truth: too true it was.
    Gold! She hoarded and hugged it first,
Longed for it, leaned o'er it, loved it—alas—
    Till the humour grew to a head and burst,
And she cried, at the final pass,—

XXIII. " Talk not of God, my heart is stone!
　　" Nor lover nor friend—be gold for both!
　" Gold I lack; and, my all, my own,
　　" It shall hide in my hair. I scarce die loth
　" If they let my hair alone! "

XXIV. Louis-d'or, some six times five,
　　And duly double, every piece.
　Now do you see? With the priest to shrive,
　　With parents preventing her soul's release
　By kisses that kept alive,—

XXV. With heaven's gold gates about to ope,
　　With friends' praise, gold-like, lingering still,
　An instinct had bidden the girl's hand grope
　　For gold, the true sort—" Gold in heaven, if you
　　　will;
　" But I keep earth's too, I hope."

XXVI. Enough! The priest took the grave's grim yield:
　　The parents, they eyed that price of sin
　As if *thirty pieces* lay revealed
　　On the place *to bury strangers in,*
　The hideous Potter's Field.

XXVII. But the priest bethought him: " ' Milk that's spilt '
　　" —You know the adage! Watch and pray!
　" Saints tumble to earth with so slight a tilt!
　　" It would build a new altar; that, we may! "
　And the altar therewith was built.

XXVIII. Why I deliver this horrible verse?
　　As the text of a sermon, which now I preach:
　Evil or good may be better or worse
　　In the human heart, but the mixture of each
　Is a marvel and a curse.

XXIX. The candid incline to surmise of late
　　That the Christian faith proves false, I find:
　For our Essays-and-Reviews' debate
　　Begins to tell on the public mind,
　And Colenso's words have weight:

XXX. I still, to suppose it true, for my part,
　　See reasons and reasons; this, to begin:
　'Tis the faith that launched point-blank her dart
　　At the head of a lie—taught Original Sin.
　The Corruption of Man's Heart.

THE WORST OF IT.

I. WOULD it were I had been false, not you!
 I that am nothing, not you that are all:
I, never the worse for a touch or two
 On my speckled hide: not you, the pride
Of the day, my swan, that a first fleck's fall
 On her wonder of white must unswan, undo!

II. I had dipped in life's struggle and, out again,
 Bore specks of it here, there, easy to see,
When I found my swan and the cure was plain;
 The dull turned bright as I caught your white
On my bosom: you saved me—saved in vain
 If you ruined yourself, and all through me!

III. Yes, all through the speckled beast that I am,
 Who taught you to stoop; you gave me yourself,
And bound your soul by the vows that damn:
 Since on better thought you break, as you ought,
Vows—words, no angel set down, some elf
 Mistook,—for an oath, an epigram!

IV. Yes, might I judge you, here were my heart,
 And a hundred its like, to treat as you pleased!
I choose to be yours, for my proper part,
 Yours, leave or take, or mar me or make;
If I acquiesce, why should you be teased
 With the conscience-prick and the memory-smart?

V. But what will God say? Oh, my sweet,
 Think, and be sorry you did this thing
Though earth were unworthy to feel your feet,
 There's a heaven above may deserve your love:
Should you forfeit heaven for a snapt gold ring
 And a promise broke, were it just or meet?

VI. And I to have tempted you! I, who tired
 Your soul, no doubt, till it sank! Unwise,
I loved and was lowly, loved and aspired,
 Loved, grieving or glad, till I made you mad,
And you meant to have hated and despised—
 Whereas, you deceived me nor inquired!

VII. She, ruined? How? No heaven for her?
　　Crowns to give, and none for the brow
　That looked like marble and smelt like myrrh?
　　Shall the robe be worn, and the palm-branch borne,
　And she go graceless, she graced now
　　Beyond all saints, as themselves aver?

VIII. Hardly! That must be understood!
　　The earth is your place of penance, then;
　And what will it prove? I desire your good,
　　But, plot as I may, I can find no way
　How a blow should fall such as falls on men,
　　Nor prove too much for your womanhood.

IX. It will come, I suspect, at the end of life,
　　When you walk alone, and review the past;
　And I, who so long shall have done with strife,
　　And journeyed my stage and earned my wage
　And retired as was right,—I am called at last,
　　When the devil stabs you, to lend the knife.

X. He stabs for the minute of trivial wrong,
　　Nor the other hours are able to save,
　The happy, that lasted my whole life long:
　　For a promise broke, not for first words spoke,
　The true, the only, that turn my grave
　　To a blaze of joy and a crash of song.

XI. Witness beforehand! Off I trip
　　On a safe path gay through the flowers you flung:
　My very name made great by your lip,
　　And my heart a-glow with the good I know
　Of a perfect year when we both were young,
　　And I tasted the angels' fellowship.

XII. And witness, moreover . . . Ah, but wait!
　　I spy the loop whence an arrow shoots!
　It may be for yourself, when you meditate,
　　That you grieve—for slain ruth, murdered truth.
　" Though falsehood escape in the end, what boots?
　　" How truth would have triumphed!"—you sigh too
　　　late.

XIII. Ay, who would have triumphed like you, I say!
　　Well, it is lost now; well, you must bear,

Abide and grow fit for a better day:
    You should hardly grudge, could I be your judge,
But hush! For you, can be no despair:
    There's amends: 'tis a secret: hope and pray!

XIV. For I was true at least—oh, true enough!
    And, Dear, truth is not as good as it seems!
Commend me to conscience!   Idle stuff!
    Much help is in mine, as I mope and pine,
And skulk through day, and scowl in my dreams
    At my swan's obtaining the crow's rebuff.

XV. Men tell me of truth now—" False! " I cry:
    Of beauty—" A mask, friend!   Look beneath! "
We take our own method, the devil and I,
    With pleasant and fair and wise and rare:
And the best we wish to what lives, is—death;
    Which even in wishing, perhaps we lie!

XVI. Far better commit a fault and have done—
    As you, Dear!—for ever; and choose the pure,
And look where the healing waters run,
    And strive and strain to be good again
And a place in the other world ensure,
    All glass and gold, with God for its sun.

XVII. Misery! What shall I say or do?
    I cannot advise, or, at least, persuade:
Most like, you are glad you deceived me—rue
    No whit of the wrong: you endured too long,
Have done no evil and want no aid,
    Will live the old life out and chance the new.

XVIII. And your sentence is written all the same,
    And I can do nothing,—pray, perhaps:
But somehow the world pursues its game,—
    If I pray, if I curse,—for better or worse:
And my faith is torn to a thousand scraps,
    And my heart feels ice while my words breathe flame.

XIX. Dear, I look from my hiding-place.
    Are you still so fair?   Have you still the eyes?
Be happy!   Add but the other grace,
    Be good!   Why want what the angels vaunt?
I knew you once: but in Paradise,
    If we meet, I will pass nor turn my face.

II—Q 42

DIS ALITER VISUM; OR, LE BYRON DE NOS JOURS.

I. Stop, let me have the truth of that!
    Is that all true?   I say, the day
Ten years ago when both of us
    Met on a morning, friends—as thus
We meet this evening, friends or what?—

II. Did you—because I took your arm
    And sillily smiled, " A mass of brass
" That sea looks, blazing underneath! "
    While up the cliff-road edged with heath,
We took the turns nor came to harm—

III. Did you consider " Now makes twice
    " That I have seen her, walked and talked
" With this poor pretty thoughtful thing,
    " Whose worth I weigh: she tries to sing;
" Draws, hopes in time the eye grows nice;

IV. " Reads verse and thinks she understands;
    " Loves all, at any rate, that's great,
" Good, beautiful; but much as we
    " Down at the bath-house love the sea,
" Who breathe its salt and bruise its sands:

V. " While . . . do but follow the fishing-gull
    " That flaps and floats from wave to cave!
" There's the sea-lover, fair my friend!
    " What then?   Be patient, mark and mend!
" Had you the making of your scull? "

VI. And did you, when we faced the church
    With spire and sad slate roof, aloof
From human fellowship so far,
    Where a few graveyard crosses are,
And garlands for the swallows' perch,—

VII. Did you determine, as we stepped
    O'er the lone stone fence, " Let me get
" Her for myself, and what's the earth
    " With all its art, verse, music, worth—
" Compared with love, found, gained, and kept?

VIII. " Schumann's our music-maker now;
    " Has his march-movement youth and mouth?
" Ingres's the modern man that paints;
    " Which will lean on me, of his saints?
" Heine for songs; for kisses, how? "

IX. And did you, when we entered, reached
    The votive frigate, soft aloft
Riding on air this hundred years,
    Safe-smiling at old hopes and fears,—
Did you draw profit while she preached?

X. Resolving, " Fools we wise men grow!
    " Yes, I could easily blurt out curt
" Some question that might find reply
    " As prompt in her stopped lips, dropped eye,
" And rush of red to cheek and brow:

XI. " Thus were a match made, sure and fast,
    " Mid the blue weed-flowers round the mound
" Where, issuing, we shall stand and stay
    " For one more look at baths and bay,
" Sands, sea-gulls, and the old church last—

XII. " A match 'twixt me, bent, wigged and lamed,
    " Famous, however, for verse and worse,
" Sure of the Fortieth spare Arm-chair
    " When gout and glory seat me there,
" So, one whose love-freaks pass unblamed,—

XIII. " And this young beauty, round and sound
    " As a mountain-apple, youth and truth
" With loves and doves, at all events
    " With money in the Three per Cents;
" Whose choice of me would seem profound:—

XIV. " She might take me as I take her.
    " Perfect the hour would pass, alas!
" Climb high, love high, what matter? Still,
    " Feet, feelings, must descend the hill:
" An hour's perfection can't recur.

XV. " Then follows Paris and full time
    " For both to reason: ' Thus with us!'
" She'll sigh, ' Thus girls give body and soul
    " ' At first word, think they gain the goal,
" ' When 'tis the starting-place they climb!

XVI.   "'My friend makes verse and gets renown;
    "'Have they all fifty years, his peers?
  "'He knows the world, firm, quiet and gay;
    "'Boys will become as much one day:
  "'They're fools; he cheats, with beard less brown.

XVII.   "'For boys say, *Love me or I die !*
    "'He did not say, *The truth is, youth*
  "'*I want, who am old and know too much ;*
    "'*I'd catch youth : lend me sight and touch !*
  "'*Drop heart's blood where life's wheels grate dry !*'

XVIII.   " While I should make rejoinder "—(then
It was, no doubt, you ceased that least
Light pressure of my arm in yours)
    "'I can conceive of cheaper cures
  "'For a yawning-fit o'er books and men.

XIX.   "'What? All I am, was, and might be,
    "'All, books taught, art brought, life's whole strife,
  "'Painful results since precious, just
    "'Were fitly exchanged, in wise disgust,
  "'For two cheeks freshened by youth and sea?

XX.   "'All for a nosegay!—what came first;
    "'With fields on flower, untried each side;
  "'I rally, need my books and men,
    "'And find a nosegay': drop it, then,
  " No match yet made for best or worst!"

XXI. That ended me. You judged the porch
We left by, Norman; took our look
At sea and sky; wondered so few
Find out the place for air and view;
Remarked the sun began to scorch;

XXII. Descended, soon regained the baths,
And then, good-bye! Years ten since then:
Ten years! We meet: you tell me, now,
By a window-seat for that cliff-brow,
On carpet-stripes for those sand-paths.

XXIII. Now I may speak: you fool, for all
Your lore! WHO made things plain in vain?
What was the sea for? What, the grey
Sad church, that solitary day,
Crosses and graves and swallows' call?

XXIV. Was there nought better than to enjoy?
  No feat which, done, would make time break
 And let us pent-up creatures through
  Into eternity, our due?
 No forcing earth teach heaven's employ?

XXV. No wise beginning, here and now,
  What cannot grow complete (earth's feat)
 And heaven must finish, there and then?
  No tasting earth's true food for men,
 Its sweet in sad, its sad in sweet?

XXVI. No grasping at love, gaining a share
  O' the sole spark from God's life at strife
 With death, so, sure of range above
  The limits here? For us and love,
 Failure; but, when God fails, despair.

XXVII. This you call wisdom? Thus you add
  Good unto good again, in vain?
 You loved, with body worn and weak;
  I loved, with faculties to seek:
 Were both loves worthless since ill-clad?

XXVIII. Let the mere star-fish in his vault
  Crawl in a wash of weed, indeed,
 Rose-jacynth to the finger-tips:
  He, whole in body and soul, outstrips
 Man, found with either in default.

XXIX. But what's whole, can increase no more,
  Is dwarfed and dies, since here's its sphere.
 The devil laughed at you in his sleeve!
  You knew not? That I well believe;
 Or you had saved two souls: nay, four.

XXX. For Stephanie sprained last night her wrist,
  Ankle or something. "Pooh," cry you?
 At any rate she danced, all say,
  Vilely; her vogue has had its day.
 Here comes my husband from his whist.

TOO LATE.

I. HERE was I with my arm and heart
  And brain, all yours for a word, a want
Put into a look—just a look, your part,—
  While mine, to repay it . . . vainest vaunt,
Were the woman, that's dead, alive to hear,
  Had her lover, that's lost, love's proof to show!
But I cannot show it; you cannot speak
  From the churchyard neither, miles removed,
Though I feel by a pulse within my cheek,
  Which stabs and stops, that the woman I loved
Needs help in her grave and finds none near,
  Wants warmth from the heart which sends it—so!

II. Did I speak once angrily, all the drear days
  You lived, you woman I loved so well,
Who married the other? Blame or praise,
  Where was the use then? Time would tell,
And the end declare what man for you,
  What woman for me, was the choice of God.
But, Edith dead! no doubting more!
  I used to sit and look at my life
As it rippled and ran till, right before,
  A great stone stopped it: oh, the strife
Of waves at the stone some devil threw
  In my life's midcurrent, thwarting God!

III. But either I thought, " They may churn and chide
  " Awhile, my waves which came for their joy
" And found this horrible stone full-tide:
  " Yet I see just a thread escape, deploy
" Through the evening-country, silent and safe,
  " And it suffers no more till it finds the sea."
Or else I would think, " Perhaps some night
  " When new things happen, a meteor-ball
" May slip through the sky in a line of light,
  " And earth breathe hard, and landmarks fall,
" And my waves no longer champ nor chafe,
  " Since a stone will have rolled from its place: let be!"

Too Late

IV. But, dead! All's done with: wait who may,
    Watch and wear and wonder who will.
Oh, my whole life that ends to-day!
    Oh, my soul's sentence, sounding still,
" The woman is dead that was none of his;
    " And the man that was none of hers may go!"
There's only the past left: worry that!
    Wreak, like a bull, on the empty coat,
Rage, its late wearer is laughing at!
    Tear the collar to rags, having missed his throat;
Strike stupidly on—" This, this and this,
    " Where I would that a bosom received the blow!"

v. I ought to have done more: once my speech,
    And once your answer, and there, the end,
And Edith was henceforth out of reach!
    Why, men do more to deserve a friend,
Be rid of a foe, get rich, grow wise,
    Nor, folding their arms, stare fate in the face.
Why, better even have burst like a thief
    And borne you away to a rock for us two,
In a moment's horror, bright, bloody and brief:
    Then changed to myself again—" I slew
" Myself in that moment: a ruffian lies
    " Somewhere: your slave, see, born in his place!"

vi. What did the other do? You be judge!
    Look at us, Edith! Here are we both!
Give him his six whole years: I grudge
    None of the life with you, nay, loathe
Myself that I grudged his start in advance
    Of me who could overtake and pass.
But, as if he loved you! No, not he,
    Nor anyone else in the world, 'tis plain:
Who ever heard that another, free
    As I, young, prosperous, sound and sane,
Poured life out, proffered it—" Half a glance
    " Of those eyes of yours and I drop the glass!"

vii. Handsome, were you? 'Tis more than they held,
    More than they said; I was 'ware and watched:
I was the 'scapegrace, this rat belled
    The cat, this fool got his whiskers scratched:

The others?   No head that was turned, no heart
  Broken, my lady, assure yourself!
Each soon made his mind up; so and so
  Married a dancer, such and such
Stole his friend's wife, stagnated slow,
  Or maundered, unable to do as much,
And muttered of peace where he had no part:
  While, hid in the closet, laid on the shelf,—

VIII. On the whole, you were let alone, I think!
  So, you looked to the other, who acquiesced;
My rival, the proud man,—prize your pink
  Of poets!   A poet he was!   I've guessed:
He rhymed you his rubbish nobody read,
  Loved you and doved you—did not I laugh!
There was a prize!   But we both were tried.
  Oh, heart of mine, marked broad with her mark,
Tekel, found wanting, set aside,
  Scorned!   See, I bleed these tears in the dark
Till comfort come and the last he bled:
  He?   He is tagging your epitaph.

IX. If it would only come over again!
  —Time to be patient with me, and probe
This heart till you punctured the proper vein,
  Just to learn what blood is: twitch the robe
From that blank lay-figure your fancy draped,
  Prick the leathern heart till the—verses spirt!
And late it was easy; late, you walked
  Where a friend might meet you; Edith's name
Arose to one's lip if one laughed or talked;
  If I heard good news, you heard the same;
When I woke, I knew that your breath escaped;
  I could bide my time, keep alive, alert.

X. And alive I shall keep and long, you will see!
  I knew a man, was kicked like a dog
From gutter to cesspool; what cared he
  So long as he picked from the filth his prog?
He saw youth, beauty and genius die,
  And jollily lived to his hundredth year.
But I will live otherwise: none of such life!
  At once I begin as I mean to end.

Go on with the world, get gold in its strife,
  Give your spouse the slip and betray your friend!
There are two who decline, a woman and I,
  And enjoy our death in the darkness here.

XI. I liked that way you had with your curls
  Wound to a ball in a net behind:
Your cheek was chaste as a quaker-girl's,
  And your mouth—there was never, to my mind,
Such a funny mouth, for it would not shut;
  And the dented chin too—what a chin!
There were certain ways when you spoke, some words
  That you know you never could pronounce:
You were thin, however; like a bird's
  Your hand seemed—some would say, the pounce
Of a scaly-footed hawk—all but!
  The world was right when it called you thin.

XII. But I turn my back on the world: I take
  Your hand, and kneel, and lay to my lips.
Bid me live, Edith! Let me slake
  Thirst at your presence! Fear no slips:
'Tis your slave shall pay, while his soul endures,
  Full due, love's whole debt, *summum jus*.
My queen shall have high observance, planned
  Courtship made perfect, no least line
Crossed without warrant. There you stand,
  Warm too, and white too: would this wine
Had washed all over that body of yours,
  Ere I drank it, and you down with it, thus!

ABT VOGLER.

(AFTER HE HAS BEEN EXTEMPORIZING UPON THE MUSICAL INSTRUMENT OF HIS INVENTION.)

I.

WOULD that the structure brave, the manifold music I build,
  Bidding my organ obey, calling its keys to their work,
Claiming each slave of the sound, at a touch, as when Solomon
    willed
  Armies of angels that soar, legions of demons that lurk,
II—*Q 42

Man, brute, reptile, fly,—alien of end and of aim,
 Adverse, each from the other heaven-high, hell-deep
  removed,—
Should rush into sight at once as he named the ineffable Name,
 And pile him a palace straight, to pleasure the princess
  he loved!

II.

Would it might tarry like his, the beautiful building of mine,
 This which my keys in a crowd pressed and importuned
  to raise!
Ah, one and all, how they helped, would dispart now and
  now combine,
 Zealous to hasten the work, heighten their master his
  praise!
And one would bury his brow with a blind plunge down to
  hell,
 Burrow awhile and build, broad on the roots of things,
Then up again swim into sight, having based me my palace
  well,
 Founded it, fearless of flame, flat on the nether springs.

III.

And another would mount and march, like the excellent
  minion he was,
 Ay, another and yet another, one crowd but with many a
  crest,
Raising my rampired walls of gold as transparent as glass,
 Eager to do and die, yield each his place to the rest:
For higher still and higher (as a runner tips with fire,
 When a great illumination surprises a festal night—
Outlining round and round Rome's dome from space to
  spire)
 Up, the pinnacled glory reached, and the pride of my soul
  was in sight.

IV.

In sight? Not half! for it seemed, it was certain, to match
  man's birth,
 Nature in turn conceived, obeying an impulse as I;
And the emulous heaven yearned down, made effort to reach
  the earth,
 As the earth had done her best, in my passion, to scale the
  sky:

Novel splendours burst forth, grew familiar and dwelt with
    mine,
   Not a point nor peak but found and fixed its wandering
     star;
Meteor-moons, balls of blaze: and they did not pale nor pine,
   For earth had attained to heaven, there was no more near
     nor far.

v.

Nay more; for there wanted not who walked in the glare
    and glow,
   Presences plain in the place; or, fresh from the Protoplast,
Furnished for ages to come, when a kindlier wind should blow,
   Lured now to begin and live, in a house to their liking at
     last;
Or else the wonderful Dead who have passed through the
    body and gone,
   But were back once more to breathe in an old world worth
     their new;
What never had been, was now; what was, as it shall be
    anon;
   And what is,—shall I say, matched both? for I was made
     perfect too.

vi.

All through my keys that gave their sounds to a wish of my
    soul,
   All through my soul that praised as its wish flowed visibly
     forth,
All through music and me! For think, had I painted the
    whole,
   Why, there it had stood, to see, nor the process so wonder-
     worth;
Had I written the same, made verse—still, effect proceeds
    from cause,
   Ye know why the forms are fair, ye hear how the tale is
     told;
It is all triumphant art, but art in obedience to laws,
   Painter and poet are proud in the artist-list enrolled:—

vii.

But here is the finger of God, a flash of the will that can,
   Existent behind all laws, that made them and, lo, they
     are!

And I know not if, save in this, such gift be allowed to man,
    That out of three sounds he frame, not a fourth sound,
        but a star,
Consider it well: each tone of our scale in itself is nought;
    It is everywhere in the world—loud, soft, and all is said:
Give it to me to use! I mix it with two in my thought:
    And, there! Ye have heard and seen: consider and bow
        the head!

VIII.

Well, it is gone at last, the palace of music I reared;
    Gone! and the good tears start, the praises that come too
        slow;
For one is assured at first, one scarce can say that he feared,
    That he even gave it a thought, the gone thing was to go.
Never to be again! But many more of the kind
    As good, nay, better perchance: is this your comfort to me
To me, who must be saved because I cling with my mind
    To the same, same self, same love, same God: ay, what
        was, shall be.

IX.

Therefore to whom turn I but to thee, the ineffable Name?
    Builder and maker, thou, of houses not made with hands!
What, have fear of change from thee who art ever the same?
    Doubt that thy power can fill the heart that thy power
        expands?
There shall never be one lost good! What was, shall live
    as before;
    The evil is null, is nought, is silence implying sound;
What was good shall be good, with, for evil, so much good
    more;
    On the earth the broken arcs; in the heaven, a perfect
    round.

X.

All we have willed or hoped or dreamed of good shall exist;
    Not its semblance, but itself; no beauty, nor good, nor
    power
Whose voice has gone forth, but each survives for the melodist
    When eternity affirms the conception of an hour.
The high that proved too high, the heroic for earth too hard,
    The passion that left the ground to lose itself in the sky,
Are music sent up to God by the lover and the bard;
    Enough that he heard it once: we shall hear it by-and-by.

XI.

And what is our failure here but a triumph's evidence
  For the fulness of the days? Have we withered or
    agonized?
Why else was the pause prolonged but that singing might
  issue thence?
  Why rushed the discords in but that harmony should be
    prized?
Sorrow is hard to bear, and doubt is slow to clear,
  Each sufferer says his say, his scheme of the weal and woe:
But God has a few of us whom he whispers in the ear;
  The rest may reason and welcome: 'tis we musicians know.

XII.

Well, it is earth with me; silence resumes her reign:
  I will be patient and proud, and soberly acquiesce.
Give me the keys. I feel for the common chord again,
  Sliding by semitones, till I sink to the minor,—yes,
And I blunt it into a ninth, and I stand on alien ground,
  Surveying awhile the heights I rolled from into the deep;
Which, hark, I have dared and done, for my resting-place is
    found,
  The C Major of this life: so, now I will try to sleep.

RABBI BEN EZRA

   I. GROW old along with me!
     The best is yet to be,
The last of life, for which the first was made:
    Our times are in His hand
    Who saith " A whole I planned,
" Youth shows but half; trust God: see all nor be afraid! "

   II. Not that, amassing flowers,
     Youth sighed " Which rose make ours,
" Which lily leave and then as best recall? "
    Not that, admiring stars,
    It yearned " Nor Jove, nor Mars;
" Mine be some figured flame which blends, transcends them
    all! "

III. Not for such hopes and fears
    Annulling youth's brief years,
Do I remonstrate: folly wide the mark!
    Rather I prize the doubt
    Low kinds exist without,
Finished and finite clods, untroubled by a spark.

IV. Poor vaunt of life indeed,
    Were man but formed to feed
On joy, to solely seek and find and feast:
    Such feasting ended, then
    As sure an end to men;
Irks care the crop-full bird? Frets doubt the maw-crammed
      beast?

V. Rejoice we are allied
    To That which doth provide
And not partake, effect and not receive!
    A spark disturbs our clod;
    Nearer we hold of God
Who gives, than of His tribes that take, I must believe.

VI. Then, welcome each rebuff
    That turns earth's smoothness rough,
Each sting that bids nor sit nor stand but go!
    Be our joys three-parts pain!
    Strive, and hold cheap the strain;
Learn, nor account the pang; dare, never grudge the throe.

VII. For thence,—a paradox
    Which comforts while it mocks,—
Shall life succeed in that it seems to fail:
    What I aspired to be,
    And was not, comforts me:
A brute I might have been, but would not sink i' the
      scale.

VIII. What is he but a brute
    Whose flesh has soul to suit,
Whose spirit works lest arms and legs want play?
    To man, propose this test—
    Thy body at its best,
How far can that project thy soul on its lone way?

IX. Yet gifts should prove their use:
    I own the Past profuse
Of power each side, perfection every turn:
    Eyes, ears took in their dole,
    Brain treasured up the whole;
Should not the heart beat once " How good to live and
    learn? "

X. Not once beat " Praise be Thine!
    " I see the whole design,
" I, who saw power, see now love perfect too:
    " Perfect I call Thy plan:
    " Thanks that I was a man!
" Maker, remake, complete,—I trust what Thou shalt do! "

XI. For pleasant is this flesh;
    Our soul, in its rose-mesh
Pulled ever to the earth, still yearns for rest;
    Would we some prize might hold
    To match those manifold
Possessions of the brute,—gain most, as we did best!

XII. Let us not always say
    " Spite of this flesh to-day
" I strove, made head, gained ground upon the whole! "
    As the bird wings and sings,
    Let us cry " All good things
" Are ours, nor soul helps flesh more, now, than flesh helps
    soul! "

XIII. Therefore I summon age
    To grant youth's heritage,
Life's struggle having so far reached its term:
    Thence shall I pass, approved
    A man, for aye removed
From the developed brute; a god though in the germ.

XIV. And I shall thereupon
    Take rest, ere I be gone
Once more on my adventure brave and new:
    Fearless and unperplexed,
    When I wage battle next,
What weapons to select, what armour to indue.

xv. Youth ended, I shall try
            My gain or loss thereby;
Leave the fire ashes, what survives is gold:
            And I shall weigh the same,
            Give life its praise or blame:
Young, all lay in dispute; I shall know, being old.

xvi. For note, when evening shuts,
            A certain moment cuts
The deed off, calls the glory from the grey:
            A whisper from the west
            Shoots—" Add this to the rest,
" Take it and try its worth: here dies another day."

xvii. So, still within this life,
            Though lifted o'er its strife,
Let me discern, compare, pronounce at last,
            " This rage was right i' the main,
            " That acquiescence vain:
" The Future I may face now I have proved the Past."

xviii. For more is not reserved
            To man, with soul just nerved
To act to-morrow what he learns to-day:
            Here, work enough to watch
            The Master work, and catch
Hints of the proper craft, tricks of the tool's true play.

xix. As it was better, youth
            Should strive, through acts uncouth,
Toward making, than repose on aught found made:
            So, better, age, exempt
            From strife, should know, than tempt
Further.   Thou waitedest age: wait death nor be afraid!

xx. Enough now, if the Right
            And Good and Infinite
Be named here, as thou callest thy hand thine own,
            With knowledge absolute,
            Subject to no dispute
From fools that crowded youth, nor let thee feel alone.

xxi. Be there, for once and all,
            Severed great minds from small,

Announced to each his station in the Past!
   Was I, the world arraigned,
   Were they, my soul disdained,
Right? Let age speak the truth and give us peace at last!

 XXII. Now, who shall arbitrate?
   Ten men love what I hate,
Shun what I follow, slight what I receive;
   Ten, who in ears and eyes
   Match me: we all surmise,
They this thing, and I that: whom shall my soul believe?

 XXIII. Not on the vulgar mass
   Called " work," must sentence pass,
Things done, that took the eye and had the price;
   O'er which, from level stand,
   The low world laid its hand,
Found straightway to its mind, could value in a trice:

 XXIV. But all, the world's coarse thumb
   And finger failed to plumb,
So passed in making up the main account;
   All instincts immature,
   All purposes unsure,
That weighed not as his work, yet swelled the man's amount:

 XXV. Thoughts hardly to be packed
   Into a narrow act,
Fancies that broke through language and escaped;
   All I could never be,
   All, men ignored in me,
This, I was worth to God, whose wheel the pitcher shaped.

 XXVI. Ay, note that Potter's wheel,
   That metaphor! and feel
Why time spins fast, why passive lies our clay,—
   Thou, to whom fools propound,
   When the wine makes its round,
" Since life fleets, all is change; the Past gone, seize to-day! "

 XXVII. Fool! All that is, at all,
   Lasts ever, past recall;
Earth changes, but thy soul and God stand sure:
   What entered into thee,
   That was, is, and shall be:
Time's wheel runs back or stops: Potter and clay endure.

XXVIII. He fixed thee mid this dance
    Of plastic circumstance,
This Present, thou, forsooth, wouldst fain arrest:
    Machinery just meant
    To give thy soul its bent,
Try thee and turn thee forth, sufficiently impressed.

XXIX. What though the earlier grooves
    Which ran the laughing loves
Around thy base, no longer pause and press?
    What though, about thy rim,
    Scull-things in order grim
Grow out, in graver mood, obey the sterner stress?

XXX. Look not thou down but up!
    To uses of a cup,
The festal board, lamp's flash and trumpet's peal,
    The new mine's foaming flow,
    The Master's lips a-glow!
Thou, heaven's consummate cup, what need'st thou with
    earth's wheel?

XXXI. But I need, now as then,
    Thee, God, who mouldest men;
And since, not even while the whirl was worst,
    Did I,—to the wheel of life
    With shapes and colours rife,
Bound dizzily,—mistake my end, to slake Thy thirst:

XXXII. So, take and use Thy work:
    Amend what flaws may lurk,
What strain o' the stuff, what warpings past the aim!
    My times be in Thy hand!
    Perfect the cup as planned!
Let age approve of youth, and death complete the same!

A DEATH IN THE DESERT.

[SUPPOSED of Pamphylax the Antiochene:
It is a parchment, of my rolls the fifth,
Hath three skins glued together, is all Greek
And goeth from *Epsilon* down to *Mu* :
Lies second in the surnamed Chosen Chest,

Stained and conserved with juice of terebinth,
Covered with cloth of hair, and lettered *Xi*,
From Xanthus, my wife's uncle, now at peace:
Mu and *Epsilon* stand for my own name.
I may not write it, but I make a cross
To show I wait His coming, with the rest,
And leave off here: beginneth Pamphylax.]

I said, " If one should wet his lips with wine,
" And slip the broadest plantain-leaf we find,
" Or else the lappet of a linen robe,
" Into the water-vessel, lay it right,
" And cool his forehead just above the eyes,
" The while a brother, kneeling either side,
" Should chafe each hand and try to make it warm,—
" He is not so far gone but he might speak."

This did not happen in the outer cave,
Nor in the secret chamber of the rock
Where, sixty days since the decree was out,
We had him, bedded on a camel-skin,
And waited for his dying all the while;
But in the midmost grotto: since noon's light
Reached there a little, and we would not lose
The last of what might happen on his face.

I at the head, and Xanthus at the feet,
With Valens and the Boy, had lifted him,
And brought him from the chamber in the depths,
And laid him in the light where we might see:
For certain smiles began about his mouth,
And his lids moved, presageful of the end.

Beyond, and half way up the mouth o' the cave,
The Bactrian convert, having his desire,
Kept watch, and made pretence to graze a goat
That gave us milk, on rags of various herb,
Plantain and quitch, the rocks' shade keeps alive:
So that if any thief or soldier passed,
(Because the persecution was aware)
Yielding the goat up promptly with his life,
Such man might pass on, joyful at a prize,
Nor care to pry into the cool o' the cave.
Outside was all noon and the burning blue.

" Here is wine," answered Xanthus,—dropped a drop;
I stooped and placed the lap of cloth aright,
Then chafed his right hand, and the Boy his left:
But Valens had bethought him, and produced
And broke a ball of nard, and made perfume.
Only, he did—not so much wake, as—turn
And smile a little, as a sleeper does
If any dear one call him, touch his face—
And smiles and loves, but will not be disturbed.
Then Xanthus said a prayer, but still he slept:
It is the Xanthus that escaped to Rome,
Was burned, and could not write the chronicle.

Then the Boy sprang up from his knees, and ran,
Stung by the splendour of a sudden thought,
And fetched the seventh plate of graven lead
Out of the secret chamber, found a place,
Pressing with finger on the deeper dints,
And spoke, as 'twere his mouth proclaiming first,
" I am the Resurrection and the Life."

Whereat he opened his eyes wide at once,
And sat up of himself, and looked at us;
And thenceforth nobody pronounced a word;
Only, outside, the Bactrian cried his cry
Like the lone desert-bird that wears the ruff,
As signal we were safe, from time to time.

First he said, " If a friend declared to me,
" This my son Valens, this my other son,
" Were James and Peter,—nay, declared as well
" This lad was very John,—I could believe!
" —Could, for a moment, doubtlessly believe:
" So is myself withdrawn into my depths,
" The soul retreated from the perished brain
" Whence it was wont to feel and use the world
" Through these dull members, done with long ago.
" Yet I myself remain; I feel myself:
" And there is nothing lost. Let be, awhile! "

[This is the doctrine he was wont to teach,
How divers persons witness in each man,
Three souls which make up one soul: first, to wit,
A soul of each and all the bodily parts,

Seated therein, which works, and is what Does,
And has the use of earth, and ends the man
Downward: but, tending upward for advice,
Grows into, and again is grown into
By the next soul, which, seated in the brain,
Useth the first with its collected use,
And feeleth, thinketh, willeth,—is what Knows:
Which, duly tending upward in its turn,
Grows into, and again is grown into
By the last soul, that uses both the first,
Subsisting whether they assist or no,
And, constituting man's self, is what Is—
And leans upon the former, makes it play,
As that played off the first: and, tending up,
Holds, is upheld by, God, and ends the man
Upward in that dread point of intercourse,
Nor needs a place, for it returns to Him.
What Does, what Knows, what Is; three souls, one man.
I give the glossa of Theotypas.]

And then, " A stick, once fire from end to end
" Now, ashes save the tip that holds a spark!
" Yet, blow the spark, it runs back, spreads itself
" A little where the fire was: thus I urge
" The soul that served me, till it task once more
" What ashes of my brain have kept their shape,
" And these make effort on the last o' the flesh,
" Trying to taste again the truth of things—"
(He smiled)—" their very superficial truth;
" As that ye are my sons, that it is long
" Since James and Peter had release by death,
" And I am only he, your brother John,
" Who saw and heard, and could remember all.
" Remember all! It is not much to say.
" What if the truth broke on me from above
" As once and oft-times? Such might hap again:
" Doubtlessly He might stand in presence here,
" With head wool-white, eyes flame, and feet like brass,
" The sword and the seven stars, as I have seen—
" I who now shudder only and surmise
" ' How did your brother bear that sight and live? '

" If I live yet, it is for good, more love
" Through me to men: be nought but ashes here

" That keep awhile my semblance, who was John,—
" Still, when they scatter, there is left on earth
" No one alive who knew (consider this !)
" —Saw with his eyes and handled with his hands
" That which was from the first, the Word of Life.
" How will it be when none more saith ' I saw '?

" Such ever was love's way: to rise, it stoops.
" Since I, whom Christ's mouth taught, was bidden **teach,**
" I went, for many years, about the world,
" Saying ' It was so; so I heard and saw,'
" Speaking as the case asked: and men believed.
" Afterward came the message to myself
" In Patmos isle; I was not bidden teach,
" But simply listen, take a book and write,
" Nor set down other than the given word,
" With nothing left to my arbitrament
" To choose or change: I wrote, and men believed.
" Then, for my time grew brief, no message more.
" No call to write again, I found a way,
" And, reasoning from my knowledge, merely taught
" Men should, for love's sake, in love's strength believe;
" Or I would pen a letter to a friend
" And urge the same as friend, nor less nor more:
" Friends said I reasoned rightly, and believed.
" But at the last, why, I seemed left alive
" Like a sea-jelly weak on Patmos strand,
" To tell dry sea-beach gazers how I fared
" When there was mid-sea, and the mighty things:
" Left to repeat, ' I saw, I heard, I knew,'
" And go all over the old ground again,
" With Antichrist already in the world,
" And many Antichrists, who answered prompt
" ' Am I not Jasper as thyself art John?
" ' Nay, young, whereas through age thou mayest forget:
" ' Wherefore, explain, or how shall we believe?'
" I never thought to call down fire on such,
" Or, as in wonderful and early days,
" Pick up the scorpion, tread the serpent dumb;
" But patient stated much of the Lord's life
" Forgotten or misdelivered, and let it work:
" Since much that at the first, in deed and word,
" Lay simply and sufficiently exposed,

" Had grown (or else my soul was grown to match,
" Fed through such years, familiar with such light,
" Guarded and guided still to see and speak)
" Of new significance and fresh result;
" What first were guessed as points, I now knew stars,
" And named them in the Gospel I have writ.
" For men said, ' It is getting long ago:
" ' Where is the promise of His coming? '—asked
" These young ones in their strength, as loth to wait,
" Of me who, when their sires were born, was old.
" I, for I loved them, answered, joyfully,
" Since I was there, and helpful in my age;
" And, in the main, I think such men believed.
" Finally, thus endeavouring, I fell sick,
" Ye brought me here, and I supposed the end,
" And went to sleep with one thought that, at least,
" Though the whole earth should lie in wickedness,
" We had the truth, might leave the rest to God.
" Yet now I wake in such decrepitude
" As I had slidden down and fallen afar,
" Past even the presence of my former self,
" Grasping the while for stay at facts which snap,
" Till I am found away from my own world,
" Feeling for foot-hold through a blank profound,
" Along with unborn people in strange lands,
" Who say—I hear said or conceive they say—
" ' Was John at all, and did he say he saw?
" ' Assure us, ere we ask what he might see! '

" And how shall I assure them?   Can they share
" —They, who have flesh, a veil of youth and strength
" About each spirit, that needs must bide its time,
" Living and learning still as years assist
" Which wear the thickness thin, and let man see—
" With me who hardly am withheld at all,
" But shudderingly, scarce a shred between,
" Lie bare to the universal prick of light?
" Is it for nothing we grow old and weak,
" We whom God loves?   When pain ends, gain ends too.
" To me, that story—ay, that Life and Death
" Of which I wrote ' it was '—to me, it is;
" —Is, here and now: I apprehend nought else.
" Is not God now i' the world His power first made?

" Is not His love at issue still with sin
" Visibly when a wrong is done on earth?
" Love, wrong, and pain, what see I else around?
" Yea, and the Resurrection and Uprise
" To the right hand of the throne—what is it beside,
" When such truth, breaking bounds, o'erfloods my soul,
" And, as I saw the sin and death, even so
" See I the need yet transiency of both,
" The good and glory consummated thence?
" I saw the power; I see the Love, once weak,
" Resume the Power: and in this word ' I see,'
" Lo, there is recognized the Spirit of both
" That moving o'er the spirit of man, unblinds
" His eye and bids him look.   These are, I see;
" But ye, the children, His beloved ones too,
" Ye need,—as I should use an optic glass
" I wondered at erewhile, somewhere i' the world,
" It had been given a crafty smith to make;
" A tube, he turned on objects brought too close,
" Lying confusedly insubordinate
" For the unassisted eye to master once:
" Look through his tube, at distance now they lay,
" Become succinct, distinct, so small, so clear!
" Just thus, ye needs must apprehend what truth
" I see, reduced to plain historic fact,
" Diminished into clearness, proved a point
" And far away: ye would withdraw your sense
" From out eternity, strain it upon time,
" Then stand before that fact, that Life and Death
" Stay there at gaze, till it dispart, dispread,
" As though a star should open out, all sides,
" Grow the world on you, as it is my world.

" For life, with all it yields of joy and woe,
" And hope and fear,—believe the aged friend,—
" Is just our chance o' the prize of learning love,
" How love might be, hath been indeed, and is;
" And that we hold thenceforth to the uttermost
" Such prize despite the envy of the world,
" And, having gained truth, keep truth: that is all.
" But see the double way wherein we are led,
" How the soul learns diversely from the flesh!
" With flesh, that hath so little time to stay,

" And yields mere basement for the soul's emprise,
" Expect prompt teaching. Helpful was the light,
" And warmth was cherishing and food was choice
" To every man's flesh, thousand years ago,
" As now to yours and mine; the body sprang
" At once to the height, and stayed: but the soul,—no!
" Since sages who, this noontide, meditate
" In Rome or Athens, may descry some point
" Of the eternal power, hid yestereve;
" And, as thereby the power's whole mass extends,
" So much extends the æther floating o'er,
" The love that tops the might, the Christ in God,
" Then, as new lessons shall be learned in these
" Till earth's work stop and useless time run out,
" So duly, daily, needs provision be
" For keeping the soul's prowess possible,
" Building new barriers as the old decay,
" Saving us from evasion of life's proof,
" Putting the question ever, ' Does God love,
" ' And will ye hold that truth against the world? '
" Ye know there needs no second proof with good
" Gained for our flesh from any earthly source:
" We might go freezing, ages,—give us fire,
" Thereafter we judge fire at its full worth,
" And guard it safe through every chance, ye know!
" That fable of Prometheus and his theft,
" How mortals gained Jove's fiery flower, grows old
" (I have been used to hear the pagans own)
" And out of mind; but fire, howe'er its birth,
" Here is it, precious to the sophist now
" Who laughs the myth of Æschylus to scorn,
" As precious to those satyrs of his play,
" Who touched it in gay wonder at the thing.
" While were it so with the soul,—this gift of truth
" Once grasped, were this our soul's gain safe, and sure
" To prosper as the body's gain is wont,—
" Why, man's probation would conclude, his earth
" Crumble; for he both reasons and decides,
" Weighs first, then chooses: will he give up fire
" For gold or purple once he knows its worth?
" Could he give Christ up were His worth as plain?
" Therefore, I say, to test man, the proofs shift,
" Nor may he grasp that fact like other fact,

" And straightway in his life acknowledge it,
" As, say, the indubitable bliss of fire.
" Sigh ye, ' It had been easier once than now '?
" To give you answer I am left alive;
" Look at me who was present from the first!
" Ye know what things I saw; then came a test,
" My first, befitting me who so had seen:
" ' Forsake the Christ thou sawest transfigured, Him
" ' Who trod the sea and brought the dead to life?
" ' What should wring this from thee!'—ye laugh and ask.
" What wrung it? Even a torchlight and a noise,
" The sudden Roman faces, violent hands,
" And fear of what the Jews might do! Just that,
" And it is written, ' I forsook and fled:'
" There was my trial, and it ended thus.
" Ay, but my soul had gained its truth, could grow:
" Another year or two,—what little child,
" What tender woman that had seen no least
" Of all my sights, but barely heard them told,
" Who did not clasp the cross with a light laugh,
" Or wrap the burning robe round, thanking God?
" Well, was truth safe for ever, then? Not so.
" Already had begun the silent work
" Whereby truth, deadened of its absolute blaze,
" Might need love's eye to pierce the o'erstretched doubt.
" Teachers were busy, whispering ' All is true
" ' As the aged ones report; but youth can reach
" ' Where age gropes dimly, weak with stir and strain,
" ' And the full doctrine slumbers till to-day.'
" Thus, what the Roman's lowered spear was found,
" A bar to me who touched and handled truth,
" Now proved the glozing of some new shrewd tongue,
" This Ebion, this Cerinthus or their mates,
" Till imminent was the outcry ' Save our Christ!'
" Whereon I stated much of the Lord's life
" Forgotten or misdelivered, and let it work.
" Such work done, as it will be, what comes next?
" What do I hear say, or conceive men say,
" ' Was John at all, and did he say he saw?
" ' Assure us, ere we ask what he might see!'

" Is this indeed a burthen for late days,
" And may I help to bear it with you all,

A Death in the Desert

" Using my weakness which becomes your strength?
" For if a babe were born inside this grot,
" Grew to a boy here, heard us praise the sun,
" Yet had but yon sole glimmer in light's place,—
" One loving him and wishful he should learn,
" Would much rejoice himself was blinded first
" Month by month here, so made to understand
" How eyes, born darkling, apprehend amiss:
" I think I could explain to such a child
" There was more glow outside than gleams he caught,
" Ay, nor need urge ' I saw it, so believe!'
" It is a heavy burthen you shall bear
" In latter days, new lands, or old grown strange,
" Left without me, which must be very soon.
" What is the doubt, my brothers?   Quick with it!
" I see you stand conversing, each new face,
" Either in fields, of yellow summer eves,
" On islets yet unnamed amid the sea;
" Or pace for shelter 'neath a portico
" Out of the crowd in some enormous town
" Where now the larks sing in a solitude;
" Or muse upon blank heaps of stone and sand
" Idly conjectured to be Ephesus:
" And no one asks his fellow any more
" ' Where is the promise of His coming?' but
" ' Was he revealed in any of His lives,
" ' As Power, as Love, as Influencing Soul?'

" Quick, for time presses, tell the whole mind out,
" And let us ask and answer and be saved!
" My book speaks on, because it cannot pass;
" One listens quietly, nor scoffs but pleads
" ' Here is a tale of things done ages since;
" ' What truth was ever told the second day?
" ' Wonders, that would prove doctrine, go for nought.
" ' Remains the doctrine, love; well, we must love,
" ' And what we love most, power and love in one,
" ' Let us acknowledge on the record here,
" ' Accepting these in Christ: must Christ then be?
" ' Has He been?   Did not we ourselves make Him?
" ' Our mind receives but what it holds, no more.
" ' First of the love, then; we acknowledge Christ—
" ' A proof we comprehend His love, a proof

" ' We had such love already in ourselves,
" ' Knew first what else we should not recognize.
" ' 'Tis mere projection from man's inmost mind,
" ' And, what he loves, thus falls reflected back,
" ' Becomes accounted somewhat out of him;
" ' He throws it up in air, it drops down earth's,
" ' With shape, name, story added, man's old way.
" ' How prove you Christ came otherwise at least?
" ' Next try the power: He made and rules the world:
" ' Certes there is a world once made, now ruled,
" ' Unless things have been ever as we see.
" ' Our sires declared a charioteer's yoked steeds
" ' Brought the sun up the east and down the west,
" ' Which only of itself now rises, sets,
" ' As if a hand impelled it and a will,—
" ' Thus they long thought, they who had will and hands:
" ' But the new question's whisper is distinct,
" ' Wherefore must all force needs be like ourselves?
" ' We have the hands, the will; what made and drives
" ' The sun is force, is law, is named, not known,
" ' While will and love we do know; marks of these,
" ' Eye-witnesses attest, so books declare—
" ' As that, to punish or reward our race,
" ' The sun at undue times arose or set
" ' Or else stood still: what do not men affirm?
" ' But earth requires as urgently reward
" ' Or punishment to-day as years ago,
" ' And none expects the sun will interpose:
" ' Therefore it was mere passion and mistake,
" ' Or erring zeal for right, which changed the truth.
" ' Go back, far, farther, to the birth of things;
" ' Ever the will, the intelligence, the love,
" ' Man's!—which he gives, supposing he but finds,
" ' As late he gave head, body, hands and feet,
" ' To help these in what forms he called his gods.
" ' First, Jove's brow, Juno's eyes were swept away,
" ' But Jove's wrath, Juno's pride continued long;
" ' As last, will, power, and love discarded these,
" ' So law in turn discards power, love, and will.
" ' What proveth God is otherwise at least?
" ' All else, projection from the mind of man! '
" Nay, do not give me wine, for I am strong,
" But place my gospel where I put my hands.

A Death in the Desert 497

" I say that man was made to grow, not stop;
" That help, he needed once, and needs no more,
" Having grown but an inch by, is withdrawn:
" For he hath new needs, and new helps to these.
" This imports solely, man should mount on each
" New height in view; the help whereby he mounts,
" The ladder-rung his foot has left, may fall,
" Since all things suffer change save God the Truth.
" Man apprehends Him newly at each stage
" Whereat earth's ladder drops, its service done;
" And nothing shall prove twice what once was proved.
" You stick a garden-plot with ordered twigs
" To show inside lie germs of herbs unborn,
" And check the careless step would spoil their birth,
" But when herbs wave, the guardian twigs may go,
" Since should ye doubt of virtues, question kinds,
" It is no longer for old twigs ye look,
" Which proved once underneath lay store of seed,
" But to the herb's self, by what light ye boast,
" For what fruit's signs are.   This book's fruit is plain,
" Nor miracles need prove it any more.
" Doth the fruit show?   Then miracles bade 'ware
" At first of root and stem, saved both till now
" From trampling ox, rough boar and wanton goat.
" What?   Was man made a wheelwork to wind up,
" And be discharged, and straight wound up anew?
" No!—grown, his growth lasts; taught, he ne'er forgets:
" May learn a thousand things, not twice the same.

" This might be pagan teaching: now hear mine.

" I say, that as the babe, you feed awhile,
" Becomes a boy and fit to feed himself,
" So, minds at first must be spoon-fed with truth:
" When they can eat, babe's-nurture is withdrawn.
" I fed the babe whether it would or no:
" I bid the boy or feed himself or starve.
" I cried once, ' That ye may believe in Christ,
" ' Behold this blind man shall receive his sight!'
" I cry now, ' Urgest thou, *for I am shrewd*
" ' *And smile at stories how John's word could cure*
" ' *Repeat that miracle and take my faith?*'
" I say, that miracle was duly wrought
" When, save for it, no faith was possible.

" Whether a change were wrought i' the shows o' the world,
" Whether the change came from our minds which see
" Of shows o' the world so much as and no more
" Than God wills for His purpose,—(what do I
" See now, suppose you, there where you see rock
" Round us?)—I know not; such was the effect,
" So faith grew, making void more miracles
" Because too much: they would compel, not help.
" I say, the acknowledgment of God in Christ
" Accepted by thy reason, solves for thee
" All questions in the earth and out of it,
" And has so far advanced thee to be wise.
" Wouldst thou unprove this to re-prove the proved?
" In life's mere minute, with power to use that proof,
" Leave knowledge and revert to how it sprung?
" Thou hast it: use it and forthwith, or die!

" For I say, this is death and the sole death,
" When a man's loss comes to him from his gain,
" Darkness from light, from knowledge ignorance,
" And lack of love from love made manifest;
" A lamp's death when, replete with oil, it chokes:
" A stomach's when, surcharged with food, it starves
" With ignorance was surety of a cure.
" When man, appalled at nature, questioned first
" ' What if there lurk a might behind this might?'
" He needed satisfaction God could give,
" And did give, as ye have the written word:
" But when he finds might still redouble might,
" Yet asks, ' Since all is might, what use of will?'
" —Will, the one source of might,—he being man
" With a man's will and a man's might, to teach
" In little how the two combine in large,—
" That man has turned round on himself and stands
" Which in the course of nature is, to die.

" And when man questioned, ' What if there be love
" ' Behind the will and might, as real as they?'—
" He needed satisfaction God could give,
" And did give, as ye have the written word:
" But when, beholding that love everywhere,
" He reasons, ' Since such love is everywhere,
" ' And since ourselves can love and would be loved,
" ' We ourselves make the love, and Christ was not,'—

" How shall ye help this man who knows himself,
" That he must love and would be loved again,
" Yet, owning his own love that proveth Christ,
" Rejecteth Christ through very need of Him?
" The lamp o'erswims with oil, the stomach flags
" Loaded with nurture, and that man's soul dies.

" If he rejoin, ' But this was all the while
" ' A trick; the fault was, first of all, in thee,
" ' Thy story of the places, names and dates,
" ' Where, when and how the ultimate truth had rise,
" ' —Thy prior truth, at last discovered none,
" ' Whence now the second suffers detriment.
" ' What good of giving knowledge if, because
" ' O' the manner of the gift, its profit fail?
" ' And why refuse what modicum of help
" ' Had stopped the after-doubt, impossible
" ' I' the face of truth—truth absolute, uniform?
" ' Why must I hit of this and miss of that,
" ' Distinguish just as I be weak or strong,
" ' And not ask of thee and have answer prompt,
" ' Was this once, was it not once?—then and now
" ' And evermore, plain truth from man to man.
" ' Is John's procedure just the heathen bard's?
" ' Put question of his famous play again
" ' How for the ephemerals' sake Jove's fire was filched,
" ' And carried in a cane and brought to earth;
" ' *The fact is in the fable*, cry the wise,
" ' *Mortals obtained the boon, so much is fact,*
" ' *Though fire be spirit and produced on earth.*
" ' As with the Titan's, so now with thy tale:
" ' Why breed in us perplexity, mistake,
" ' Nor tell the whole truth in the proper words?'

" I answer, Have ye yet to argue out
" The very primal thesis, plainest law,
" —Man is not God but hath God's end to serve,
" A master to obey, a course to take,
" Somewhat to cast off, somewhat to become?
" Grant this, then man must pass from old to new,
" From vain to real, from mistake to fact,
" From what once seemed good, to what now proves best.
" How could man have progression otherwise?
" Before the point was mooted ' What is God?'

" No savage man inquired ' What am myself? '
" Much less replied, ' First, last, and best of things.'
" Man takes that title now if he believes
" Might can exist with neither will nor love,
" In God's case—what he names now Nature's Law—
" While in himself he recognizes love
" No less than might and will: and rightly takes.
" Since if man prove the sole existent thing
" Where these combine, whatever their degree,
" However weak the might or will or love,
" So they be found there, put in evidence,—
" He is as surely higher in the scale
" Than any might with neither love nor will,
" As life, apparent in the poorest midge,
" (When the faint dust-speck flits, ye guess its wing)
" Is marvellous beyond dead Atlas' self—
" Given to the nobler midge for resting-place!
" Thus, man proves best and highest—God, in fine,
" And thus the victory leads but to defeat,
" The gain to loss, best rise to the worst fall,
" His life becomes impossible, which is death.

" But if, appealing thence, he cower, avouch
" He is mere man, and in humility
" Neither may know God nor mistake himself;
" I point to the immediate consequence
" And say, by such confession straight he falls
" Into man's place, a thing nor God nor beast,
" Made to know that he can know and not more:
" Lower than God who knows all and can all,
" Higher than beasts which know and can so far
" As each beast's limit, perfect to an end,
" Nor conscious that they know, nor craving more;
" While man knows partly but conceives beside,
" Creeps ever on from fancies to the fact,
" And in this striving, this converting air
" Into a solid he may grasp and use,
" Finds progress, man's distinctive mark alone,
" Not God's, and not the beasts': God is, they are,
" Man partly is and wholly hopes to be.
" Such progress could no more attend his soul
" Were all it struggles after found at first
" And guesses changed to knowledge absolute,

" Than motion wait his body, were all else
" Than it the solid earth on every side,
" Where now through space he moves from rest to rest.
" Man, therefore, thus conditioned, must expect
" He could not, what he knows now, know at first;
" What he considers that he knows to-day,
" Come but to-morrow, he will find misknown;
" Getting increase of knowledge, since he learns
" Because he lives, which is to be a man,
" Set to instruct himself by his past self:
" First, like the brute, obliged by facts to learn,
" Next, as man may, obliged by his own mind,
" Bent, habit, nature, knowledge turned to law.
" God's gift was that man should conceive of truth
" And yearn to gain it, catching at mistake,
" As midway help till he reach fact indeed.
" The statuary ere he mould a shape
" Boasts a like gift, the shape's idea, and next
" The aspiration to produce the same;
" So, taking clay, he calls his shape thereout,
" Cries ever ' Now I have the thing I see ':
" Yet all the while goes changing what was wrought,
" From falsehood like the truth, to truth itself.
" How were it had he cried ' I see no face,
" ' No breast, no feet i' the ineffectual clay '?
" Rather commend him that he clapped his hands,
" And laughed ' It is my shape and lives again ! '
" Enjoyed the falsehood, touched it on to truth,
" Until yourselves applaud the flesh indeed
" In what is still flesh-imitating clay.
" Right in you, right in him, such way be man's !
" God only makes the live shape at a jet.
" Will ye renounce this pact of creatureship?
" The pattern on the Mount subsists no more,
" Seemed awhile, then returned to nothingness;
" But copies, Moses strove to make thereby,
" Serve still and are replaced as time requires:
" By these, make newest vessels, reach the type !
" If ye demur, this judgment on your head,
" Never to reach the ultimate, angels' law,
" Indulging every instinct of the soul
" There where law, life, joy, impulse are one thing !
" Such is the burthen of the latest time.

" I have survived to hear it with my ears,
" Answer it with my lips: does this suffice?
" For if there be a further woe than such,
" Wherein my brothers struggling need a hand,
" So long as any pulse is left in mine,
" May I be absent even longer yet,
" Plucking the blind ones back from the abyss,
" Though I should tarry a new hundred years!"

But he was dead; 'twas about noon, the day
Somewhat declining: we five buried him
That eve, and then, dividing, went five ways,
And I, disguised, returned to Ephesus.

By this, the cave's mouth must be filled with sand.
Valens is lost, I know not of his trace;
The Bactrian was but a wild childish man,
And could not write nor speak, but only loved:
So, lest the memory of this go quite,
Seeing that I to-morrow fight the beasts,
I tell the same to Phœbas, whom believe!
For many look again to find that face,
Beloved John's to whom I ministered,
Somewhere in life about the world; they err:
Either mistaking what was darkly spoke
At ending of his book, as he relates,
Or misconceiving somewhat of this speech
Scattered from mouth to mouth, as I suppose.
Believe ye will not see him any more
About the world with his divine regard!
For all was as I say, and now the man
Lies as he lay once, breast to breast with God.

[Cerinthus read and mused; one added this:

" If Christ, as thou affirmest, be of men
" Mere man, the first and best but nothing more,—
" Account Him, for reward of what He was,
" Now and for ever, wretchedest of all.
" For see; Himself conceived of life as love,
" Conceived of love as what must enter in,
" Fill up, make one with His each soul He loved
" Thus much for man's joy, all men's joy for Him.
" Well, He is gone, thou sayest, to fit reward.
" But by this time are many souls set free,

" And very many still retained alive:
" Nay, should His coming be delayed awhile,
" Say, ten years longer (twelve years, some compute)
" See if, for every finger of thy hands,
" There be not found, that day the world shall end,
" Hundreds of souls, each holding by Christ's word
" That He will grow incorporate with all,
" With me as Pamphylax, with him as John,
" Groom for each bride! Can a mere man do this?
" Yet Christ saith, this He lived and died to do.
" Call Christ, then, the illimitable God,
" Or lost!"

But 'twas Cerinthus that is lost.]

CALIBAN UPON SETEBOS; OR, NATURAL
THEOLOGY IN THE ISLAND.

" Thou thoughtest that I was altogether such a one as thyself."

['WILL sprawl, now that the heat of day is best,
Flat on his belly in the pit's much mire,
With elbows wide, fists clenched to prop his chin.
And, while he kicks both feet in the cool slush,
And feels about his spine small eft-things course,
Run in and out each arm, and make him laugh:
And while above his head a pompion-plant,
Coating the cave-top as a brow its eye,
Creeps down to touch and tickle hair and beard,
And now a flower drops with a bee inside,
And now a fruit to snap at, catch and crunch,—
He looks out o'er yon sea which sunbeams cross
And recross till they weave a spider-web
(Meshes of fire, some great fish breaks at times)
And talks to his own self, howe'er he please,
Touching that other, whom his dam called God.
Because to talk about Him, vexes—ha,
Could He but know! and time to vex is now,
When talk is safer than in winter-time.
Moreover Prosper and Miranda sleep
In confidence he drudges at their task,
And it is good to cheat the pair, and gibe,
Letting the rank tongue blossom into speech.]

Setebos, Setebos, and Setebos!
'Thinketh, He dwelleth i' the cold o' the moon.

'Thinketh He made it, with the sun to match,
But not the stars; the stars came otherwise;
Only made clouds, winds, meteors, such as that:
Also this isle, what lives and grows thereon,
And snaky sea which rounds and ends the same.

'Thinketh, it came of being ill at ease:
He hated that He cannot change His cold,
Nor cure its ache. 'Hath spied an icy fish
That longed to 'scape the rock-stream where she lived,
And thaw herself within the lukewarm brine
O' the lazy sea her stream thrusts far amid,
A crystal spike 'twixt two warm walls of wave;
Only, she ever sickened, found repulse
At the other kind of water, not her life,
(Green-dense and dim-delicious, bred o' the sun)
Flounced back from bliss she was not born to breathe,
And in her old bounds buried her despair,
Hating and loving warmth alike: so He.

'Thinketh, He made thereat the sun, this isle,
Trees and the fowls here, beast and creeping thing.
Yon otter, sleek-wet, black, lithe as a leech;
Yon auk, one fire-eye in a ball of foam,
That floats and feeds; a certain badger brown
He hath watched hunt with that slant white-wedge eye
By moonlight; and the pie with the long tongue
That pricks deep into oakwarts for a worm,
And says a plain word when she finds her prize,
But will not eat the ants; the ants themselves
That build a wall of seeds and settled stalks
About their hole—He made all these and more,
Made all we see, and us, in spite: how else?
He could not, Himself, make a second self
To be His mate: as well have made Himself:
He would not make what he mislikes or slights,
An eyesore to Him, or not worth His pains:
But did, in envy, listlessness or sport,
Make what Himself would fain, in a manner, be—
Weaker in most points, stronger in a few,

Worthy, and yet mere playthings all the while,
Things He admires and mocks too,—that is it.
Because, so brave, so better though they be,
It nothing skills if He begin to plague.
Look now, I melt a gourd-fruit into mash,
Add honeycomb and pods, I have perceived,
Which bite like finches when they bill and kiss,—
Then, when froth rises bladdery, drink up all,
Quick, quick, till maggots scamper through my brain;
Last, throw me on my back i' the seeded thyme,
And wanton, wishing I were born a bird.
Put case, unable to be what I wish,
I yet could make a live bird out of clay:
Would not I take clay, pinch my Caliban
Able to fly?—for, there, see, he hath wings,
And great comb like the hoopoe's to admire,
And there, a sting to do his foes offence,
There, and I will that he begin to live,
Fly to yon rock-top, nip me off the horns
Of grigs high up that make the merry din,
Saucy through their veined wings, and mind me not.
In which feat, if his leg snapped, brittle clay,
And he lay stupid-like,—why, I should laugh;
And if he, spying me, should fall to weep,
Beseech me to be good, repair his wrong,
Bid his poor leg smart less or grow again,—
Well, as the chance were, this might take or else
Not take my fancy: I might hear his cry,
And give the mankin three sound legs for one,
Or pluck the other off, leave him like an egg,
And lessoned he was mine and merely clay.
Were this no pleasure, lying in the thyme,
Drinking the mash, with brain become alive,
Making and marring clay at will?   So He.

'Thinketh, such shows nor right nor wrong in Him,
Nor kind, nor cruel: He is strong and Lord.
'Am strong myself compared to yonder crabs
That march now from the mountain to the sea;
'Let twenty pass, and stone the twenty-first,
Loving not, hating not, just choosing so.
'Say, the first straggler that boasts purple spots
Shall join the file, one pincer twisted off;

'Say, this bruised fellow shall receive a worm,
And two worms he whose nippers end in red;
As it likes me each time, I do: so He.

Well then, 'supposeth He is good i' the main,
Placable if His mind and ways were guessed,
But rougher than His handiwork, be sure!
Oh, He hath made things worthier than Himself,
And envieth that, so helped, such things do more
Than He who made them!   What consoles but this?
That they, unless through Him, do nought at all,
And must submit: what other use in things?
'Hath cut a pipe of pithless elder joint
That, blown through, gives exact the scream o' the jay
When from her wing you twitch the feathers blue:
Sound this, and little birds that hate the jay
Flock within stone's throw, glad their foe is hurt:
Put case such pipe could prattle and boast forsooth
" I catch the birds, I am the crafty thing,
" I make the cry my maker cannot make
" With his great round mouth; he must blow through mine! "
Would not I smash it with my foot?   So He.

But wherefore rough, why cold and ill at ease?
Aha, that is a question!   Ask, for that,
What knows,—the something over Setebos
That made Him, or He, may be, found and fought,
Worsted, drove off and did to nothing, perchance.
There may be something quiet o'er His head,
Out of His reach, that feels nor joy nor grief,
Since both derive from weakness in some way.
I joy because the quails come; would not joy
Could I bring quails here when I have a mind:
This Quiet, all it hath a mind to, doth.
'Esteemeth stars the outposts of its couch,
But never spends much thought nor care that way.
It may look up, work up,—the worse for those
It works on! 'Careth but for Setebos
The many-handed as a cuttle-fish,
Who, making Himself feared through what He does,
Looks up, first, and perceives he cannot soar
To what is quiet and hath happy life;
Next looks down here, and out of very spite

Makes this a bauble-world to ape yon real,
These good things to match those as hips do grapes.
'Tis solace making baubles, ay, and sport.
Himself peeped late, eyed Prosper at his books
Careless and lofty, lord now of the isle:
Vexed, 'stitched a book of broad leaves, arrow-shaped,
Wrote thereon, he knows what, prodigious words;
Has peeled a wand and called it by a name;
Weareth at whiles for an enchanter's robe
The eyed skin of a supple oncelot;
And hath an ounce sleeker than youngling mole,
A four-legged serpent he makes cower and couch,
Now snarl, now hold its breath and mind his eye,
And saith she is Miranda and my wife:
'Keeps for his Ariel a tall pouch-bill crane
He bids go wade for fish and straight disgorge;
Also a sea-beast, lumpish, which he snared,
Blinded the eyes of, and brought somewhat tame,
And split its toe-webs, and now pens the drudge
In a hole o' the rock and calls him Caliban;
A bitter heart that bides its time and bites.
'Plays thus at being Prosper in a way,
Taketh his mirth with make-believes: so He.

His dam held that the Quiet made all things
Which Setebos vexed only: 'holds not so.
Who made them weak, meant weakness He might vex.
Had He meant other, while His hand was in,
Why not make horny eyes no thorn could prick,
Or plate my scalp with bone against the snow,
Or overscale my flesh 'neath joint and joint,
Like an orc's armour? Ay,—so spoil His sport!
He is the One now: only He doth all.

'Saith, He may like, perchance, what profits Him.
Ay, himself loves what does him good; but why?
'Gets good no otherwise. This blinded beast
Loves whoso places flesh-meat on his nose,
But, had he eyes, would want no help, but hate
Or love, just as it liked him: He hath eyes.
Also it pleaseth Setebos to work,
Use all His hands, and exercise much craft,
By no means for the love of what is worked.

'Tasteth, himself, no finer good i' the world
When all goes right, in this safe summer-time,
And he wants little, hungers, aches not much,
Than trying what to do with wit and strength.
'Falls to make something: 'piled yon pile of turfs,
And squared and stuck there squares of soft white chalk,
And, with a fish-tooth, scratched a moon on each,
And set up endwise certain spikes of tree,
And crowned the whole with a sloth's skull a-top,
Found dead i' the woods, too hard for one to kill.
No use at all i' the work, for work's sole sake;
'Shall some day knock it down again: so He.

'Saith He is terrible: watch His feats in proof!
One hurricane will spoil six good months' hope.
He hath a spite against me, that I know,
Just as He favours Prosper, who knows why?
So it is, all the same, as well I find.
'Wove wattles half the winter, fenced them firm
With stone and stake to stop she-tortoises
Crawling to lay their eggs here: well, one wave,
Feeling the foot of Him upon its neck,
Gaped as a snake does, lolled out its large tongue,
And licked the whole labour flat: so much for spite.
'Saw a ball flame down late (yonder it lies)
Where, half an hour before, I slept i' the shade:
Often they scatter sparkles: there is force!
'Dug up a newt He may have envied once
And turned to stone, shut up inside a stone.
Please Him and hinder this?—What Prosper does?
Aha, if He would tell me how! Not He!
There is the sport: discover how or die!
All need not die, for of the things o' the isle
Some flee afar, some dive, some run up trees;
Those at His mercy,—why, they please Him most
When . . . when . . . well, never try the same way twice!
Repeat what act has pleased, He may grow wroth.
You must not know His ways, and play Him off,
Sure of the issue. 'Doth the like himself:
'Spareth a squirrel that it nothing fears
But steals the nut from underneath my thumb,
And when I threat, bites stoutly in defence:
'Spareth an urchin that contrariwise,

Curls up into a ball, pretending death
For fright at my approach: the two ways please.
But what would move my choler more than this,
That either creature counted on its life
To-morrow and next day and all days to come,
Saying, forsooth, in the inmost of its heart,
" Because he did so yesterday with me,
" And otherwise with such another brute,
" So must he do henceforth and always."—Ay?
Would teach the reasoning couple what " must " means!
'Doth as he likes, or wherefore Lord? So He.

'Conceiveth all things will continue thus,
And we shall have to live in fear of Him
So long as He lives, keeps His strength: no change,
If He have done His best, make no new world
To please Him more, so leave off watching this,—
If He surprise not even the Quiet's self
Some strange day,—or, suppose, grow into it
As grubs grow butterflies: else, here are we,
And there is He, and nowhere help at all.

'Believeth with the life, the pain shall stop.
His dam held different, that after death
He both plagued enemies and feasted friends:
Idly! He doth His worst in this our life,
Giving just respite lest we die through pain,
Saving last pain for worst,—with which, an end.
Meanwhile, the best way to escape His ire
Is, not to seem too happy. 'Sees, himself,
Yonder two flies, with purple films and pink,
Bask on the pompion-bell above; kills both.
'Sees two black painful beetles roll their ball
On head and tail as if to save their lives:
Moves them the stick away they strive to clear.

Even so, 'would have Him misconceive, suppose
This Caliban strives hard and ails no less,
And always, above all else, envies Him;
Wherefore he mainly dances on dark nights,
Moans in the sun, gets under holes to laugh,
And never speaks his mind save housed as now:
Outside, 'groans, curses. If He caught me here,
O'erheard this speech, and asked " What chucklest at? "
II—*R 42

'Would, to appease Him, cut a finger off,
Or of my three kid yearlings burn the best,
Or let the toothsome apples rot on tree,
Or push my tame beast for the orc to taste:
While myself lit a fire, and made a song
And sung it, " *What I hate, be consecrate*
" *To celebrate Thee and Thy state, no mate*
" *For Thee ; what see for envy in poor me ?* "
Hoping the while, since evils sometimes mend,
Warts rub away and sores are cured with slime,
That some strange day, will either the Quiet catch
And conquer Setebos, or likelier He
Decrepit may doze, doze, as good as die.

[What, what? A curtain o'er the world at once!
Crickets stop hissing; not a bird—or, yes,
There scuds His raven that has told Him all!
It was fool's play, this prattling! Ha! The wind
Shoulders the pillared dust, death's house o' the move,
And fast invading fires begin! White blaze—
A tree's head snaps—and there, there, there, there, there,
His thunder follows! Fool to gibe at Him!
Lo! 'Lieth flat and loveth Setebos!
'Maketh his teeth meet through his upper lip,
Will let those quails fly, will not eat this month
One little mess of whelks, so he may 'scape!]

CONFESSIONS.

I. WHAT is he buzzing in my ears?
    " Now that I come to die,
   " Do I view the world as a vale of tears? "
    Ah, reverend sir, not I!

II. What I viewed there once, what I view again
    Where the physic bottles stand
   On the table's edge,—is a suburb lane,
    With a wall to my bedside hand.

III. That lane sloped, much as the bottles do,
    From a house you could descry
   O'er the garden-wall: is the curtain blue
    Or green to a healthy eye?

IV. To mine, it serves for the old June weather
     Blue above lane and wall;
    And that farthest bottle labelled " Ether "
     Is the house o'ertopping all.

V. At a terrace, somewhere near the stopper,
     There watched for me, one June,
    A girl: I know, sir, it's improper,
     My poor mind's out of tune.

VI. Only, there was a way . . . you crept
     Close by the side, to dodge
    Eyes in the house, two eyes except;
     They styled their house " The Lodge."

VII. What right had a lounger up their lane?
      But, by creeping very close,
     With the good wall's help,—their eyes might strain
      And stretch themselves to Oes.

VIII. Yet never catch her and me together,
       As she left the attic, there,
      By the rim of the bottle labelled " Ether,"
       And stole from stair to stair,

IX. And stood by the rose-wreathed gate.   Alas,
     We loved, sir—used to meet:
    How sad and bad and mad it was—
     But then, how it was sweet!

MAY AND DEATH.

I. I WISH that when you died last May,
    Charles, there had died along with you
   Three parts of spring's delightful things;
    Ay, and, for me, the fourth part too.

II. A foolish thought, and worse, perhaps!
     There must be many a pair of friends
    Who, arm in arm, deserve the warm
     Moon-births and the long evening-ends.

III. So, for their sake, be May still May!
    Let their new time, as mine of old,
Do all it did for me: I bid
    Sweet sights and sounds throng manifold.

IV. Only, one little sight, one plant,
    Woods have in May, that starts up green
Save a sole streak which, so to speak,
    Is spring's blood, spilt its leaves between,—

V. That, they might spare; a certain wood
    Might miss the plant; their loss were small:
But I,—whene'er the leaf grows there,
    Its drop comes from my heart, that's all.

DEAF AND DUMB.

A GROUP BY WOOLNER.

ONLY the prism's obstruction shows aright
The secret of a sunbeam, breaks its light
Into the jewelled bow from blankest white;
    So may a glory from defect arise:
Only by Deafness may the vexed Love wreak
Its insuppressive sense on brow and cheek,
Only by Dumbness adequately speak
    As favoured mouth could never, through the eyes.

PROSPICE.

FEAR death?—to feel the fog in my throat,
    The mist in my face,
When the snows begin, and the blasts denote
    I am nearing the place,
The power of the night, the press of the storm,
    The post of the foe;
Where he stands, the Arch Fear in a visible form,
    Yet the strong man must go:
For the journey is done and the summit attained,
    And the barriers fall,
Though a battle's to fight ere the guerdon be gained,
    The reward of it all.

I was ever a fighter, so—one fight more,
    The best and the last!
I would hate that death bandaged my eyes, and forbore,
    And bade me creep past.
No! let me taste the whole of it, fare like my peers
    The heroes of old,
Bear the brunt, in a minute pay glad life's arrears
    Of pain, darkness and cold.
For sudden the worst turns the best to the brave,
    The black minute's at end,
And the elements' rage, the fiend-voices that rave,
    Shall dwindle, shall blend,
Shall change, shall become first a peace out of pain,
    Then a light, then thy breast,
O thou soul of my soul! I shall clasp thee again,
    And with God be the rest!

EURYDICE TO ORPHEUS.

A PICTURE BY LEIGHTON.

But give them me, the mouth, the eyes, the brow!
Let them once more absorb me! One look now
    Will lap me round for ever, not to pass
Out of its light, though darkness lie beyond:
Hold me but safe again within the bond
    Of one immortal look! All woe that was,
Forgotten, and all terror that may be,
Defied,—no past is mine, no future: look at me!

YOUTH AND ART.

I. It once might have been, once only:
    We lodged in a street together,
You, a sparrow on the housetop lonely,
    I, a lone she-bird of his feather.

II. Your trade was with sticks and clay,
    You thumbed, thrust, patted and polished,
Then laughed " They will see some day
    " Smith made, and Gibson demolished."

III. My business was song, song, song;
    I chirped, cheeped, trilled and twittered,
  " Kate Brown's on the boards ere long,
    And Grisi's existence embittered!"

IV. I earned no more by a warble
    Than you by a sketch in plaster;
  You wanted a piece of marble,
    I needed a music-master.

V. We studied hard in our styles,
    Chipped each at a crust like Hindoos,
  For air looked out on the tiles,
    For fun watched each other's windows.

VI. You lounged, like a boy of the South,
    Cap and blouse—nay, a bit of beard too;
  Or you got it, rubbing your mouth
    With fingers the clay adhered to.

VII. And I—soon managed to find
    Weak points in the flower-fence facing,
  Was forced to put up a blind
    And be safe in my corset-lacing.

VIII. No harm! It was not my fault
    If you never turned your eye's tail up
  As I shook upon E *in alt*,
    Or ran the chromatic scale up:

IX. For spring bade the sparrows pair,
    And the boys and girls gave guesses,
  And stalls in our street looked rare
    With bulrush and watercresses.

X. Why did not you pinch a flower
    In a pellet of clay and fling it?
  Why did not I put a power
    Of thanks in a look, or sing it?

XI. I did look, sharp as a lynx,
    (And yet the memory rankles)
  When models arrived, some minx
    Tripped up-stairs, she and her ankles.

XII. But I think I gave you as good!
    " That foreign fellow,—who can know
  " How she pays, in a playful mood,
    " For his tuning her that piano?"

XIII. Could you say so, and never say,
    " Suppose we join hands and fortunes,
  " And I fetch her from over the way,
    " Her, piano, and long tunes and short tunes?"

XIV. No, no; you would not be rash,
    Nor I rasher and something over:
  You've to settle yet Gibson's hash,
    And Grisi yet lives in clover.

XV. But you meet the Prince at the Board,
    I'm queen myself at *bals-paré*,
  I've married a rich old lord,
    And you're dubbed knight and an R.A.

XVI. Each life unfulfilled, you see;
    It hangs still, patchy and scrappy:
  We have not sighed deep, laughed free,
    Starved, feasted, despaired,—been happy.

XVII. And nobody calls you a dunce,
    And people suppose me clever:
  This could but have happened once,
    And we missed it, lost it for ever.

A FACE.

IF one could have that little head of hers
  Painted upon a background of pale gold,
Such as the Tuscan's early art prefers!
  No shade encroaching on the matchless mould
Of those two lips, which should be opening soft
  In the pure profile; not as when she laughs,
For that spoils all: but rather as if aloft
  Yon hyacinth, she loves so, leaned its staff's
Burthen of honey-coloured buds to kiss

And capture 'twixt the lips apart for this.
Then her lithe neck, three fingers might surround,
How it should waver on the pale gold ground
Up to the fruit-shaped, perfect chin it lifts!
I know, Correggio loves to mass, in rifts
Of heaven, his angel faces, orb on orb
Breaking its outline, burning shades absorb:
But these are only massed there, I should think,
    Waiting to see some wonder momently
    Grow out, stand full, fade slow against the sky
    (That's the pale ground you'd see this sweet face by),
    All heaven, meanwhile, condensed into one eye
Which fears to lose the wonder, should it wink.

A LIKENESS.

Some people hang portraits up
In a room where they dine or sup:
    And the wife clinks tea-things under,
And her cousin, he stirs his cup,
    Asks " Who was the lady, I wonder? "
" 'Tis a daub John bought at a sale,"
    Quoth the wife,—looks black as thunder:
" What a shade beneath her nose!
" Snuff-taking, I suppose,—"
Adds the cousin, while John's corns ail.

Or else, there's no wife in the case,
But the portrait's queen of the place,
Alone mid the other spoils
Of youth,—masks, gloves and foils,
And pipe-sticks, rose, cherry-tree, jasmine,
    And the long whip, the tandem-lasher,
And the cast from a fist (" not, alas! mine,
    " But my master's, the Tipton Slasher "),
And the cards where pistol-balls mark ace,
And a satin shoe used for cigar-case,
And the chamois-horns (" shot in the Chablais ")
    And prints—Rarey drumming on Cruiser,
    And Sayers, our champion, the bruiser,
And the little edition of Rabelais:

A Likeness

Where a friend, with both hands in his pockets,
  May saunter up close to examine it,
  And remark a good deal of Jane Lamb in it,
" But the eyes are half out of their sockets:
" That hair's not so bad, where the gloss is,
" But they've made the girl's nose a proboscis:
" Jane Lamb, that we danced with at Vichy!
" What, is not she Jane? Then, who is she?"

All that I own is a print,
An etching, a mezzotint;
'Tis a study, a fancy, a fiction,
Yet a fact (take my conviction)
Because it has more than a hint
  Of a certain face, I never
Saw elsewhere touch or trace of
In women I've seen the face of:
  Just an etching, and, so far, clever.

I keep my prints, an imbroglio,
Fifty in one portfolio.
When somebody tries my claret,
We turn round chairs to the fire,
Chirp over days in a garret
  Chuckle o'er increase of salary,
Taste the good fruits of our leisure,
Talk about pencil and lyre,
  And the National Portrait Gallery:
Then I exhibit my treasure.
After we've turned over twenty,
  And the debt of wonder my crony owes
  Is paid to my Marc Antonios,
He stops me—" *Festina lentè !*
" What's that sweet thing there, the etching?"
How my waistcoat-strings want stretching,
  How my cheeks grow red as tomatos,
How my heart leaps! But hearts, after leaps, ache.

" By the by, you must take, for a keepsake,
  " That other, you praised, of Volpato's."
The fool! would he try a flight further and say—
He never saw, never before to-day,
What was able to take his breath away,

A face to lose youth for, to occupy age
With the dream of, meet death with,—why, I'll not engage
But that, half in a rapture and half in a rage,
I should toss him the thing's self—" 'Tis only a duplicate,
" A thing of no value!   Take it, I supplicate! "

MR. SLUDGE, " THE MEDIUM."

Now, don't, sir!   Don't expose me!   Just this once!
This was the first and only time, I'll swear,—
Look at me,—see, I kneel,—the only time,
I swear, I ever cheated,—yes, by the soul
Of Her who hears—(your sainted mother, sir!)
All, except this last accident, was truth—
This little kind of slip!—and even this,
It was your own wine, sir, the good champagne,
(I took it for Catawba, you're so kind)
Which put the folly in my head!

                                   " Get up? "
You still inflict on me that terrible face?
You show no mercy?—Not for Her dear sake,
The sainted spirit's, whose soft breath even now
Blows on my cheek—(don't you feel something, sir?)
You'll tell?

                Go tell, then!   Who the devil cares
What such a rowdy chooses to . . .

                                   Aie—aie—aie!
Please, sir! your thumbs are through my windpipe, sir!
Ch—ch!

                Well, sir, I hope you've done it now!
Oh Lord!   I little thought, sir, yesterday,
When your departed mother spoke those words
Of peace through me, and moved you, sir, so much,
You gave me—(very kind it was of you)
These shirt-studs—(better take them back again,
Please, sir)—yes, little did I think so soon
A trifle of trick, all through a glass too much
Of his own champagne, would change my best of friends
Into an angry gentleman!

                        Though, 'twas wrong.
I don't contest the point: your anger's just:

Whatever put such folly in my head,
I know 'twas wicked of me. There's a thick
Dusk undeveloped spirit (I've observed)
Owes me a grudge—a negro's, I should say,
Or else an Irish emigrant's; yourself
Explained the case so well last Sunday, sir,
When we had summoned Franklin to clear up
A point about those shares i' the telegraph:
Ay, and he swore . . . or might it be Tom Paine? . . .
Thumping the table close by where I crouched,
He'd do me soon a mischief: that's come true!
Why, now your face clears! I was sure it would!
Then, this one time . . . don't take your hand away,
Through yours I surely kiss your mother's hand . . .
You'll promise to forgive me? —or, at least,
Tell nobody of this? Consider, sir!
What harm can mercy do? Would but the shade
Of the venerable dead-one just vouchsafe
A rap or tip! What bit of paper's here?
Suppose we take a pencil, let her write,
Make the least sign, she urges on her child
Forgiveness? There now! Eh? Oh! 'Twas your foot,
And not a natural creak, sir?

                              Answer, then!
Once, twice, thrice . . . see, I'm waiting to say "thrice!"
All to no use? No sort of hope for me?
It's all to post to Greeley's newspaper?

What? If I told you all about the tricks?
Upon my soul?—the whole truth, and nought else,
And how there's been some falsehood—for your part,
Will you engage to pay my passage out,
And hold your tongue until I'm safe on board?
England's the place, not Boston—no offence!
I see what makes you hesitate: don't fear!
I mean to change my trade and cheat no more,
Yes, this time really it's upon my soul!
Be my salvation!—under Heaven, of course.
I'll tell some queer things. Sixty Vs must do.
A trifle, though, to start with! We'll refer
The question to this table?

                              How you're changed!
Then split the difference; thirty more, we'll say.

Ay, but you leave my presents! Else I'll swear
'Twas all through those: you wanted yours again,
So, picked a quarrel with me, to get them back!
Tread on a worm, it turns, sir! If I turn,
Your fault! 'Tis you'll have forced me! Who's obliged
To give up life yet try on self-defence?
At all events, I'll run the risk. Eh?

                                        Done!

May I sit, sir? This dear old table, now!
Please, sir, a parting egg-nogg and cigar!
I've been so happy with you! Nice stuffed chairs,
And sympathetic sideboards; what an end
To all the instructive evenings! (It's alight.)
Well, nothing lasts, as Bacon came and said.
Here goes,—but keep your temper, or I'll scream!

Fol-lol-the-rido-liddle-iddle-ol!
You see, sir, it's your own fault more than mine;
It's all your fault, you curious gentlefolk!
You're prigs,—excuse me,—like to look so spry,
So clever, while you cling by half a claw
To the perch whereon you puff yourselves at roost,
Such piece of self-conceit as serves for perch
Because you chose it, so it must be safe.
Oh, otherwise you're sharp enough! You spy
Who slips, who slides, who holds by help of wing,
Wanting real foothold,—who can't keep upright
On the other perch, your neighbour chose, not you:
There's no outwitting you respecting him!
For instance, men love money—that, you know
And what men do to gain it: well, suppose
A poor lad, say a help's son in your house,
Listening at keyholes, hears the company
Talk grand of dollars, V-notes, and so forth,
How hard they are to get, how good to hold,
How much they buy,—if, suddenly, in pops he—
" *I've* got a V-note!"—what do you say to him?
What's your first word which follows your last kick?
" Where did you steal it, rascal? " That's because
He finds you, fain would fool you, off your perch,
Not on the special piece of nonsense, sir,
Elected your parade-ground: let him try

Lies to the end of the list,—" He picked it up,
" His cousin died and left it him by will,
" The President flung it to him, riding by,
" An actress trucked it for a curl of his hair,
" He dreamed of luck and found his shoe enriched,
" He dug up clay, and out of clay made gold "—
How would you treat such possibilities?
Would not you, prompt, investigate the case
With cow-hide?   " Lies, lies, lies," you'd shout: and why?
Which of the stories might not prove mere truth?
This last, perhaps, that clay was turned to coin!
Let's see, now, give him me to speak for him!
How many of your rare philosophers,
In plaguy books I've had to dip into,
Believed gold could be made thus, saw it made
And made it?   Oh, with such philosophers
You're on your best behaviour!   While the lad—
With him, in a trice, you settle likelihoods,
Nor doubt a moment how he got his prize:
In his case, you hear, judge and execute,
All in a breath: so would most men of sense.

But let the same lad hear you talk as grand
At the same keyhole, you and company,
Of signs and wonders, the invisible world;
How wisdom scouts our vulgar unbelief
More than our vulgarest credulity;
How good men have desired to see a ghost,
What Johnson used to say, what Wesley did,
Mother Goose thought, and fiddle-diddle-dee:—
If he break in with, " Sir, I saw a ghost!"
Ah, the ways change!   He finds you perched and prim;
It's a conceit of yours that ghosts may be:
There's no talk now of cow-hide.   " Tell it out!
" Don't fear us!   Take your time and recollect!
" Sit down first: try a glass of wine, my boy!
" And, David, (is not that your Christian name?)
" Of all things, should this happen twice—it may—
" Be sure, while fresh in mind, you let us know!"
Does the boy blunder, blurt out this, blab that,
Break down in the other, as beginners will?
All's candour, all's considerateness—" No haste!
" Pause and collect yourself!   We understand!

" That's the bad memory, or the natural shock,
" Or the unexplained *phenomena !* "

                    Egad,
The boy takes heart of grace; finds, never fear,
The readiest way to ope your own heart wide,
Show—what I call your peacock-perch, pet post
To strut, and spread the tail, and squawk upon!
" Just as you thought, much as you might expect!
" There be more things in heaven and earth, Horatio," . . .
And so on.   Shall not David take the hint,
Grow bolder, stroke you down at quickened rate?
If he ruffle a feather, it's " Gently, patiently!
" Manifestations are so weak at first!
" Doubting, moreover, kills them, cuts all short,
" Cures with a vengeance! "

                 There, sir, that's your style!
You and your boy—such pains bestowed on him,
Or any headpiece of the average worth,
To teach, say, Greek, would perfect him apace,
Make him a Person (" Porson? " thank you, sir!)
Much more, proficient in the art of lies.
You never leave the lesson!   Fire alight,
Catch you permitting it to die!   You've friends;
There's no withholding knowledge,—least from those
Apt to look elsewhere for their souls' supply:
Why should not you parade your lawful prize?
Who finds a picture, digs a medal up,
Hits on a first edition,—he henceforth
Gives it his name, grows notable: how much more,
Who ferrets out a " medium "?   " David's yours,
" You highly-favoured man?   Then, pity souls
" Less privileged!   Allow us share your luck! "
So, David holds the circle, rules the roast,
Narrates the vision, peeps in the glass ball,
Sets-to the spirit-writing, hears the raps,
As the case may be.

            Now mark!   To be precise—
Though I say, " lies " all these, at this first stage,
'Tis just for science' sake: I call such grubs
By the name of what they'll turn to, dragonflies.

Strictly, it's what good people style untruth;
But yet, so far, not quite the full-grown thing:
It's fancying, fable-making, nonsense-work—
What never meant to be so very bad—
The knack of story-telling, brightening up
Each dull old bit of fact that drops its shine.
One does see somewhat when one shuts one's eyes,
If only spots and streaks; tables do tip
In the oddest way of themselves: and pens, good Lord,
Who knows if you drive them or they drive you?
'Tis but a foot in the water and out again;
Not that duck-under which decides your dive.
Note this, for it's important: listen why.
I'll prove, you push on David till he dives
And ends the shivering. Here's your circle, now:
Two-thirds of them, with heads like you their host,
Turn up their eyes, and cry, as you expect,
" Lord, who'd have thought it!" But there's always one
Looks wise, compassionately smiles, submits
" Of your veracity no kind of doubt,
" But—do you feel so certain of that boy's?
" Really, I wonder! I confess myself
" More chary of my faith!" That's galling, sir!
What, he the investigator, he the sage,
When all's done? Then, you just have shut your eyes,
Opened your mouth, and gulped down David whole,
You! Terrible were such catastrophe!
So, evidence is redoubled, doubled again,
And doubled besides; once more, " He heard, we heard,
" You and they heard, your mother and your wife,
" Your children and the stranger in your gates:
" Did they or did they not?" So much for him,
The black sheep, guest without the wedding-garb,
The doubting Thomas! Now's your time to crow:
" He's kind to think you such a fool: Sludge cheats?
" Leave you alone to take precautions!"
                                        Straight
The rest join chorus. Thomas stands abashed,
Sips silent some such beverage as this,
Considers if it be harder, shutting eyes
And gulping David in good fellowship,
Than going elsewhere, getting, in exchange,
With no egg-nogg to lubricate the food,

Some just as tough a morsel. Over the way,
Holds Captain Sparks his court: is it better there?
Have not you hunting-stories, scalping-scenes,
And Mexican War exploits to swallow plump
If you'd be free o' the stove-side, rocking-chair,
And trio of affable daughters?

                             Doubt succumbs!
Victory! All your circle's yours again!
Out of the clubbing of submissive wits,
David's performance rounds, each chink gets patched,
Every protrusion of a point's filed fine,
All's fit to set a-rolling round the world,
And then return to David finally,
Lies seven-feet thick about his first half-inch.
Here's a choice birth o' the supernatural,
Poor David's pledged to! You've employed no tool
That laws exclaim at, save the devil's own,
Yet screwed him into henceforth gulling you
To the top o' your bent,—all out of one half-lie!

You hold, if there's one half or a hundredth part
Of a lie, that's his fault,—his be the penalty!
I dare say! You'd prove firmer in his place?
You'd find the courage,—that first flurry over,
That mild bit of romancing-work at end,—
To interpose with " It gets serious, this;
" Must stop here. Sir, I saw no ghost at all.
" Inform your friends I made . . . well, fools of them,
" And found you ready-made. I've lived in clover
" These three weeks: take it out in kicks of me! "
I doubt it. Ask your conscience! Let me know,
Twelve months hence, with how few embellishments
You've told almighty Boston of this passage
Of arms between us, your first taste o' the foil
From Sludge who could not fence, sir! Sludge, your boy!
I lied, sir,—there! I got up from my gorge
On offal in the gutter, and preferred
Your canvas-backs: I took their carver's size,
Measured his modicum of intelligence,
Tickled him on the cockles of his heart
With a raven feather, and next week found myself
Sweet and clean, dining daintily, dizened smart,
Set on a stool buttressed by ladies' knees,

Every soft smiler calling me her pet,
Encouraging my story to uncoil
And creep out from its hole, inch after inch,
" How last night, I no sooner snug in bed,
" Tucked up, just as they left me,—than came raps!
" While a light whisked " . . . " Shaped somewhat like a
    star ? "
" Well, like some sort of stars, ma'am."—" So we thought!
" And any voice? Not yet? Try hard, next time,
" If you can't hear a voice; we think you may:
" At least, the Pennsylvanian ' mediums ' did."
Oh, next time comes the voice! " Just as we hoped! "
Are not the hopers proud now, pleased, profuse
O' the natural acknowledgment?

                                        Of course!
So, off we push, illy-oh-yo, trim the boat,
On we sweep with a cataract ahead,
We're midway to the Horseshoe: stop, who can,
The dance of bubbles gay about our prow!
Experiences become worth waiting for,
Spirits now speak up, tell their inmost mind,
And compliment the " medium " properly,
Concern themselves about his Sunday coat,
See rings on his hand with pleasure. Ask yourself
How you'd receive a course of treats like these!
Why, take the quietest hack and stall him up,
Cram him with corn a month, then out with him
Among his mates on a bright April morn,
With the turf to tread; see if you find or no
A caper in him, if he bucks or bolts!
Much more a youth whose fancies sprout as rank
As toadstool-clump from melon-bed. 'Tis soon,
" Sirrah, you spirit, come, go, fetch and carry,
" Read, write, rap, rub-a-dub, and hang yourself! "
I'm spared all further trouble; all's arranged;
Your circle does my business; I may rave
Like an epileptic dervish in the books,
Foam, fling myself flat, rend my clothes to shreds;
No matter: lovers, friends and countrymen
Will lay down spiritual laws, read wrong things right
By the rule o' reverse. If Francis Verulam
Styles himself Bacon, spells the name beside

With a *y* and a *k*, says he drew breath in York,
Gave up the ghost in Wales when Cromwell reigned,
(As, sir, we somewhat fear he was apt to say,
Before I found the useful book that knows)
Why, what harm's done?   The circle smiles apace,
" It was not Bacon, after all, you see!
" We understand; the trick's but natural:
" Such spirits' individuality
" Is hard to put in evidence: they incline
" To gibe and jeer, these undeveloped sorts.
" You see, their world's much like a jail broke loose,
" While this of ours remains shut, bolted, barred,
" With a single window to it.   Sludge, our friend,
" Serves as this window, whether thin or thick,
" Or stained or stainless; he's the medium-pane
" Through which, to see us and be seen, they peep:
" They crowd each other, hustle for a chance,
" Tread on their neighbour's kibes, play tricks enough!
" Does Bacon, tired of waiting, swerve aside?
" Up in his place jumps Barnum—' I'm your man,
" ' I'll answer you for Bacon!' Try once more!"

Or else it's—" What's a 'medium'?   He's a means,
" Good, bad, indifferent, still the only means
" Spirits can speak by; he may misconceive,
" Stutter and stammer,—he's their Sludge and drudge,
" Take him or leave him; they must hold their peace,
" Or else, put up with having knowledge strained
" To half-expression through his ignorance.
" Suppose, the spirit Beethoven wants to shed
" New music he's brimful of; why, he turns
" The handle of this organ, grinds with Sludge,
" And what he poured in at the mouth o' the mill
" As a Thirty-third Sonata, (fancy now!)
" Comes from the hopper as bran-new Sludge, nought else,
" The Shakers' Hymn in G, with a natural F,
" Or the ' Stars and Stripes ' set to consecutive fourths."
Sir, where's the scrape you did not help me through,
You that are wise?   And for the fools, the folk
Who came to see,—the guests, (observe that word!)
Pray do you find guests criticize your wine,
Your furniture, your grammar, or your nose?
Then, why your " medium "?   What's the difference?

Prove your madeira red-ink and gamboge,—
Your Sludge, a cheat—then, somebody's a goose
For vaunting both as genuine. "Guests!" Don't fear!
They'll make a wry face, nor too much of that,
And leave you in your glory.

                         "No, sometimes
"They doubt and say as much!" Ay, doubt they do!
And what's the consequence? "Of course they doubt"—
(You triumph) "that explains the hitch at once!
"Doubt posed our 'medium,' puddled his pure mind;
"He gave them back their rubbish: pitch chaff in,
"Could flour come out o' the honest mill?" So, prompt
Applaud the faithful: cases flock in point,
"How, when a mocker willed a 'medium' once
"Should name a spirit James whose name was George,
"'James' cried the 'medium,'—'twas the test of truth!"
In short, a hit proves much, a miss proves more.
Does this convince? The better: does it fail?
Time for the double-shotted broadside, then—
The grand means, last resource. Look black and big!
"You style us idiots, therefore—why stop short?
"Accomplices in rascality; this we hear
"In our own house, from our invited guest
"Found brave enough to outrage a poor boy
"Exposed by our good faith! Have you been heard?
"Now, then, hear us; one man's not quite worth twelve.
"You see a cheat? Here's some twelve see an ass!
"Excuse me if I calculate: good day!"
Out slinks the sceptic, all the laughs explode.
Sludge waves his hat in triumph!

                        Or—he don't.
There's something in real truth (explain who can!)
One casts a wistful eye at, like the horse
Who mopes beneath stuffed hay-racks and won't munch
Because he spies a corn-bag: hang that truth,
It spoils all dainties proffered in its place!
I've felt at times when, cockered, cosseted
And coddled by the aforesaid company,
Bidden enjoy their bullying,—never fear,
But o'er their shoulders spit at the flying man,—
I've felt a child, only a fractious child

That, dandled soft by nurse, aunt, grandmother,
Who keep him from the kennel, sun and wind,
Good fun and wholesome mud,—enjoined be sweet,
And comely and superior,—eyes askance
The ragged sons o' the gutter at their game,
Fain would be down with them i' the thick o' the filth,
Making dirt-pies, laughing free, speaking plain,
And calling granny the grey old cat she is.
I've felt a spite, I say, at you, at them,
Huggings and humbug—gnashed my teeth to mark
A decent dog pass! It's too bad, I say,
Ruining a soul so!

                  But what's " so," what's fixed,
Where may one stop? Nowhere! The cheating's nursed
Out of the lying, softly and surely spun
To just your length, sir! I'd stop soon enough:
But you're for progress. " All old, nothing new?
" Only the usual talking through the mouth,
" Or writing by the hand? I own, I thought
" This would develop, grow demonstrable,
" Make doubt absurd, give figures we might see,
" Flowers we might touch. There's no one doubts you,
    Sludge!
" You dream the dreams, you see the spiritual sights,
" The speeches come in your head, beyond dispute.
" Still, for the sceptics' sake, to stop all mouths,
" We want some outward manifestation!—well,
" The Pennsylvanians gained such; why not Sludge?
" He may improve with time!"

                       Ay, that he may!
He sees his lot: there's no avoiding fate.
'Tis a trifle at first. " Eh, David? Did you hear?
" You jogged the table, your foot caused the squeak,
" This time you're . . . joking, are you not, my boy?"
" N-n-no!"—and I'm done for, bought and sold henceforth.
The old good easy jog-trot way, the . . . eh?
The . . . not so very false, as falsehood goes,
The spinning out and drawing fine, you know,—
Really mere novel-writing of a sort,
Acting, or improvising, make-believe,
Surely not downright cheatery,—any how,

'Tis done with and my lot cast; Cheat's my name:
The fatal dash of brandy in your tea
Has settled what you'll have the souchong's smack:
The caddy gives way to the dram-bottle.

Then, it's so cruel easy!   Oh, those tricks
That can't be tricks, those feats by sleight of hand,
Clearly no common conjuror's!—no indeed!
A conjuror?   Choose me any craft i' the world
A man puts hand to; and with six months' pains
I'll play you twenty tricks miraculous
To people untaught the trade: have you seen glass blown,
Pipes pierced?   Why, just this biscuit that I chip,
Did you ever watch a baker toss one flat
To the oven?   Try and do it!   Take my word,
Practise but half as much, while limbs are lithe,
To turn, shove, tilt a table, crack your joints,
Manage your feet, dispose your hands aright,
Work wires that twitch the curtains, play the glove
At end o' your slipper,—then put out the lights
And . . . there, there, all you want you'll get, I hope!
I found it slip, easy as an old shoe.

Now, lights on table again!   I've done my part,
You take my place while I give thanks and rest.
" Well, Judge Humgruffin, what's your verdict, sir?
" You, hardest head in the United States,—
" Did you detect a cheat here?   Wait!   Let's see!
" Just an experiment first, for candour's sake!
" I'll try and cheat you, Judge?   The table tilts:
" Is it I that move it?   Write!   I'll press your hand:
" Cry when I push, or guide your pencil, Judge!"
Sludge still triumphant!   " That a rap, indeed?
" That, the real writing?   Very like a whale!
" Then, if, sir, you—a most distinguished man,
" And, were the Judge not here, I'd say, . . . no matter!
" Well, sir, if you fail, you can't take us in,—
" There's little fear that Sludge will!"

                                     Won't he, ma'am?
But what if our distinguished host, like Sludge,
Bade God bear witness that he played no trick,
While you believed that what produced the raps
Was just a certain child who died, you know,

And whose last breath you thought your lips had felt?
Eh? That's a capital point, ma'am; Sludge begins
At your entreaty with your dearest dead,
The little voice set lisping once again,
The tiny hand made feel for yours once more,
The poor lost image brought back, plain as dreams,
Which image, if a word had chanced recall,
The customary cloud would cross your eyes,
Your heart return the old tick, pay its pang!
A right mood for investigation, this!
One's at one's ease with Saul and Jonathan,
Pompey and Cæsar: but one's own lost child . . .
I wonder, when you heard the first clod drop
From the spadeful at the grave-side, felt you free
To investigate who twitched your funeral scarf
Or brushed your flounces? Then, it came of course
You should be stunned and stupid; then, (how else?)
Your breath stopped with your blood, your brain struck work.
But now, such causes fail of such effects,
All's changed,—the little voice begins afresh,
Yet you, calm, consequent, can test and try
And touch the truth. " Tests? Didn't the creature tell
" Its nurse's name, and say it lived six years,
" And rode a rocking-horse? Enough of tests!
" Sludge never could learn that!"

                                    He could not, eh?
You compliment him. " Could not?" Speak for yourself!
I'd like to know the man I ever saw
Once,—never mind where, how, why, when,—once saw,
Of whom I do not keep some matter in mind
He'd swear I " could not " know, sagacious soul!
What? Do you live in this world's blow of blacks,
Palaver, gossipry, a single hour
Nor find one smut has settled on your nose,
Of a smut's worth, no more, no less?—one fact
Out of the drift of facts, whereby you learn
What someone was, somewhere, somewhen, somewhy?
You don't tell folk—" See what has stuck to me!
" Judge Humgruffin, our most distinguished man,
" Your uncle was a tailor, and your wife
" Thought to have married Miggs, missed him, hit you!"—
Do you, sir, though you see him twice a-week?
" No," you reply, " what use retailing it?

"Why should I?" But, you see, one day you *should*,
Because one day there's much use,—when this fact
Brings you the Judge upon both gouty knees
Before the supernatural; proves that Sludge
Knows, as you say, a thing he "could not" know:
Will not Sludge thenceforth keep an outstretched face
The way the wind drives?

               "Could not!" Look you now,
I'll tell you a story! There's a whiskered chap,
A foreigner, that teaches music here
And gets his bread,—knowing no better way:
He says, the fellow who informed of him
And made him fly his country and fall West
Was a hunchback cobbler, sat, stitched soles and sang,
In some outlandish place, the city Rome,
In a cellar by their Broadway, all day long;
Never asked questions, stopped to listen or look,
Nor lifted nose from lapstone; let the world
Roll round his three-legged stool, and news run in
The ears he hardly seemed to keep pricked up.
Well, that man went on Sundays, touched his pay,
And took his praise from government, you see;
For something like two dollars every week,
He'd engage tell you some one little thing
Of some one man, which led to many more,
(Because one truth leads right to the world's end)
And make you that man's master—when he dined
And on what dish, where walked to keep his health
And to what street. His trade was, throwing thus
His sense out, like an ant-eater's long tongue,
Soft, innocent, warm, moist, impassible,
And when 'twas crusted o'er with creatures—slick,
Their juice enriched his palate. "Could not Sludge!"

I'll go yet a step further, and maintain,
Once the imposture plunged its proper depth
I' the rotten of your natures, all of you,—
(If one's not mad nor drunk, and hardly then)
It's impossible to cheat—that's, be found out!
Go tell your brotherhood this first slip of mine,
All to-day's tale, how you detected Sludge,
Behaved unpleasantly, till he was fain confess,
And so has come to grief! You'll find, I think,

Why Sludge still snaps his fingers in your face.
There now, you've told them!   What's their prompt reply?
" Sir, did that youth confess he had cheated me,
" I'd disbelieve him.   He may cheat at times;
" That's in the ' medium '-nature, thus they're made,
" Vain and vindictive, cowards, prone to scratch.
" And so all cats are; still, a cat's the beast
" You coax the strange electric sparks from out,
" By rubbing back its fur; not so a dog,
" Nor lion, nor lamb: 'tis the cat's nature, sir!
" Why not the dog's?   Ask God, who made them beasts!
" D'ye think the sound, the nicely-balanced man
" (Like me "—aside)—" like you yourself,"—(aloud)
" —He's stuff to make a ' medium '?   Bless your soul,
" 'Tis these hysteric, hybrid half-and-halfs,
" Equivocal, worthless vermin yield the fire!
" We take such as we find them, 'ware their tricks,
" Wanting their service.   Sir, Sludge took in you—
" How, I can't say, not being there to watch:
" He was tried, was tempted by your easiness,—
" He did not take in me! "

                                   Thank you for Sludge!
I'm to be grateful to such patrons, eh,
When what you hear's my best word?   'Tis a challenge
" Snap at all strangers, half-tamed prairie-dog,
" So you cower duly at your keeper's beck!
" Cat, show what claws were made for, muffling them
" Only to me!   Cheat others if you can,
" Me, if you dare! "   And, my wise sir, I dared—
Did cheat you first, did make you cheat others next,
And had the help o' your vaunted manliness
To bully the incredulous.   You used me?
Have not I used you, taken full revenge,
Persuaded folk they knew not their own name,
And straight they'd own the error!   Who was the fool
When, to an awe-struck wide-eyed open-mouthed
Circle of sages, Sludge would introduce
Milton composing baby-rhymes, and Locke
Reasoning in gibberish, Homer writing Greek
In noughts and crosses, Asaph setting psalms
To crotchet and quaver?   I've made a spirit squeak
In sham voice for a minute, then outbroke
Bold in my own, defying the imbeciles—

Have copied some ghost's pothooks, half a page,
Then ended with my own scrawl undisguised.
" All right! The ghost was merely using Sludge,
" Suiting itself from his imperfect stock! "
Don't talk of gratitude to me! For what?
For being treated as a showman's ape,
Encouraged to be wicked and make sport,
Fret or sulk, grin or whimper, any mood
So long as the ape be in it and no man—
Because a nut pays every mood alike.
Curse your superior, superintending sort,
Who, since you hate smoke, send up boys that climb
To cure your chimney, bid a " medium " lie
To sweep you truth down! Curse your women too,
Your insolent wives and daughters, that fire up
Or faint away if a male hand squeeze theirs,
Yet, to encourage Sludge, may play with Sludge
As only a " medium," only the kind of thing
They must humour, fondle . . . oh, to misconceive
Were too preposterous! But I've paid them out!
They've had their wish—called for the naked truth,
And in she tripped, sat down and bade them stare;
They had to blush a little and forgive!
" The fact is, children talk so; in next world
" All our conventions are reversed,—perhaps
" Made light of: something like old prints, my dear!
" The Judge has one, he brought from Italy,
" A metropolis in the background,—o'er a bridge,
" A team of trotting roadsters,—cheerful groups
" Of wayside travellers, peasants at their work,
" And, full in front, quite unconcerned, why not?
" Three nymphs conversing with a cavalier,
" And never a rag among them: ' fine,' folk cry—
" And heavenly manners seem not much unlike!
" Let Sludge go on; we'll fancy it's in print! "
If such as came for wool, sir, went home shorn,
Where is the wrong I did them? 'Twas their choice;
They tried the adventure, ran the risk, tossed up
And lost, as some one's sure to do in games;
They fancied I was made to lose,—smoked glass
Useful to spy the sun through, spare their eyes:
And had I proved a red-hot iron plate
They thought to pierce, and, for their pains, grew blind,

Whose were the fault but theirs?   While, as things go,
Their loss amounts to gain, the more's the shame!
They've had their peep into the spirit-world,
And all this world may know it!   They've fed fat
Their self-conceit which else had starved: what chance
Save this, of cackling o'er a golden egg
And compassing distinction from the flock,
Friends of a feather?   Well, they paid for it,
And not prodigiously; the price o' the play,
Not counting certain pleasant interludes,
Was scarce a vulgar play's worth.   When you buy
The actor's talent, do you dare propose
For his soul beside?   Whereas my soul you buy!
Sludge acts Macbeth, obliged to be Macbeth,
Or you'll not hear his first word!   Just go through
That slight formality, swear himself's the Thane,
And thenceforth he may strut and fret his hour,
Spout, spawl, or spin his target, no one cares!
Why hadn't I leave to play tricks, Sludge as Sludge?
Enough of it all!   I've wiped out scores with you—
Vented your fustian, let myself be streaked
Like tom-fool with your ochre and carmine,
Worn patchwork your respectable fingers sewed
To metamorphose somebody,—yes, I've earned
My wages, swallowed down my bread of shame,
And shake the crumbs off—where but in your face?

As for religion—why, I served it, sir!
I'll stick to that!   With my *phenomena*
I laid the atheist sprawling on his back,
Propped up Saint Paul, or, at least, Swedenborg!
In fact, it's just the proper way to baulk
These troublesome fellows—liars, one and all,
Are not these sceptics?   Well, to baffle them,
No use in being squeamish: lie yourself!
Erect your buttress just as wide o' the line,
Your side, as they build up the wall on theirs;
Where both meet, midway in a point, is truth
High overhead: so, take your room, pile bricks,
Lie!   Oh, there's titillation in all shame!
What snow may lose in white, snow gains in rose;
Miss Stokes turns—Rahab,—nor a bad exchange!
Glory be on her, for the good she wrought,

Breeding belief anew 'neath ribs of death,
Browbeating now the unabashed before,
Ridding us of their whole life's gathered straws
By a live coal from the altar! Why, of old,
Great men spent years and years in writing books
To prove we've souls, and hardly proved it then:
Miss Stokes with her live coal, for you and me!
Surely, to this good issue, all was fair—
Not only fondling Sludge, but, even suppose
He let escape some spice of knavery,—well,
In wisely being blind to it! Don't you praise
Nelson for setting spy-glass to blind eye
And saying . . . what was it—that he could not see
The signal he was bothered with? Ay, indeed!

I'll go beyond: there's a real love of a lie,
Liars find ready-made for lies they make,
As hand for glove, or tongue for sugar-plum.
At best, 'tis never pure and full belief;
Those furthest in the quagmire,—don't suppose
They strayed there with no warning, got no chance
Of a filth-speck in their face, which they clenched teeth,
Bent brow against! Be sure they had their doubts,
And fears, and fairest challenges to try
The floor o' the seeming solid sand! But no!
Their faith was pledged, acquaintance too apprised,
All but the last step ventured, kerchiefs waved,
And Sludge called "pet": 'twas easier marching on
To the promised land join those who, Thursday next,
Meant to meet Shakespeare; better follow Sludge—
Prudent, oh sure!—on the alert, how else?—
But making for the mid-bog, all the same!
To hear your outcries, one would think I caught
Miss Stokes by the scruff o' the neck, and pitched her flat,
Foolish-face-foremost! Hear these simpletons,
That's all I beg, before my work's begun,
Before I've touched them with my finger-tip!
Thus they await me (do but listen, now!
It's reasoning, this is,—I can't imitate
The baby voice, though) "In so many tales
"Must be some truth, truth though a pin-point big,
"Yet, some: a single man's deceived, perhaps—
"Hardly, a thousand: to suppose one cheat

" Can gull all these, were more miraculous far
" Than aught we should confess a miracle "—
And so on.   Then the Judge sums up—(it's rare)
Bids you respect the authorities that leap
To the judgment-seat at once,—why don't you note
The limpid nature, the unblemished life,
The spotless honour, indisputable sense
Of the first upstart with his story?   What—
Outrage a boy on whom you ne'er till now
Set eyes, because he finds raps trouble him?
Fools, these are: ay, and how of their opposites
Who never did, at bottom of their hearts,
Believe for a moment?—Men emasculate,
Blank of belief, who played, as eunuchs use,
With superstition safely,—cold of blood,
Who saw what made for them i' the mystery,
Took their occasion, and supported Sludge
—As proselytes?   No, thank you, far too shrewd!
—But promisers of fair play, encouragers
O' the claimant; who in candour needs must hoist
Sludge up on Mars' Hill, get speech out of Sludge
To carry off, criticize, and cant about!
Didn't Athens treat Saint Paul so?—at any rate,
It's " a new thing " philosophy fumbles at.
Then there's the other picker-out of pearl
From dung-heaps,—ay, your literary man,
Who draws on his kid gloves to deal with Sludge
Daintily and discreetly,—shakes a dust
O' the doctrine, flavours thence, he well knows how,
The narrative or the novel,—half-believes,
All for the book's sake, and the public's stare,
And the cash that's God's sole solid in this world!
Look at him!   Try to be too bold, too gross
For the master!   Not you!   He's the man for muck;
Shovel it forth, full-splash, he'll smooth your brown
Into artistic richness, never fear!
Find him the crude stuff; when you recognize
Your lie again, you'll doff your hat to it,
Dressed out for company!   " For company,"
I say, since there's the relish of success:
Let all pay due respect, call the lie truth,
Save the soft silent smirking gentleman
Who ushered in the stranger: you must sigh

" How melancholy, he, the only one
" Fails to perceive the bearing of the truth
" Himself gave birth to!"—There's the triumph's smack!
That man would choose to see the whole world roll
I' the slime o' the slough, so he might touch the tip
Of his brush with what I call the best of browns—
Tint ghost-tales, spirit-stories, past the power
Of the outworn umber and bistre!

                    Yet I think
There's a more hateful form of foolery—
The social sage's, Solomon of saloons
And philosophic diner-out, the fribble
Who wants a doctrine for a chopping-block
To try the edge of his faculty upon,
Prove how much common sense he'll hack and hew
I' the critical minute 'twixt the soup and fish!
These were my patrons: these, and the like of them
Who, rising in my soul now, sicken it,—
These I have injured!   Gratitude to these?
The gratitude, forsooth, of a prostitute
To the greenhorn and the bully—friends of hers,
From the wag that wants the queer jokes for his club,
To the snuff-box decorator, honest man,
Who just wants at his wits' end where to find
So genial a Pasiphæ!   All and each
Pay, compliment, protect from the police:
And how she hates them for their pains, like me!
So much for my remorse at thanklessness
Toward a deserving public!

                  But, for God?
Ay, that's a question!   Well, sir, since you press—
(How you do tease the whole thing out of me!
I don't mean you, you know, when I say " them ":
Hate you, indeed!   But that Miss Stokes, that Judge!
Enough, enough—with sugar: thank you, sir!)
Now for it, then!   Will you believe me, though?
You've heard what I confess; I don't unsay
A single word: I cheated when I could,
Rapped with my toe-joints, set sham hands at work,
Wrote down names weak in sympathetic ink,
Rubbed odic lights with ends of phosphor-match,
And all the rest; believe that: believe this,

By the same token, though it seem to set
The crooked straight again, unsay the said,
Stick up what I've knocked down; I can't help that,
It's truth! I somehow vomit truth to-day.
This trade of mine—I don't know, can't be sure
But there was something in it, tricks and all!
Really, I want to light up my own mind.
They were tricks,—true, but what I mean to add
Is also true. First,—don't it strike you, sir?
Go back to the beginning,—the first fact
We're taught is, there's a world beside this world,
With spirits, not mankind, for tenantry;
That much within that world once sojourned here,
That all upon this world will visit there,
And therefore that we, bodily here below,
Must have exactly such an interest
In learning what may be the ways o' the world
Above us, as the disembodied folk
Have (by all analogic likelihood)
In watching how things go in the old home
With us, their sons, successors, and what not.
Oh yes, with added powers probably,
Fit for the novel state,—old loves grown pure,
Old interests understood aright,—they watch!
Eyes to see, ears to hear, and hands to help,
Proportionate to advancement: they're ahead,
That's all—do what we do, but noblier done—
Use plate, whereas we eat our meals off delf,
(To use a figure).

        Concede that, and I ask
Next what may be the mode of intercourse
Between us men here, and those once-men there?
First comes the Bible's speech; then, history
With the supernatural element,—you know—
All that we sucked in with our mothers' milk,
Grew up with, got inside of us at last,
Till it's found bone of bone and flesh of flesh.
See now, we start with the miraculous,
And know it used to be, at all events:
What's the first step we take, and can't but take,
In arguing from the known to the obscure?
Why this: " What was before, may be to-day.
" Since Samuel's ghost appeared to Saul, of course

" My brother's spirit may appear to me."
Go tell your teacher that! What's his reply?
What brings a shade of doubt for the first time
O'er his brow late so luminous with faith?
" Such things have been," says he, " and there's no doubt
" Such things may be: but I advise mistrust
" Of eyes, ears, stomach, and, more than all, your brain,
" Unless it be of your great-grandmother,
" Whenever they propose a ghost to you!"
The end is, there's a composition struck;
'Tis settled, we've some way of intercourse
Just as in Saul's time; only, different:
How, when and where, precisely,—find it out!
I want to know, then, what's so natural
As that a person born into this world
And seized on by such teaching, should begin
With firm expectancy and a frank look-out
For his own allotment, his especial share
I' the secret,—his particular ghost, in fine?
I mean, a person born to look that way,
Since natures differ: take the painter-sort,
One man lives fifty years in ignorance
Whether grass be green or red,—" No kind of eye
" For colour," say you; while another picks
And puts away even pebbles, when a child,
Because of bluish spots and pinky veins—
" Give him forthwith a paint-box!" Just the same
Was I born . . . " medium," you won't let me say,—
Well, seer of the supernatural
Everywhen, everyhow and everywhere,—
Will that do?

I and all such boys of course
Started with the same stock of Bible-truth;
Only,—what in the rest you style their sense,
Instinct, blind reasoning but imperative,
This, betimes, taught them the old world had one law
And ours another: " New world, new laws," cried they:
" None but old laws, seen everywhere at work,"
Cried I, and by their help explained my life
The Jews' way, still a working way to me.
Ghosts made the noises, fairies waved the lights,
Or Santa Claus slid down on New Year's Eve
And stuffed with cakes the stocking at my bed,

Changed the worn shoes, rubbed clean the fingered slate
O' the sum that came to grief the day before.
This could not last long: soon enough I found
Who had worked wonders thus, and to what end:
But did I find all easy, like my mates?
Henceforth no supernatural any more?
Not a whit: what projects the billiard-balls?
" A cue," you answer: " Yes, a cue," said I:
" But what hand, off the cushion, moved the cue?
" What unseen agency, outside the world,
" Prompted its puppets to do this and that,
" Put cakes and shoes and slates into their mind,
" These mothers and aunts, nay even schoolmasters? "
Thus high I sprang, and there have settled since.
Just so I reason, in sober earnest still,
About the greater godsends, what you call
The serious gains and losses of my life.
What do I know or care about your world
Which either is or seems to be? This snap
O' my fingers, sir! My care is for myself;
Myself am whole and sole reality
Inside a raree-show and a market-mob
Gathered about it: that's the use of things.
'Tis easy saying they serve vast purposes,
Advantage their grand selves: be it true or false,
Each thing may have two uses. What's a star?
A world, or a world's sun: doesn't it serve
As taper also, time-piece, weather-glass,
And almanac? Are stars not set for signs
When we should shear our sheep, sow corn, prune trees?
The Bible says so.
                              Well, I add one use
To all the acknowledged uses, and declare
If I spy Charles's Wain at twelve to-night,
It warns me, " Go, nor lose another day,
" And have your hair cut, Sludge! " You laugh: and why?
Were such a sign too hard for God to give?
No: but Sludge seems too little for such grace:
Thank you, sir! So you think, so does not Sludge!
When you and good men gape at Providence,
Go into history and bid us mark
Not merely powder-plots prevented, crowns
Kept on kings' heads by miracle enough,

But private mercies—oh, you've told me, sir,
Of such interpositions! How yourself
Once, missing on a memorable day
Your handkerchief—just setting out, you know,—
You must return to fetch it, lost the train,
And saved your precious self from what befell
The thirty-three whom Providence forgot.
You tell, and ask me what I think of this?
Well, sir, I think then, since you needs must know,
What matter had you and Boston city to boot
Sailed skyward, like burnt onion-peelings? Much
To you, no doubt: for me—undoubtedly
The cutting of my hair concerns me more,
Because, however sad the truth may seem,
Sludge is of all-importance to himself.
You set apart that day in every year
For special thanksgiving, were a heathen else:
Well, I cannot boast the like escape,
Suppose I said " I don't thank Providence
" For my part, owing it no gratitude "?
" Nay, but you owe as much "—you'd tutor me,
" You, every man alive, for blessings gained
" In every hour o' the day, could you but know!
" I saw my crowning mercy: all have such,
" Could they but see! " Well, sir, why don't they see?
" Because they won't look,—or perhaps, they can't."
Then, sir, suppose I can, and will, and do
Look, microscopically as is right,
Into each hour with its infinitude
Of influences at work to profit Sludge?
For that's the case: I've sharpened up my sight
To spy a providence in the fire's going out,
The kettle's boiling, the dime's sticking fast
Despite the hole i' the pocket. Call such facts
Fancies, too petty a work for Providence,
And those same thanks which you exact from me
Prove too prodigious payment: thanks for what,
If nothing guards and guides us little men?
No, no, sir! You must put away your pride,
Resolve to let Sludge into partnership!
I live by signs and omens: looked at the roof
Where the pigeons settle—" If the further bird,
" The white, takes wing first, I'll confess when thrashed;

" Not, if the blue does "—so I said to myself
Last week, lest you should take me by surprise:
Off flapped the white,—and I'm confessing, sir!
Perhaps 'tis Providence's whim and way
With only me, i' the world: how can you tell?
" Because unlikely!"   Was it likelier, now,
That this our one out of all worlds beside,
The what-d'you-call-'em millions, should be just
Precisely chosen to make Adam for,
And the rest o' the tale?   Yet the tale's true, you know:
Such undeserving clod was graced so once;
Why not graced likewise undeserving Sludge?
Are we merit-mongers, flaunt we filthy rags?
All you can bring against my privilege
Is, that another way was taken with you,—
Which I don't question.   It's pure grace, my luck:
I'm broken to the way of nods and winks,
And need no formal summoning.   You've a help;
Holloa his name or whistle, clap your hands,
Stamp with your foot or pull the bell: all's one,
He understands you want him, here he comes.
Just so, I come at the knocking: you, sir, wait
The tongue o' the bell, nor stir before you catch
Reason's clear tingle, nature's clapper brisk,
Or that traditional peal was wont to cheer
Your mother's face turned heavenward: short of these
There's no authentic intimation, eh?
Well, when you hear, you'll answer them, start up
And stride into the presence, top of toe,
And there find Sludge beforehand, Sludge that sprang
At noise o' the knuckle on the partition-wall!
I think myself the more religious man.
Religion's all or nothing; it's no mere smile
O' contentment, sigh of aspiration, sir—
No quality o' the finelier-tempered clay
Like its whiteness or its lightness; rather, stuff
O' the very stuff, life of life, and self of self.
I tell you, men won't notice; when they do,
They'll understand.   I notice nothing else:
I'm eyes, ears, mouth of me, one gaze and gape,
Nothing eludes me, everything's a hint,
Handle and help.   It's all absurd, and yet
There's something in it all, I know: how much?

No answer! What does that prove? Man's still man,
Still meant for a poor blundering piece of work
When all's done; but, if somewhat's done, like this,
Or not done, is the case the same?   Suppose
I blunder in my guess at the true sense
O' the knuckle-summons, nine times out of ten,—
What if the tenth guess happen to be right?
If the tenth shovel-load of powdered quartz
Yield me the nugget?   I gather, crush, sift all,
Pass o'er the failure, pounce on the success.
To give you a notion, now—(let who wins, laugh!)
When first I see a man, what do I first?
Why, count the letters which make up his name,
And as their number chances, even or odd,
Arrive at my conclusion, trim my course:
Hiram H. Horsefall is your honoured name,
And haven't I found a patron, sir, in you?
"Shall I cheat this stranger?"   I take apple-pips,
Stick one in either canthus of my eye,
And if the left drops first—(your left, sir, stuck)
I'm warned, I let the trick alone this time.
You, sir, who smile, superior to such trash,
You judge of character by other rules:
Don't your rules sometimes fail you?   Pray, what rule
Have you judged Sludge by hitherto?

                Oh, be sure,
You, everybody blunders, just as I,
In simpler things than these by far!   For see:
I knew two farmers,—one, a wiseacre
Who studied seasons, rummaged almanacs,
Quoted the dew-point, registered the frost,
And then declared, for outcome of his pains,
Next summer must be dampish: 'twas a drought.
His neighbour prophesied such drought would fall,
Saved hay and corn, made cent. per cent. thereby,
And proved a sage indeed: how came his lore?
Because one brindled heifer, late in March,
Stiffened her tail of evenings, and somehow
He got into his head that drought was meant!
I don't expect all men can do as much:
Such kissing goes by favour. You must take
A certain turn of mind for this,—a twist
I' the flesh, as well. Be lazily alive,

Open-mouthed, like my friend the ant-eater,
Letting all nature's loosely-guarded motes
Settle and, slick, be swallowed! Think yourself
The one i' the world, the one for whom the world
Was made, expect it tickling at your mouth!
Then will the swarm of busy buzzing flies,
Clouds of coincidence, break egg-shell, thrive,
Breed, multiply, and bring you food enough.

I can't pretend to mind your smiling, sir!
Oh, what you mean is this! Such intimate way,
Close converse, frank exchange of offices,
Strict sympathy of the immeasurably great
With the infinitely small, betokened here
By a course of signs and omens, raps and sparks,—
How does it suit the dread traditional text
O' the " Great and Terrible Name "? Shall the Heaven of
    Heavens
Stoop to such child's play?

                 Please, sir, go with me
A moment, and I'll try to answer you.
The " *Magnum et terribile* " (is that right?)
Well, folk began with this in the early day;
And all the acts they recognized in proof
Were thunders, lightnings, earthquakes, whirlwinds, dealt
Indisputably on men whose death they caused.
There, and there only, folk saw Providence
At work,—and seeing it, 'twas right enough
All heads should tremble, hands wring hands amain,
And knees knock hard together at the breath
O' the Name's first letter; why, the Jews, I'm told,
Won't write it down, no, to this very hour,
Nor speak aloud; you know best if 't be so.
Each ague-fit of fear at end, they crept
(Because somehow people once born must live)
Out of the sound, sight, swing and sway o' the Name,
Into a corner, the dark rest of the world,
And safe space where as yet no fear had reached;
'Twas there they looked about them, breathed again,
And felt indeed at home, as we might say.
The current o' common things, the daily life,
This had their due contempt; no Name pursued
Man from the mountain-top where fires abide,

To his particular mouse-hole at its foot
Where he ate, drank, digested, lived in short:
Such was man's vulgar business, far too small
To be worth thunder: " small," folk kept on, " small,"
With much complacency in those great days!
A mote of sand, you know, a blade of grass—
What was so despicable as mere grass,
Except perhaps the life o' the worm or fly
Which fed there?   These were " small " and men were great.
Well, sir, the old way's altered somewhat since,
And the world wears another aspect now:
Somebody turns our spyglass round, or else
Puts a new lens in it: grass, worm, fly grow big:
We find great things are made of little things,
And little things go lessening till at last
Comes God behind them.   Talk of mountains now?
We talk of mould that heaps the mountain, mites
That throng the mould, and God that makes the mites.
The Name comes close behind a stomach-cyst,
The simplest of creations, just a sac
That's mouth, heart, legs and belly at once, yet lives
And feels, and could do neither, we conclude,
If simplified still further one degree:
The small becomes the dreadful and immense
Lightning, forsooth?   No word more upon that!
A tin-foil bottle, a strip of greasy silk,
With a bit of wire and knob of brass, and there's
Your dollar's-worth of lightning!   But the cyst—
The life of the least of the little things?

                           No, no!
Preachers and teachers try another tack,
Come near the truth this time: they put aside
Thunder and lightning: " That's mistake," they cry,
" Thunderbolts fall for neither fright nor sport,
" But do appreciable good, like tides,
" Changes o' the wind, and other natural facts—
" ' Good ' meaning good to man, his body or soul.
" Mediate, immediate, all things minister
" To man,—that's settled: be our future text
" ' We are His children!' "   So, they now harangue
About the intention, the contrivance, all
That keeps up an incessant play of love,—
See the Bridgewater book.

Amen to it!
Well, sir, I put this question: I'm a child?
I lose no time, but take you at your word:
How shall I act a child's part properly?
Your sainted mother, sir,—used you to live
With such a thought as this a-worrying you?
" She has it in her power to throttle me,
" Or stab or poison: she may turn me out,
" Or lock me in,—nor stop at this to-day,
" But cut me off to-morrow from the estate
" I look for " (long may you enjoy it, sir!)
" In brief, she may unchild the child I am."
You never had such crotchets?   Nor have I!
Who, frank confessing childship from the first
Cannot both fear and take my ease at once,
So, don't fear,—know what might be, well enough
But know too, child-like, that it will not be,
At least in my case, mine, the son and heir
O' the kingdom, as yourself proclaim my style.
But do you fancy I stop short at this?
Wonder if suit and service, son and heir
Needs must expect, I dare pretend to find?
If, looking for signs proper to such an one,
I straight perceive them irresistible?
Concede that homage is a son's plain right,
And, never mind the nods and raps and winks,
'Tis the pure obvious supernatural
Steps forward, does its duty: why, of course!
I have presentiments; my dreams come true:
I fancy a friend stands whistling all in white
Blithe as a boblink, and he's dead I learn.
I take dislike to a dog my favourite long,
And sell him; he goes mad next week and snaps.
I guess that stranger will turn up to-day
I have not seen these three years; there's his knock
I wager " sixty peaches on that tree! "—
That I pick up a dollar in my walk,
That your wife's brother's cousin's name was George--
And win on all points.   Oh, you wince at this?
You'd fain distinguish between gift and gift,
Washington's oracle and Sludge's itch
O' the elbow when at whist he ought to trump?
With Sludge it's too absurd? *Fine, draw the line*
Somewhere, but, sir, your somewhere is not mine!

Bless us, I'm turning poet! It's time to end.
How you have drawn me out, sir! All I ask
Is—am I heir or not heir? If I'm he,
Then, sir, remember, that same personage
(To judge by what we read i' the newspaper)
Requires, beside one nobleman in gold
To carry up and down his coronet,
Another servant, probably a duke,
To hold egg-nogg in readiness: why want
Attendance, sir, when helps in his father's house
Abound, I'd like to know?

                         Enough of talk!
My fault is that I tell too plain a truth.
Why, which of those who say they disbelieve,
Your clever people, but has dreamed his dream,
Caught his coincidence, stumbled on his fact
He can't explain, (he'll tell you smilingly)
Which he's too much of a philosopher
To count as supernatural indeed,
So calls a puzzle and problem, proud of it
Bidding you still be on your guard, you know,
Because one fact don't make a system stand,
Nor prove this an occasional escape
Of spirit beneath the matter: that's the way!
Just so wild Indians picked up, piece by piece,
The fact in California, the fine gold
That underlay the gravel—hoarded these,
But never made a system stand, nor dug!
So wise men hold out in each hollowed palm
A handful of experience, sparkling fact
They can't explain; and since their rest of life
Is all explainable, what proof in this?
Whereas I take the fact, the grain of gold,
And fling away the dirty rest of life,
And add this grain to the grain each fool has found
O' the million other such philosophers,—
Till I see gold, all gold and only gold,
Truth questionless though unexplainable,
And the miraculous proved the commonplace!
The other fools believed in mud, no doubt—
Failed to know gold they saw: was that so strange?
Are all men born to play Bach's fiddle-fugues,
" Time " with the foil in carte, jump their own height,

Cut the mutton with the broadsword, skate a five,
Make the red hazard with the cue, clip nails
While swimming, in five minutes row a mile,
Pull themselves three feet up with the left arm,
Do sums of fifty figures in their head,
And so on, by the scores of instances?
The Sludge with luck, who sees the spiritual facts
His fellows strive and fail to see, may rank
With these, and share the advantage.

                                     Ay, but share
The drawback! Think it over by yourself;
I have not heart, sir, and the fire's gone grey.
Defect somewhere compensates for success,
Everyone knows that. Oh, we're equals, sir!
The big-legged fellow has a little arm
And a less brain, though big legs win the race:
Do you suppose I 'scape the common lot?
Say, I was born with flesh so sensitive,
Soul so alert, that, practice helping both,
I guess what's going on outside the veil,
Just as a prisoned crane feels pairing-time
In the islands where his kind are, so must fall
To capering by himself some shiny night,
As if your back-yard were a plot of spice—
Thus am I 'ware o' the spirit world: while you,
Blind as a beetle that way,—for amends,
Why, you can double fist and floor me, sir!
Ride that hot hardmouthed horrid horse of yours,
Laugh while it lightens, play with the great dog,
Speak your mind though it vex some friend to hear,
Never brag, never bluster, never blush,—
In short, you've pluck, when I'm a coward—there!
I know it, I can't help it,—folly or no,
I'm paralyzed, my hand's no more a hand,
Nor my head a head, in danger: you can smile
And change the pipe in your cheek. Your gift's not mine.
Would you swap for mine? No! but you'd add my gift
To yours: I dare say! I too sigh at times,
Wish I were stouter, could tell truth nor flinch,
Kept cool when threatened, did not mind so much
Being dressed gaily, making strangers stare,
Eating nice things; when I'd amuse myself,
I shut my eyes and fancy in my brain

I'm—now the President, now Jenny Lind,
Now Emerson, now the Benicia Boy—
With all the civilised world a-wondering
And worshipping. I know it's folly and worse;
I feel such tricks sap, honeycomb the soul,
But I can't cure myself: despond, despair,
And then, hey, presto, there's a turn o' the wheel,
Under comes uppermost, fate makes full amends;
Sludge knows and sees and hears a hundred things
You all are blind to,—I've my taste of truth,
Likewise my touch of falsehood,—vice no doubt,
But you've your vices also: I'm content.

What, sir? You won't shake hands? " Because I cheat!"
" You've found me out in cheating!" That's enough
To make an apostle swear! Why, when I cheat,
Mean to cheat, do cheat, and am caught in the act,
Are you, or, rather, am I sure o' the fact?
(There's verse again, but I'm inspired somehow.)
Well then I'm not sure! I may be, perhaps,
Free as a babe from cheating: how it began,
My gift,—no matter; what 'tis got to be
In the end now, that's the question; answer that!
Had I seen, perhaps, what hand was holding mine,
Leading me whither, I had died of fright:
So, I was made believe I led myself.
If I should lay a six-inch plank from roof
To roof, you would not cross the street, one step,
Even at your mother's summons: but, being shrewd,
If I paste paper on each side the plank
And swear 'tis solid pavement, why, you'll cross
Humming a tune the while, in ignorance
Beacon Street stretches a hundred feet below:
I walked thus, took the paper-cheat for stone.
Some impulse made me set a thing o' the move
Which, started once, ran really by itself;
Beer flows thus, such the siphon; toss the kite,
It takes the wind and floats of its own force.
Don't let truth's lump rot stagnant for the lack
Of a timely helpful lie to leaven it!
Put a chalk-egg beneath the clucking hen,
She'll lay a real one, laudably deceived,
Daily for weeks to come. I've told my lie,
And seen truth follow, marvels none of mine;

All was not cheating, sir, I'm positive!
I don't know if I move your hand sometimes
When the spontaneous writing spreads so far,
If my knee lifts the table all that height,
Why the inkstand don't fall off the desk a-tilt,
Why the accordion plays a prettier waltz
Than I can pick out on the piano-forte,
Why I speak so much more than I intend,
Describe so many things I never saw.
I tell you, sir, in one sense, I believe
Nothing at all,—that everybody can,
Will, and does cheat: but in another sense
I'm ready to believe my very self—
That every cheat's inspired, and every lie
Quick with a germ of truth.

                You ask perhaps
Why I should condescend to trick at all
If I know a way without it?   This is why!
There's a strange secret sweet self-sacrifice
In any desecration of one's soul
To a worthy end,—isn't it Herodotus
(I wish I could read Latin!) who describes
The single gift o' the land's virginity,
Demanded in those old Egyptian rites,
(I've but a hazy notion—help me, sir!)
For one purpose in the world, one day in a life,
One hour in a day—thereafter, purity,
And a veil thrown o'er the past for evermore!
Well, now, they understood a many things
Down by Nile city, or wherever it was!
I've always vowed, after the minute's lie,
And the end's gain,—truth should be mine henceforth.
This goes to the root o' the matter, sir,—this plain
Plump fact: accept it and unlock with it
The wards of many a puzzle!

              Or, finally,
Why should I set so fine a gloss on things?
What need I care?   I cheat in self-defence,
And there's my answer to a world of cheats!
Cheat? To be sure, sir! What's the world worth else?
Who takes it as he finds, and thanks his stars?
Don't it want trimming, turning, furbishing up

And polishing over? Your so-styled great men,
Do they accept one truth as truth is found,
Or try their skill at tinkering? What's your world?
Here are you born, who are, I'll say at once,
Of the luckiest kind, whether in head and heart,
Body and soul, or all that helps them both.
Well, now, look back: what faculty of yours
Came to its full, had ample justice done
By growing when rain fell, biding its time,
Solidifying growth when earth was dead,
Spiring up, broadening wide, in seasons due?
Never! You shot up and frost nipped you off,
Settled to sleep when sunshine bade you sprout;
One faculty thwarted its fellow: at the end,
All you boast is " I had proved a topping tree
" In other climes "—yet this was the right clime
Had you foreknown the seasons. Young, you've force
Wasted like well-streams: old,—oh, then indeed,
Behold a labyrinth of hydraulic pipes
Through which you'd play off wondrous waterwork;
Only, no water's left to feed their play.
Young,—you've a hope, an aim, a love: it's tossed
And crossed and lost: you struggle on, some spark
Shut in your heart against the puffs around,
Through cold and pain; these in due time subside,
Now then for age's triumph, the hoarded light
You mean to loose on the altered face of things,—
Up with it on the tripod! It's extinct.
Spend your life's remnant asking, which was best,
Light smothered up that never peeped forth once,
Or the cold cresset with full leave to shine?
Well, accept this too,—seek the fruit of it
Not in enjoyment, proved a dream on earth,
But knowledge, useful for a second chance,
Another life,—you've lost this world—you've gained
Its knowledge for the next. What knowledge, sir,
Except that you know nothing? Nay, you doubt
Whether 'twere better have made you man or brute,
If aught be true, if good and evil clash.
No foul, no fair, no inside, no outside,
There's your world!

        Give it me! I slap it brisk
With harlequin's pasteboard sceptre: what's it now?

Changed like a rock-flat, rough with rusty weed,
At first wash-over o' the returning wave!
All the dry dead impracticable stuff
Starts into life and light again; this world
Pervaded by the influx from the next.
I cheat, and what's the happy consequence?
You find full justice straightway dealt you out,
Each want supplied, each ignorance set at ease,
Each folly fooled.   No life-long labour now
As the price of worse than nothing!   No mere film
Holding you chained in iron, as it seems,
Against the outstretch of your very arms
And legs i' the sunshine moralists forbid!
What would you have?   Just speak and, there, you see!
You're supplemented, made a whole at last,
Bacon advises, Shakespeare writes you songs,
And Mary Queen of Scots embraces you.
Thus it goes on, not quite like life perhaps,
But so near, that the very difference piques,
Shows that e'en better than this best will be—
This passing entertainment in a hut
Whose bare walls take your taste since, one stage more,
And you arrive at the palace: all half real,
And you, to suit it, less than real beside,
In a dream, lethargic kind of death in life,
That helps the interchange of natures, flesh
Transfused by souls, and such souls!   Oh, 'tis choice!
And if at whiles the bubble, blown too thin,
Seem nigh on bursting,—if you nearly see
The real world through the false,—what *do* you see?
Is the old so ruined?   You find you're in a flock
O' the youthful, earnest, passionate—genius, beauty,
Rank and wealth also, if you care for these:
And all depose their natural rights, hail you,
(That's me, sir) as their mate and yoke-fellow,
Participate in Sludgehood—nay, grow mine,
I veritably possess them—banish doubt,
And reticence and modesty alike!
Why, here's the Golden Age, old Paradise
Or new Eutopia!   Here's true life indeed,
And the world well won now, mine for the first time!

And all this might be, may be, and with good help
Of a little lying shall be: so, Sludge lies!

Why, he's at worst your poet who sings how Greeks
That never were, in Troy which never was,
Did this or the other impossible great thing!
He's Lowell—it's a world (you smile applause),
Of his own invention—wondrous Longfellow,
Surprising Hawthorne!   Sludge does more than they,
And acts the books they write: the more his praise!

But why do I mount to poets?   Take plain prose—
Dealers in common sense, set these at work,
What can they do without their helpful lies?
Each states the law and fact and face o' the thing
Just as he'd have them, finds what he thinks fit,
Is blind to what missuits him, just records
What makes his case out, quite ignores the rest.
It's a History of the World, the Lizard Age,
The Early Indians, the Old Country War,
Jerome Napoleon whatsoever you please,
All as the author wants it.   Such a scribe
You pay and praise for putting life in stones,
Fire into fog, making the past your world.
There's plenty of " How did you contrive to grasp
" The thread which led you through this labyrinth?
" How build such solid fabric out of air?
" How on so slight foundation found this tale?
" Biography, narrative? " or, in other words,
" How many lies did it require to make
" The portly truth you here present us with? "
" Oh," quoth the penman, purring at your praise,
" 'Tis fancy all; no particle of fact:
" I was poor and threadbare when I wrote that book
" ' Bliss in the Golden City.' I, at Thebes?
" We writers paint out of our heads, you see! "
" —Ah, the more wonderful the gift in you,
" The more creativeness and godlike craft! "
But I, do I present you with my piece,
It's " What, Sludge?   When my sainted mother spoke
" The verses Lady Jane Grey last composed
" About the rosy bower in the seventh heaven
" Where she and Queen Elizabeth kept house,—
" You made the raps?   'Twas your invention that?
" Cur, slave and devil! "—eight fingers and two thumbs
Stuck in my throat!

                              Well, if the marks seem gone
'Tis because stiffish cock-tail, taken in time,
Is better for a bruise than arnica.
There, sir! I bear no malice: 'tisn't in me.
I know I acted wrongly: still, I've tried
What I could say in my excuse,—to show
The devil's not all devil . . . I don't pretend,
He's angel, much less such a gentleman
As you, sir! And I've lost you, lost myself,
Lost all-l-l-l- . . .

                              No—are you in earnest, sir?
O yours, sir, is an angel's part! I know
What prejudice prompts, and what's the common course
Men take to soothe their ruffled self-conceit:
Only you rise superior to it all!
No, sir, it don't hurt much; it's speaking long
That makes me choke a little: the marks will go!
What? Twenty V-notes more, and outfit too,
And not a word to Greeley? One—one kiss
O' the hand that saves me! You'll not let me speak,
I well know, and I've lost the right, too true!
But I must say, sir, if She hears (she does)
Your sainted . . . Well, sir,—be it so! That's, I think,
My bedroom candle. Good-night! Bl-l-less you, sir.

R-r-r, you brute-beast and blackguard! Cowardly scamp!
I only wish I dared burn down the house
And spoil your sniggering! Oh what, you're the man?
You're satisfied at last? You've found out Sludge?
We'll see that presently: my turn, sir, next!
I too can tell my story: brute,——do you hear?—
You throttled your sainted mother, that old hag,
In just such a fit of passion: no, it was . . .
To get this house of hers, and many a note
Like these . . . I'll pocket them, however . . . five,
Ten, fifteen . . . ay, you gave her throat the twist,
Or else you poisoned her! Confound the cuss!
Where was my head? I ought to have prophesied
He'll die in a year and join her: that's the way.
I don't know where my head is: what had I done?
How did it all go? I said he poisoned her,
And hoped he'd have grace given him to repent,
Whereon he picked this quarrel, bullied me

And called me cheat: I thrashed him,—who could help?
He howled for mercy, prayed me on his knees
To cut and run and save him from disgrace:
I do so, and once off, he slanders me.
An end of him! Begin elsewhere anew!
Boston's a hole, the herring-pond is wide,
V-notes are something, liberty still more.
Beside, is he the only fool in the world?

APPARENT FAILURE.

" We shall soon lose a celebrated building."—*Paris Newspaper.*

I. No, for I'll save it! Seven years since,
    I passed through Paris, stopped a day
To see the baptism of your Prince;
    Saw, made my bow, and went my way:
Walking the heat and headache off,
    I took the Seine-side, you surmise,
Thought of the Congress, Gortschakoff,
    Cavour's appeal and Buol's replies,
So sauntered till—what met my eyes?

II. Only the Doric little Morgue!
    The dead-house where you show your drowned:
Petrarch's Vaucluse makes proud the Sorgue,
    Your Morgue has made the Seine renowned.
One pays one's debt in such a case;
    I plucked up heart and entered,—stalked,
Keeping a tolerable face
    Compared with some whose cheeks were chalked:
Let them! No Briton's to be baulked!

III. First came the silent gazers; next,
    A screen of glass, we're thankful for;
Last, the sight's self, the sermon's text,
    The three men who did most abhor
Their life in Paris yesterday,
    So killed themselves: and now, enthroned
Each on his copper couch, they lay
    Fronting me, waiting to be owned.
I thought, and think, their sin's atoned.

IV. Poor men, God made, and all for that!
    The reverence struck me; o'er each head
Religiously was hung its hat,
    Each coat dripped by the owner's bed,
Sacred from touch: each had his berth,
    His bounds, his proper place of rest,
Who last night tenanted on earth
    Some arch, where twelve such slept abreast,—
Unless the plain asphalte seemed best.

V. How did it happen, my poor boy?
    You wanted to be Buonaparte
And have the Tuileries for toy,
    And could not, so it broke your heart?
You, old one by his side, I judge,
    Were, red as blood, a socialist,
A leveller! Does the Empire grudge
    You've gained what no Republic missed?
Be quiet, and unclench your fist!

VI. And this—why, he was red in vain,
    Or black,—poor fellow that is blue!
What fancy was it turned your brain?
    Oh, women were the prize for you!
Money gets women, cards and dice
    Get money, and ill-luck gets just
The copper couch and one clear nice
    Cool squirt of water o'er your bust,
The right thing to extinguish lust!

VII. It's wiser being good than bad;
    It's safer being meek than fierce:
It's fitter being sane than mad.
    My own hope is, a sun will pierce
The thickest cloud earth ever stretched;
    That, after Last, returns the First,
Though a wide compass round be fetched;
    That what began best, can't end worst,
Nor what God blessed once, prove accurst.

EPILOGUE.

FIRST SPEAKER, *as David.*

I. On the first of the Feast of Feasts,
  The Dedication Day,
When the Levites joined the Priests
  At the Altar in robed array,
Gave signal to sound and say,—

II. When the thousands, rear and van,
  Swarming with one accord
Became as a single man
  (Look, gesture, thought and word)
In praising and thanking the Lord,—

III. When the singers lift up their voice,
  And the trumpets made endeavour,
Sounding, " In God rejoice! "
  Saying, " In Him rejoice
" Whose mercy endureth for ever! "—

IV. Then the Temple filled with a cloud,
  Even the House of the Lord;
Porch bent and pillar bowed:
  For the presence of the Lord,
In the glory of His cloud,
  Had filled the House of the Lord.

SECOND SPEAKER, *as Renan.*

Gone now! All gone across the dark so far,
  Sharpening fast, shuddering ever, shutting still,
Dwindling into the distance, dies that star
  Which came, stood, opened once! We gazed our fill
With upturned faces on as real a Face
  That, stooping from grave music and mild fire,
Took in our homage, made a visible place
  Through many a depth of glory, gyre on gyre,
For the dim human tribute. Was this true?
  Could man indeed avail, mere praise of his,
To help by rapture God's own rapture too,
  Thrill with a heart's red tinge that pure pale bliss?
Why did it end? Who failed to beat the breast,
  And shriek, and throw the arms protesting wide,

When a first shadow showed the star addressed
　　Itself to motion, and on either side
The rims contracted as the rays retired;
　　The music, like a fountain's sickening pulse,
Subsided on itself; awhile transpired
　　Some vestige of a Face no pangs convulse,
No prayers retard; then even this was gone,
　　Lost in the night at last.   We, lone and left
Silent through centuries, ever and anon
　　Venture to probe again the vault bereft
Of all now save the lesser lights, a mist
　　Of multitudinous points, yet suns, men say—
And this leaps ruby, this lurks amethyst,
　　But where may hide what came and loved our clay?
How shall the sage detect in yon expanse
　　The star which chose to stoop and stay for us?
Unroll the records! Hailed ye such advance
　　Indeed, and did your hope evanish thus?
Watchers of twilight, is the worst averred?
　　We shall not look up, know ourselves are seen,
Speak, and be sure that we again are heard,
　　Acting or suffering, have the disk's serene
Reflect our life, absorb an earthly flame,
　　Nor doubt that, were mankind inert and numb,
Its core had never crimsoned all the same,
　　Nor, missing ours, its music fallen dumb?
Oh, dread succession to a dizzy post,
　　Sad sway of sceptre whose mere touch appals,
Ghastly dethronement, cursed by those the most
　　On whose repugnant brow the crown next falls!

THIRD SPEAKER.

I. Witless alike of will and way divine,
　　How heaven's high with earth's low should intertwine!
　　Friends, I have seen through your eyes: now use mine!

II. Take the least man of all mankind, as I;
　　Look at his head and heart, find how and why
　　He differs from his fellows utterly:

III. Then, like me, watch when nature by degrees
　　Grows alive round him, as in Arctic seas
　　(They said of old) the instinctive water flees

IV. Toward some elected point of central rock,
   As though, for its sake only, roamed the flock
   Of waves about the waste: awhile they mock

V. With radiance caught for the occasion,—hues
   Of blackest hell now, now such reds and blues
   As only heaven could fitly interfuse,—

VI. The mimic monarch of the whirlpool, king
   O' the current for a minute: then they wring
   Up by the roots and oversweep the thing,

VII. And hasten off, to play again elsewhere
   The same part, choose another peak as bare,
   They find and flatter, feast and finish there.

VIII. When you see what I tell you,—nature dance
   About each man of us, retire, advance,
   As though the pageant's end were to enhance

IX. His worth, and—once the life, his product, gained—
   Roll away elsewhere, keep the strife sustained,
   And show thus real, a thing the North but feigned—

X. When you acknowledge that one world could do
   All the diverse work, old yet ever new,
   Divide us, each from other, me from you,—

XI. Why, where's the need of Temple, when the walls
   O' the world are that? What use of swells and falls
   From Levites' choir, Priests' cries, and trumpet-calls?

XII. That one Face, far from vanish, rather grows,
   Or decomposes but to recompose,
   Become my universe that feels and knows.

BEN KARSHOOK'S WISDOM.

[KARSHOOK = THISTLE.]

" WOULD a man 'scape the rod? "
　　Rabbi Ben Karshook saith,
" See that he turn to God
　　The day before his death."

" Ay could a man enquire
　　When it shall come! " I say,
The Rabbi's eye shoots fire—
　　" Then let him turn to-day! "

Quoth a young Sadducee:
　　" Reader of many rolls,
Is it so certain we
　　Have, as they tell us, souls? "

" Son, there is no reply! "
　　The Rabbi bit his beard:
" Certain, a soul have *I*—
　　We may have none," he sneer'd.

Thus Karshook, the Hiram's-Hammer,
　　The Right-hand Temple-column,
Taught babes in grace their grammar,
　　And struck the simple, solemn.

Rome, April 27, 1854.

SONNET.

EYES, calm beside thee, (Lady, could'st thou know!)
   May turn away thick with fast-gathering tears:
I glance not where all gaze: thrilling and low
   Their passionate praises reach thee—my cheek wears
Alone no wonder when thou passest by;
Thy tremulous lids bent and suffused reply
To the irrepressible homage which doth glow
   On every lip but mine: if in thine ears
Their accents linger—and thou dost recall
   Me as I stood, still, guarded, very pale,
Beside each votarist whose lighted brow
Wore worship like an aureole, " O'er them all
   My beauty," thou wilt murmer, " did prevail
Save that one only: "—Lady, couldst thou know!

Was written on August 17th, 1834, and published in
" The Monthly Repository," 1834.